The City in S

The City in Slang

New York Life and Popular Speech

Irving Lewis Allen

Oxford University Press

New York   *Oxford*

*With very few exceptions, indeed, slang terms are
sociologically valuable and historically revealing.*
ERIC PARTRIDGE

Oxford University Press

Oxford   New York
Athens   Auckland   Bangkok   Bombay
Calcutta   Cape Town   Dar es Salaam   Delhi
Florence   Hong Kong   Istanbul   Karachi
Kuala Lampur   Madras   Madrid   Melbourne
Mexico City   Nairobi   Paris   Singapore
Taipei   Tokyo   Toronto

and associated companies in
Berlin   Ibadan

Copyright © 1993 by Oxford University Press, Inc.

First published in 1993 by Oxford University Press, Inc.,
200 Madison Avenue, New York, New York 10016

First issued as an Ocford University Press paperback, 1995

Oxford is a registered trademark of Oxford University Press

Library of Congress Cataloging-in-Publication Data
Allen, Irving L.
The city in slang : New York life and popular speech / Irving Lewis Allen.
p. cm   Includes bibliographical references and indexes.
ISBN 0-19-507591-9
ISBN 0-19-509265-1 (PBK.)
1. English language—Spoken English—New York (N.Y.)
2. English language—Social aspects—New York (N.Y.)
3. New York (N.Y.)—Social life and customs.
4. English language—New York (N.Y.)—Slang.
5. New York (N.Y.)—Popular culture.
6. City and town life—Terminology.
7. Americanisms—New York (N.Y.)
I. Title. PE3101.N7A45 1993
427'.97471—dc20   92-9377

1 2 3 4 5 6 7 8 9 10
Printed in the United states of America

Preface

American city life, especially that of New York, left an abundant cultural legacy of words and phrases of slang and other popular speech about life at the center of the metropolis. Many of these popular expressions either originated in or have close associations with Manhattan's social and cultural history. This vocabulary constitutes a distinctive lexical culture—a coherent, comprehensive, collective view of the social city—that echoes the whole metropolitan experience. These expressions enlivened the speech of their day and many still have popular use. Slang and other popular speech yield their own special picture of New York and more generally of other large American cities. Contrary to the old wisdom, New York has always been and remains an integral part of America. Yet the extreme diversity and commercial vigor of New York have also given it a special quality that is evident in its culture, including its abundant talk about itself.

In this book on words about the city, I want to show how American popular speech responded to the emerging metropolis of New York in particular. Once prompted, this vocabulary and its multiple subtexts, allusions, and implicit metaphors also directed social perceptions of the urban world and behavior toward it. The social contexts of lexical innovation and diffusion, histories of key words and phrases, and the implicit meanings and subtexts of whole vocabularies as systems of popular thought reveal a new set of cultural interactions with the urban experience. We make words, but to an extent words also make us and our social realities.

Nearly every form of human expression in word and image—save language itself—has been used to explore the historical city of the mind. Images of the big city in intellectual thought, novels, poetry, painting, and travel accounts of visitors tell us how the metropolis was seen by articulate cultural elites. Popular images of the modern city have been viewed through the selective and coloring filters of the mass media in old newspapers, magazines, popular fiction, popular music, and movies. Reconstructions of past urban culture and society with these materials have increased our understanding of the thoughtways of the people who made the images and, though with more caution, of the people who consumed them. The body of popular speech about the experience of social life in the city adds to this story.

Since the 1850s and even earlier American slang and other urban street speech have been extensively and systematically collected by scholars, usually lexicographers and dialectologists, including some amateurs, and compiled into dictionaries and other word lists. Some of these words and phrases were first gathered in their own day by people who actually heard them in everyday use. In later years the vocabulary was collected retrospectively from surviving printed sources. Today, sample surveys are also used to collect popular speech, and they show that many of the older expressions are still in living memory and use.

Etymologists have researched the origins of most of these expressions and dated their first appearance in print, which usually follows oral use by several years. Many of the expressions are Americanisms of native origin. A good many, too, are loanwords borrowed from British English and other languages and put into American service, often with new or variant meanings. As a result of all these efforts, the vocabulary is now abundantly recorded, dated, and etymologized in the latest editions of major unabridged dictionaries of the English language. I supplemented these sources with social histories, sociological studies, memoirs, accounts of journalists, fictional impressions of New York life, and many other studies and observations of popular speech. These distinctively urban lexical innovations now can be connected with general and often specific places and events, many of them in New York.

"Butterfly collecting" has great value as well as its charms, and many specimens of slang etymology are both beautiful and fascinating. But a further step is required to make a coherent and general story of the mass of lexical data and etymological research on words and phrases about the city. At a very broad level, most historical slang can be associated with urbanization—the settlement and development of cities—and more directly with urbanism—the distinctive culture that emerges from this social form. This larger picture is seen here in the rise and decentralization of a single great metropolitan community—New York—and its influence on the vocabulary that emerged to express the urban experience from the view at the center.

New York's classic cycle of urbanization is the supreme American case, some would say the only case, for a complete study of city and word. The city's urban, social, and cultural history is a concise story of metropolitan America during this period and elucidates the general relationship between popular speech and all large cities of the urban society. New York's urban culture also led that of the nation. For this reason, many popular words and phrases about big city life have origins in New York or came in the course of things to have strong associations with the city. The interplay of metropolitan life in New York with the popular lexicons about the city and its street life enables us to see especially well a fascinating instance of the interaction of society, culture, and language.

This word image of a great metropolis in popular speech brings full circle the many studies of city life in literature, journalism, art and illustration, popular music, and movies. The popular vocabulary, taken as a whole, is an aggregate, alternative, more rough-and-tumble view of city life that tugs against more conventional views seen through the lenses of standard usages. In the social context of their urban origins, these words and phrases of popular speech show us in a new way how metropolitan life was socially constructed in the minds of millions of ordinary city dwellers.

The overarching interpretive scheme of the book is the response of lexical innovation to the century-long cycle of urbanization from roughly 1850 to 1950. Yet the story was gathering momentum well before 1850 and continues in important respects down to the present. Chapter 1 reviews the ways that popular speech, first of all, rises from the facts of social structure and change. Popular expressions then reflect, refract, and help shape metropolitan social reality. Slang is both a constraining and generating medium of thought about the public aspect of city life. A subsidiary theme is also developed throughout the book. Naturalist or realist city literature, realist art, and popular culture are expressive forms, along with popular speech, of a unitary urban culture and each has influenced all the others. Mass communication, as one of the integrative forces of diverse modern society, also interacts with and diffuses popular speech into the national culture.

The mass of lexical data, when sorted by my lights, falls into the subsequent nine chapters of New York metropolitan life. These chapters divide to represent the themes of lexical innovation in response to the symbolism of city streets, nightlife, new forms of transportation and communication, the vertical city of tall buildings, the worlds of poverty, common vices, the array of social types in city streets, and the names of social divisions of class, neighborhood, and of town and country. The book can be read in either of two ways, and I hope it will be read in both. It is a slice of the history of popular speech through the development of the modern metropolis, specifically New York, and it is a slice of the social and cultural history of New York through the material of popular speech. More generally, I hope to add to the understanding of the social context of the origin and use of these words and, so, allow a different look at city life through the lenses of popular speech.

Storrs, Conn.   I. L. A.
August 1992

⅋ ⅋ ⅋ ⅋ ⅋

Acknowledgments

I thank my friends and colleagues who read and commented so helpfully on early drafts: Leonard R. N. Ashley, Gerald L. Cohen, Connie C. Eble, Barry Glassner, and Barry Schwartz. Polly Reynolds Allen, especially, gave much time and advised me wisely on every aspect of the book.

Frederic G. Cassidy and the staff of the *Dictionary of American Regional English* made available computer data from their national surveys. Randy Roberts at the Ellis Library of the University of Missouri-Columbia responded graciously to my inquiries concerning materials in the Peter Tamony Collection. I also think the officers and members of the American Dialect Society, the American Name Society, the American Society of Geolinguistics, the Modern Language Association, and the Names Institute for letting me air sections of the emerging manuscript at meetings and for being such good and supportive audiences. The University of Connecticut Research Foundation generously provided financial support to obtain the book's illustrations and various permissions.

The William Benton Museum of Art gave their gratis permission to reproduce several prints by Reginald Marsh from their collection. The Delaware Art Museum similarly made available three prints by John Sloan from their collection, a gift from Helen Farr Sloan. For their generous permission to quote brief excerpts, I also thank Ruth Ellington Boatwright and Tempo Music, Inc., for Billy Strayhorn's "Take the 'A' Train," copyright 1941 by Tempo Music, Inc.; the Estate of James F. Hanley for "The Gold-Digger," copyright 1923; and Random House, Inc., and Harold Ober, Associates, for Langston Hughes's "Harlem Sweeties" in *Shakespeare in Harlem,* Alfred A. Knopf, copyright 1942.

Credits for the use of excerpts from Lorenz Hart's song lyrics are: "Give It Back to the Indians" (Lorenz Hart), copyright 1939 Chappell & Co. (renewed). All rights reserved. Used by permission. "Lady Is a Tramp" (Lorenz Hart), copyright 1939 Chappell & Co. (renewed). All rights reserved. Used by permission. "Give That Little Girl A Hand" (Richard Rodgers, Lorenz Hart), copyright 1927 Warner Bros. Inc. (renewed) and Marlin Enterprises. All rights on behalf of Marlin Enterprises administered by WB Music Corp. All rights reserved. Used by permission.

Illustrations

1. John Sloan. *Sixth Avenue, Greenwich Village* 7

2. Outline Map of Manhattan in the 1930s 30–31

3. Berenice Abbott. *Court of the First Model Tenement* 33

4. Reginald Marsh. *East Tenth Street Jungle* 37

5. Reginald Marsh. *Chop Suey Dancers #2* 68

6. *A Rubbernecker Bus* 82

7. John Sloan. *Seeing New York* 83

8. T. de Thulstrup. *A Station Scene in the "Rush" Hours* 91

9. Isabel Bishop. *Single Straphanger* 94

10. Charles Broughton. *A New York Charity—Distributing Bread* 144

11. John Sloan. *Bandits Cave* 147

12. Reginald Marsh. *Diana Dancing Academy* 173

13. Reginald Marsh. *New Gotham Burlesk* 175

14. Serrell and Perkins. *Hooking a Victim* 184

15. B. West Clinedinst. *The Shop-Girl Released from Toil* 193

16. W. A. Rogers. *Shop-Girls Buying Easter Bonnets* 202

17. G. A. Davis. *A Harbinger of Spring on the East Side* 208

Contents

PART I *Manhattan in the Mirror of Slang*

    1. New York City Life and Popular Speech   3

    2. The Social Meaning of City Streets   27

PART II *The Modern Ruptures of Traditional Life*

    3. The Bright Lights   57

    4. New Ways of Urban Living   85

    5. Tall Buildings   113

PART III *The Shadow Worlds of Social Class in City Life*

    6. Mean Streets   139

    7. The Sporting Life   163

PART IV *The Naming of Social Differences*

    8. Social Types in City Streets   189

    9. Us and Them   217

    10. The Contempt for Provincial Life   241

    Notes   261

    References and Bibliography   275

    Index of Words and Phrases   289

    Author and Subject Index   301

PART I
Manhattan in the Mirror of Slang

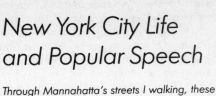

New York City Life and Popular Speech

Through Mannahatta's streets I walking, these things gathering.
WALT WHITMAN, "Our Old Feuillage"

The hundreds, even thousands, of words and phrases of slang and other popular speech about life in New York, especially Manhattan, are a treasure trove of social and cultural history. A distinctive word culture of social life in the city flowed from the modern cycle of urban growth that started significantly in the 1840s. These words about the city, individually and taken together, retell in a new voice the story of metropolitan life down to the 1950s, when so much national attention began to turn away from the culture of the old metropolitan core and toward the suburbs. Many of these word images of the city are still in our speechways and, more important, in our thoughtways.

New words and new meanings of old words, even flippant and ephemeral ones, are cultural creations that burst upon a silence and bring new thoughts and new ways of seeing into existence. What indeed can slangy, frivolous, fanciful, but undeniably popular expressions of the urban experience tell us about the history and culture of cities in general and of New York in particular? Just consider the city lore prompted by the mere mention of names like *The Big Apple, The Great White Way, butter-and-egg man, gold-digger, rubbernecker, Sugar Hill, rent party, The Tenderloin, the urban jungle, hooker, straphanger, hot dog, cliff dweller, tar beach, spieler, yellow journalism, breadline, hokey-pokey man, The Upper Ten, The Four Hundred, herkimer jerkimer,* or *appleknocker*—to mention only several.

The popular culture of big American cities, including its speechways, historically has been led by New York, which by the middle of the nineteenth century was emerging to lead the national urban culture in many other ways as well. New York became the preeminent national city and swelled with pride and talk of itself. The city's word images of itself, with the early help of print and journalism, diffused and influenced the nation's image of New York and, by extension, of all big cities. The city's nineteenth-century dominance of publishing, popular music, minstrelsy, vaudeville, and, early in this century, movies and radio all amplified the New York idiom and took it across the nation.

Other large American cities had a similar urban experience in the same period and made their own contributions. These words spread to New York and elsewhere, just as New York idioms diffused to other parts of the country. New Yorkers took some of these expressions from other cities, such as *skid row* from Seattle, and gave them their own special meanings. Just as readily, other cities adopted and adapted New York's words. San Francisco today calls its nightclub district *The Tenderloin*. That evocative name originated in the 1880s for the notorious area of nightlife and vice on the west side of Manhattan. Many other popular expressions about life in American cities either originated in or had close associations with Manhattan. The city's history is the archetype of metropolitan development and most fully represents the American experience of city life. New York, of all American cities, most profusely made up words and phrases about the metropolitan experience and created the most distinctive word image of its urban world.

The historian Thomas Bender has written that the culture of New York is "based on premises not quite shared by the dominant American culture." Further, "this very different history became the material for an alternative vision of society, one that embraced difference, diversity, and conflict."[1] The popular speech and slang of historical New York, I will add, both grew from and helped to construct the climate of social difference, diversity, and conflict. The emergent structure of social difference and inequality in the American metropolis, especially its class, ethnic, and regional variety, alone spawned perhaps two thousand words and phrases of slang that name the particulars of that diversity and the conflict it bred.

Slang also provided names for every other aspect of big-city life. The wellsprings of these lexical innovations include social releases from the constraints of traditional society; sheer urban excitement—the bright lights, and the contrasts of life in town and country; the social symbolism of the rectangular grid of city streets; nineteenth-century street talk of common vices; the parade of colorful social types seen in city streets; reactions to new technologies, consumer styles, and quickened tempos of life in the rapidly expanding city; the appearance of the new vertical city of tall buildings and the early middle-class ambivalences about apartment living; the moral confrontation with tenements, slums, and poverty; reactions to class and ethnic diversity and the spatial expressions of segregated diversity on the grid of streets; and cultural strains between the center and the periphery of the metropolitan region.

Most of these words and phrases are still known today; all were known in their time; some have become standard usage and no longer seem so unusual or fresh. The historical arrays of these words display a rich popular imagery of cities and of city life and can be made, in their own words, to retell an old story in a new medium.

The story begins in history and is resolved primarily in the economic and social workings of the Great City. Popular speech and slang about city life in New York, or for that matter in any large city, anywhere in the world, or in any language, derives ultimately from the economic engine of the metropolis. Great cities, the most intense and generative manifestations of modern society, are often likened to a machine, some would say an infernal machine, for economic growth, production, specialization, technological innovation, consumption, and all the attendant social variegation. A new social order and its culture, or what the social scientists call urbanism, arose from the urban industrial economy.

The basic influence of this new society on language is the first story to tell. The distinctive culture of the city and its ways of life, or urbanism, arose directly from the population characteristics mandated and assembled by the new capitalist economy. The city's large population size, its density of settlement, the diversity of its social groups, and, especially, how they made a living created a new quality of social interaction and new states of mind. Urbanism as a way of life was viewed as a curse or a blessing depending on whether one focused on the supposed loss of community in the city or on the joys of release from tradition afforded by city life. In either case, the new culture of urbanism included lexical culture. Some of it was slang that expressed new social categories, new forms of social inequality, new institutions, new relationships, new technologies, new ways of life, and other ruptures of tradition.

Great cities by their nature create differences of every kind, and difference is the source of lexical innovation. The very idea of difference and conflict, not sameness and harmony, is key to understanding the special quality of New York life and the way it described itself—and still describes itself—in popular speech. By the 1840s the great American market cities of free-flowing capital had produced a disturbing new social order of rich and poor and amazing new ways of life. New social classes, statuses, ethnic groups, and styles of life appeared as a result. The tensions of these new inequalities and their culture clashes prompted a slang lexicon that captured these unfolding events in surprising detail and nuance. The city's economic machine was also dividing the people of the metropolitan region into two other interdependent social classes—the city people at the urban-industrial center and the country people on the rural-agrarian periphery. This division, too, is richly recorded in popular speech.

The dynamic economic city also generated a corresponding spatial diversity—new commercial districts and residential neighborhoods—that both accommodated and symbolized the new social order. The location of individuals, families, and social groups in the spatial order testified to and validated their statuses, either high or low.[2] Personifying social types, who symbolized these new social roles and their physical location, were named and stereotyped with Runyonesque flair. The Bowery and Bowery life early symbolized working-class and immigrant New York. Broadway symbolized the middle and upper classes and their patterns of consumption, and to be seen there, especially in fine dress, was a marker of high status. The two societies led parallel lives on almost parallel streets, just several blocks but worlds apart. Bowery Boys seldom mixed socially with Broadway Belles, except in fiction.

In short, the whole historical and social process of modern urbanization and urbanism was richly expressed in slang and other popular speech—and it was better said in New York than in any other American city.

Slang and Other Popular Speech

Slang is the raw material for this book. But what is it exactly, and how is it different from other kinds of vocabulary in everyday use? Slang is, at bottom, just a highly informal register of speech and does not differ from standard usages in any purely linguistic way. Slang shares indistinct boundaries with other informal levels of vocabulary, such as colloquial usages, subgroup argots, and regional, class, and ethnic dialects. Slang is such a slippery concept that the idea of "popular speech," a broader concept that includes slang, is now preferred by many writers on language. Popular speech, most simply put, may be said to be those words and phrases that are *not* standard, formal, or academic, or at least were not in their bloom. The related idea of "street speech" lays stress on the urban side of popular speech.

Yet a certain sociological idea of slang underlies the consideration of metropolitan life and popular speech.[3] General slang is mostly words and phrases that have escaped from the myriad subcultures of society and found favor in wider usage.[4] Slang emerges from the plural structure of society and, in subsequent usage, helps in small ways to maintain as well as to modify social diversity, usually toward more diversity. Slang is a necessary and inevitable cultural product of diverse, complex, and highly interdependent modern society. Slang grew where diverse peoples met at the cultural crossroads of the ancient market city; it flourished in the more diverse and occupationally interdependent medieval city.[5] For the same but now infinitely more complex reasons, slang is part of the life of modern cities, or more correctly today, of modern society in general. In this sense most slang is urban; slang about the city is a special case of it.

Slang grows from, depends on, and marks social differences in its everyday use. The subgroup or subcultural origins of general slang include social classes, genders, sexual interests, all majority and minority ethnic groups, regional groups, age groups, many occupational specialties, a host of lifestyle and consumer cultures, and all of the so-called deviant subcultures. Everyone, especially city people, belongs to a variety of these overlapping subgroups. Some of the most intense subcultures have their own dialects or varieties of English that exist in degrees of distinction from standard speech. Each variety, and most are merely nascent, may include distinctive pronunciations, special words or special meanings of ordinary words, or even grammatical differences. There is no single New York dialect or accent of English, but there are as many varieties of speech as there are major social differences.[6]

Special and restricted subcultural words and phrases become general slang if and when they diffuse through the word-of-mouth networks and between the intersecting social circles that lace together much of the whole society. Slang diffuses among social groups in the process of being used to manage the multiple, overlapping, and shifting identities of urban life—a world of masks and mirrors. These special words, often ordinary words with special meanings, sometimes thus escape their little social circles or leak into one or more intersecting or tangential circles, where they are provisionally adopted. The adoption of subgroup talk often signals the acceptance of subgroup values, and this is sometimes the prelude to real social change, for good or bad.

If the word or phrase proves useful or amusing in its new social setting, it may pass further into more and more circles until it reaches a wide enough

FIGURE 1.   John Sloan. *Sixth Avenue, Greenwich Village* (1923). Slang about city life was coined, reinforced, and diffused by word-of-mouth among ordinary people in countless millions of social interactions, such as in this scene on the sidewalks of New York.
(*Courtesy of Delaware Art Museum*)

audience, who at least understand its meaning, to say that it is in general slang and part of the general culture. Certain expressions from gay talk, drug jargon, and black street vernacular have all made this journey in recent decades. If such slang stays in wide use for decades, it may lose its subcultural associations and seem to be part of the language, its subgroup origins remote or forgotten. But etymology frequently reminds us of slang's social origins.

The diffusion of lexical innovation, including slang and other popular speech, follows the same principles that govern the diffusion of any cultural innovation: it spreads in direct proportion to population density, intensity of communication, and perceived usefulness. The mass media augments and amplifies this process and can bring almost instantaneous diffusion of new expressions, introducing them at once into many thousands of local social circles, from which they spread further by word of mouth. In modern societies laced together by the mass media, folk lexical culture (categories invented by people) blends with mass lexical culture (categories invented by media writers for the people). This is no less true of slang about New York.

The Social Construction of Urban Reality

Language also influences society, or at least people's perception of it, and cognition is the stuff of social reality. The popular words and phrases that frame the social life of the city can be read to elucidate its meaning. Clusters of words and their meanings in historical slang disclose popular systems of thought and values. Language is culture, and through language and vocabulary the social world in the mind's eye is revealed. Words and phrases about city life are only a special case. Vocabulary, including popular speech, is a way of seeing—or rather constructing—the urban social world. Art and literature can be cognate ways of interpreting the same world. Clearly, language and other cultural expressions are not perfect reflections of the real world. Language, rather, is a prism that refracts the cognitive world and breaks down the continua of social life into colored bands of perception, categories, or words.

The critic Kenneth Burke once wrote that a name is a fetishistic representation of the named thing. Naming things, uttering the names, and then arranging and changing those names seem to give us magical power over objects in the social world.[7] Once names or categories exist, and to the extent that we accept them as valid, we tend to reason from them as models of reality. Once a part of the city is defined as *Hell's Kitchen*, a *slum*, or a *ghetto*, we go on to infer many things about the residents and the meaning of life in these areas. New and variant meanings of the particulars of awareness continually emerge in everyday talk. We make the world increasingly meaningful throughout life by dividing it into—naming—increasingly complicated categories, dropping or collapsing old categories, and substituting

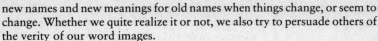
new names and new meanings for old names when things change, or seem to change. Whether we quite realize it or not, we also try to persuade others of the verity of our word images.

City people name their urban surroundings just as they name other things of interest in each of their other social worlds. Knowing the names of things and being able to name seemingly new social experiences enable people to direct and control their behavior and, as the process is elaborated, make possible complicated programs of social action, such as dealing with everyday life in the city. Different, seemingly predatory types in city streets, such as *mashers, panhandlers, mushroom fakers, muggers,* and *pullers-in,* are distinguished in language in part so that we can infer their motives toward us. Naming the urban social world—ascribing meaning to it—is a coping strategy necessary for understanding and for moving freely and effectively in a complicated social world of anonymity, tangential social relations, and extreme diversity.[8]

The historical accumulation of lexical expressions about a particular aspect of urban social reality constitutes a "lexical field," as the linguists call it, or a collective folk model of reality. These composite images are especially apparent in lists of near synonyms with all their various connotations, together with their real and folkloristic etymologies—all viewed in their temporal, spatial, and social context. For instance, slang names for female prostitutes who solicited in the streets went beyond the single name *streetwalkers* to take account of other major aspects of their folk image. These women search for men by strolling about (*cruisers*) at night (*ladies of the night, little night birds*), as though innocently (*star gazers*), on city streets (*nymphs of the pave, pavement princesses*), and catch them like fish (*hookers*).

The model becomes cultural knowledge of the urban world, a knowing shaped and directed by the cognition of language. These linguistic constructs frame experience, direct perception, suggest yet other near synonyms, call forth stereotypes that the words themselves helped to create, and imply appropriate attitudes and behavior toward the objects. Various urban entities (e.g., *skid row*), social types and roles (e.g., *straphangers*), certain land uses (e.g., *The Tenderloin*), and distinctly urban activities (e.g., *nightlife*) are significantly interpreted through the popular speech that denotes and, especially, characterizes them.

Popular speech that has grown up around certain aspects of city life also shows how city folk see the categories of standard terminology differently. The police, for example, have inspired a variety of slang names, such as *pigs, bulls,* and *flatfoot,* that speak to an image at variance with the standard word *police*—the City's "Finest." The number of slang synonyms for *police* and other street types, such as toughs and roughs, also suggests their level of real and symbolic conflict with slangsters, as well as their prominence in the public world of the streets.

The folk model of linguistic reality frames experience on a bias and suggests somewhat different attitudes toward experience from those in-clined by standard, formal, or elite language. The study of slang discovers a skewed view of the urban world—a view from the streets, and of the streets. Slang is deliberately and perversely connotative; it strikes a contrary attitude and expresses a cocked opinion. *Rubbernecker* for an out-of-town sightseer is one of the funniest words in the vocabulary and reveals New Yorkers' sardonic attitude toward tourists, as well as a graphically comic image of their behavior. Popular speech, especially slang, while greatly overlapping more formal and conventional presuppositions about the urban world, tugs against them for a view of a different slant and color—a slightly different refraction.

Talking about the City

Popular speech about the city is mostly about its public and semi-public life. By public I usually mean things that can be seen in, or from, the streets, things accessible to all, and things otherwise associated with the common knowledge of the town. Lifelong residents of New York do not feel much need to acquire the language of the city because they already speak it. As with the casual acquisition of any language, they learn it as they need it. Day by day they accumulate enough terminology and other new meanings to get along, at least in their own little social worlds.

But visitors and other outsiders must learn strange sign systems or codes, including verbal ones, and they are culturally disadvantaged until they do. Guidebooks for tourists in foreign lands, which travelers significantly call survival manuals, often contain a short lexicon of the local lingo. The list is chosen, as in tourists' phrase-books, to orient visitors to essential elements of their new surroundings. Guidebooks for visitors to New York, like guides to a foreign country, sometimes used to contain a short, usually humorous lexicon of New York locutions that purported to explain the native speech habits and, generally, to help the visitor to impart meaning to the new surroundings. One published in the early 1930s saw fit to include *hotsy-totsy, Annie Oakley* (a theater pass), *schmuck, up the river, rent party, clip joint, whoopee, sheet* and *tab* (for a tabloid newspaper), and more than a hundred others.[9] Many such expressions, once thought peculiar to New York, have since spread into general, national slang. But how many Ameri-cans today know, say, the meaning of *skell?* (It is an old word of recent revival and today is on the lips of many New Yorkers to denote a particularly down-and-out homeless man or woman in the streets.)

After the Civil War, when New York became even more of a focus of national life and a magnet for travelers, a rash of books were published that claimed to explain the Great City to visitors. These enormously popu-lar books were read in the provinces for vicarious experience and by visi-tors to the city to prepare for real experience in the streets. One author in

1868 wrote in his Preface: "His [the vicarious traveler's] curiosity can be satisfied in these pages, and he can know the Great City from them, without incurring the danger attending an effort to see it."[10] The books explained the political, economic, and social workings of the city and described the many social traps that befell even the natives. They gave dire warnings about skin games to cheat the tourists and about tantalizing but dangerous attractions. In doing all this, the books were sprinkled with unusual words and phrases, often in quotation marks, that helped the visitor to ascribe additional meaning to unusual things and activities and generally to decode the environment.

The historical, accumulated vocabulary of popular expressions about the urban world can be arranged and read like a text by a collective author. The great French novelist Honoré de Balzac read Paris as a city of signs— gestures, physiognomies, body language, dress, and speechways—a text that yielded meanings of social difference below its surface of apparent nondifferentiation.[11] A middle-class Parisian social type called *flâneurs* made an art and avocation of strolling and sitting about the public places of Paris and, from an elite perspective, reading the visible and often subtle signs of social difference to discern the social order of the city.[12] To the speakers of slang in the streets, these words and phrases were one of their ways to read the city and comprehend the whole city in its diversity. The ideologies implicit in popular speech are a demotic view of the order of things.

Like all language, slang is rich in metaphors, which guide our thought-ways more than most people realize.[13] Slang metaphors tend to be a bit newer, or seem so to the users, and thus express the new, extended, or contrary meanings for which speakers are striving. Some fairly elaborate metaphors are the city's public life expressed as *the streets;* the city's social organization as an *urban jungle;* and the cityscape as a stone and steel landscape of *canyons, cliffs,* and *mesas,* inhabited by *cliff dwellers* and *cave dwellers.* The metaphors are used, as often as not, for the connotations so essential to the rhetorical effect of slang. Popular speech about the city, like all speech, encodes many hidden meanings and deeper visions of the world.

The City Seen as Sets of Opposites

The social strains of the metropolitan experience, and hence the structure of a world view, are reflected in the tendency of popular speech to express the urban social world as sets of opposites, usually with a hierarchy implied. These implied vertical stratifications in slang usually hark back to the various social structures generated by the political economy. A similar duality is also expressed in other popular and even intellectual social thought about the city. The Christian dualisms of Heaven and Hell, of light and dark, and of sunshine and shadow shaped the concerned rhetoric of nineteenth-century urban reform. The secular city turned the dualism on its head and redefined the artificial light of night—the *bright lights*—as positive and the dark of provincial righteousness as negative. A rich lexical culture of night-life flowed from this popular, more demotic view of the urban world.

Dual oppositions are also expressed in language as ends of a continuum, usually with one end valued over the other, and each end taking part of its meaning from opposition to the other. Popular speech about the city more broadly expresses folk perceptions of rural-urban continua and marks cultural strains between the multiple sets of polarities. The core oppositions are discernible in many lexical connotations of high and low (both spatial and social), social pluralism and unity, deviance and conventionality, chaos and order, center and periphery, motion and stillness, fastness and slowness, complexity and simplicity, density and sparseness, and the boundaries between group ego and social others. This is certainly not the only structure of culture, and much of this naming phenomenon in slang is only a reflection of the universal human inclination to oversimplify reality to a minimum number of differences, namely two.

A large class of generic names, which I call the oppositions of Us and Them, divides the world into two kinds of things and thoroughly demonstrates the principle. Looking across the whole historical vocabulary of popular speech and slang in American English, we find a remarkable tendency in culturally stressful areas to divide the social world into oppositions, one usually presumed superior to the other. And this has another wrinkle. The slang names that denote those people traveling, usually upwardly, between the two positions—assimilators, apostates, social climbers, and rural immigrants—can even be taken as indicating a third position that mediates and resolves the dichotomy. Altogether, slang about the city seems to be yet more evidence of the human tendency to divide the social world into vertically stratified dualities.[14] This perceived structure of social life is then read onto reality and, to various degrees, becomes social reality.

A number of cultural oppositions or dialectal tensions can be located in the whole urban lexicon of popular speech. These can be reduced to several general oppositions: high and low, front and back, open and closed, order and chaos, and center and periphery. Some are ancient metaphorical extensions of the human body onto the social body, projected into space and, as a cultural exercise in orthogonality, onto the rectangular grid of American city streets. The most pervasive and general theme I hear in these thousands of words and phrases is vertical stratification on the horizontal field of city streets and neighborhoods. The relations of class, social mobility, and their conflicts in the historical city are expressed, among other ways, in metaphors of the American city street grid and in the informal names of neighborhoods and their residents.

The rich imagery of the bright lights and its associated cultures have symbolized the city as a place of individualism and social release in contrast to the constraints of traditional rural society. The lexical reactions to new ways of urban living, especially accommodations to technological innovations, dramatize in yet other ways the distinction between rural and urban society. The imaging of tall buildings in popular speech as *skyscrapers,* to take another instance, reveals the ambivalent feelings of urbanites toward their stark world of steel and concrete and its endless, upward growth.

The predominant dichotomous structure in historical popular speech about the city is the rhetorical setting apart of social outgroups and the parts of the city in which they live—Them versus Us. The cleavages of social class, high and low status in the community, and the closely related fact of ethnic inequality are among the most stringent ordering principles of modern life and are elaborately expressed in popular speech. Urbanites, too, have a history of derogating their country cousins (*hicks*) and small towns and rural areas (*the sticks*), drawing a sharp distinction between center and periphery in the metropolitan region. People name in slang, usually pejoratively, all sorts of social others as a way to establish and maintain social boundaries and, reflexively, assert their own identities.

Culture and Popular Speech

Literature, art and illustration, mass culture, and popular speech about the city all define a similar set of social objects, for all are part of the same cultural cake. Urban realist art and literature have most often been correlated.[15] In New York all four of these expressive forms found much the same places, activities, and social types in the public life of city streets and in nearby semi-public enclosures. All depicted the elevated trains, cafés, theaters, saloons, speakeasies, breadlines, and so on. All showed keen awarenesses of skyscrapers and apartment houses and found social significance in their height, walls, doors, windows, basements, and rooftops. All categorized and characterized the same array of urban social types in city streets—beggars, homeless men and women, peddlers, well-dressed loafers and dandies, strutting toughs, streetwalkers, ethnic types, policemen, country hicks, swells, and other sorts that made up the Steinbergian cast of characters on the city pave.

These awarenesses of the urban surrounds are much the same in the culture of any large city, though they take special flavor from particular cities, in this case New York. Awareness of the physical city, for example, tends to focus on certain symbolic places in the city, such as famous downtown promenades of various social groups (Broadway and the Bowery), public squares and other outdoor social hubs (Union, Madison, and Times squares and Central Park), rich neighborhoods (the Silk-Stocking District and Millionaires' Row), slums (Hell's Kitchen, The Gashouse District, The Dead End) and ethnic neighborhoods (Chinatown, Harlem, or Little Italy), the vital financial districts in a capitalist economy (Wall Street), and specialized land uses of nightlife and vice (The Great White Way and The Tenderloin).

American realist and naturalist literature used popular speech to evoke social surroundings. City literature and realist art owe much to the spirit of Walt Whitman, a street-level democrat who reveled in the humanity of New York and its panoply of street life, including its popular speech. Whitman loved and used in his writing the natural, spoken cadences and vocabulary of everyday speech. "Slang," Whitman wrote, "profoundly consider'd, is the lawless germinal element, below all words and sentences, and behind all poetry, and proves a certain perennial rankness and protestantism in speech."[16] He urged his followers to find essentially American themes and expressions as demotic as slang.

In the much-analyzed, so-called city novel, the city itself, its social diversity, its impersonality, its harsh stratification, its exacting quality, and the magic of its unpredictability are, so to speak, characters in the narrative and interact with human characters to influence their lives.[17] The human characters sometimes speak the slang of their urban social worlds, naming people, places, and things in the city around them. City novelists are a wide and disparate class, notably including William Dean Howells, Stephen Crane, Theodore Dreiser, Edith Wharton, John Dos Passos, and Thomas Wolfe. Most eventually came to and wrote about New York. Several city novelists started with newspapers and, like some of their urban realist counterparts in art who began their careers as newspaper illustrators, came to share a similar gritty view of the city.

Certain novelists, such as Crane, used street speech as raw material before it was generally accepted as a fundamental tool in literature and taken for granted by readers. Around 1900, the reading public was fascinated with slang and social dialect. Racy popular speech signaled a break with Victorian proprieties of usage and with those who clung to them. Slang also seemed to open the curious worlds of low city life. Stories written in the dialect of the Bowery, complete with its slang, were widely read in the 1890s. Edward W. Townsend's "Chimmie Fadden" stories were enormously popular and were first written for and published in the New York *Sun*. Chimmie, a scrapping newsboy from Park Row, rose in the world to make his wry observations on New York high life from his incorruptible Bowery point of view. Stephen Crane's *Maggie: A Girl of the Streets,* first published in 1893, used Bowery dialect for a much more somber effect.

Slang, especially after the First World War, had a cachet for many urbanites. Using slang signaled familiarity with the many excitingly deviant social worlds of the city and it was a necessary tool in the vocabulary of the man—or woman—about town. Urban color writers in the 1920s and 1930s, such as Damon Runyon and Ring Lardner, established styles of writing in slang. In the 1930s egalitarian sentiments among intellectuals and the quest for the proletarian novel, such as Albert Halper's *Union Square* (1933), helped make it fashionable to view slang as the natural speech of the common man. Howard Hawks' movie *Ball of Fire* (1941), starring Gary Cooper and Barbara Stanwyck, played with the notion of slang as the authentic, up-to-the-minute speech of real people, and Stanwyck taught it to Cooper.

The short stories of O. Henry (the famous pseudonym of William Sydney Porter) evoked many of the popular symbols of New York life, typically in the first paragraphs, and he usually nailed them down with the popular expressions of his day. His New York stories were all written during his brief residence in the city between 1902 and 1908, just before his death in 1910 at age 47. His best New York stories are in *The Four Million* (1906), *The Trimmed Lamp* (1907), and *The Voice of the City* (1908). He lived most of his time in New York at 55 Irving Place, just south of Gramercy Park. From his front parlor-floor window, he viewed street life and passersby, imagining their lives to make story characters. Most of his New York stories took their locales—streets, parks, bars, and restaurants—within a radius of about half a mile, an easy stroll, from his rooms on Irving Place. Within this world, O. Henry was an acute if sentimental observer of the city's social scene, populated as it was with his beloved shopgirls, waitresses, factory girls, typists, clerks, rounders, con men, cops, transients, and park bums.

O. Henry's anonymous urbanites from all walks of life, going their separate ways, somehow manage to cross paths and are revealed and redeemed in their humanity. He subjects his characters to the "magic" of city life, as sociologist Peter Berger has called the feeling, if not the fact, that "anything can happen here—and it could happen right now."[18] O. Henry did, after all, call New York "Bagdad on the Subway." The magic of O. Henry's city lies in romantic hope. He made it happen in his stories, and that is his charm, even today. He draws on the uniquely urban situation to get sweet coincidence into the cold world of strangers. In "The Green Door" (1906), a romantic urban adventurer, through a random turn in an urban maze, finds the love of his life. This elusive, magical quality of city life, ignoring its dark side, still attracts many people, especially the young and socially adventurous.

By the 1950s the classic city novel and similar literature had gone into near eclipse in favor of indoor and backyard suburban settings and unidentifiable locales. The successor *urban* novel, and that modifier now seems fitting, turned to negative themes of urban despair, alienation, poverty, and violence. The city was not abandoned as a theme but continued darkly alongside the new suburban novels. The new suburban setting, now in contrast to the receding city, simply reflected the new environs of growing numbers of writers and their middle-class readers, or reflected the setting to which they aspired.

The suburban novel became introverted and psychological, preoccupied with the interiors of personalities and with the minutiae of personal relations, largely because of its middle-class preoccupations. Characters seemed largely unaware of, or at least unaffected by, their social surroundings, though sometimes they were influenced by suburban homogeneity and boredom. People talked informally or even slangily, but to evoke character and attitude, not surroundings. The city in the suburban novel, reflecting the national mind, had ceased to be a factor, a character, and had become a given, and one largely ignored.

A similar relationship exists between the visual arts and popular speech in their symbolization of the old metropolitan core. Around 1905, a group of urban realist painters and printmakers, later facetiously called the Ashcan School, emerged in New York and were counterparts of the naturalist and realist writers. Robert Henri, John Sloan, William J. Glackens, Everett Shinn, and George Luks studied at the Pennsylvania Academy of Fine Arts. All were in a social group around Henri and met frequently at his Philadelphia studio.[19] Henri, Sloan, Glackens, Luks, and Shinn later moved to and settled in New York. All but Henri had been newspaper illustrators in Philadelphia and, so, had followed the tradition of Winslow Homer. Like certain of their literary counterparts with early careers in newspaper work, they were especially close to street vernaculars of both image and word. The spirit of Walt Whitman generally inspired this group of young artists.

In 1908 Henri established a school in New York and subsequently taught George Bellows, Edward Hopper, Glenn O. Coleman, and Stuart Davis, all of whom had Ashcan aspects or periods. Robert Henri taught his circle to follow the example of Whitman and to find American subjects and idioms for their art in the most ordinary and everyday life of the city. John Sloan, who admired Walt Whitman's "Song of Myself," became the preeminent realist of New York street life. In the next half century these artists and their successors portrayed tenement life, crowded sidewalk scenes, ordinary people interspersed with down-and-outs in city parks and squares, workers and shoppers riding mass transit, and sometimes even ashcans. Not surprisingly, they often used words and phrases of popular speech about the city to title their pictures and further evoke their subject.

The Armory Show of 1913 marked the turn to modernism in American art and shifted attention from realism. But the realists and similarly inspired artists continued to pursue their vision of city life. The Fourteenth Street School, the next group of urban realists, were so called because many of their studios were located on or near 14th Street around Union Square and because several of the group drew and painted street, park, shop, and subway scenes of the neighborhood. Almost as an anachronism, they carried forward the tradition of gritty street realism into the early 1950s and toward the end of the modernist period. Kenneth Hayes Miller, who also once taught Edward Hopper, was the mentor of the group that included Reginald Marsh, Isabel Bishop, and the Soyer brothers. Reginald Marsh was the most consistently oriented toward grimy street life and gnarled, sweaty crowd scenes.

The first wave of American modernism in the 1910s, especially the art of John Marin, Max Weber, and Joseph Stella, also dealt intensely with city images. Photographers, such as Jacob Riis (in the documentary style) and

Edward Steichen, Paul Strand, and Berenice Abbott (as self-conscious fine artists), recorded many of the same scenes in much the same spirit. The urban artists and writers, along with the people who used corresponding categories of popular speech, all found much the same city in each of their mediums. It was always Whitman's city of "shifting tableaux."

The City, Mass Communications, and Popular Speech

Popular speech and mass communications have always been interactive, each borrowing from the other, each spreading further the other's locutions. Stories, articles, and columns in newspapers and magazines, minstrelsy and vaudeville, popular song titles and lyrics, the dialogue of radio and movies, and the bubbles over the heads of comic-strip characters—all borrowed words of slang and, in circular ways, modified and returned them to slang. Slang in general, and slang about the big city in particular, flowed profusely from the early popular arts and, later, from the mass entertainment that grew as an integral part of the new industrial order. The new mass culture responded to its consumers' new social experience and to the new requirements of metropolitan life. Mass communication traded in the *lingua franca* of slang when they wanted to speak as one with the city. Millions were reading, listening, laughing, and learning—all the while talking.

Writers and performers who worked in the early mass media were mostly of city origins, in touch with urban worlds of discourse, and consequently knew a great deal of slang. They naturally incorporated this social knowledge into their products of mass culture and with it won wide acceptance. Some of the slang-makers in show business, journalism, radio, and movies drew their words from their own ethnic backgrounds, especially Yiddish-American and Irish-American vernaculars, and sent along the words and phrases they had heard as children in the streets of New York. The diffusion of popular vocabulary was hastened by Tin Pan Alley, gag writers, comedians, press agents, promoters, headline writers for sensational tabloids, Broadway columnists, cartoonists, and advertising people. In one sense, the business of all these writers, lyricists, and jingle-makers was to coin bright new catchpennies, a few of which met a real need in popular expression. If the fresh words were fun, they might be picked up and used widely.

Newspapers, the first mass medium, were tremendously interactive with popular speech. In the 1880s the metropolitan dailies in New York and other large cities became highly competitive and they grasped for wider readership by abandoning their staid old formal styles and using livelier language, including many popular expressions. The papers entered a direct, reciprocal relationship with popular speech. Newspaper writers invented whole genres of slang, a few items of which became actually popular. Broadway columnists, forever seeking a novel turn of phrase, coined scores of slangy synonyms for 42nd Street and The Great White Way. The columnists slanged up everything. The newspapers, says urban historian Gunther Barth, "coined new words that shaped urban patterns of speaking and thinking, gave old words new meanings, and wore others out."[20]

Columnists like Walter Winchell, Arthur (Bugs) Baer, and Damon Runyon both coined and borrowed slang, but in either event sometimes popularized catchy expressions.[21] The columnist O. O. McIntyre exaggerated in 1929 when he wrote that Thomas A. "TAD" Dorgan, the cartoonist, was "also the genius who has furnished ninety percent of the slang that has enlivened Broadway and the out country for twenty years."[22] TAD did help popularize hundreds of slang expressions and probably coined some of them, though today he is credited with coining more than he really did. Walter Winchell also traded in bright new slang, and much of it was from whole cloth.

The newspapers' syndicated comic strips early in this century were a powerful force for spreading slang.[23] It is easy to forget the enormous popularity of the comics in the days before television. Sociologist Leo Bogart reported that in 1949 the comics were "read by four of every five urban adults in America." In New York 85 percent of those interviewed read them; 60 percent said they "talked about the things happening in the comics."[24] Television has all but supplanted this role of the newspaper comic strips in the talk of the town.

As New York and other large cities became larger and internally more diverse, especially through immigration, the popular forms of stage entertainment reflected more and more the concerns, the interests, the social worlds, and so the speech of their urban audiences.[25] Minstrelsy and variety in the nineteenth century, continuing as vaudeville and burlesque in this century, borrowed from city slang, invigorated it, and gave it back to audiences to be taken again into the streets. Vaudeville, as a more genteel American version of variety came to be called in New York after about 1893, was the chief medium of live, oral entertainment and was part of the web of social life—until radio came along after 1920. Vaudeville drew a diverse urban audience and through its comedy and songs gave city people an image of their own diversity.

New York's old Palace Theater, O. O. McIntyre remarked, was "where one got the latest slang, smart cracks and popular tunes."[26] Robert W. Snyder, in his recent history of vaudeville in New York, suggested that vaudeville was, so to speak, "the voice of the city."[27] Indeed, the tangled etymology of *vaudeville,* in one phase at least, suggests the French *voix de ville,* "voices of the city," though that is not its most direct source.[28] From the stage routines at the Palace and many earlier houses, wrote urban historian Gunther Barth, "the audience also distilled models for everyday behavior and guides for living in the modern city."[29] Vaudeville acts made audiences aware of the tensions of ethnic, social, and regional diversities with blatant stereotypes, often labeled with slang names. Vaudeville and the slang it spread surely can be taken as voices of the city.

The lyrics of popular songs and musical comedies, really forms of light verse, interacted closely with popular speech about the city. The publication of popular songs about New York began in the late nineteenth century and increased to a peak in the 1920s and 1930s, but fell off sharply after 1950. The old songs extolled the romance of the bright lights, the fun, and the style of Manhattan. Through the decades, the neighborhoods named in the lyrics shifted with the northward growth of the city, from the Bowery, to midtown, especially to Broadway and Times Square, and finally uptown to Harlem in the 1920s and 1930s.[30] The publication of popular songs about New York increased again in the 1970s and 1980s, probably reflecting the interest of young people in the style of Downtown.

Tin Pan Alley was exceedingly quick to pick up any new expression and make it a song title or work it into the lyrics. Tony Pastor and years later Irving Berlin followed the newspapers to stay in touch with the voice of the city and to get themes and phrases for song lyrics.[31] By about 1940, at least two hundred songs about New York and its social life had been published, a quarter of them extolling Broadway. Sheet music familiarized millions of Americans with the words and music of Broadway, as well as with the antics of *playboys, chorus girls, gold diggers, cigarette girls, stage-door johnnies, champagne charlies,* and *butter-and-egg men.* Lyricists like George M. Cohan, Irving Berlin, Lorenz Hart, and Cole Porter wrote songs about New York and singably fixed many popular expressions in the American mind. Finley Peter Dunne, better known as Mr. Dooley, said, "when we Americans get through with the English language, it will look like it had been run over by a musical comedy."

Commercial radio broadcasting after 1920 and the talking movies a decade later continued and deepened the interplay between mass culture and popular speech and eventually carried the message simultaneously into every town and city in the country. The talking pictures of the 1930s and 1940s used big city slang, real or imagined, to simulate the tenor of city life, real or imagined. More than any other medium of the period, the movies popularized and occasionally coined underworld argot. Many early script writers had city backgrounds and knew street talk; later ones actually searched scholarly works on slang for authentic locutions.

Other movies of that period—musicals, screwball comedies, and boy-meets-loses-gets-girl romances—were often set in New York and, much more than today, celebrated the variety, romance, opportunities, adventure, surprises, and incongruities of city life. These movies, often as not, had at least one character who was a fast-talking, wise-cracking Broadway Joe or Jane, a show-biz type, or a hardboiled newspaper reporter on the city beat who spouted a dazzling array of slang. For that matter, everybody talked slang, except of course stuffy parents, school teachers, judges, wardens, and other inhibited people. The Dead End Kids and the Bowery Boys in the

Hollywood movies gave America a gentle and largely incorrect version of New York street gangs and how they talked—"*Cheese it*, duh cops."[32] But some of their stagetalk stuck in the speech of young people who sat on Saturday afternoons in the movie houses of Middletown, USA.

The Cycle of New York Metropolitan Life

The proliferation of popular speech about the city and life at the center rose and fell in the century roughly between 1850 and 1950. This cycle was in close correlation with the rise and decline of the modern industrial phase of American urbanization. This is wholly expectable, for this class of words and the culture of urbanism that gave them birth, including its art, literature, and mass culture, are part of this cycle of urbanization. A rough plotting of the words and phrases in this book indicates that lexical innovation about the metropolitan core rose quickly after about 1850 to a peak between 1880 and 1920, thereafter declining, rapidly after about 1950. The metropolis remains a fact of national life and new slang about the city is still appearing. Increasingly, though, new popular speech comes from the centerless matrix of national life, especially through television.

After 1814, when the still new nation had found its own pace, the industrial cities on the northeastern seaboard, especially New York, Boston, and Philadelphia, grew rapidly and their urban cultures deepened. The distinguished language scholar Allen Walker Read has shown how the slang term *O.K.*, the quintessential Americanism that went on to worldwide success in many languages, emerged in the late 1830s from the social and political contexts of Boston as well as New York.[33] In 1868 New York's songwriters first used *O.K.* in a popular song, William Horace Lingard and Charles E. Pratt's "Walking Down Broadway." The lyric goes: "The O.K. thing on Saturday is walking down Broadway."

By the 1840s New York life had already begun to develop a distinctive lexical culture of new slang about city life that was to pass into the American language. *Smart aleck,* an obnoxiously conceited person or wise guy, was most likely coined by the city's police in reference to the reputation of the famous thief Aleck Hoag, who was well known to New Yorkers in the mid-1840s.[34] *Shyster,* an unprofessional and unethical lawyer, does not derive from a surname, despite the many stories. *Shyster* most certainly came from American German *Scheisser,* "shitter," from *Scheisse,* excrement, and was used to describe certain New York lawyers in the 1840s.[35]

Nearly as well known are *Brodie* and *Buttinsky,* which are related to surnames. *Brodie,* as in *to do a Brodie,* meaning to take a wild dive or leap, especially one that results in failure, a flop, is from the name of the self-promoting Bowery saloon owner Steve Brodie who built his reputation on a specious claim to have dived from the Brooklyn Bridge in 1886. Brodie's claim excited public interest mainly because a real stunt leap in 1885 had killed Robert E. Odlum, whose name is ironically forgotten. *Buttinsky* is a mock surname formed by attaching the Slavic ending *-sky* to *butt in,* 'intrude,' and was in use by 1902. Classically, a *Buttinsky* was a busybody who walked the streets of the Lower East Side asking "How's business?"

H. L. Mencken, along with other language scholars, argued that the old American frontier set the emerging tone of American speech, with "its disdain of all scholastic rules and precedents, its tendency toward bold and often bizarre tropes, its rough humors, its not infrequent flights of what might be called poetic fancy, its love of neologisms for their own sake." Mencken added that "to the immigrants who poured in after 1850, even the slums of the great Eastern cities presented essentially frontier conditions."[36] This urban frontier was in its own way every bit as wild and woolly as the West, and popular speech sometimes saw it exactly that way, too.

By 1850 or thereabouts several important trends, especially well illustrated in New York, had reached thresholds that stimulated new popular vocabulary about the urban world. The expanding national economy, the spectacular growth of wealth in the 1850s, new technologies, and soon the Civil War were to change the country permanently. Large industrial cities in the North created situations that prompted a groundswell of new words and new meanings for old words as a result of cultural adaptation to these new circumstances. American slang, contrary to what is sometimes said, is not by its very nature more inclined to coinage, but simply found in history more of the rapid social change that required coinage. "And," said Kenneth Burke, " 'slang' was the result. It is, by this analysis, simply *proverbs not so named,* a kind of 'folk criticism'."[37]

New York at mid-century was emerging as the world metropolis it would become by 1900. The city's population had increased nearly fourfold between 1820 and 1850. The Crystal Palace Exhibition of 1853, the nation's first World's Fair, enlivened the city's commerce and opened a new era of tourism. New York soon exerted its metropolitan influence over a wider region and over the nation. For a century thereafter New York dominated the nation's popular and media images of the dynamic, diverse, glamorous, wicked big city. The city's concentration of mass media portrayed for the whole nation New York's social types, consumer and leisure styles, urban folkways, vanities, sins, wealth, squalor, and traps—and in doing so carried many locutions of and about those social worlds into national popular speech.

The new industrialization and unfettered capitalism, while generally raising levels of living for the masses in the long run, in the short run created a huge urban proletariat that cyclically fell on hard times. Disturbing numbers were always unemployed, which served to remind the employed of their precarious status. The new economy also created an enlarged class of commercial and industrial wealth whose interests and ways of life sharply diverged from those of the working class. The half-truth of our national mythology promised steady upward mobility for virtually all who were willing to work hard, if not personally, then at least for their children. But upward mobility in cities of this period, as history shows us, was less general than many have presumed.[38] For the most part the social classes stood—and remained generation after generation—in stark contrast. By the 1850s the social diversity of New York and other cities and the gulf between the classes were further increased by the migration from the farm to town. The great Irish immigration in the 1840s and immigrants fleeing the European revolts of 1848 settled in the large industrial cities of the East and further enlarged the working classes. These arrivals were echoed with considerable pungency in popular speech.

Until mid-century, New York, as well as Boston and Philadelphia, were densely settled and surprisingly compact "walking cities," as the historians now call them. One could walk from the center to the periphery in half an hour, or through all the neighborhoods in a day. Most of New York was still in the Old City below 14th Street and business activity concentrated along lower Broadway. The walking city began to expand by new means of public transportation, which changed city life with new commuting patterns. In addition, the wealthier residents could now remove themselves from the congested center and add physical distance to social distance. A multitude of epithets for the upper classes and lexical scorn for social climbers emerged from this process. Because of the shape of the skinny island of Manhattan, the wealthy generally moved uptown, fanning out along the spine of Fifth Avenue, and were derided as *Avenoodles*. The compact Old City, with its close mix of rich, poor, and commercial activity, now became dispersed and reformed into large homogeneous areas. The trend eventually reshaped metropolitan life and is abundantly reflected in popular speech.

Even before mid-century poverty was discovered in the slums of big American cities, and it was "novel in kind and alarming in size."[39] The new urban poverty had developed in the wake of industrialization, rapid urbanization, and heavy but unabsorbed immigration in the first half of the century. New York was the most densely settled big city and its slums were the worst. Charles Dickens visited the United States in 1842 and in *American Notes* described the already infamous New York slum of Five Points, a squalid quarter near today's Chinatown. (The area was named for its center at the intersection of five streets.) Dickens, with a police escort, made a night visit to one of the hovels of Five Points and watched as the miserable, surprised sleepers stirred from their corners "as if the judgement hour were near at hand, and every obscene grave were giving up its dead."[40] Dickens, and fifty years later Jacob Riis writing of the Bend of Mulberry Street, made the Five Points and its "worst" building, the Old Brewery, world-famous symbols of American industrial poverty. The slum was largely razed by the 1890s.

Around 1850 the word *slang*, while in English a century earlier, became the accepted term for "illegitimate" and other unconventional speech.[41] Disapproving comment on low speech forms, fueled by class anxieties in the changing city, probably helped establish the word *slang* in the United States. By 1900 the term had all its present meanings, including that of a vocabulary regarded as below standard and that threatened proper, genteel usages. The huge and troubling social diversity of New York was manifest by 1850. Proximity and common knowledge among urban subgroups, augmented and amplified by newspapers and popular art forms, were increasing. Street speech of the period expressed the troublesome spirit of the social underside of the industrial city: unconventional, experimental without license, insubordinate, scornful of—or merely careless of—authority. These locutions spread rapidly and began to be noticed, recorded, and deemed something of a social problem.

American scholars at this time were also trying to standardize spelling and grammar and to establish usages they considered proper and correct from their elite perspectives. The more brazen forms of popular speech were their bugbears. The attempt to codify formal speech and thus to express middle-class solidarity drew popular speech into critical relief. Criminal cant, from which much slang derived, seemed even more threatening to the social order. Herman Melville in his novel *Pierre* (1852) created an evening's adventure for his hero in a New York police station. Pierre, upon arriving in the darkened city and in charge of two provincial young ladies, stopped at the station to ask assistance. Pierre reflected on the lower-class street speech he and his charges heard among the detainees in the station as "the foulest of all human lingoes, that dialect of sin and death, known as the Cant language, or the Flash."[42]

The most important record of this New York street speech, which so shocked Melville's characters, was collected by George Washington Matsell in his dictionary titled *Vocabulum,* published in 1859. Indigenous New York street vernacular is mixed in with imported British criminal cant or flash language, which had already become part of the low speech of New York streets. Understanding underworld cant was believed to give insights into the lower-class world of the "dangerous classes" and, for the police, insights into criminal behavior and social control. For instance, the police could know that the cant expression *Coves, let us frog and toe* translates as "Lads, let's go to New York; *frog and toe,* wrote Matsell, meant 'New York.' More generally, the particulars of this and other street vernaculars were of great interest and usefulness in the new plural city. Some of this restricted vocabulary of the underworld thus escaped into the slang of the period.

Matsell was an unlikely lexicographer, a politician who rose through the ranks of Tammany Hall to become New York's first Chief of Police in 1845. He remained in that post until 1857 when the New York Police Department was abolished in favor of the Metropolitan Police Department; he was in later years a Commissioner of Police. At the same time, obviously with a conflict of interests, he published the *National Police Gazette,* a successful paper that reported tales of crime and boxing news. Matsell was a notorious and colorful character, weighing over 300 pounds, reportedly corrupt, and a lover of the sporting life.[43] Whatever Matsell's lexicographical abilities and character, his *Vocabulum* has been through the years a source for scholars, a rare voice from the mean streets.[44]

In the 1880s and 1890s, the writings of journalists such as Jacob Riis and the early efforts of Progressivism fired wide public indignation and curiosity about the problems and lives of the urban poor. Literature and, especially, journalism more intensely explored and publicized the contrasting life ways of high and low society. Numerous city newspapers bound the diverse community with common knowledge and made the complexity of the modern city comprehensible. Conspicuous consumption by the rich, always good news copy, and blatant vice, equally saleable news, rose to new heights in the Gilded Age. The press reported the scandals of fashionable society and the garden-variety crime of the poor and immigrant. The more sensational newspapers used the liveliest terms of the urban vernacular.

The middle period between about 1880 and the end of the First World War was most abundant in the appearance of new words about city life. New York (i.e., Manhattan) reached a population of one million in the census of 1880. The following four decades saw the enormous New Immigration from eastern and southern Europe before the Golden Door was closed. Greater New York, the metropolitan consolidation of Manhattan, Brooklyn, the Bronx, Queens, and Staten Island, was established in 1898 and doubled the population of the city. The population rose to a new high before the First World War and the New Immigration immensely increased ethnic diversity. In 1910, the bulk of the city's population was of foreign birth or had been born of immigrant parents. This new diversity in New York and other cities sprinkled American popular speech with borrowings from foreign tongues and again stirred names for the new social perceptions of ethnic and class diversity.

These four decades also saw the quickening of communication, modern advertising, mass consumerism, and other dramatic developments. New electric streetcar lines reached to the suburbs and allowed the city to grow horizontally at a faster rate. The new, true skyscrapers—towers with full-steel frames, curtain walls, and electric elevators—and large apartment buildings now allowed the city to grow vertically, ever more densely, and at a faster rate. Rapid transit, especially elevated trains and subways, quickened travel within the city. The main streets—starting with Broadway—were lighted by electricity, intensely so at entertainment centers, to create a spectacle that was to give new meaning to the old symbol of urban gaiety—the *bright lights.*

The Federal Census of 1920 marked the end of the middle period and the close of a historical era. For the first time in American history over half of the U.S. population was living in towns and cities. We were no longer chiefly an agrarian society. The wide use of Henry Ford's mass-produced automobile after 1920 allowed all cities to spread rapidly into the countryside. The telephone, by then becoming common, reknit social networks that had been dispersed by new forms of transportation and made convenient the suburb's promise of a better life. The automobile, telephone, phonograph, radio, and the motion pictures tied the metropolitan region as well as the whole country closer together with an overlay of popular culture. These innovations changed the pace and quality of life for many urbanites, and the experience of them is richly reflected in popular speech.

The relaxing of certain ethnic and class barriers in the large cities, especially after the First World War, brought conventional, middle-class people into contact with a variety of formerly isolated urban subcultures, such as bohemians, theater people, socialists, ethnic minorities, gangsters, and drug users. The divergent economic interests of rural and urban economies, however interdependent their welfares, once again heightened the contrast between rural and urban life and prompted urbanites to celebrate even more the bright lights while disparaging even more the dullness of small-town and rural life. In the 1930s, the Great Depression, the rise of organized labor, and the uprooting of regional labor forces and troublesome resettlement of homeless men in the skid rows of large cities widened public consciousness of these ways of life. The mass media and literature celebrated slang as the speech of the common people and so of their spirit.

New York and other cities in the North had clearly reached a certain plateau—a maturity—by the late 1940s. The older, downtown housing stock had deteriorated and little new urban housing had been built during the Depression and the Second World War; neighborhood services and the quality of life at the core of cities had deteriorated. Savings built up from wartime prosperity, the postwar baby boom, all abetted by pro-suburban federal housing policy, set the country on the newest, biggest wave ever of middle-class suburbanization. Escaping urbanites were followed first by their everyday service facilities and eventually by their jobs. By the early 1960s, the New York sociologist Herbert Gans could write that most urbanites remained in cities because of poverty, unemployment, or ties to family and ethnic neighborhood. The only people who actually liked living in the big city, said Gans, were a minority of young, unmarried, childless people, and an even smaller number of "cosmopolites"—artists, intellectuals, and the like.[45]

Slang innovation about life at the metropolitan center dropped off sharply after about 1950, and a smaller—and somehow less vital—popular vocabulary about the suburbs arose. The dictionaries of current slang published in the 1970s and 1980s, while containing many old expressions, are largely devoid of old or new words and phrases about life at the metropolitan center. Social historians seem in agreement that the country underwent a profound change of life after the Second World War. The country as a whole, at least after the end of the Korean War in 1953, was in a period of prosperity, optimism, and confidence. But the great cities—New York among them—languished and their cultures of the center seemed to undergo a loss of confidence as lifelong urbanites turned their backs on the city and looked toward the future and a better life in suburbia and exurbia.

Popular culture generally reflected the decline of the metropolitan center. Until the mid-1950s, the movies had portrayed the big city as a place of middle-class excitement, romance, and adventure. But then, along with television, the movies began to portray the big city, New York in particular, as a sinkhole of poverty, crime, violence, and drugs. Fewer words about the city's core and its ways of life, except those about the new order of ghetto life and its social problems, came into popular speech, and some of the older words fell into disuse. As early as the mid-1950s, new slang began to reflect this spatial pulling apart. The old city was sometimes disparaged from the suburban sidelines, but mostly the attitude was one of growing indifference.

New slang today is as likely to come from suburban malls as from the cities. The young people who frequent the suburban shopping malls in search of social life are themselves the object of slang, in the late 1980s called *mall rats* or *mallies,* collectively a *malling* of young people in a debased quest for urban excitement. Popular speech, like the culture of the suburbs, noticeably lost its fancy for the hurly-burly and variety at the center. Some of the old city words, no longer so useful, will be forgotten.

The lexicon of popular speech about New York life leads us in a time-walk through the historical city of the mind. Following the trail of these words and phrases, we will go where they take us, East Side, West Side, and all around the town, into all the city's neighborhoods, and into the haunts of its low and high life. The people of the city in every walk of life spoke their collective minds about the urban world around them. If we listen carefully, we can hear an unusual account of the cultural and social history of the greatest American metropolis.

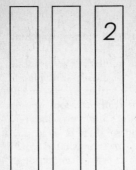

2

The Social Meaning
of City Streets

The blab of the pave. . . .
WALT WHITMAN, "Song of Myself," Canto 8

Word images of city streets in popular speech have in several ways echoed the major tensions of New York social life. First of all, the fundamental opposition of public and private social worlds is abundantly apparent in many references to city streets in the historical lexicon. Many popular expressions imaged the peculiarly American grid-iron plan of city streets. In Manhattan especially, the grid served as metaphors and mental maps of social class and social mobility. The grid and deviations from it gave social meanings to its main thoroughfares, intersections, cross streets, and backstreets. Even the physical constructions of the modern city street—sidewalks, curbs, gutters, and sewers—have stood for increments of social status at the lower end of the scale. In a number of other popular expressions the grid served as a larger, more implicit metaphor for the advances, frustrations, deviations, successes, and failures in competitive urban life.

A primary tension in urban culture exists between the seeming chaos of the public world of strangers, the merciless marketplace and the encroachments of threatening lower-class life, on the one hand, and the secure, predictable, and ordered private world of middle-class life, on the other.[1] The streets are the preeminent metaphor for unrestricted, socially diverse public places as opposed to restricted, socially homogeneous private spaces. In a civil, or perhaps a romantic, view of city life, writes the geographer and philosopher of cities Yi-Fu Tuan, "open space signifies freedom, the promise of adventure, light, the public realm, formal and unchanging beauty; enclosed space signifies the cozy security of the womb, privacy, darkness, biologic life. . . . The appeal of cities lies in large part [in] the juxtaposition of the cozy and grand, of darkness and light, the intimate and the public."[2] But the industrial city was a harsher matter, and popular culture makes this clear.

For the middle class, the meaning of failure was to fall from, or to be cast out of, the private sphere without the shields of either status or money—*naked in the streets,* as the expression has it. The phrases *to be out on* (or *in*) *the streets,* possibly *to be thrown out on* (or *in*) *the streets,* is to say that one has fallen from the protection and comfort of the private and the semi-private spheres of city life and is without money, a job, middle-class respectability, or choices. One is then completely vulnerable to the city. Anything can happen in the streets, and it is usually bad.

Popular speech for the most part expresses the public and semi-public side of urban life, especially that of the streets—the most public places. Slang, in its essential urbanism, is a view of society from the streets—and of the streets. The streets are the arena in which the confrontations among diverse social elements of the city take place. People are admitted selectively to the semi-private areas of the city, and social control there is great, ultimately enforced by bouncers or the police. But the streets are shared by all; social control has always been a problem. The streets symbolize the rough and tumble of city life itself. The streets are full of surprises, often rude starts, if not violent or criminal ones. Largely for these reasons the streets are the most threatening places. Streets of the modern city are busy with many and diverse people, relating in segmental and anonymous ways, and pursuing a multitude of personal goals, including predatory ones.

A number of popular expressions have used the adjective and noun *street(s)* to signify the public sphere of urban life. The streets are populated with the greatest cross section of the social scale, often skewed toward the low end. *The man in the street* since the early nineteenth century has been the common man, the average, ordinary, anonymous person whom one might pass in the street. *The street* also has long meant the street life of a city, that is, public life at the most common, accessible level. A few expressions use the idea of the street as a metaphor for the correspondence between private and public life. *To take it to the streets* is a political expression that means to extend a private conflict to a public arena. Simply *to take to the streets* or *to go on the streets* means to reject conventional, institutional channels of conflict resolution, especially the law, and to pursue direct action. In a related sense *the streets* and *on the streets* have been used to mean 'in public life,' when said of a politician or political appointee. But these are middle-class expressions that romantically allude to the idea of mean streets. Middle-class people, except for occasional slumming adventures, did not have much to do with "the streets."

The street has long symbolized social destruction in American urban literature and popular speech. Sociologist Anselm Strauss identified two related literary themes in novels about city life down to the 1960s: the encroachment of the changing city on middle-class life and the sheer destructiveness of lower-class street life. From a middle-class perspective, the lower classes invaded middle-class neighborhoods in the incessantly changing city. The middle classes then struggled to stay in city neighborhoods and to keep family and culture together. From the view of the lower classes, moving to better neighborhoods was upward social mobility. "For those left behind, there is 'The Street,' endowed with metaphorical malignancy, symbolizing all the environmental forces massed to degrade its residents, destroy their potentialities, and prevent their rising to better status."[3] Stephen Crane wrote *Maggie: A Girl of the Streets* (1893) around the street-as-destruction theme, and more recent novelists, especially black and Latino authors, have addressed the same issue.

Popular speech also specifies various aspects of the public world of the streets, such as the highly informal, even outcast status of people and activities. Things associated in name with the out-of-doors world of streets, sidewalks, and curbs are never quite legitimate. In several popular expressions, the adjective *street* denotes activities, practices, and people who exist or operate outside of regular, middle-class institutions, such as *street arab, street Christian* or *street ministry, street fighter, street money, street name* (a *nom de pavé*), *street people,* and *street theater.* The modifiers *sidewalk,* as in *sidewalk superintendent,* and *curb* or *curbstone,* as in *curbstone broker,* do about the same with a variety of other expressions.

Stoops are halfway between private and public in working-class life and represent the intersection of both worlds. City streets, continuous with tenement stoops, also served as a social center for the working classes and an extension of their crowded living spaces. The American word *stoop,* from Dutch *stoep,* 'step,' denoted the short stairway and landing leading from sidewalk level to the raised, main floor of New York's row houses and some tenements. The Dutch colonials introduced this architectural feature from the Netherlands where it served to prevent flooding of the ground floor. New Yorkers grew accustomed to it and liked its appearance. In the tight street-grid arrangement that did not allow space for back alleys, the stoop also came to serve the unexpected function of allowing an entrance under the stairs into the kitchen of the brownstone fronts.[4]

The stoop has had an important real and symbolic role in New York's street and neighborhood life, which was noticed as early as the 1820s. Mainly, the stoops were used for sitting and socializing with neighbors, as a place to escape the steaming tenements in the summer, and as a perch from which to watch the passing scene. The stoops of converted row houses and tenements were—and remain—a social center midway between home and street. O. Henry in "Rus in Urbe" (1909) captures the scene where "in the cross-town streets the steps of old brown-stone houses were swarming with 'stoopers,' that motley race hailing from skylight room and basement, bringing out their straw door-step mats to sit and fill the air with strange noises and opinions."

The stoop and its social life are usually present in art, literary, and popular-cultural images of New York's old tenement life. Rows of stoops, often occupied by "stoopers," flanked by women leaning on window sills, have long served as a cinematic symbol of an old-fashioned kind of street life

FIGURE 2. (overleaf) Outline Map of Manhattan in the 1930s.
(From *The WPA Guide to New York City* by the Federal Writers Project. Copyright © 1982 by Random House, Inc. Permission of Pantheon Books, a division of Random House, Inc.)

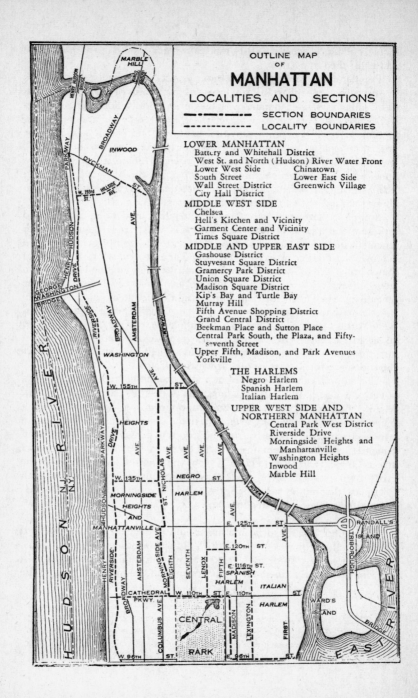

OUTLINE MAP
OF
MANHATTAN
LOCALITIES AND SECTIONS

▬▬▬▬▬▬ SECTION BOUNDARIES
▬ ▬ ▬ ▬ ▬ LOCALITY BOUNDARIES

LOWER MANHATTAN
Battery and Whitehall District
West St. and North (Hudson) River Water Front
Lower West Side   Chinatown
South Street   Lower East Side
Wall Street District   Greenwich Village
City Hall District
MIDDLE WEST SIDE
Chelsea
Hell's Kitchen and Vicinity
Garment Center and Vicinity
Times Square District
MIDDLE AND UPPER EAST SIDE
Gashouse District
Stuyvesant Square District
Gramercy Park District
Union Square District
Madison Square District
Kip's Bay and Turtle Bay
Murray Hill
Fifth Avenue Shopping District
Grand Central District
Beekman Place and Sutton Place
Central Park South, the Plaza, and Fifty-
  seventh Street
Upper Fifth, Madison, and Park Avenues
Yorkville
      THE HARLEMS
        Negro Harlem
        Spanish Harlem
        Italian Harlem
      UPPER WEST SIDE AND
        NORTHERN MANHATTAN
          Central Park West District
          Riverside Drive
          Morningside Heights and
            Manhattanville
          Washington Heights
          Inwood
          Marble Hill

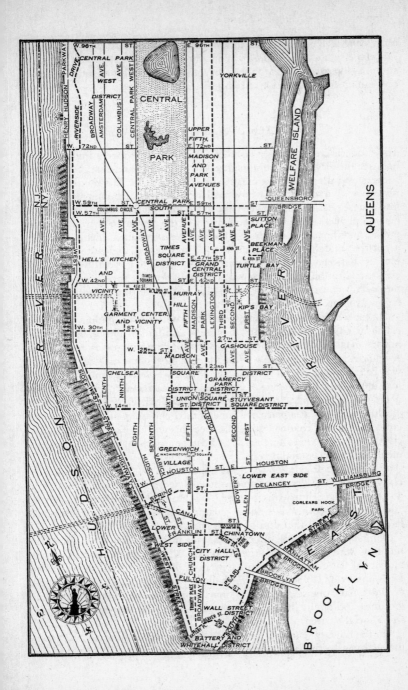

on a generic East Side. The image sometimes contains a child playing *stoopball,* bounding a *spaldeen* (a Spalding brand of rubber ball) against a stoop. Stoop sitting, even today, is an enduring New York institution, especially in more self-conscious neighborhoods.

Public Versus Private Social Worlds

The modern city of laissez-faire capitalism became increasingly divided between the private and public spheres of ownership and of social life. This process and the tensions it creates are still going on. The modern city in many ways is a social form whose total life is polarized, though reciprocally, into a tense relationship between its private and public spheres. The dialectal tension in part comes from the tendency of the private to encroach on the public, and the converse. It is now fashionable in certain academic circles to argue that middle-class interests fostered an ideology and culture of sharp barriers between private and public social worlds to conceal the results of class exploitation.[5] Yet the evidence from all popular speech suggests that the socially constructed reality of city life was just as often negotiated from below as imposed from above.

In the worlds of Henry James and Edith Wharton the middle and upper classes lived, for the most part, in large, single-family houses, usually row houses, in fashionable sections, such as Washington Square or, later, on Fifth Avenue. A large single-family house through most of the nineteenth century was considered essential for respectable and wholesome family life. Near invisibility in the private life of cavernous mansions marked the upper class of old money as much as their wealth. The newly rich wanted to display their wealth and status at a place and time of their choosing, and the privacy of large houses and country estates assured this choice. The best of middle-class apartment living after the 1870s did not much change the basic arrangement between class and privacy.

The lack of privacy, on the other hand, was a mark of crowded, lower-class city life. The first large tenement in New York was built about 1850 and for the next century was the mode of working-class housing. The private and the public worlds were not so separate in the early tenements. Personal lives were open to the scrutiny of the neighbors. Jacob Riis, in *How the Other Half Lives* (1890), discerned that the three marks of a true tenement building were an unlocked street door, no bells at front entrances to ring individual flats, and hallways that were "a highway for all the world by night and by day."[6] Sometimes the hallways were used as extensions of the crowded flats, one stage closer to home than the stoops. Doors were often left open and family life exposed; the threshold and door here were much less a social barrier.

In the Bowery tenement of Crane's *Maggie,* family quarrels were completely open to the observation and even the participation of neighbors.

FIGURE 3. Berenice Abbott. *Court of the First Model Tenement in New York City* (1936). Scenes of the family wash, including underwear and bed linen, hung out to dry in view of the whole neighborhood prompted the expression *on the clothesline,* meaning to make public intimate family affairs.
(*Museum of the City of New York*)

When fallen Maggie came home from the streets to face her family, "women came into the hallways" and the neighbors' "children ventured into the room and ogled her as if they formed the front row at a theatre. . . . Maggie's mother paced to and fro, addressing the doorful of eyes, expounding like a glib showman." As the defeated Maggie for the last time finally left home through the tenement hallway, "she went before open doors framing more eyes strangely microscopic."[7]

Common knowledge about private lives was great among neighbors. The preeminent sign of intensely interactive tenement life was the familiar clotheslines for the family's wash—strung on pulleys over the backyards of tenements, from a back window to either a mast or the opposite building. In yet earlier years the wash was hung out on horizontal poles, like flags, in front of the house and over the street.[8] The image of family wash flapping over the backyards of tenements is seen in countless art and cinematic scenes. Howells in his essay "New York Streets" wrote of "the lines thickly woven from the windows . . . and fluttering with drying clothes as with banners."[9] Banners of significance they were. The family wash, undies and all, drying in full view of the neighborhood, became a metaphor in popular speech for the particulars of personal lives "hung out" for the scrutiny of all the world, for all in the streets. Indeed, the slang expression *clothesline* once meant gossip or rumor.

Personal and family problems in this century also have been called a *clothesline*. Before family troubles and intimate concerns, "stains on the linens," reached the "clothesline" for all to see, they were potentially embarrassing *dirty wash* or *soiled linen*. Airing (or *washing*) *dirty linen in public*, that is, arguing about private matters in public, is the act of deliberately and indifferently exposing intimate family problems to public view.[10] The only worse thing one could do would be *to shout it from the rooftops* (or *from the housetops*) where all the world, that is, everyone in the streets, could hear the scandal. The streets, especially in working-class neighborhoods, also represent a face-to-face social network. One meaning of *the street* (singular) is that of a metonym for residents of a street who gossip: "The whole street is talking about it."

In the late nineteenth century, semi-private places (or semi-public places, wherever the emphasis) emerged as especially important arenas for social life and presented special problems of social control. Semi-private places are privately owned, but publicly attended, and operated for commercial gain. Most are enclosed places such as hotels, restaurants, bars, theaters, night clubs, dance halls, gambling establishments, and brothels. They are, so to speak, extensions of the street toward the private sphere and the reverse. Most historical popular speech denoting urban enclosures and their activities refers to these kinds of semi-private establishments, not least because of their popular attendance and often illegitimate activities. Schools, libraries, hospitals, museums, and other respectable places inspired few if any pejorative slang names.

The public and the private areas of life in modern cities are marked by the opposition of streets to private houses, businesses, and other places with limited or no public access. The boundary between house and street in middle-class city life is symbolized by the threshold and the door and secured by the lock. These form the last line separating the private and the public worlds. The old common law against "breaking and entering" denotes violating the lock and crossing the threshold into the private realm. In the traditional western city, most houses of the middle and upper classes and other private establishments face the streets. The two worlds are but a step away from each other.

The opposition of street and house, the boundary of the threshold, the barriers of the door and lock, and the controlled interpretation of the window have served fiction well, especially in novels of city life. In the New York novels of Henry James and Edith Wharton, the door was a symbol of the line between the private and public worlds. For these writers, the door most often closed against the city and its chaos. In Wharton's short story, "Pomegranate Seed," Charlotte Ashby "paused on her doorstep [while at her back the] grinding, rasping street life of the city was at its highest. . . . The contrast between the soulless roar of New York, its devouring blaze of lights, the oppression of its congested traffic, congested houses, lives, minds and this veiled sanctuary she called home, always stirred her profoundly."[11]

The window is an architectural feature, actually a social device, that qualifies the absolute seal between private and public life. The boundary would lose some of its social usefulness, especially for the higher classes, if the seal were complete. The window allows limited views from the private to the public world and, to the extent that householders wish to display their way of life and level of consumption, a view from the street into their homes. What can't be seen from without, can't be envied; and the envy that can't be seen from within can't be fully enjoyed.

New Yorkers of all social classes almost traditionally watch one another through windows and form impressions of how others live. O. Henry glanced into city windows for intimations of private worlds to use in his stories. He also looked out his windows on Irving Place and imagined the intimate lives of the passersby. Edward Hopper painted lonely interior scenes he glimpsed through open and undraped windows while riding the New York elevated. The March couple in Howells's *A Hazard of New Fortunes* (1890) liked to ride the elevated, especially at night. For fleeting instances, they identified with the touching domestic tableaux they saw in the lighted second and third story windows and compared the whole panorama to a theatrical experience.[12]

Surveillance of the street through windows has served a need for informal social control. Mrs. Grundy watches the doings in Main Street for evidence of impropriety. One of Wharton's New York matrons "belonged to the generation which still surveyed its world from an upper window, like the Dutch ancestresses to whom the doings of the street were reported by a little mirror."[13] In tenement districts, women traditionally lean on window sills, elbows on cushions, and watch over activities in the streets. John Sloan rendered the scene in an oil, *A Window on the Street* (1912), and in a drawing, *Woman at a Window* (1913). The urban-planning critic Jane Jacobs in *The Death and Life of Great American Cities* (1961) pointed out that this surveillance by women served a useful function in the old Italian section of Greenwich Village. From their windows, the women supervised children at play, monitored adult behavior in the streets, and generally contributed to safety in the streets of dense working-class neighborhoods.[14]

The Urban Jungle

The jungle is the metaphorical social condition of the streets after the rise of the industrial city. "Images are reversed so that the wilderness stands for order (ecological order) and freedom whereas the central city is chaotic, a jungle ruled by social outcasts," writes Yi-Fu Tuan.[15] The term in a related sense became especially popular after the publication in 1906 of Upton Sinclair's influential novel about the Chicago stockyards, *The Jungle*. Sinclair wrote at a time when the ethos of social Darwinism and its facile justification of the survival of the fittest still reigned in an economy of laissez-faire capitalism. Industrial workers labored at subsistence wages and were pitted against one another for jobs—for survival—like animals in a jungle of savage competition. Sinclair, a socialist, made abundantly clear throughout the novel that he viewed the packinghouses, the stockyards, the city of Chicago, and all of capitalist society as a "jungle." Two years later he wrote about New York in *The Metropolis* (1908), a novel about the conspicuous consumption, vanity, and venality of the city's rich upper classes— a different sort of jungle.

Popular word imagery in a like way has seen the public sphere of city life, especially the streets, as a jungle—an uncivilized place where human predators are free to roam. The predators may be economic, creating a climate of barbarous competition, or criminal, creating a climate of fear for one's life, limb, or property. In tenement life, the streets were also an arena of courtship where male conquest and lost feminine virtue were at stake. Caroline Ware in her study of ethnic life in Greenwich Village of the 1920s described Italian-American courtship behavior as "a jungle in which the game was women," a game ruled by "the law of the jungle which dominated the street."[16]

Popular culture now and then trades on the metaphor of the city as jungle. King Kong, displaced and atop the Empire State Building, briefly ruled over a city beyond his ken. The movie of 1933 makes clear in multiple ways that the city is an atavistic urban jungle.[17] Popular uses of the idea of the jungle illustrate the variety of this characteristic imputed to city life in the public sphere. The popular imagery of a real jungle is that of a tangled web of diverse organisms, a buzz of mysterious communication, dog-eat-dog competition, lawlessness (except the *law of the jungle,* which is lawlessness), unpredictability, and imminent danger.[18]

A related meaning of *the jungle* is revealed through informal place names, mostly of journalistic origin. The big-city saying, "It's a jungle out there!," means that the competition is rough, the way to success a perilous maze, and the situation seemingly chaotic. New York's *Wall Street Jungle* and the former downtown electronics *Jungle* suggest keen competition as well as a maze to the uninitiated. If the human actors, made animal-like trying to survive in the urban jungle, are not "trapped," or going around and around in a "squirrel cage," then they are in the "rat race," the mindless competition with everyone else who is trying to get ahead. Other informal place names also suggest that a "jungle" morality prevails, as in the *Hollywood Jungle,* or in the *Washington Jungle,* a specification of the *political jungle.*

Slum neighborhoods where street life is threatening were called *urban jungles* and, by the 1960s, *inner-city jungles.* In this sense, such neighbor-

FIGURE 4. Reginald Marsh. *East Tenth Street Jungle* (1934). During the Great Depression, in-town *jungles* of the unemployed and homeless appeared in New York's vacant lots and other unused open spaces. The notion of the whole city as an "urban jungle" may have been influenced by this hobo and tramp slang. (Courtesy of the William Benton Museum of Art)

hoods, or even whole cities, are perceived as *asphalt jungles*—a notion also marking the cultural transition to the anti-urban 1950s. John Huston's movie *The Asphalt Jungle* (1950) is about crime in an unnamed middlewestern city and is based on W. R. Burnett's 1949 novel of the same title. Several other popular novels and movies used the jungle metaphor in their titles: *The Blackboard Jungle* (1955) is about big city high-school violence and is from Evan Hunter's 1954 novel of the same title. *The Garment Jungle* (1957) is about union corruption and gangsters in New York's garment industry, the "rag trade," on "Fashion Avenue," as the street signs on that part of Seventh Avenue now read.

All these usages were influenced by an older hobo and tramp sense of a *jungle,* a settlement of the unemployed, often on the edge of a town near the railroad tracks and, incidentally, also perversely called a *suburb.* Hobo jungles came into public consciousness in the 1930s. Despite having a certain etiquette, the jungles were rough, dangerous, lawless places, much like the image of city streets. Other hobo jungles were in the center of cities. The feel of a hobo jungle in lower Manhattan is conveyed in Reginald Marsh's Depression-era etching *East Tenth Street Jungle* (1934).

Mean Streets. The unregulated world of criminals and of the lower classes is, in the old phrase, *mean streets.* In underworld and lower-class street talk, the metaphor of the city street has long meant personal freedom from institutional restraints, especially prison, and freedom to pursue the occupation of theft and the preoccupation of drugs. Many of these terms have now found their place in general slang and even in more accepted locutions.

By 1900 *the street(s)* and *on the streets* were criminals' expressions for the world outside of prison, where drugs and other vice were available. *Street time* is the interim periods when one is on parole and in town between prison terms. *On the sidewalk* and *on the pavement* also allude to the criminal life. In the speech of drug users *pounding the pavement* is the relentless search for drugs; *the street* and *on the street* is the social world of the drug addicts and the constant search for drugs.[19] *Street money* is the gain from drug dealing or from prostitution—or *street walking.*

In the black ghettoes the street is a central and inescapable fact of life. For decades *the street* has referred to a society of lawlessness and violence. Black teenage vernacular uses *the streets* for any place other than home, school, or work. The term also refers to the source of practical experience and of skills needed for survival in lower-class neighborhoods of big cities. Social workers more than a century ago realized that the streets were, in effect, a school for young people, an important arena for socialization, often exerting more influence than family, church, or schools.

In slums, streets are the locus of information and rumor, which exerts its own kind of social control.[20] In this sense *the street* is a metaphor for neighborhood rumor networks or, generally, any situation where rumors are heard and information exchanged. *To put it on the street* is an expression for disclosing usually damaging information for the rumor network; *to hear it on the street* is to receive such information *on the grapevine*.[21] Such rumor is then said to be *street talk* and generally carries negative value in lower-class culture. (In middle-class cultures, to be *the talk of the town* is to be favorably discussed, socially successful, and sought after.)

The adjectives *street-smart* and *street-wise* describe tough, cunning, cynical attitudes and special knowledge by which one not only survives but also thrives in predatory social surroundings, such as in the streets of the urban jungle. The knowledge is called *street smarts*. These terms were first recorded in the 1960s and early 1970s, probably from the concerned discussions of destructive street life in black and Latino slums. William Safire writes that he heard *street smarts* yet earlier in the 1950s to describe a politician's ability to deal with the rough and tumble of the real world, often with a sassy and anti-intellectual air.[22] *Street smarts* has since come into general slang to mean highly practical savvy about political or economic matters, especially those of the Washington Jungle or of New York's Wall Street Jungle.

The Street also is a nickname for sections of New York with a concentration of certain high-flying professions or trades, especially of entertainment, advertising, or finance, which can be jungle-like. Those several Manhattan street names that became metonyms for their most important businesses— Wall Street, Madison Avenue, Broadway, 52nd Street—have been called *The Street* by insiders. Madison Avenue was sometimes called *The Street* or *The Avenue* by its workers; the Broadway theater district was called *The Street* in its glamour days early in this century. In the late 1930s and 1940s, the two-block stretch of 52nd Street, especially between Fifth and Sixth avenues, and beyond the El at Sixth, toward Seventh Avenue, was famous for its jazz clubs and was called *The Street* by jazzmen, taxi drivers, and other hep sorts. The strip was even more popularly known as *Swing Street* and, with more funk, as *Swing Alley*.

Wall Street is today most famously called *The Street,* just as the British use *The Alley* for London's Exchange Alley.[23] The popular nickname for Wall Street goes back to the 1840s at least. *Wall Streeters* were soon speaking of working *on The Street* and greeting one another with "What's new on The Street." The *Wall Street Journal* runs a stock-market column titled "Heard on the Street." In the context of Wall Street, *street smarts* recalls the low origins of the term to make a double meaning—the low tactics of high finance by what used to be called Wall Street plungers and sharks. The inside traders of the high-rolling 1980s carried forward these reputations in the worst tradition of Wall Street.

Hitting the Bricks.   The city street—or more exactly the sidewalk—was symbolized in urban vernaculars of itinerants by the synecdoches *bricks, pavement,* and very slangily *rocks*. Some of these and related expressions leaked into popular speech. To enter on the street and to walk on the sidewalk, especially when looking for something to do, in the logic of slang, is *to hit, to pad, to pound,* or *to beat the bricks, the pavement,* or sometimes *the macadam.* The several senses of the related noun *beat,* a neighborhood area, as in a policeman's beat and a beggar's beat, or an area of endeavor, as in a newspaper reporter's beat, date to the eighteenth century and are possibly Americanisms.

To hit the bricks, one of the more enduring variations, has had several meanings.[24] The phrase has meant to go onto the sidewalk or to start walking, to leave a public place by withdrawing into the street, to be released from prison, to go on strike, and to walk the streets all night because of homelessness. The idea of taking leave by striking with the feet the hard surface of the sidewalk has gone the rounds and, with variations, appeared in other subcultural speech. A variant in 1940s black speech was *to beat the rocks,* 'to walk on the sidewalk.'[25] *To hit the sidewalks* and *to pound the pavement* especially have meant looking for a job. Merely *to press the bricks,* however, is to stand loafing in the streets.

To be *on the pavement, on the sidewalks,* or *on the street* meant to hustle, especially as a prostitute. A *streetwalker* works "the streets," where she was known as a *nymph of the pave* or a *pavement princess. To hit the bricks, to hit the sidewalks,* and *to hit the turf* have all had various prison and underworld meanings of getting paroled and going out to steal again. Then one may have *to hit the road,* to flee a town to avoid getting sent *out of town,* that is, to prison.

The New York state prison was built in 1828 near the town of Sing Sing, north of New York City and up the Hudson River. The prison, informally called Sing Sing, soon became known in the City for its harsh discipline and *up the river* was a dreaded destination for criminals. In the town of Sing Sing itself, the reputation of the prison was considered a blight and the citizens changed the town's name to Ossining in 1901. By 1850 or thereabouts New York City criminals were speaking of being *sent up the river,* as in "doin' time up de river," or just being *sent up,* all referring to Sing Sing prison up the Hudson River.[26] In 1858 Walt Whitman, perhaps with conscious irony, used the apparently otherwise popular expression "up the river" in quotation marks to denote the vacations on the Hudson taken by well-to-do and law-abiding New Yorkers, but they went, and were not sent, up the river.[27]

The Main Drag. Most slang terms for main streets in American towns and cities derive from the speech of hoboes, tramps, and bums. These expressions came to New York, along with some of the drifters. Hoboes began to concentrate in larger American cities after the Civil War. The several severe economic depressions in the late nineteenth century increased their numbers and set them farther adrift in search of work. They gravitated to cities and, then, to or near the central business district, where they sometimes panhandled. In large cities they often gathered on the decaying main street, as New York's Bowery, which by the 1890s was well into its decline.

By 1900 some of their argot, including *main drag* and *main stem*—or, extended to any street, just a *drag* or a *stem*—had begun to leak into popular speech. Today, these terms are widely used, informal expressions for the streets of a town or city. The main drag or main stem originally was the main thoroughfare of hobohemias, such as the Bowery, rather than the principal and most central street of a town, such as Fifth Avenue or 42nd Street. But the terms in slang were generalized to the main street of a city, or to the main thoroughfare of some part of a large city. The theater district along Broadway was once called *The Main Stem*.

Drag is old British cant that emerged in American slang meaning a road or street. It is of uncertain origin and allusion. Godfrey Irwin in *American Tramp and Underworld Slang* wrote in 1931 that a "street or railroad line [is called a *drag*] since a tramp drags his weary way over these means of communication," and that is as good a thought as any.[28] The phrase *on the stem* is hobo jargon for walking the main street of a town, sometimes panhandling and begging, or, as they said, *mooching the stem* or *piping the stem*. The main street in hobo talk was sometimes the *the big alley* or *the main alley*. Each term was an image of Main Street and other city streets in the eyes of homeless men. Carnies similarly projected a word image of their world, *the midway,* onto the main street of a town. Slang came to use it for any brightly lighted thoroughfare, especially an entertainment *strip,* such as Sunset Strip in Hollywood and The Strip in Las Vegas.

Often a major street in a big city deteriorated into a skid row. New York's Bowery, which prospered before the Civil War, is the most famous example of this transition. The Bowery's history almost recapitulates the history of all lower Manhattan.[29] The broad, busy commercial street peaked as a center of working-class community life in the 1860s. The Bowery was a famous promenade or *crawl* for "Bowery B'hoys" and their "G'hals." The street was a recreational magnet for the working class and a precursor of Coney Island. It was no mere coincidence that in later years one of the most famous midways at Coney Island was called the Bowery.

New Yorkers always have uttered the name of the street with the definite article, *the* Bowery, and not to do so was and remains a shibboleth. In 1871 an anonymous writer in *Harper's* warned: "Let no unlettered rustic win derision to himself by calling this great thoroughfare Bowery *Street,* for it is 'The Bowery,' and nothing more." Around 1900 some of the locals on the Bowery also called it "De Lane," referring to the old formal name, Bowery Lane, of the eighteenth century, a name still borne in a yet older form by the Bouwerie Lane Theatre at 330 Bowery.

Broadway, several blocks to the west, served some of the same promenading, shopping, and recreational functions for the middle classes. Philip Stoner's 1872 song lyrics, *The Broadway, Opera and Bowery Crawl* ("I'll show you the Broadway [or "Bowery"] afternoon crawl.") draws the social parallels of afternoon promenades of belles and swells on the Bowery, Broadway, and Fifth Avenue.[30] Such finely dressed street types were called *The Fancy*. The Bowery and lower Broadway prospered side by side, each serving different social groups in similar ways. But by 1900 the Bowery was in deep decline and becoming a main drag of hoboes, and lower Broadway in its own way also declined. Both streets are now recovering through gentrification; expensive condos are appearing along the old skid row and the gloomier parts of Broadway above City Hall are brightening.

Between 1865 and about 1900, the city's African Americans were greatly concentrated on the West Side, from about 26th Street to 63rd, and Seventh Avenue was their main thoroughfare. In the 1890s fashionable blacks promenaded on Seventh Avenue, especially from 23rd to 34th streets, and whites, just a stone's throw away, derisively called it *African Broadway*. In an older black street vernacular, *the stroll* alluded to the social use of the main street as a promenade, just as the Bowery and Broadway were *crawls* for whites. In the 1920s, after the blacks moved to Harlem, Seventh Avenue farther uptown between 131st and 132nd was called The Stroll. In its glory days, the promenade of Harlem's Seventh Avenue was described in the "Prologue" of Carl Van Vechten's controversial novel *Nigger Heaven* (1926).

Social Class and the Meaning of *Main Street*

Social stratification is a universal in modern societies and the systems are in many ways encoded in culture and language. Relative to traditional emblems, such as clothing, and personal reputations of rank, exactly where one lived in the modern city became more important as a marker of class and status. A *good address* was near the center of a settlement, especially on the main street, and lesser status was measured roughly on a gradient with declining distance from the center. In New York, a city of many "urban villages" and other symbolic areas, the generic *main street* often has been used to denote a chief thoroughfare and social center. Streets and avenues such as Broadway, Fifth Avenue, or Seventh Avenue, in sequential periods and for different social sets, were the "main streets," the centers of fashionable New York life. Manhattan offers an especially well-developed, richly illustrated symbolic system based on the grid, always with one of its main streets at its center.

The story of the elaborate symbolic relationship between the grid of city streets and social status begins in the early villages and small towns of America, not in the big cities. Main Street in American towns and cities had—and still has—a special significance in the symbolic life of the community, one that sets it apart from main streets in the urban histories of other countries. The High Streets of Britain and of certain Commonwealth nations are not quite the same thing; their chief social meaning is that of the focus of commerce and shopping, and the American connotations are generally lacking. Almost every American town seems to have its Main Street, though it may not bear that exact name. The main street is sometimes called Center Street, Broad Street—or for that matter Broadway—or some other name that denoted its status as the principal thoroughfare. When the town faced on a river or other water front, the main street was often called Front Street, which connoted that the street was not only at the front, but was the face of the town. Yet it is striking how often the main thoroughfare is actually named Main Street. Whatever its name, Main Street was, and to some extent remains, an American institution.

Carole Rifkind, an architectural historian, found the origins of the American Main Street in the colonial villages of New England in the seventeenth century and traced the spread of the spatial form to New Jersey and New York in the eighteenth century.[31] By the second half of the nineteenth century, the physical and cultural model of Main Street as the axis of the town was stamped on nearly every town and city in the country. Early in this century the epitome of Main Street in popular imagery was seen in the small towns of the great Middle West. Sinclair Lewis's 1920 novel *Main Street* commented on the physical as well as the moral drabness of many midwestern Main Streets.[32] The title of Lewis's novel thrust the name *Main Street,* with all these connotations, into popular speech, much as other of his fictional placenames and personal names (e.g., *Babbitt*) entered slang in the 1920s as popular labels of their types.

Main Street, as it was ideally conceived, built, and lived, signified an established way of doing things that articulated the social order, reflected the hierarchy of values, and had moral significance for the social life of the community. Main Street typically intersected the settlement and was the political, economic, and social center of the town. The edifices and monuments that reflected the official and usually prevailing values of local society were usually located about midway along the length of Main Street and at the center of the community. These symbolic structures expressed the town's integration with the regional and national societies. The courthouse square or the town square, the successor to the green in colonial villages, was the symbolic heart of the community and the site of such collective representations as monuments, public observances, recognitions, and other celebrations of common values.

Main Street was further the center of social prestige in the settlement. The largest and most prestigious residences traditionally were closest to the center and the lesser dwellings at a farther distance or on cross, side, or back streets. In the ideal arrangement, the placement of buildings and institutions descended from the center in a predictable order of values: institutions of law at the center, flanked by a zone of commerce, all buttressed by the large houses of the middle classes, mostly merchants and the professionals. Other, lesser streets bore equally agreed-upon and predictable relations to Main Street and extended the spatial metaphor. Some towns, keeping certain activities in their place, relegated saloons and brothels to side streets and back streets; worse things were tolerated or escaped notice in alleys. The middle-class dominance of Main Street and the social meaning of all these arrangements caused Main Street to become the popular symbol of public scrutiny, social approval, and middle-class respectability. Mrs. Grundy, had she lived in America, would certainly have lived on and overseen the affairs of Main Street.

The corners of Main Street, significantly the intersections of cross streets and side streets, attracted socially marginal elements in the town and gave the language several new expressions. Street corners, often furnished with a lamp post that could be leaned against, became a favored hangout for *corner boys*, a term used since about 1855. An ethnographic tradition in sociology, beginning significantly with William Foote Whyte's *Street Corner Society* (1943), studied the social world of working-class corner boys in large cities. In this century corner boys who met on street corners, gossiped, and ogled women became known as *corner cowboys* and sometimes *corner wolves*, a low variety of street masher. By about 1925 *drugstore cowboys* were young men who loafed in and outside the corner soda fountains. Big-city street corners in cartoon images are also associated with tuxedoed drunks hanging onto lamp posts or with ladies of the night basking in circles of light cast by street lamps.

By the 1890s, when street paving and lighting had become common across the country, *Main Street* had become a metaphor for the dominant social order of the community; in syntax, other streets and their corners stood for variance from it. Popular speech came to express the social understanding embodied in this spatial metaphor for social standing in the community and used the syntactic relation of streets in the grid as a signified idea. This was the beginning of a much more elaborate development about the meaning of city streets.

City Streets as Mental Maps of Social Class

A physically horizontal, but socially vertical, map-like metaphor underlies the ordering of Main Street and lesser streets on the grid. The classification is from centrality to peripherality and, so, from respectability to nonrespectability, from high to low status in the community. The metaphor obviously springs from the historical association of middle- and upper-class people living on the main, widest, most prestigious and visible streets of a town, with their social inferiors living on cross streets, side streets, back streets, or in alleys behind the main street. The system is straightforward and peculiarly American. The idea of Main Street signifies the moral center of the community while its tributary streets, back streets, and alleys imply a graded decline in social standing.

The idiom *main street* denotes—and connotes—the center or apex of the hierarchy; *cross streets* intersect the main street but are once removed in status; *side streets* join and are usually terminated by the main street and are twice removed; *back streets,* like "back-street" human lives, neither join nor cross but run parallel to and are "behind" Main Street, and are, in effect, thrice removed; in the American idiom *alleys* have the lowest status and are infinitely removed. In American English *alley* connotes low, behind-the-scenes activity, a connotation lacking in the British usage.[33]

The manifold ordering also strains toward bipolarity. The social isolation of back streets and alleys stands generally in opposition to the frontness of Main Street and its tributaries. People who chafe against the petty, gossipy constraints of community opinion never tire of pointing out that the moral code of Main Street is often hypocritical and that the pillars of the community can be found standing, often as not, in the back streets and alleys of a town. The social dichotomy of front and back, of course, follows from, as we say, the front and back of the human body; the front has higher social value.[34] The human back has the low-status "backsides" and one "turns a back" against undesirable things and people. This dichotomous value, a somatic and psychological asymmetry, is projected into space and onto rooms, houses, street grids, and whole cities, as in "the backside of town" and several scatological expressions about the worst part of town. Middle- and upper-class housing, especially, has clearly demarcated fronts and backs. Front entrances, through the face of houses and which face the street, are more respectable than back entrances.

The idioms *cross street* and *side street* in fact have never been prominent in the metaphor; they suggest only a short step away from Main Street. But the far removed *back street,* a noun phrase in English since 1638, has been long used to label unacceptable people and behavior. A mistress was once disparaged as a *back-street wife.* She was in a parallel social role in some respects but behind a respectable scene. Fannie Hurst's novel *Back Street* (1930) about the mistress of a married man was made into three movie versions and all named *Back Street* (1932, 1941, and 1961). A back street, like the life it symbolizes, usually runs parallel to but behind the main street; a back street is also usually narrower and shorter. A similar metaphor of front and back is apparent in the simplest and most conventional layout of public and semi-private buildings. The *backroom* is behind the front, public room, and is where shady, secret, and often illegal things are connived by *backroom boys.* The adjectives *backstairs* and *backdoor* have long meant secret and unofficial.

Even lower and often beyond the control of community opinion are people and behavior labeled with *alley.* The poor and deviant historically have been relegated to back streets and alleys. The lower classes used the narrow, curving back streets or alleys to escape from the main streets when they were chased by the law and generally to hide illegal activities. New York's Old City below 14th Street once had many alleys containing the hovels of the poor. Much as unruly Parisians in 1848 fled into twisting lanes of the old city to escape and hide from authorities, criminals and rioters in New York fled into the narrow, curving streets and alleys of Greenwich Village. The intense real estate development and high land prices on the pervasive grid above 14th Street, however, often precluded the use of precious space for alleys between and behind buildings and few exist in most uptown neighborhoods.

Unlike the French *allée* or the German *Allee,* an avenue, an American alley is a narrow, often dark passageway between or behind buildings. Many informal street names in slang take -*Alley,* especially to refer to a section of town or to a particular street that specializes in the residences of low-status ethnic groups or where a certain commodity, service, or activity, usually low ones, are to be found. Backrooms of buildings, by way of backstairs and backdoors, open onto alleys. Alleys are used for unobserved passage away from the prying eyes of Main Street. Alleys are also used to set out trash; they attract vermin and are generally dirty places. Derelicts sleep in alleys, and nasty things go on there. Alleys are often associated with slums and low-status ethnic groups. The early descriptions of urban reformers, such as Jacob Riis, helped create the popular image of alleys in New York's tenement districts. They condemned the overcrowded housing as "rookeries" and "warrens" to suggest that people in them lived like animals.

A poor, run-down area where squalor and vice abound is doubly pejorated as a *back alley.* The adjectival form also suggests a sordid, clandestine, and possibly illegal activity, such as *back-alley abortion.* An utterly fallen woman, especially a lower-class one, is an *alley cat* who, following the metaphor, roams back alleys. She was less often called an *alley bat,* the *bat* being a prostitute who works the street by night. Her male companion in the 1930s might have been called an *alley rat,* a low criminal who lured or forced victims into alleys and robbed them. Or the rat could be a higher social type held in low esteem. One of Will Carleton's verses from *City Ballads* of 1885 exclaims "Oh, heaven's! there runs a great big Norway rat,/ Sleek as a banker, and almost as fat." The epithet *rat,* as in "you dirty rat," eventually lost its bite, and a man held in complete contempt came to be called a *cockroach,* another, even lower denizen of alleys and other slimy places. And lower still is one who is *lower than the belly of a cockroach,* perhaps an original New Yorkism for the low of the low.

Lower-class ethnic groups in the middle of the nineteenth century were closely identified with the streets, especially alleys. A slang term for a city street, making an ethnic slur, was once *Irishman's sidewalk,* perhaps an assertion that in the street, or more exactly in the roadway, rather than on the sidewalk, was a more suitable place for the hated Irish to walk, or that perhaps they were too dumb to know the difference. The slur continued with *Irish confetti,* a popular term for paving stones or Belgian bricks that were laid in New York streets beginning about 1832.[35] These brickbats were pried loose and thrown as weapons in the mid nineteenth-century street riots of Irish gangs that sometimes raged for days in the Five Points and the Bowery. The police sometimes wore thick, curving slabs of rubber on their helmets to protect them from Irish confetti dropped from tenement roofs. By the 1920s Irish confetti was also known as *alley apples,* referring similarly to violent lower-class behavior associated with brawls in alleys and with back-alley ways of life.

The Manhattan Grid. The social structure of New York is expressed in several map-like metaphors that use the image of the typical grid plan of American city streets, especially as they were designed, paved, and lighted after about 1850. The stark and nearly pervasive Manhattan grid is the archetype. The city's master plan was published in 1811 and officially adopted in 1820; its essentials are fulfilled in the present-day layout, especially in the New City north of 14th Street that developed after about 1850. In the new federal republic, the grid was designed to make uniform parcels of land to facilitate their egalitarian disposal as private property. The concept of land use as community asset and public responsibility, by and large, was not yet in the reckoning and there was no royalty, as in Europe, to set aside park preserves or to dictate master plans of urban growth.

The street grid has influenced the perception of American city life, and its attendant language is yet another way the economic imperative of market society reaches down in subtle ways to organize the culture of everyday life. But the grid also expressed existing social values of the early nineteenth century. The very rectangularity and uniformity of the grid seemed to express, or at least to facilitate, the rationality and emphasis on production in the market society. The supporting Calvinist moral order of society and conventionality in social life have long been expressed in the metaphorical nouns and adjectives *straight, square,* and *flat.* On the other hand, deviance from these norms has been anciently expressed in the metaphorical noun *crook* and the adjectives *crooked, bent, kinky,* and the like. The Manhattan grid above 14th Street is eminently straight, square, and flat, or so it was intended.

The historical direction of urban development and of social mobility in New York has been from the earlier, older settlements downtown toward newer, higher status neighborhoods farther uptown. The site of the earliest settlement at the southern tip of Manhattan and the narrow shape of the Island were the first constraints. Urban growth, and the social mobility it represented, was concentrated first along Broadway and then along the major north-south avenues. Fifth Avenue was most centrally at the spine, and prestige declined on a gradient east and west along its cross streets. A long popular cliché about New York is that the grid is boring, too predictable, even dehumanizing—a gigantic chessboard on which a game of real estate, development, demolition, and redevelopment is played out.

Foreign visitors have always been struck by the longitudinality of Manhattan, sometimes viewing it as parallel strips of social meaning. In 1941 writer Jules Romains saw each Manhattan avenue pursuing "its growth by itself, always from south to north, preserving its own character." In 1945 Jean-Paul Sartre saw Manhattan as a complex of "longitudinal worlds," a city "striped with parallel, uncommunicable meanings."[36] More conventional, less mindful European criticisms simply regarded the grid as alienating and soulless and New York as an anti-city. In one of his "mythologies," Roland Barthes criticizes one such view (Bernard Buffet's painted New York scenes) as a "folklore New York" that "confirms the Frenchman in the excellence of his [Parisian] habitat." Barthes argues that the Manhattan grid, to the contrary, allows people to grasp, possess, and "rule effectively over this enormous urban nature" and "to master the distances and orientations by the mind, to put at one man's disposal the space of these twelve million, this fabulous reservoir, this world emporium in which *all* goods exist except the metaphysical variety. This is the purpose of New York's geometry: that each individual should be *poetically* the owner of the capital of the world."[37]

The image of the Manhattan grid is also, writes the critic Peter Conrad, "a map of social esteem."[38] In the city novels of Henry James, Edith Wharton, William Dean Howells, F. Scott Fitzgerald, and others, references and allusions to the Manhattan grid symbolize social class and mobility, and this is the popular image, too. The avenues are "ladders of ascent" and the cross streets, if one goes too far aside, can mean deviations from the life-course and social obscurity. "The grid is a dual convenience for the novelists," writes Conrad. "Longitudinally, it permits social display; latitudinally, it provides for social exclusion."[39] For Dos Passos in *Manhattan Transfer,* even the sidewalks, divided by lines into cement squares, represented a miniature grid that measured aimless movement. "Parlorsnakes and flappers joggle hugging downtown uptown, hug joggling gray square after gray square."[40] The literary and closely related popular word images of city streets are a grammar of social stratification in the modern city.

Henry James's Washington Square, once a potter's field and with 22,000 souls still lying there in unmarked graves, is at the foot of the great uptown stretch of Fifth Avenue. In the 1830s the new townhouses around the square were a fashionable neighborhood for affluent families moving up from the dense, pestilent, and socially declining downtown. Later movement continued up Fifth Avenue with miles of brownstone fronts. F. Scott Fitzgerald in *The Beautiful and Damned,* published in 1922 but mostly set before the First World War, wrote, "Fifth and Sixth Avenues, it seemed to Anthony, were the uprights of a gigantic ladder stretching from Washington Square to Central Park. Coming up-town on top of a bus toward Fifty-second Street invariably gave him the sensation of hoisting himself hand by hand on a series of treacherous rungs."[41] In 1930 the French novelist Paul Morand in his travel account, *New York,* wrote that "the streets were arranged like the rungs of a ladder, and one socially climbs them, like a parrot, with the help of beak and claws. At thirty, one is in Thirtieth Street, at seventy, in Seventieth Street. The word 'climber' here takes on its fullest sense."[42]

The cross streets and the corners they formed also had iconographic value in art and literature, as well as in the imagery of popular speech. Street corners are literary and sometimes pictorial metaphors for individual and social turning points. Corners symbolized beginnings of biographical asides, more serious social deviations, or simply crossroads in the life-trip uptown. The visual effects yielded by intersections on the grid interact with their social meanings. Benjamin de Casseres remarked that "corners are the elbows of the mind" and that "the corners of New York are doorknobs that open up to the eye the long vestibule of the streets which always end at a river."[43] Deviations to either the east or west were socially descending ones. Ultimately, jumping off a pier at the end of one of these cross-town streets into the Hudson or the East rivers, I might add, was in parables of New York life the melodramatic fate of many doomed heroes and heroines, like Stephen Crane's poor Maggie.

Corners are the windows of city life. Corners are also an ideal location for social voyeurs, both low and high. In his paintings of towns, Edward Hopper was fond of corners as an artistic vantage point, and when they harbored glass-paned diners and the like, he took full advantage of their see-through potential to see, as it were, around corners. Every great city center has at least one famous corner that stands for the crossroads of metropolitan life and has collected its bit of folklore. In the mid-nineteenth century the northeast corner of Broadway and Fulton Street was said to be "the most crowded point in the city." Benjamin de Casseres quipped that Walt Whitman "was a professional corner loafer" and that some "profess to be able to see his epical heel-prints even unto this day at the corner of Broadway and Fulton, where he stood and mentally bagged the human race."[44] It used to be said in New York that, if one stood long enough at the Flatiron corner at 23rd Street and Broadway or, in later years, at the corner of 42nd Street and Broadway (or sometimes it is Fifth Avenue and 42nd Street), one would meet again everybody one ever knew. Publicists called Times Square the "Crossroads of the World," a name borrowed from London's Picadilly Circus. Watching the crowds pass a busy street corner is like a review of life itself, ultimately one's own.

Manhattanites live, moreover, in a rectangular, "carpentered" environment, which influences perception and world view.[45] The artists Piet Mondrian and Stuart Davis were influenced by the New York grid to see the city as rectangles and cubistically. The old idiom *to go in circles,* or *to go in a circle,* to wander without purpose and getting nowhere, when said in the city seems to take on a new meaning of not having the line of the grid to follow toward a goal. O. Henry saw the Manhattan grid as a metaphor for the citifying effects of urban life, making life orthogonal. In "Squaring the Circle" (1908), he writes that the

> natural is rounded; the artificial is made up of angles. A man lost in the snow wanders, in spite of himself, in perfect circles; the city man's feet, denaturalized by rectangular streets and floors, carry him ever away from himself. . . . When we begin to move in straight lines and turn sharp corners our natures begin to change. . . . Nature is lost quickest in a big city. The cause is geometrical not moral. . . . Wherefore, it may be said that the big city has demonstrated the problem of squaring the circle.

The regularity of the grid dominates the imagination in most of Manhattan. New Yorkers who value social variances in general also usually value variances in the grid and seek them out as places to live, visit, or just to think about. Streets that deviate from the strict grid take on special value in those old sections of the city that were settled in the eighteenth century before the grid plan and have escaped its later penetrations. Upper Broadway and the Bowery, both discarded in the original plan of 1811, were in modern times celebrated for having defied the plan and overridden the grid. Parts of Greenwich Village also escaped the grid, though the extension of Seventh Avenue in the 1910s cut through its heart with a straight line.

O. Henry in the "The Lost Blend" (1907) and "The Last Leaf" (1907) took these odd-shaped corners, which tend to be called "places," and imbued them with a magical quality where very human things might happen. (The saloon of "The Lost Blend," Kenealy's café, was in fact Healy's Tavern on the corner diagonally across the street from O. Henry's rooms at 55 Irving Place; it still stands as Pete's Tavern.) Residents of Greenwich Village never tire of pointing out to visitors old nooks and crannies formed before the grid, or ones left in the interstices where the grid varied its rectangularity. The curious, paradoxical intersections of curving West 4th Street with West 10th, 11th, and 12th Streets seem a minor miracle, as though the rationality of the grid was made to relent, to do a contradictory, human thing, at least once.

The Curbside of City Life. A second and complementary metaphor of social stratification, but in microscale, is drawn from a mental cross section of the city street—down from the *sidewalk,* onto the *curb,* into the *gutter,* and down the *sewer.* This vertical metaphor emerged directly from the way streets developed and were built after about 1850. In Europe the urban street was not clearly allocated between vehicular and pedestrian traffic until the middle ages; today this distinction remains confused in some developing countries. At one time in the European city, pedestrians used the center of the passageway while vehicular traffic kept to the side with the animals, garbage, and sewage. But the lack of pavement in the center eventually forced pedestrians to the sides and animals and vehicles claimed the center. The modern street design, with raised sidewalks paved differently from the road surfaces, strictly separating and protecting pedestrian from vehicular traffic with curbs, did not become the norm in American cities until roughly 1850.[46]

The sidewalk, thus formed, was shared by high and low alike, though the low were often expected to defer to the passage of their betters, and in the case of extreme social distance even to step into the gutter. Middle-class elements in the community tried to keep the sidewalks respectable places in the public life of the city. The sidewalk, like the rest of Main Street, was scrutinized, at least in daylight hours, by the agents of respectable forces. The slang phrase *spitting on the sidewalk,* originally a hobo term alluding to police harassment and the ostensible reason for an arrest, leaked into popular speech to mean any trivial offense for which one has been confronted by the law.

"Curbstones," says Carole Rifkind, "marked off the street from the sidewalk; this interface also served as a sometime market and informal resting place."[47] The curb is also the margin between the controlled sidewalk and the chaotic roadway, and the curb is just above but very near the gutter, the place of unspeakable things. Some urban dog owners still do not honor the distinction; they were once commanded by street signs to "curb your dog." These clever exhortations had the double if unclear meaning of restraining the dog and leading it not to the curb but beyond to the gutter—at least.

The curb became a figure of speech for social marginality as well. The adjective *curbstone* generally meant "of the street" as a public arena and came to modify a number of activities that were only quasi-legal at best. *Curbstone justice,* before the days of Miranda, was an old-fashioned, informal discipline meted out by the cop on the beat to kids in poor neighborhoods. *Curbstone singers* were nineteenth-century street singers, sometimes whole impoverished families, who sang for their supper. A *curbstone philosopher* was an urban successor to the cracker-barrel philosopher of the country general store. Some curbstone philosophers surely were speakers at *curbstone meetings,* which in the 1890s were planned but informal gatherings on the sidewalk rather than in a hired hall.

A *curbstone broker* or just *curbstoner*—or any *curbstone* business—is one operating informally and perhaps shadily.[48] When the New York Stock Exchange was initially organized and went indoors, many excluded brokers were left on the street (in both senses) and called *curbstone brokers* by 1848 and *street brokers* by 1856. "A group of them formed *the New York Curb Exchange* in 1842, simply called the *curb market* or *the curb* by 1890, and the members then called *curb brokers,* which became *the New York Curb Market Association* in 1911 and finally *the American Stock Exchange* in 1953," having discarded all reference to their low-status origins at the curbside.[49]

The early curbstone brokers usually did their business on the sidewalks, but sometimes they were allowed to assemble in the middle of Broad Street in the financial district—al fresco in either case. Some worked out of doors as late as 1921. William Glackens's painting *Curb Exchange* (1907–10) shows a crowd of curb brokers trading securities in the street outside the New York Stock Exchange.[50] Scenes of such squalid capitalism offended finer sensibilities. Early in this century, Florence Wilkinson Evans began her verse "The Curb-Brokers," with "Hail, ye frenzied creatures, antic, mask-like figures,/ Shouting gibberish symbols, wheat and corn and cotton." Some things modified by *curbstone* meant still lower activities and nearer the gutter. The noun *curbstone,* in another sense, was bums' argot for a cigarette hand-rolled from the tobacco taken from stubs picked up in the street.

Just below the curb is the *gutter,* which is the metaphorical state and abode of the lowest orders of humanity. A young individual of this class, a street urchin or ragamuffin, by 1869 was called a *guttersnipe,* less often a *gutter rat,* and, more gently, a *gutterpup.* Guttersnipes were also the youngest members of gangs of homeless boys, the older of whom were called *street arabs.* Many guttersnipes and street arabs were well voiced from hawking newspapers and noted for their foul language and, so, were said to speak *gutter language* and probably also *to have their minds in the gutter.* Members of the New York Stock Exchange once ridiculed the curb market as the *gutter market* and its members as *guttersnipes.*

Guttersnipe was also extended to a street beggar and to a street musician who passed the hat. There were yet other musical associations. "A 'mud-gutter' [i.e., curbstone] band in front of one of the dance-halls was making discordant music," said a New York social commentator in 1892.[51] In musicians' talk around 1900 *gutter music* was funeral and parade music played in the streets, that is, marching in the gutter. Jazz musicians later took the expression to comment ironically on the low esteem in which the public held early ragtime and jazz.[52] An even lower, filthier place is the sewer. There dirty rats from the alley can work their way down to the status of *sewer rats* and speak, I suppose, with *sewer mouths.*

The Street Grid as the Gameboard of City Life

A number of other idiomatic, informal, and slang expressions, taken together, seem to speak to a common cultural image of city streets, though each expression arose independently and at different times. Such expressions, like any aggregate of words and phrases, could be construed to tell many different stories. Yet they all too easily tell a certain story of competitive striving on the giant Monopoly board of the street grid. Their cumulative image of the city streets seems to metaphorize the cultural anxiety related to class, status, and mobility in urban society, where money and success all too often are the measures of social worth. Indeed, the grid for many urbanites is not an ordered, predictable course upwards, like a ladder, but a horizontal maze of hazards, dead-ends, frustrating turns, lost opportunities, mixed fortunes, surprises, and always the possibility of failure.

Several imaginary street names in popular speech symbolize the dual opposition of success or failure. Success meant to be on *Easy Street,* which by about 1900 meant a personal situation of ease and affluence, especially a recently acquired or anticipated state. Facing the sun-like goal of success, wealth, happiness, and optimism, the right side to be on is the *sunny side of the street,* an urban expression dating from sometime before 1905. Any city walker knows that the sunny side is the preferred side on a clear, cold winter's day, whether the climate is meteorological or social.

The opposite state of affairs is to end up on *Poverty Row,* the most popular metaphorical state of poverty in late nineteenth-century New York. Old British slang gave us a few specific street names in the neighborhood of Poverty Row. In the literary life, one can end up *in Grub Street* working as a hack.[53] In any walk of life, if things get bad enough one can land *in Queer Street,* that is, in trouble, especially financial, and in certain American usages it seems extended to any awkward, embarrassing situation. Indigenous American slang offers *Shit Street* as a rough equivalent; it seems adapted from the name of the creek up which one, moreover, is said not to have a paddle. A person can end up in Grub Street by straying into a *one-way street,* or worse, into Queer Street by straying down a *dead-end street,* or *up a blind alley,* and in the locution of public transport finding oneself at the *end of the line.* In this situation, one is said *to have been driven to the wall, to be up against the wall,* or *to have one's back against the wall.*

Relations with city life, like all in life, are a *two-way street.* One usually starts at the beginning of the endeavor, or from *Jump Street.* The object of the competitive game is not to stay *in the same street* with everyone else, but *to explore every avenue* and to break away and *get streets ahead* of them, even if one has *to work both sides of the street* and even *to cut corners* in order, as we say today, *to be the first (kid) on one's block* with a better idea. Only the very cautious stick to the *middle of the road;* successful urbanites *get off the beaten path,* work hard, and *pave their own way to success.* The important thing is not *to step off the curb,* figuratively to die, to fail. The urban world is changeable and unpredictable and success may be *just around the corner,* though some are frustrated at every turn. One hopes to get *the green light* as one approaches the crossroads of urban life. Success is often a matter of finding a niche, or something just *down* or right *up one's street* (or *alley*). If we get good enough at a particular thing, we might find ourselves in *Fat City* and all set to enjoy the bright lights of city life.

PART II

The Modern Ruptures of Traditional Life

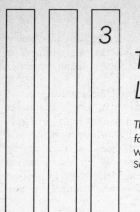

3

The Bright Lates

The life of the theatre, bar-room, huge hotel, for me!
WALT WHITMAN, "Give Me the Splendid Silent Sun," 1865

The lights of the city are the ancient symbol of the contrast of city life to the dullness of rural areas and small towns. In the modern, industrial city, the brilliant artificial lights were, further, a symbol of transcendence—and deliverance—from tradition. The bright lights stood for gaiety, pleasure, and new style in contrast to the boredom and strictures of traditional social roles and ways of life. The righteous may have seen the bright lights as just a new form of darkness. But many city people saw them as illuminating the path to the good life.

From the time in ancient cities when houses and shops were illuminated with oil lamps and public squares lit with torches, city lights have been to approaching travelers a beacon and a symbol of urban respite. The bright lights of the city's center at night have always beckoned to the young and adventurous, whether from rural areas or from quarters of tradition within the city itself. To this day, lights of a city—seen approaching from land, sea, or air—signify the warmth and buzz of human activity, against the surrounding darkness. Painters and photographers have long charmed us with romantic images of the lighted city—the shining jewel—viewed from approaches that suggest imminent arrival, or opportunity held in abeyence for the moment.

The City That Never Sleeps

Artificial street lighting in New York and other cities—gaslights after the mid-1820s and electric lights beginning in the 1880s—enabled street life to go on as late as it would sustain business, or as late as customary rhythms of day and night in the community would tolerate. Artificial lighting in cities, indoors and out, created a new urban frontier that enabled the economy to "colonize" the world after dark, with far-reaching social and economic consequences that are still with us.[1] The modern city has for more than a century continually reorganized to accommodate production and consumption around the clock. Cities long ago ceased *to roll up the sidewalks* at sunset, but stay open to the limits dictated by the demands of production and consumption. The brightest blaze of lights was in the entertainment or *white-light district,* an area of a city given over to and symbolizing consumption, luxury, success, and entertainment.

Nightlife, the word itself from the early 1850s and the beginnings of the modern city, may be defined as after-dark entertainment and gaiety under artificial light in various public establishments. The phrase *bright lights* became meaningful in the modern sense only after the introduction of gas-lit streets, first in the busiest commercial quarters of cities and their nearby entertainment areas. In 1823 the first gaslights in the city were installed along Broadway, from the Battery to Canal Street, and the Bowery was soon gas-lit as well.[2] Lights from carriages, shops, hotels, restaurants, and theaters added to the illumination of the streets.

The early public interest in street lighting was for the convenience of elites and social control of the streets but eventually became more a matter of civic pride and promotion of commerce.[3] Electric-arc street lighting was introduced in New York on December 20, 1880, to the delight of New Yorkers and the amazement of visitors. The first stretch was up Broadway from 14th Street to 23rd Street and, at each end, in Union and Madison squares—the city's first *white way.* Arc lamps also blazed on the Bowery after 1884, making it into a working-class white way. The culmination of the bright lights was to be farther uptown.

The Great White Way

Broadway became the city's—and the nation's—symbol of the bright lights. New York's center of nightlife gradually moved uptown, from Union Square to Madison Square, then to Herald Square, and finally to Times Square. Broadway was celebrated with many epithets at different periods of its development. By 1890 Broadway was ablaze with electric lights. The stretch between 23rd and 34th streets was the liveliest spot in the city, though the action even then was rapidly moving northward toward 42nd Street. Diamond Jim Brady, city lore has it, once stepped out into the lights of Broadway and declared it "The Street of the Midnight Sun."

The Great White Way, the most famous of the popular names for Broadway, dates from about 1900. Broadway from Herald Square through Longacre Square, soon to be Times Square, was by then a blazing canyon of lights and a fantasia of many-colored electrical advertising signs. The coinage of *The Great White Way* in reference to Broadway is variously attributed. The naming is traditionally credited, though without proof, to Oscar J. Gude, the New York advertising man who foresaw the possibilities of electric signs and in 1892 erected over Madison Square the first truly spectacular electrical advertising sign of the sort that later made Times Square famous. He began erecting electrical signs on Longacre Square in 1900 and reportedly dubbed the stretch of Broadway through the square *The Great White Way* in 1901.

The earliest found printed instance of *The Great White Way* in reference to Broadway, however, is the headline usage, "Found on The Great White Way," by an anonymous reporter for the New York *Evening Telegram* on February 3, 1902.[4] The reporter, it is said, borrowed the name of Albert Bigelow Paine's novel, *The Great White Way*, which had been published late in 1901. Paine's novel was about a fantastic adventure in the Antarctic and had nothing to do with Broadway. In early February of 1902, New York lay under a heavy snowfall that the city was slow to remove. The spectacle of Broadway covered with snow apparently reminded the reporter of Paine's Great White Way to the Antarctic and he used the phrase once to headline his regular column of Broadway news. One account says that his readers, many show people among them, liked the new nickname for Broadway and that their usage soon propelled it into wide usage.

Yet the name might have emerged in popular speech about 1900 or earlier and referred first to the bright, white lights above, not to white snow beneath. *The Great White Way* might have been just a specification of *white way*—any street of white lights—and took the modifier *Great*, much as *Gay* soon modified the expression in *The Gay White Way*, a form popular after about 1910. "This glittering trail along upper Broadway, the 'Great White Way,' is celebrated all over the world," wrote the New York *Herald* on September 22, 1906. A line from a 1908 song by Charles K. Harris goes: "She's a little white girl on the Great White Way/ In the city where nobody cares."

By 1910, the blocks of Broadway just above 42nd Street were at the very heart of the Great White Way. The glow of Times Square symbolized the center of New York, if not of the world. Names for the white-light districts in other cities, such as Chicago's *The Little White Way* on North Clark Street, were but extensions of the image of Broadway as *The* Great White Way. H. L. Mencken wrote that "every American town of any airs has a *Great White Way*."[5] The spectacle of The Great White Way, a bit paradoxically, always had as much to do with its many colored lights as with its white lights. Actually, the first colored advertising lights on Broadway appeared in 1828 at the opening of Niblo's Garden on the northeast corner at Prince Street—gas jets in red-, white-, and blue-glass cups—arrayed along an iron pipe spelled out "NIBLO."

Electrical advertising signs appeared on a large scale in the early 1890s, and many people were struck by the new feeling of the city at night. William Dean Howells in his *Letters of an Altrurian Traveller* (1893–94) lamented the signs that spoiled the cityscape. Even "the darkness does not shield you from them, and by night the very sky is starred with the electric bulbs that spell out, on the roofs of the lofty city edifices, the frantic announcement of this or that business enterprise."[6] "By the close of the century," wrote the historian Bayard Still, "the 'omnipresence of electricity' already offered a foretaste of the glamor which was to suffuse Broadway in the ensuing years."[7]

Stephen Crane in 1902 wrote that "Broadway of late years has fallen heir to countless signs illuminated with red, blue, green, and gold electric lamps, and the people certainly fly to these as moths go to a candle."[8] By 1905 or so the city had several thousand electrical advertising signs with hundreds of thousands of incandescent bulbs. In 1914 Vachel Lindsay addressed his much-anthologized "A Rhyme About An Electrical Advertising Sign" to this image of the new electrified city: "I look on the specious electrical light/ Blatant, mechanical, crawling and white,/ Wickedly red or malignantly green."

Broadway became brighter and brighter and the theatrical district seemed to settle down permanently in and around Longacre Square. In 1904 the name was changed to Times Square upon completion of the *New York Times* newspaper building at the south end. The renaming followed the example of Herald Square, which was obligingly so named by the city in 1895 to note the presence of the offices of the New York *Herald*. Times Square became world famous for its garish "crawling" lights. Journalists and travel writers exhausted their vocabularies trying to capture the blazing, multi-colored, dazzling, animated, fantastic, monstrous, absurd spectacle. In the bitterly cold winter of 1917–18, coal shortages and electrical blackouts caused the Great White Way to become "a yawning black chasm," wrote the historian Henry Collins Brown. "For awhile it almost seemed as if we were doomed to live in Philadelphia."[9] But that was not for long.

The 1920s saw the introduction of the neon advertising sign. This medium was to give American downtowns a shimmering, romantic glow in the 1930s and 1940s, a memory now held in nostalgic esteem. New York's first neon sign is said to have appeared in 1923 either on a movie marquee in Times Square or, another story has it, a little farther north in Columbus Circle on the marquee of William Randolph Hearst's Cosmopolitan Theatre where Marion Davies opened in *Little Old New York*. As an adjective, *neon* came to denote a tawdry or gaudy nightlife district in any city. Colored neon cast a wicked, sensuous light that stood in contrast to the light of day, and even to the white street lights that were supposed to control social behavior. Of this atmosphere in other cities, Nelson Algren titled his collection of short stories *The Neon Wilderness* (1947) and John D. McDonald his novel *The Neon Jungle* (1953).

The reputation of Times Square's bubbly nightlife and the gaiety of its visitors soon equaled the fame of its bright lights. The gin-soaked Great White Way was punningly referred to as the *Great Tight Way* in the 1910s. Benjamin de Casseres called 42nd Street and Broadway "the corner of the Rue de Booze and the Great Wine Way."[10] The stretch of Broadway through Times Square was also called the *Roaring Forties,* or (in everyday use) just *The Forties.* Syndicated newspaper columnists between the world wars

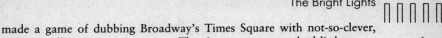
made a game of dubbing Broadway's Times Square with not-so-clever, punning, alliterative stunt names. The sixty or so names had little or no currency beyond their columns, but serve to suggest the word images of Broadway the mass media purveyed to the rest of the country. Bright lights, hokum, and drink are the major allusions.[11] Of these many names for Broadway, only *The Great White Way* has survived with vigor in popular speech.

The Rialto.   Broadway for well over a century has been the main street of the theater district, the location of many theatrical agents, a promenade of employed and unemployed actors, and generally a meeting place of show people; Tin Pan Alley was always nearby on various cross streets. Until the 1880s, the south side of Union Square on 14th Street was called *The Rialto,* after the name of the busy commercial district in Venice. In the 1860s, actors lounged around the base of the great equestrian statue of George Washington, and there they had what they and passersby called the *slave market* for those seeking employment through the theatrical offices in the area.

Among show people, 14th Street was "the street" in the sense of an informal network of news and gossip. Hence, the famous New York phrase "What's new on the Rialto?"—an inquiry about what was going on in show biz and later by extension in any world of endeavor. The question echoes the line in *The Merchant of Venice,* "What news on the Rialto?"[12] So, it is not surprising that the perennial inquiry found favor with actors. Other nearby streets also served as rialtos, such as Irving Place in the 1870s and early 1880s. In later years Second Avenue south of 14th was called the Yiddish Rialto and the Yiddish Broadway, alluding to the many Yiddish theaters and supporting enterprises that once lined the street. Its social center was the Café Royal—sometimes called "the Yiddish Sardi's"—which opened in 1920 on the southeast corner of Second Avenue and 12th Street.

After about 1890 the stretch of Broadway between Union Square and Madison Square became the Rialto. But the vanguard of new theaters was already pressing it farther uptown. By 1905 the Rialto centered on Herald Square. By 1910 the Rialto was between 34th and 47th streets and soon the name referred chiefly to the stretch through Times Square. By the 1930s, movies and the pull of Hollywood for many actors, as well as the crush of tourists in Times Square, pushed the Rialto onto the blocks along 42nd Street and finally dispersed it altogether.

People in show business also called the blocks of Broadway through Times Square *The Street,* representing the concentration of their industry. For young hopefuls, however, The Street was 47th Street between Sixth and Seventh Avenues—*Dream Street,* as Damon Runyon named it. Just off Broadway, this was the block with the offices and stagedoor of the B. F. Keith's Palace Theater, the mecca of American vaudeville from its opening in

1913 until it became a movie house in 1932. *Panic Beach* was the sidewalk in front of the Palace and was so named for the unemployed performers who waited and milled about there.

The Big Apple.   Today's universally known and boosterish nickname for New York, *The Big Apple,* was in 1971 successfully promoted by Charles Gillett, then president of the New York Convention and Visitors Bureau. *The Big Apple* was the happy successor to the much ridiculed, short-lived *Fun City,* which had become an ironic epithet by the late 1960s. A controversy ensued over the origin, date, and the first meaning of *The Big Apple,* but the story is now getting straightened out through the efforts of slang etymologist Gerald L. Cohen and of Barry Popik.[13]

The name is best known and most noted as an expression of jazz musicians in the 1930s and 1940s, referring to bookings in New York. The best Harlem places and the clubs on 52nd Street were the pinnacles of success— *The* Big Apple. Yet the expression was used earlier and in other enterprises. As early as 1909, the expression had been used in print as a critical metaphor for the city as the dominant metropolis in the nation. "New York [was] merely one of the fruits of that great tree whose roots go down in the Mississippi Valley, and whose branches spread from one ocean to the other. . . . [But] the big apple [New York] gets a disproportionate share of the national sap."[14]

By the early 1920s *The Big Apple* was being used to name the acme of certain endeavors, such as appearing on Broadway as the height of success in show business, getting jazz bookings in top Manhattan clubs, or in horse racing competing for big purses at New York tracks. The name was also extended to the main stems and commercial societies that located and supported these endeavors, such as Broadway and Seventh Avenue in Harlem. Because so many of these businesses, the greatest professional achievement in them, and their symbolic streets were in New York, the city itself came to symbolize the acme of various fields. *The Big Apple* in several of these connections was appearing in print by the late 1920s. In 1927 Walter Winchell wrote that "Broadway is the Big Apple, the Main Stem, the goal of all ambition, the pot of gold at the end of a drab and somewhat colorless rainbow." Soon the columnist O. O. McIntyre also was using *The Big Apple* for Broadway.[15]

The notion of the Big Apple as the height of success is a fitting culmination to the deep metaphor of Manhattan streets suggested in the previous chapter. The business culture influenced a popular imagery in which Times Square (and the surrounding entertainment district) was the crown of a great tree whose trunk was the Great White Way that stretched down to 34th Street. One Broadway businessman wrote of the Great White Way as "that portion of Broadway from 34th to 59th Streets, (which can be likened unto the trunk of a great tree, the cross streets representing its many branches)."[16] Another wrote that "Broadway is the trunk of the tree and its

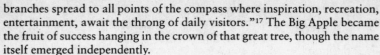
branches spread to all points of the compass where inspiration, recreation, entertainment, await the throng of daily visitors."[17] The Big Apple became the fruit of success hanging in the crown of that great tree, though the name itself emerged independently.

To make it in New York was to make it in The Big Apple. Gradually, the sense of *The Big Apple* was expanded from New York as success in a particular endeavor to a nickname for the city itself, but it remained in special and restricted usage, mostly in the entertainment business. The first known printed instance of *The Big Apple* as a nickname for New York City is found in a glossary, "The Slang of Film Men," in the New York *Times* on March 11, 1928.[18] But the expression was not known to the general public and was barely kept alive by jazz musicians in the 1930s and 1940s. The name was all but forgotten until its revival in 1971. *The Big Apple* is a fitting sobriquet for New York. It is closely associated with the city's public life in the early decades of this century, speaks to its status as a premier national and world city, and has a rich history of meaning that is just now coming to light.

The Great White Way of Broadway, whether hailed as The Rialto or The Big Apple, had its heyday and went into slow decline. As early as the 1910s people were saying that Broadway and Times Square seemed grey and tawdry by day. In the early 1930s, a visitor compared Broadway to "a lady of the evening. In the sunlight she looks like a suddenly awakened chorus girl who went to bed with her make-up on." By the end of the Second World War, much of the Broadway and Times Square area had become blighted, even sordid. Today the police and denizens of Times Square call the block of 42nd Street between Seventh and Eighth avenues *The Deuce,* referring to the "two" in the street name of this crime- and vice-ridden area. In the 1960s the building of Lincoln Center twenty blocks to the north further detracted from Times Square. But the old center, despite the forces of age and decay, has held as the theater district and as a magnet for tourists. Times Square is now undergoing controversial commercial and civic redevelopment that promises to revive the area as the Great White Way.

Tin Pan Alley. The bright lights illuminate Broadway, but music animates it. *Tin Pan Alley,* the popular name since the 1890s for music-publishers' row in New York, served show business from the wings of the theater district, usually one or two cross streets just off Broadway. Tin Pan Alley followed the moving center of show business uptown along Broadway, from Union Square at 14th Street by 1880, to the short block of West 28th Street between Broadway and Fifth Avenue by 1900, to Herald and Greeley squares at 34th Street by the 1910s, and to just above Times Square by the 1920s. The Alley was then concentrated in old brownstone fronts to the west of Broadway in 46th and 47th streets where, wrote O. O. McIntyre, "the strident jangle of a hundred pianos rises above the street din."[19]

By 1950 Tin Pan Alley was dispersed nationwide to Chicago, Los Angeles, and even so-called in London, where it was near Charing Cross. But the name is of New York origin and became generic for the popular music business—song writing, selling, publishing—though it is now seldom used in the business. New York's cluster of music publishers, agents, composers, and arrangers is today located between Broadway and Seventh Avenue a few blocks north of Times Square. The Brill Building at 1619 Broadway, between 49th and 50th streets, has a number of such offices.

Tin Pan Alley was greatly important in the diffusion of city slang into the national mainstream of popular speech. Writers such as Irving Berlin would hear a bit of new slang, work it into a song, and it would go out from there. From the professional jargon of Tin Pan Alley we also learned to speak of pop songs as "numbers," of sentimental songs as "ballads," of love songs as "torches," all of which were shamelessly and aggressively "plugged" in any way to get public attention.

The name *Tin Pan Alley* first appeared in print about 1899, though the industry itself was already well established. Most evidence points to its origin in the name and sound of the cheap, tinny pianos used in many studios of music publishers' row. In 1890s musicians' argot such a piano was called a *tin-pan,* alluding to the thinness and cheapness of tin pans. The adjective *tin-pan,* a harsh, clanging noise, is also an Americanism from the 1840s, possibly from the sound of beating on a tin pan. "All music publishers had a tinny piano available for auditions, whence the whimsical notion of an actual alley lined with tinny pianos," wrote John Ciardi.[20] This seems the most likely story.

Yet the music-business historian Kenneth Aaron Kanter cautiously attributes *Tin Pan Alley* to journalist-songwriter Monroe Rosenfeld.[21] Harry Von Tilzer, a song writer turned publisher, later claimed coinage of the name. But Rosenfeld, says Kanter, "made it stick by giving it large circulation." As Kanter tells the story, in the late 1890s Rosenfeld visited Von Tilzer's office on West 28th Street to gather material for an article on the music business. Von Tilzer, he noticed, had wound pieces of paper over the piano strings (a kid's trick) to make the tinny sound he was fond of. That sound gave Rosenfeld the idea for the title of his article, "Tin Pan Alley," which supposedly launched the popular name. But the name may have had oral use in the trade before Rosenfeld used it.

On the Town

Lewis A. Erenberg, the author of *Steppin' Out,* shows how the history of New York nightlife is "a window to the process of transformation of social and cultural attitudes and behavior."[22] Public nightlife, along with the bright lights, grew in the 1890s and accompanied the decline of the old social order and its values. The new period also saw a relaxation of certain boundaries between the sexes, social statuses, and ethnic groups. By participating in nightlife, middle-class men and women escaped the social tensions of their traditional roles of spouses and economic producers. First men and then women used the arena of nightlife and its fantasy world to express their desire for new and freer lives, sometimes trying to project the fantasy onto reality.

The nightlife of New York and Broadway was richly productive of slang and popular speech. These words and phrases give insight into the social categories of that bygone world. Fanciful, popular speech named various kinds of establishments that could be visited, what could be done and seen there, and all the social types and social roles associated with the scene. Older words, too, were brought into the service of new experience. The vocabulary, constantly invigorated by journalism, was known to participants, vicarious nightlifers, and most city people. These words and phrases soon entered the national mainstream of popular speech.

The vocabulary can be construed to reconstruct the experience of nightlife as a coherent whole, beginning with the idea of getting dressed up, putting on one's top hat, and *steppin' out,* going out *on the town,* and ending with an anxious consideration of the social consequences. Most popular expressions of dressing for the occasion contain the idea of, and often the word *up,* to express elevating the appearance of the person to fit the aspiration of the evening. Men and women, and there is gender allusion in the terms, got *togged-up* (mid-nineteenth century), *duded-up* (late nineteenth century), *(all) dolled-up* (or *-out*) (turn of the century), or *gussied-up* (the late 1940s). Some of the terms survive from the day when country cousins got dressed up to go *into* town.

The old phrase *to go to town,* 'to let go,' to do something well, with great ease, enthusiasm, and without constraint, seems to derive from a rural view that associated personal freedom and unrestrained achievement with urban life. Slurred as *goin' to town,* the expression seems, further, to speak to the enthusiasm of anticipating, getting dressed up for, and the whole experience of, visiting town. In another rural view, a trip to town often entailed *going on a spree* or *painting the town red.* The latter, first found in print in 1884, is of uncertain origin but seems to be of the Old West, recalling some form of violence, such as the red of flames or blood.[23] New York rhetoric often found such comparisons of city life and the Wild West.

Bourgeois life tempered violent inclinations while on the town and reduced them to symbolism. In polite company, at least, abandon in public was usually little more than swinging on a chandelier, wearing a lampshade, blowing a noise-maker, or dancing on a piano. Or, when better organized, the fun may have spilled out for *dancing in the streets,* or for a snake dance, a rhumba-line that coiled out of the night clubs in their heyday. *To go on a tear, to take a flyer,* or especially *to make whoopee* was the way nightlifers spoke of these tamer sprees in the 1920s. *Whoopee!,* a cry of exuberant joy and abandon and an Americanism from the 1870s, announces that the crowd is about to go on a spree and get naughty. Walter Donaldson's popular song of

1928, "Making Whoopee," from the Ziegfeld show *Whoopee!,* was a cultural theme song of the Roaring Twenties. The lyrics of "Making Whoopee" clearly allude to extramarital sex, though the expression seems to have been extended to a variety of other breaks with straight behavior. The 1930 movie *Whoopie!,* the song now sung by Eddie Cantor, reinforced the gay ethos of the unzipped Prohibition Era. Walter Winchell used *whoopee* in his columns so much that some thought he coined it.

Urban revelers were less likely "to go to town" than, from their city residences, just *to step out on the town.* The phrase *on the town,* for men at least, has since the early eighteenth century meant seeking a good time at various fashionable places around town, or *making the rounds.* The expression *On the Town* was in the 1940s taken for the title of Leonard Bernstein's musical and subsequent movie about sailors on shore leave chasing girls all over New York. An obsolete but perhaps fuller form of the expression is *up on the town.*

"I Wanna Dance!"

By 1900 young single women, despite risks to their reputations, were joining the fun too, and it usually meant going dancing. Working-class young women were often liberated in this respect before their middle-class counterparts and took the first dance steps away from Victorian social constraints. Hutchins Hapgood described the evening activities of New York's shopgirls in the years just after 1900:

> There are many adventurous spirits among shop-girls; some of them are climbers on a lark. . . . They are fierce, independent spirits, as daring as men, full of the joy of life. They "rubber" about at night, and generally hunt in pairs. They go to the dance-halls and academies and are easily approached by "decent-looking" men; with whom they drink, and talk all round forbidden subjects. They are endowed, many of them, with wit and are very entertaining. With the men they "pick up" they will go to the theater, to late suppers, will be as jolly as they like; altho . . . they remain conventionally virtuous. . . .
>
> The dance-hall is truly a passion with working-girls. The desire to waltz is bred in the feminine bone. It is a familiar thing to see little girls on the East Side dancing rhythmically on the street, to the music of some hand-organ, while heavy wagons roll by unheeded. When those little girls grow older and become shop-girls they often continue to indulge their passion for the waltz. Some of them dance every night, and are so confirmed in it that they are technically known as "spielers."[24]

They were called *spielers* in the street vernacular of the East Side and the Bowery dance halls because of their enthusiasm for a frenetic, twirling dance style, akin to the waltz, in which the female partner is swung high off the floor. The dance itself was called the *spiel* and to do the dance was *to spiel,* whence the gerund *spieling* and the agentive form *spieler*. It is from German *spielen,* "to play," "to perform," especially in a musical way, and was probably borrowed from the city's vigorous German culture by 1880. A popular song of the 1880s by J. L. Feeney, sung to the tune of "Sweet Forget-Me-Not," was "The Spielers": "They go to parties and soirees, and almost every ball;/ You're sure to find the 'spielers' there who take the shine of all." The men dancers were occasionally also called spielers but it was more often applied to the women. These word senses of a dance style and of its performers were obsolescent by the First World War or so.

By the turn of the century, dance halls were respectable and important arenas of neighborhood social life and were enormously popular with immigrant groups on the Lower East Side and elsewhere in the city. Some thirty-one dance halls, one for every two and one-half blocks, could be counted in the small area east of the Bowery and between Houston and Grand streets. Respectable young women of the working class favored dances organized by ethnic social clubs and amusement societies, for they were one of the few places where they could safely meet unattached young men and flirt. In the slang of the day, these affairs were called *rackets, blow outs,* or *hops*. The neighborhood dance hall, according to social historian Kathy Peiss, introduced young people to the nightlife of the city and gave them an arena to work out their own style and experiment with nontraditional social roles.[25] O. Henry takes the setting of an Irish "hop" on Orchard Street for his story "The Coming-Out of Maggie" (1906). Young Maggie, who works in a paper-box factory by day, is asked by a local hero of the Irish if she would step out to the next week's dance, and she replies "Say—will a duck swim?"

New dancing styles began to reflect the loosened constraints on public sexual expression, becoming less formal and more provocative with body contact. The titillating idea of contact in dancing also seems to be behind a few slang terms of the period. A low dancing party was known as a *rub;* a cheap dance hall was sometimes called a *rub joint* because body contact was allowed and encouraged. Kathy Peiss writes that

> The sexual emphasis of the dance was even more pronounced in a style known as 'tough dancing,' which became popular after 1905. Tough dancing had its origins in the houses of prostitution on San Francisco's Barbary Coast and gradually spread, in the form of the slow rag, the lovers' two-step, turkey trot, and bunny hug, to the 'low resorts' and dance halls of major metropolitan areas. . . . Tough dancing not only permitted physical contact, it celebrated it. Indeed, the essence of tough dancing was its suggestion of sexual intercourse.[26]

In 1911 New York passed licensing laws that opened a new age of dance halls. The Grand Palace opened that year, while licenses were denied to many low establishments. The city soon had 500 licensed dance halls, some of the largest in Times Square. Roseland Ballroom, one of the grander establishments, still thrives today. The 1910s were also the time of a middle-class dance craze sparked by black and working-class dance styles. The theatrical dancers Irene and Vernon Castle translated, muted, and popularized black and Barbary Coast (San Francisco) dancing styles for the white middle classes, as well as introduced other styles and fashions for the coming Jazz Age.

Flappers. No one was more enamored of the new dance styles than the *flappers*. After the First World War, these mainly middle-class young women made the much-publicized break, at least in personal styles, with old-fashioned social behavior, dress, grooming, and attitude. The flappers were also very much a part of the gay scene in Times Square. By 1919 or so these fast young women with bobbed hair, bound breasts, skimpy dresses, and cupid-bow lips were, with their male companions, a regular part of the dance scene in cafés, cabarets, night clubs, at tea dances, matinées, and in dance halls. One of the more unlikely places flappers danced, sometimes during their lunch hour, was in certain *chop-*

FIGURE 5. Reginald Marsh. *Chop Suey Dancers #2* (1929). On their lunch hour, some young women went to midtown *chop suey dance joints*, Chinese restaurants with a jazz band, to practice the latest dance steps with their friends. (*Courtesy of the William Benton Museum of Art*)

suey dance joints, or those Chinese restaurants in the 1920s and 1930s where very spirited, very bad Chinese jazz bands played for dancing. Flappers in cloche hats and skirts above their knees are depicted dancing together in Reginald Marsh's 1929 etching *Chop Suey Dancers No. 2,* evidently practicing some of the more extreme steps of the day under the impassive eye of a Chinese waiter.

Flapper is of uncertain origin, though it is probably and remotely from the image of a young duck experimentally flapping its wings, and in the eighteenth century *flapper* did mean a fledgling duck. This image is certainly evoked by a flapper dancing the Charleston, usually paired side-by-side with her *jelly bean, boyfriend, sheik,* or *jazz bo.* And the fad one season of wearing open-top, flapping galoshes fanned the notion, too. Anyhow, the flapper flaunted staid convention. More proximately the term may have come from British speech of the late 1880s when a flapper was a girl still too young to put up her hair. She was a teenage girl of the awkward age who "flapped" in the sense of having little of the poise and composure of a mature woman. To cover her awkwardness, she was supposed to need a certain type of long, straight, loose-fitting dress, which British shops once advertised as "flapper dresses."

At about the same time in the United States, *flapper* was occasionally used for a frighteningly independent young woman, whom some too loosely thought of as a prostitute, or nearly so. But by 1910 the sense of the word had been softened to mean any pert or headstrong young woman, especially one of suffragette inclinations.[27] By 1919 the meaning of *flapper* was at one with the quintessential young woman of the Jazz Age. Scott Fitzgerald in his essay about New York, "My Lost City," wrote that the type "had become *passé* by 1923—anyhow in the East."[28] Yet the flapper danced all through the 1920s, alive and well in New York City.

Because of her fondness for nightlife, jazz, and dancing, she was also called a *jazz baby, whoopee mama,* or *hot mama.* This strange jazz family of randy "daddies," hot "mommas," and eager "babies" were word images that middle-class whites got from the song lyrics that sifted down from Harlem. The flapper was fixed in visual imagery by the enormously popular cartoons and stories of John Held, Jr.[29] In a review of a biography of Held, his colleague Al Hirschfeld describes her in Held's drawings as "flat-chested . . . with open galoshes, cloche hat, miniskirt and long-stemmed spread legs drawn from a worm's-eye view; the boy is a racooned College Joe with patent-leather hair, pork-pie hat, ukulele and a hip flask bulging from bell-bottomed trousers."

Night Spots

By the middle of the nineteenth century, evening resorts favored by the affluent classes were called *watering places.* Walt Whitman in 1858 mentioned the "watering places" of the rich in New York, many of them in the great hotels and restaurants of Broadway. They were much later called *watering holes* and later still *watering spots*. The slangier forms seem especially to allude to thirsty "jungle" animals that at dusk drift in from the hot, dusty plain and gather at a watering hole. Indeed, nightlife was a time and place to seek relief from business and other dry responsibilities with wine, women, and song. Public drinking is a subject that generated many colorful terms; other names for lower-status drinking places in other parts of town are discussed in later chapters.

Fashionable nightlife on and near Broadway went through several overlapping phases after about 1890. Each phase can be characterized by the type of establishment that set its tone. The so-called lobster palaces and roof gardens were the favored resorts of affluent nightlifers from about 1890 to 1910. Better Broadway hotels and certain other commercial buildings, such as Madison Square Garden, opened *roof gardens*, the name itself a coinage of the early 1890s. Some were fairylands of greenery and cultivated flowers; all were high above the city. In those summer evenings before air conditioning, open-air dinner and dancing were extremely popular with those who could afford the price. Down in the brightly lit canyon of Broadway the most elegant and gay restaurants were called *lobster palaces*, noted Lewis A. Erenberg, "because of their gilded interiors and gay late-night lobster suppers."[30] Rector's at Broadway and 43rd Street was a premier lobster palace from about 1905 to 1910 or so. The new lobster palaces were successors to the *oyster houses* along Sixth Avenue that had earlier entertained the chic theater and sporting crowd.

For the many upwardly mobile people in the city, it was an eye-popping experience to visit the more sumptuous establishments, such as the gilded lobster palaces. One mark of a fine place was carpeted floors, which gave rise to *rug joint*. In the minds of initiates to the high life, such watering places stood in contrast to the *sawdust joints* or *sawdust parlors* of their social origins. To visit such an elegant establishment, it was said among men by the 1920s, was *to piss on ice,* because of the old practice of fine places to put blocks of ice in the urinals to give continuous flush and keep down the odor.

The cabaret and café period of nightlife in New York was from about 1910 to 1920. Modern cabarets and evening cafés were the social centers of a popular and fashionable type of nightlife in those years. The cafés once had claim to serving coffee and light meals, whence their name, but liquor, music, and dancing later set their tone. The cabaret style was imported from Paris and Americanized in San Francisco after the earthquake and fire of 1906. The cabaret and its dance styles, such as the Turkey Trot and the Bunny Hop, soon moved to New York and took on a new local style. The cabaret period in New York may have begun specifically in 1911 when the restaurateur Jacques Bustanoby at his Café des Beaux-Arts introduced dancing with supper, an astounding idea at the time.

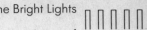
Jazz. The 1920s were called the Jazz Age, and jazz is a fitting symbol of the spirit of the modern city and its nightlife. The word *jazz*, first found in print in 1913, is of uncertain origin. Jazz music and probably the word itself came from New Orleans early in this century. This prime Americanism has a rich history of meaning and many, many connotations, two of which are speed and sexuality. The word was once spelled both *jass* and *jazz*, with the typographically more emphatic form *jazz* winning out, as though to connote the fast, vibrant, sexually charged new dance music. In 1915 jazz was introduced to New Yorkers in a vaudeville theater by Freddie Keppard's Creole Band, but few took notice.[31] In January of 1917 the Original Dixieland Jazz Band played for dancing at Reisenweber's Restaurant in Columbus Circle and there jazz captured the heart of the city.

Jazz quickly replaced ragtime as the fashionable music in the city's night spots. In the 1920s the spirit of jazz seemed to catch the essence of New York life, its vitality, releases, rhythms, and the emphasis of its nightlife on unabashed pleasure. The spirit of jazz was soon translated into a variety of broader, modernist cultural meanings for the city. Even a certain art deco style of design and architecture popular in the 1920s was retrospectively named "jazz modern." William Van Alen's ebullient Chrysler Building of 1930, detailed with insignia and hubcap designs from the 1929 model Chrysler automobile, is an exquisite example and is, many think, the single building that best caught the spirit of New York in that time.

By the late 1910s cafés, cabarets, and like establishments were called *night spots,* or just *spots.* If they featured the new jazz they might be called *jazz joints.* By the 1920s, *hot spots* were especially popular, loud, glittering, action-filled places. The idea of *hot jazz,* or informal, old-fashioned jazz for dancing and drinking, probably also influenced the name *hot spots.* The *hot* in *hot jazz* probably also alluded to the old sexual connotations of *jazz.*[32] Hot spots, gathering all these meanings, were popular places for drinking and dancing to jazz in an exciting, crowded, sexually charged atmosphere.

Another word for a nightclub of the Jazz Age and used in tonier circles was the French loanword *boîte,* which was in American English by 1922; it is from *boîte,* or, fully, *boîte de nuit,* "nightclub." But we probably took it directly from French slang *boîte,* also "nightclub," but literally "box," which seems to allude suitably to the small, crowded playrooms with tiny tables, a dance band, and a dime-sized dance floor. The word has since hid out in the imaginative corners of the language. L. E. Sissman, in his poem "Luchow's and After" (1968), has an evocative phrase, "*boîtes* that promise blue." In the 1980s the French loanword once again found a certain smart usage in New York journalism. The plain English *box,* as well, has long been used in American slang for a night club or dance hall; a *shine box,* a multilayered racist pun, was such a place in Harlem.

Speakeasies. Prohibition opened the speakeasy period of nightlife on January 1, 1920, and Repeal closed it on December 31, 1933. Few drinking New Yorkers were content *to have one on the city,* as an old slang expression said of taking a glass of water. Cabarets and such places of evening entertainment went underground and began to call themselves *nightclubs,* ostensibly private clubs, including the pretense of membership cards. Most people called them *speakeasies.* The term was soon shortened to *speak* and Damon Runyon's characters in *Guys and Dolls* were soon talking about "a little speak around the corner." A flip *speako,* affixing a familiar slang device, almost an exclamation of "Oh!," also appeared.

We often associate the Americanism *speakeasy* with Prohibition, though it is decades older, dating in print to 1889. A Philadelphia journalist, Samuel Hudson, claimed that in 1889 he picked up the new expression in Pittsburgh, introduced and popularized it in Philadelphia, whence it spread to New York.[33] *Speak-easy* (it was originally hyphenated) is probably of Irish-American dialectal origin, possibly from an utterance (such as Hudson suggested): "Spake asy, now, the police are at the dure." H. L. Mencken concluded that "the Irish gave American very few words; *shillelagh, smithereens,* and possibly *speakeasy* almost exhaust the list."[34] At any rate, the idea behind *speakeasy* is clearly silence with regard to the police.

The very sound of *speakeasy* and its suggestion of intimate knowledge and of speaking softly—"easily"—to lookouts through peepholes just fitted the spirit of the new, clandestine, yet brazenly public, drinking ways. (*Whisper-low* and *hush house* were ephemeral synonyms.) The ritual of admission to a fashionable speak was no small part of the attraction to middle-class slummers out on the town and seemed to authenticate the whole experience. New York speakeasies during Prohibition were sometimes called *Judas-hole* establishments, referring to their peepholes, which were like a "Judas Hole," or peephole, into a prison cell, except that the bouncers peeped out at the revelers who wanted in. Grover Whalen, Mayor Jimmy Walker's Commissioner of Police for two years, said 32,000 speakeasies—an almost fantastic number—were in the city. Most were very low establishments.

The old terms *blind tiger* and *blind pig* were revived for humorous use during Prohibition and New Yorkers applied them to any speakeasy. *Blind tiger* dates back to the 1850s and *blind pig* was first recorded in 1887; *blind pigger,* the proprietor, was in use by 1894. Both terms are of Western and Southern origin and of obscure etymology.[35] The idea of "blind" in both terms might refer to the old custom of covering the windows of such establishments—"blinding" them. Or the idea of getting "blind drunk" might have influenced the names or their subsequent popularity. For a more fanciful explanation, consider the title of a song of 1908, *Bl——nd and P——g Spells Blind Pig,* by Junie McCrea and Albert Von Tilzer.

Manhattan's better speakeasies were concentrated between 40th and 60th streets. Brownstone fronts in the East 50s housed many speakeasies, but many were classic dives in basements. The French novelist Paul Morand thought the speakeasies imbued Manhattan "with an exciting atmosphere of mystery."[36] He found them behind florists' shops, fake telephone booths, and even undertakers' coffins. A few speakeasies survived Repeal and exist today. The famous 21 Club at 21 West 52nd, the Palm restaurant on Second Avenue near 45th Street, and Chumley's on Bedford Street in the Village were all originally speakeasies.

The elegance of some of the speakeasies, their association with famous gangsters, the drama and comedy of occasional police raids, the imaginative ways in which some concealed themselves, and the cachet of knowing one's way around the city's best drinking places caught the public's fancy. The popular image of the speakeasy was portrayed in literature, art, song, and the movies. "I was leaning against the bar in a speakeasy on Fifty-second Street, waiting for Nora to finish her Christmas shopping, when a girl got up from a table and. . . ." The opening line from Dashiell Hammett's *The Thin Man* published in 1934—the year Prohibition ended—invoked the image of the speakeasy as a symbol of urban sophistication, and *sophistication* was a catchword of the 1920s.

During the later speakeasy period, when gangsters and bootleggers were heavily involved in the nightclub business, tourists—and also big-city nightlifers—were warned of the *clip joint,* a spot where one could be overcharged, cheated, or even robbed. The term comes from the slang verb *to clip,* 'to take,' 'to cheat.' Such places, also known as *cab joints* or *steer joints,* sometimes paid cab drivers, known as *steerers* or *cappers,* to bring them victims. Most clip joints were around Broadway but were the exception rather than the rule of business practice in the clubs. This rough and risky atmosphere of speakeasies and clip joints was surely part of the fun. Even after Repeal, the late-night crowd could still drink illegally in unlicensed *bottle clubs* or in *after-hours clubs* that violated the legal closing hours.

Café Society

Café Society was especially associated with the highly visible, much photographed life in the big nightclubs that flourished after Repeal; their favorite was El Morocco. The name *Café Society* emerged in the 1930s to denote the fashionable set suited to the name, though it obviously alludes to the earlier period of nightlife in cafés where the trend began.[37] *Café Society,* first appearing in print in the late 1930s, was popularized and probably coined by *Herald Tribune* columnist Lucius Beebe. The term became synonymous with big-city chic, and in 1939 it was affirmed by the movie *Café Society* starring Madeleine Carroll.

Society columnist Maury Paul, the first "Cholly Knickerbocker," claimed that he first indicated the new Café Society, though not with that exact phrase. His claim rests on an observation made at the dining room of the Ritz-Carlton Hotel in February 1919. For the "first" time representatives of high society had sat down and broken bread with show people in a public place. He wrote: "Society isn't staying home any more. Society is going out to dinner, out to night life, and letting down the barriers."[38]

Café Society came to designate, if only in retrospect, well-to-do and fashionable people, particularly the new kind of mixed and open society, who went to the best cafés, restaurants, and speakeasies. Café Society was a clique and a style invented and sustained by the newspapers and their society reporters for the awe of the public. Fashionable New York cafés in the 1920s, wrote historian Lloyd Morris, "blended the Social Register, Broadway stars and showgirls, top-drawer racketeers, and a few intellectuals into a novel, heady mix. In the end, it produced 'café society,' which proved as dazzling to the American imagination as the sacred Four Hundred."[39] This was also the crowd that popularized the dance crazes in the 1920s, such as the Shimmy, the Charleston, the Black Bottom, the Lindy Hop, and the Shuffle. Yet it is all too easy to romanticize Prohibition and the night-club era. Even in the 1920s visitors contended that New York "did not 'flame' as much as the movies and the magazines had led them to expect."[40]

The Great Black Way

A parallel society and its nightlife had emerged in Harlem over much the same period. Writer Jervis Anderson in *This Was Harlem* (1982) called the stretch of Seventh Avenue through the heart of Harlem the "Great Black Way." On October 16, 1929, wrote *Variety,* nightlife in Harlem "now surpasses that of Broadway itself . . . in mirth and hilarity." Harlem nightlife was concentrated on and near Seventh Avenue in the 130s and 140s and, to a lesser extent, on Lenox. Seventh Avenue was Harlem's promenade—*The Stroll,* parade route, and, like Broadway through Times Square, the center of its nightlife. Jazz musicians called Seventh Avenue the *Big Red with the Long Green Stem,* a phrase requiring decoding. *Big Red* is an elliptical form of the *Big Red Apple,* green is money, *long green* is much money, and *stem,* slang for a main street, also alludes to the elongated spatial feature of the strip. Compare this imagery to the *Big Apple* of white Broadway through Times Square, conceived as the fruit of a great tree of commercial success.

White New Yorkers soon sought out Harlem in search of new experience. In the 1920s and the early 1930s, the ultimate night out on the town was *to go slumming* in Harlem and *do* the various clubs—*black joints, black-and-tan* resorts, as they were called—and maybe smoke a little marijuana. Walter Winchell called them *sepia sin spots;* a taste of forbidden fruit was exactly what the white slummers sought. Parties of handsomely dressed white slummers made the rounds of Harlem cabarets to dance the Charleston or the Black Bottom. They sought out the titillation of beautiful black show girls at the Cotton Club or Connie's Inn. They saw Harlem as their playground with the sideshow of happy-go-lucky blacks dancing all night to jazz. Harlem was a moral vacation for whites and, wrote the historian Gilbert Osofsky, "was seen as the antithesis of Main Street, Zenith and Gopher Prairie." It was a morally indifferent view. "Whatever seemed thrilling, bizarre or sensuous about Harlem life became part of the community's image; whatever was sad or tragic about it, ignored."[41]

Among the top Harlem night clubs was The Cotton Club on Lenox at 142nd, while over on Seventh Avenue was Small's Paradise at 135th, Barron Wilkins' Exclusive Club at 134th, and Connie's Inn at 131st. The Cotton Club and Connie's Inn had black entertainers but white patrons only. The Cotton Club most famously featured Duke Ellington. The popular Savoy Ballroom on Lenox Avenue between 140th and 141st streets was one of the city's great dance halls. Benny Goodman's playing of "Stompin' at the Savoy" spread its fame in the 1930s. Reginald Marsh's painting *Savoy Ballroom* (1931), a jubilant dance-floor scene, is unforgettable. A strip on 133rd Street between Seventh and Lenox had so many night clubs with supposed African decor and themes that it was called *Jungle Alley. Jungle music* was Duke Ellington's distinctive "jungle" sound of tom-toms and growling brasses. Yet white New Yorkers saw all of Harlem as a jungle of wild parties, hot jazz, and primitive passions.

One important aspect of Harlem's indigenous nightlife grew from the custom of *rent parties*. During the early days of Harlem rent gouging and the extraordinary need to raise money for rent, these affairs began as informal but public musical entertainments given in private homes or apartments, typically on Saturday nights. A small admission fee got one in; soul food and drinks were extra but cheap. Some Harlemites called these rent parties *jumps, shouts,* or *struts*. The frenetic dancing at rent parties was why they were also called *house hops* and *jump joints*. Some jazz authorities say these rollicking affairs were the source of the expressions *the house really hopped* and *the joint really jumped*. Fats Waller played and sang "The Joint Is Jumpin' " in a 1940s movie version of a Harlem rent party.

Rent party seems to be a short form of the Southernism *house-rent party,* denoting the custom among rural and small-town blacks to raise money to pay rents, or just to supplement incomes. The transplanted institution of the Harlem rent party grew in the 1920s. The practice not only paid the rent of sponsors. It also provided a modest form of nightlife for the black population who were not allowed in the big white-owned Harlem clubs to hear their own musicians. Rent parties also provided a free meal and drinks and, sometimes, a little pay for musicians. These affairs grew in importance, moved to large rooms rented for the express purpose, operated every night, had printed invitations, and attracted major jazzmen; eventually Downtown whites attended.

Harlem in all these ways served as an intersection of black and middle-class white cultures and increased whites' knowledge of black society and its speechways. Harlem locutions, especially ones pertaining to nightlife, music and dance, poured into white speech during this period. The slang of Harlem was heard in Broadway musicals, on the vaudeville stage, in the patter of the clubs, and eventually on the lips of the smart set. One of the most popular glossaries that marked this diffusion was *The New Cab Calloway's Hepster's Dictionary* of jive and other Harlem talk. It ran through six editions after its first appearance in 1936.[42]

Guys and Dolls

Back downtown on Broadway, big-city nightlife had a cast of characters—social stereotypes—each colorfully named in popular speech. The names caricature social roles and speak to the times, especially to the changing but still traditional relations between men and women. A seamier side of Broadway life and its stock of characters was also seen in literature. In the 1920s and 1930s, the short stories of Damon Runyon, a spiritual successor to O. Henry, captured the Broadway vernacular of "guys and dolls" in his distinctive "Runyonese." Regardless of whether all the locutions he recorded were genuine or not, his stories influenced our idea of Broadway and its cast of vivid characters. Runyon country was the stretch of Broadway from 42nd Street to Columbus Circle, with peninsulas in its cross streets, a world that ended with the outbreak of the Second World War.

Playboys. In the early years of Bowery and Broadway nightlife, men were clearly the principal players. In the gaslight era, *Champagne Charlie* was the ultimate irresponsible bachelor and defier of the work ethic. His folk name inspired, or was invented by, the popular song of 1867, "Champagne Charlie Is My Name," by H. J. Whymark and Alfred Lee. He was as famous in the variety shows of New York as he was in the music halls of London. Champagne Charlie debauched throughout the grand era of New York nightlife. Lorenz Hart in the lyrics of "Give It Back to the Indians" (1939) wrote of Champagne Charlie's boozy decline. "Broadway's turning into Coney,/ Champagne Charlie's drinking gin."

A *man about town* around 1900 was a bon vivant, a "high-liver," a Broadway boulevardier. O. Henry in "Man About Town" (1906) wrote a whole story that played with the futility of defining *man about town,* much less of finding a specimen. At any rate, "he makes his rounds every evening; while you and I see the elephant once a week." A particularly dissolute man about town has since the 1820s been called a *rounder*—a "swell" rounder, if rich and fashionable. He was sometimes also qualified as an "all-night" rounder, from his habit of "making the rounds," or seeking out all the sensual city's "excitements" and indulging his "artificial appetites," as they used to say. One of Hutchins Hapgood's New York types from city streets about 1910 was the *rounder,* whom he described as a sophisticated, hardened, well-to-do man about town, especially around Broadway.[43]

If a man about town or rounder did little else, he was by 1907 known as a *playboy,* a modern revival of an old word from the early seventeenth century. Lorenz Hart's lyric "Playboy" in 1919 recognized him as a man "who's willing to work at play." More slangily, he was by 1927 called a *good-time Charlie,* a descendant of Champagne Charlie.

But a woman too familiar with the same town life and its places of entertainment might be called a *woman about town,* a seeming parallel to *man about town,* but actually meaning that she was as sexually loose as her men friends. Public life historically meant freedom for men but disgrace for women. Since the eighteenth century a promiscuous woman was called a *woman of the town,* later a *lady of the town,* clear euphemisms for a prostitute. A *woman on the town* meant a prostitute in New York since at least the 1860s.[44] These phrases carry a double meaning. She is a woman who has gone *out on the town,* abandoning conventional standards of sexual behavior, and has also become public property, a *public woman,* an old term for a prostitute.

Lavish spenders in night clubs were a feature of big-city nightlife and a staple of its folklore. Around 1900 the social type was generically called a "Pittsburgh steel millionaire," from the reputation of a few for their showy spending at the old Waldorf-Astoria Hotel, a magnet for new money from all over the country. In 1920s nightclub parlance a *big spender* was also known as a *live one.* A special variety of the big spender was the *(big) butter-and-egg man.* He was a national social type, one of those out-of-town businessmen who showered night clubs with money. He always seemed to be from the Middle West and rich from a prosperous dairy business. Texas Guinan, the fabled New York night-club hostess, is often credited with giving the language *(big) butter-and-egg man,* or at least popularizing it, when she ridiculed a customer with the epithet in one of her harangues. Walter Winchell, on the other hand, attributes the expression to master of ceremonies Harry Richman and even names the original butter-and-egg man as "Uncle Sam" Balcom, a New York provisioner.[45] Whoever coined it, the expression was already popular and the title of a song in 1924, most notably sung by Louis Armstrong, and in 1925 it became the title of a play, *The Butter-and-Egg Man,* by George S. Kaufman.

Texas Guinan made the town buzz with expressions like "give the little girl a (great) big hand." Texas greeted her customers with the famous phrase "Hello, sucker!"—for which she is today conventionally credited. Eager customers at various kinds of shows had long before been called "suckers" to their faces and Texas's speakeasies were clearly in that tradition. This startling greeting was Texas's fair warning that visitors were expected to throw convention to the wind—and pay in cash for the privilege of

∏ ∏ ∏ ∏ ∏

becoming a cut-up in her arena. "He'll be happy til he sees the check," Texas said. A Lorenz Hart lyric of 1926 goes "You may be a doctor, a lawyer, or a yegg man/ But when the hostess grabs you, you're a butter and egg man."

Chorus Girls. Chorus girls, a new term in the 1890s, connoted the escapist, sexual meaning of New York nightlife. *Show girl* was an older name of similar meaning but had less currency in the early years of Broadway nightlife. By the early 1920s she was also known as a *chorine,* a new blend of *chor*us and the feminine suffix *-ine.* The New York chorus girls—*Broadway Babies*—were indeed very young. Their peak years were between ages 17 and 22; their careers seldom lasted longer than five years. The chorus girl, as a social type, has had a long history as a saloon girl, dance-hall hostess, and similar occupational roles dating to the late 1840s. She became prominent in national popular culture in the 1910s and 1920s at the pinnacle of the new nightlife. Damon Runyon called her a *chorus Judy* and H. L. Mencken once called the working chorus girl a *terpsichorine,* a pun on *terpsichorean,* from the name of the muse Terpsichore. Chorus girls were courted by men known as *stage-door Johnnys,* denoting men who waited at stagedoors with gifts for the (chorus) *line girls* when they emerged after the show. In all fairness, there were also *stage-door Jennies* or *matinée girls* who waited out matinée idols and also pursued female stars.

The appearance of the Floradora Sextette in the lobster palaces and the all-girl reviews of Florenz Ziegfield in the early days of New York's nightlife symbolized the gaiety of city life and its illusion of sexual freedom. The shows were speedy and full of action. The chorus girls, writes historian Lewis A. Erenberg, were presented as easy sexual playmates: "they were fun, not demanding."[46] Rich men tried to indulge their fantasies of chorus girls by seeking them out as wives and mistresses. Popular speech went on to characterize the several hazards and rueful ends of stepping out on the town—for both men and women.

One of the celebrated chorus girls of the time was Evelyn Nesbit, a Floradora Girl and later the wife of a Pittsburgh steel heir, Harry K. Thaw. About 1903 she had been alluringly photographed by Gertrude Käsebier, while holding near her lap a cream pitcher with its heart-shaped opening tilted toward the viewer. Will Irwin recalled her as "not quite beautiful, perhaps, but the human limit in prettiness."[47] Several years before her marriage to Thaw, she had had an affair with the architect Stanford White. Evelyn unwisely told her husband the lurid details of her seduction and swinging in the red velvet swing. In 1906 the crazed Thaw sought out White at a party on the roof of Madison Square Garden and killed him with a pistol.

In the murder trial, a sensation for the tabloids, it came out that White had upon various occasions invited Evelyn to his studio in the tower of Madison Square Garden, his apartment at 122 East 22nd Street, and his hideaway rooms at 22 West 24th Street "to see his drawings and etchings."

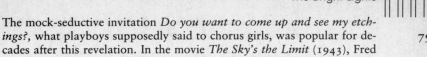
The mock-seductive invitation *Do you want to come up and see my etchings?*, what playboys supposedly said to chorus girls, was popular for decades after this revelation. In the movie *The Sky's the Limit* (1943), Fred Astaire invited Joan Leslie up to see his etching. In the portfolio on his coffee table she found and said "*The Breadline* by Reginald Marsh," and was not seduced.

The myth of the plaything chorus girl inclined middle-class men on the town—and their wives—to see them as *Dumb Doras*. They were, wrote Erenberg, "sexually charged women . . . too stupid to pose a real threat. By picturing the chorine as brainless, men found a woman who attracted, yet one whom in fantasy they could hold in check."[48] Bernard Sobel in his book *Burleycue,* a history of early burlesque published in 1931, attested that the name *Dumb Dora* was coined, apparently in the 1890s, by Anita Pines, the first woman stage manager of a burlesque theater.[49] Whatever its origin, *Dumb Dora* became a popular slang term for a bimbo. "Hardened habitués of that half-world of the Tenderloin call them [chorus girls turned gold diggers] 'Dumb Doras.' Farther uptown they are 'O.M.D.'s'—Old Men's Darlings," O. O. McIntyre reported.[50]

Unsuccessful chorus girls, it is true, sometimes drifted into cynical dependencies on older men, or *sugar daddies*. The men, seeking to go beyond the make-believe of the night clubs, sought a real-life playmate; they soon learned that the adventure carried a real-life price. The reputation of these associations accounts for the term *chorus girl* in later years becoming a euphemism for "prostitute." *Model,* for much the same reasons, was also used in yet later years for attractive young women in similar circumstances. Some ne'er-do-well chorus girls and so-called models came to be known as *party girls,* paid party-goers whose job was simply to grace and enliven social and business gatherings. Yet the party girl was not necessarily one who sought *to party*.

Many young women came to New York aspiring to be chorus girls, but few became the toast of Broadway or found the wealth, fame, and glamour they dreamed of. Some became cigarette girls in the Broadway clubs. A term of the early 1860s, *cigarette girl* was revived with new meaning in the era of public nightlife to denote the young women who, in skirts as short as possible, sashayed from table to table with trays of cigars and cigarettes for sale to customers, calling "cigars, cigarettes, cigars, cigarettes." (For a saving grace, some also sold flowers—bouquets and corsages.) The cigarette girl, too, became the subject of a popular song, "Cigars, Cigarettes," a plaintive tale, in one of Ziegfeld's *Follies*.

Stanley Walker, City Editor of the New York *Herald Tribune,* wrote in 1933 that Mavis King was "Broadway's most beautiful cigarette girl."[51] She worked at the Club Abbey on West 54th; she was earlier a flower girl at the Argonaut, also on West 54th, formerly one of Texas Guinan's joints. Several newspapermen of the day seemed smitten with her. Cigarette girls, more than the nightclub hat-check girls or camera girls (who took flash pictures for folks to take back home), or even flower girls, were the appealing, pensive waifs of Broadway mythology. McIntyre was lyrical about her:

> Broadway's cafe cigarette girl! She has never been novelized or dramatized, yet she plays a conspicuous rôle in the White Way's passing pageant. She is ever beautiful, always picturesquely dressed and in most instances has gripped the roseate dream to find it frozen. "Cigars! Cigarettes!" There is a fluted cadence to her singsong cry—a nightingale among the night hawks. About her is an air of intangible sorrow. Soggy wine guzzlers find no echoing response to their flirtatious advances. She repulses, not with scorn, but with maidenly innocence.[52]

         Gold Diggers.   *Gold digger,* in the new, slang sense, came into American English around 1915. Her type was humorously characterized in Anita Loos's best-selling novel of 1925, *Gentlemen Prefer Blondes.* The gold digger was often a none-too-successful chorus girl who got "kept"—or nearly so, exchanging sexual favors, or the promise of them for gifts, rent, and an allowance. She was then known as a *keptie,* preferably on Park Avenue in a *love nest* (a phrase of the 1910s). She was terribly spoiled. The chorus girl "takes her sweetie buy-buy," quipped McIntyre.[53] Her middle-aged friend by the 1910s was a *sugar daddy* or, perhaps significantly, just *daddy.* One of Loos's grasping blondes called her middle-aged benefactor "Daddy." The more ordinary *charity girl* of the 1920s and 1930s gave away her tender favors, usually for fun, sometimes for gifts, but never for money.

    McIntyre wrote that the "Roaring Forties is the lair of the Gold Digger. There, with pouting lips, baby stare and dégagé smile, she lies in wait for those who go intriguing incog."[54] Several years later he wrote that "the capricious cuties who live by their ability to find the 'live one' do not angle for visiting Babbitts. They know the easy marks and they flush them out of the man-made niches in Manhattan cliffs."[55]

    James F. Hanley's 1923 song "The Gold-Digger" in a Broadway musical went: Dig a little deeper, dear./ Don't mind if he's old, dig and you'll find gold./ Take a little shovel, dig a little hovel,/ On Fifth Avenue, Riverside will do, a place in the country, too." Gold diggers were usually "just a lot of good kids, trying to get along," as the lyric concluded. Busby Berkeley's movie musical, *The Gold Diggers of 1933,* its successors in 1935 and 1937, and many other movies of the 1930s were palatable caricatures of the social type. When she hit the Daddy lode, she sang "The Gold Diggers' Song," also titled "We're in the Money," written by Al Dubin and Harry Warren in 1933.

         Lounge Lizards.   By the 1910s social anxieties in the middle classes were raised when their own women began experimenting with new social freedoms. Sophisticated women started adventuring in many of the same ways that men had been doing in public nightlife since the 1890s, including outings on the town unescorted by their husbands or fiancées. The dancing craze among middle-class New Yorkers was well underway. But, as usual, the women wanted to dance and the men didn't. So even respectable women sometimes hired dancing escorts, some of them marginal types with dubious pasts. Contemporaries described them as very handsome and sleek and one said they looked more like photographs than men. They were also a dangerous factor in social life. The *tango pirate*, or *social gangster* as he was sometimes known, was thought to entrap and exploit the affluent women he met at afternoon cafés, robbing them of virtue, even living off them. The passionate tango dance itself symbolized the sexual ritual of dominance and submission and, further, connoted the raiding of class and sexual prerogatives.[56]

The epithet *lounge lizard* arose about 1915 in this new social atmosphere. They were, wrote Albert Crockett, men in "the habit of lounging in different dance resorts from tea time on, on a chance of picking up a few dollars; or they might be habitués of the place or of an outer room, described as a 'lounge,' for the purpose of picking up girls and women. In Europe, he subsequently evolved into what is now known as the *gigolo*."[57] He was originally a male counterpart to the French *gigolette*, a young woman, usually a prostitute, who solicited at public dances. *Gigolo* was securely in American English by the early 1920s.

Benjamin de Casseres wrote that "New York, like all big cities, breeds three kinds of lizards—the lounge lizard in the hotels, the corner lizard, and the bench lizard in the parks."[58] This *lizard* business is complicated. *Lounge lizard* seems to have had two lives, the second perhaps inspired by the first. The more common meaning is that of a very smooth man who, using low and slithery ways, pursues sex and fortune in tea-dance lounges and, in later years, cocktail lounges. The other sense scolds the cheapskate who courts a young woman in her own parlor, rather than taking her out on the town. He was also contemptuously known in the 1910s as a *parlor snake* or *parlor lizard*.

Slumming and Other Rubbernecking

The old song "Chinatown, My Chinatown" (1906) sang of "where the lights are low," perhaps where the wattage was lowered for romantic effect. By the 1880s, it was fashionable *to go slumming* as part of a night out on the town. The expression meant to make safe, brief outings, usually in the evening, to see how the other half lived and, especially, played. Sophisticated *slummers* ventured forth in small *slumming parties* to rub shoulders with sinners and to get a whiff of the sin prohibited in their own respectable worlds. Charles Hoyt's musical show *A Trip to Chinatown* opened November 9, 1891, and ran for 650 nights. In the 1890s commercially organized tours began taking their charges into raffish parts of town with colorful styles of life and into establishments that supposedly specialized in vice. The Bowery, or what was left of it, and "a trip to Chinatown" were favorite outings for organized slumming tours.

Modern tourism in the years around 1900 also brought many visitors to New York to see the bright lights. As cultural tourists, they came to see the modernity of the New Metropolis and the quaint survivals of pre-modernity in Chinatown and other ethnic neighborhoods. They collected, like souvenirs, the more popular locutions associated with New York and its exotic lifeways in order to authenticate the experience, and they carried back these words and phrases to show the folks at home.[59] Out-of-town tourists usually had little time and sometimes little money. They were strangers in

FIGURE 6.   *A Rubbernecker Bus (about 1910).* The bus is loaded with rubber-neckers about to go "seeing New York." H. L. Mencken said *rubberneck,* coined in the 1890s, was one of the best inventions of the American language. (*Brown Brothers*)

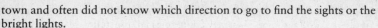
town and often did not know which direction to go to find the sights or the bright lights.

They often found their way with professional help and were noted in slang as a social type in public places. *Rubberneck*, for a gawking tourist, is a quintessential Americanism from the late 1890s. H. L. Mencken wrote that the word *rubberneck* "is almost a complete treatise on American psychology"[60] and he agreed with another appreciator that it was "one of the best words ever coined." Mencken added that "It may be homely, but it is nevertheless superb, and whoever invented it, if he could be discovered, would be worthy not only of a Harvard LL.D., but also the thanks of both Rotary and Congress, half a bushel of medals, and thirty days as the husband of Miss America."[61]

The *rubberneck wagons, -autos,* or *-buses* took sightseers around the city with a guide who shouted at them through a megaphone. The first rubberneck wagons, though they were not yet called that, were the old Fifth Avenue "stages" that traveled up and down The Avenue past the houses of millionaires. The tour became so popular with tourists and New Yorkers

FIGURE 7. John Sloan. *Seeing New York* (1917). Sloan makes a visual pun on the rubberneck bus and its load of gawking rubberneckers. He wrote in his diary: "An amusing thing—wagons loaded with coops with live poultry, on top a lot of geese with their necks poked through the slats cackling and gazing at the city." (*Courtesy of Delaware Art Museum*)

alike that the stage company issued a little booklet identifying the mansions of the rich and famous. The stage companies later installed seats on the roof so the *rubberneckers* could see better. It soon became an industry. In 1909 one travel writer mentioned the "huge cars with a crowd of out-of-towners stretching their necks, 'seeing New York,' and having misinformation shouted at them through megaphones at the same time."[62] The rubberneck wagons, or the "Seeing New York" buses, greatly amused city folk. John Sloan made a small etching of a city scene with a cartload of geese twisting their long necks through the slats of crates. He called it *Seeing New York* (1917); it was a visual pun and humorous commentary on the famous tour buses filled with rubberneckers.

O. Henry in "Sisters of the Golden Circle" (1906) describes loading one of the "Glaring-at-Gotham" cars. "The Rubberneck Auto was about ready to start. . . . The sidewalk was blockaded with sightseers who had gathered to stare at sightseers, justifying the natural law that every creature on earth is preyed upon by some other creature." In the 1920s, rubberneck wagons, by now also called *yap wagons* (from *yap,* a rustic) and *gape wagons,* picked up tourists at the Flatiron Building or in Times Square. Tour operators in Times Square used touts and steerers who worked hotel lobbies to hook tourists, and decoys were paid to occupy some seats, for the outlanders, like sheep, would hesitate to enter an empty bus. "Just starting. See the Chinese opium dens! The Bowery slums! Coney ablaze with light! Last trip of the day. One dollah the round trip."[63]

4
New Ways
of Urban Living

*—but in the artificial, the work of man too is
equally great—*
WALT WHITMAN, *Democratic Vistas*

The hustle and bustle of modern New York quickened as a result of new technologies of transportation and communication. Electric lights had extended the day into night, and the city more than ever operated around the clock. The wide application of electricity to yet other technologies, more than any other factor, was responsible for increasing the pace and tempo of city life. The decades from about 1880 to 1920 were particularly abundant in these innovations and in lexical responses to them. The new source of energy directly or indirectly made possible all the new urban developments in this period—the building boom, mass transit, modern communications, the spatial reorganization of the city, and changing ways of life. New words about new ways of living in the city were part and parcel of the aura of popular culture surrounding the new technologies.

Early forms of public transit in New York—horse-drawn omnibuses, cabs and hacks, streetcars, and steam-driven elevated railways—had for several decades serviced exchanges within and between central business districts and residential areas. The new innovations in intra-city mass transit—electrically powered streetcars, modern elevated railroads, and after 1904 the subways—moved great rhythmic streams of workers, shoppers, and entertainment-seekers to and from the center. In the expanding city, the custom that most people walked to most places was giving way to riding. The early nineteenth-century expression *the man in the street,* the ordinary, common urban person, was later in the century joined by *the man in the cars,* alluding to the riders in horsecars and other streetcars as the symbol of the common man and woman. In the years around 1900, well-to-do New Yorkers boasted that they never rode the streetcars, much as affluent New Yorkers today often say they never ride the subways.

In 1898, when Greater New York City was chartered with the present five boroughs, over 300,000 people were commuting daily to Manhattan: about 100,000 or more each from Brooklyn by bridge and ferry, from New Jersey by ferry, and from Westchester County and Connecticut by train. It is for them, Theodore Dreiser recalled of the period, "that the street cars and vehicles of transfer run thick and black."[1]

New commutation patterns necessitated new ways of eating outside the home and imaginative entrepreneurs accommodated the quickened pace of urbanites in a hurry. Innovations in electrical communications also facilitated the metropolitan flux. A few small but city-wide telephone networks were in service by 1880, and the intensified voice communication seemed to make more, not less, reason for people to move about on public transportation. The telephone began to reknit the fabric of social networks in the expanded and loosened metropolis, at least for the middle classes who could afford the new luxury. The whole urban community, in addition, was tied together by metropolitan daily newspapers that reported every news of urban life and made the big city imaginable and of a human scale for their millions of readers. In this century and in much the same way, movies made common knowledge for the whole metropolitan community and for the nation. Every one of these new ways of living prompted many new coinages, including many slangy words and phrases. The informal expressions, especially, registered the quickened pace of everyday life with a terseness and directness to match the tempo of the modern city itself.

Public Transportation

New types of conveyances and modes of within-city movement brought forth direct and often imaginative responses in popular speech. Images evoked by these vehicles, their riders, and the problematic relationships between vehicles and riders and between whole transportation systems and the city itself also entered the visions of art, music, literature, and every kind of popular culture. Formal designations of the new vehicles and systems of transportation, some of them scientific-sounding neologisms of Greek and Latin roots, were quickly contracted to slang-like names, most of which are the standard words of today. The haste in shortening the formal names also seems to testify to the hurried pace of city life: the short forms seem panted into life while people ran to catch a "bus," or a "cab," or an "el." Usually the new, demotic form was made by clipping off either the first or last part of the original word: 'bus, 'cab, hack', taxi', el', auto'. Until after the First World War, word-conscious writers used the newer of these popular forms with the elliptical apostrophe as a conservative gesture to the original word.

From mid-century, the streets of Manhattan were filled with a variety of horse-drawn, steam-driven, and later electric-powered vehicles. The term *gridlock* in its new sense of a "city-wide" traffic jam is of the late 1970s and 1980s, but traffic congestion was an everyday occurrence a century and a half earlier. A traffic *jam* or *street blockade* in the mid-nineteenth century occurred when horse-cars, lorries, cabs, private carriages, and a variety of other conveyances came to a noisy, angry impasse. The ones at Broadway and Fulton Street were famous and the subject of much folk humor.

New York was by no means the earliest adopter of all innovations in

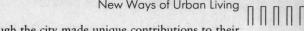
public transportation, though the city made unique contributions to their popular designations and related folklore. The horse-drawn omnibus was introduced in the 1830s, with the main line up and down Broadway. When Walt Whitman worked briefly for the New York *Aurora* in 1842, he wrote that "the noisiest things which attract attention in that part of Broadway are the omnibusses. Rumbling and bouncing along, they come, now and then stopping as some person on the sidewalk holds up his finger—a signal that he wants to take passage."[2] *Omnibus* (from Latin "for all") in most cities was contracted to *bus* by the 1840s. New Yorkers, however, continued in the 1850s to call them *stages,* "as the city people always call an omnibus," wrote Whitman in "Advice to Strangers."[3]

When the stages began running along Broadway, they were popularly and affectionately known as *Broadway Beauties*. Another major stage line operated on Fifth Avenue. The stage companies painted the exterior side panels with American landscapes, often Western ones. New Yorkers seemed to like the association of the "stages" with the West, which is perhaps why they clung to the name. The stages did most of the transportation up and down town, and survived on Broadway until the 1870s and on Fifth Avenue until after 1900. The fashionable coaching crowd in the 1880s and 1890s took suburban outings on a type of stage they called a *tally-ho*. A tally-ho much in demand left Cavanagh's restaurant in Chelsea for a ride to the countryside.

Horsecars—heavier, boxier, horse-drawn vehicles that ran on metal tracks—began operating in the early 1850s and were the common conveyance for more than half a century. The last line in the city operated on West Street and did not shut down until 1918. A famous photographic image of the era is Alfred Stieglitz's *The Terminal* (1893), picturing a horsecar with its steaming team in the snow outside the Astor House Hotel. A small one-horsecar on city streets was called a *bob-tail car*. In 1886 Brander Matthews took the name of the little horsecar for the title of a short story, "In a Bob-Tail Car," about the social customs of its passengers during a trip along 14th Street.[4] Eventually, the horsecars were called *streetcars*, a name that was later transferred to cable cars and electric trolley cars.

The advent of public transportation changed the culture of interaction with strangers in public places. The German cultural theorist Walter Benjamin noted that before the development of buses and streetcars people had never been required to sit for long minutes looking at one another but not speaking. People dealt with this new situation of uncomfortable eye, and sometimes body, contact by elaborating the culture of "civil inattention," as the sociologist Erving Goffman called it. This new civility and code of conduct required one, among other things, not to stare, and to avoid brushing and pressing against others in proscribed ways in those close quarters. A new urban folklore arose about real and imagined violations.

By the 1890s electric trolley cars, or *electrics* or *trolleys,* all across the country were replacing the old horsecars. The historian Arthur M. Schlesinger reported that the word *trolley* "probably" originated in Kansas City.⁵ At any rate, *trolley* ultimately derives from Old French, *troller,* to search, to wander. The trolleys came to Brooklyn in 1893, but not to Manhattan until 1901. The term *trolley* was used in the 1890s, but was soon replaced by *streetcar,* the enduring old word for a horsecar. Any streetcar conductor by 1900 or so was slangily called a *con* or a *conny.* About 1915 the hobble-skirt streetcars used in New York were called *Broadway battleships.* New York and other cities ended the streetcar era in the 1930s by tearing up the iron rails to clear the way for automobiles and buses.

Before they departed, the old trolleys contributed an item of enduring slang in the expression *to slip (off) one's trolley,* 'to go crazy,' or *to be off one's trolley,* 'to be crazy.' Stuart Flexner wrote that "the sight of [the motorman] getting out of the streetcar to reposition the trolley wheel back on the overhead wire was so common that by 1896 *to be off one's trolley,* to be crazy, was a popular expression."⁶ Trolley cars received their power through a grooved wheel, called a trolley, that rolled in contact with an overhead cable and carried electricity through an arm to the motor of the car. In Manhattan, overhead power lines of any kind had been strictly prohibited after so many had fallen down in the Blizzard of 1888; but overhead trolley lines were common in the City of Brooklyn. Manhattan trolleys in some cases replaced the old cable car lines and used the same tracks. The cable conduit was replaced with an underground "third rail" in the middle of the tracks, which the car's trolley contacted and got its power. At any rate, to get disconnected from one's power source is an abiding urban nightmare and tantamount to being crazy.

Urban folk humor in the 1890s about pedestrians jumping from the path of trolleys spawned in 1900 the proper name of the former Brooklyn Dodgers baseball team. Once known as the Brooklyn Trolley Dodgers, the team got its name from the joking appellation of *trolley dodgers* for Brooklynites. The name alluded to the cartoon-like spectacle of pedestrians dodging rampaging trolley cars in the streets, a favorite subject of newspaper artists. As the political theorist Marshall Berman notes, "the name expresses the way in which urban survival skills . . . can transcend utility and take on new modes of meaning and value, in sport as in art. Baudelaire would have loved this symbolism, as many of his twentieth-century successors (e. e. cummings, Marianne Moore) did."⁷ Though the old *Brooklyn Eagle* newspaper deplored the nickname for the local baseball team, the name *Brooklyn Dodgers,* minus the *Trolley,* took hold, and "Dem Bums" were proud of the monicker.

Cable cars, drawn by gripping onto a moving cable beneath the street and powered from a central source, appeared on the streets of New York in 1893 but lasted only several years. The cable cars at times proved dangerous for pedestrians. The *Tribune* wrote that "the cable car is a Juggernaut, a murderer on wheels, a maimer of men and destroyer of women and children." A bend in any road that has a history of vehicular accidents always seems to be called *Dead Man's Curve*. In New York of the 1890s, *Dead Man's Curve* was applied to the bend of the Broadway cable-car line as it turned into Union Square. Operators were under instructions, apparently because of a misunderstanding of the engineering, to build up speed, to release the grip on the cable and take the curve with the car's own momentum, while the conductor cried "Hold fast!" Journalists described the cable cars "whipping" around the corner where more than a few pedestrians were killed or maimed. The spectacle of the careening car and jumping pedestrians attracted crowds of onlookers expecting, half with horror, to witness one of the famous accidents.

Illustrators made many images of the scene of panic at Deadman's Curve as pedestrians scrambled before the cable cars. Ashcan artist George Luks, in his early days as a newspaper artist, drew satiric cartoons about the mortal perils of cable cars in Manhattan. In 1940 Reginald Marsh revived the theme in his watercolor *Dead Man's Curve*, a scene of six young women dodging trucks while crossing Broadway at 14th Street, just under his studio window. On the violent spot of Dead Man's Curve today stands a statue of Mahatma Gandhi, set in a traffic island, not without a little unintended irony.

Riding in early public transit, especially in the elevated trains, the cable cars, and the streetcars, was often uncomfortable, caused by hard-sprung suspensions and the lurching around corners, and the cars themselves made an awful, rattling noise. *Rattler* is an old English cant word for a coach, cab, or train, and found American use as well. New York and other writers since the 1840s have managed to apply the word *rattle* to the racket produced by various conveyances. O. Henry in "The Pendulum" (1907) quipped how "the cattle cars of the Manhattan Elevated rattled away." Dashiell Hammett's hero in *The Dain Curse* (1929) "grabbed a rattler," a street car, to his destination. The rough experience of riding the cable cars in the 1890s—and the whole culture of the thing—was unforgettably described by Stephen Crane in his Sketch "In the Broadway Cars."[8]

These vehicles of public transportation, especially buses and streetcars that had set routes—"lines"—and schedules, influenced the popular consciousness of everyday city life by analogy. Urban folk sayings alluding to scheduled transit attested to the irritations and frustrations of urban life generally. Expressions like *to miss the bus, to tell someone where to get off*, and *men (or women) are like buses (or streetcars); there's one by every few minutes* were inspired by the routine of waiting at stops, thinking about when the next scheduled vehicle was to arrive, and, once on, generally coping with the push and shove, often with surly and abusive motormen and conductors. Bus and streetcar lines, and the culturally prescribed routines for using them, also became a trope for the mechanized, ordered, linear, scheduled, and impersonal character of city life itself. For the last way-station of a troubled urban existence, the streetcar lines gave us *end of the* line and the *last stop*, though these expressions were perhaps carried forward and into the city from cross-country trains.

Rapid Transit. The contemporary age of mass transportation, or of "rapid transit," began in New York with electrified elevated railways in the 1880s and, after 1904, the subways, both of which carried hundreds of passengers in trains of cars. The subway especially served as a trope for city life itself. The subway is a microcosm of the cauldron of great population size, forced density, anonymity, parallel lives among strangers, and the confrontation and accommodation of social variety, all of which interact to generate urbanism as a way of life.[9]

City literature, popular music, and art took up the theme of rapid transfer of people and commented on its social meaning. Tin Pan Alley responded in the 1890s with "Rapid Transit Gallop," by A. H. Rosewig, and in 1912 with "The Subway Glide," written by Theodore Norman and Arthur Gillespie to honor the new IRT line. Popular speech responded directly to the new technologies and interacted with both art and literature. The new rapid transit was something special, a mood apart from older forms of public transportation. O. Henry wrote that "The rapid transit is poetry and art; the moon but a tedious, dry body moving by rote."

Cecilia Tichi, a literary critic, identifies a school of "rapid transit" writers, chiefly John Dos Passos and William Carlos Williams, who were under the influence of rapid-transit culture and the "rush-hour" mentality.[10] The urban realist artists drew repeatedly on images of the three-way interaction—of the city, vehicles of rapid transit, and people—to capture vignettes of city life and to comment on their meaning. The elevated trains and the subway were favorite themes of John Sloan, Edward Hopper, and Reginald Marsh. Popular speech was of the same but lighter cultural cake.

By 1890 the city was acutely conscious of the crush of daily commuters and the phrase *rush hour*, informally just *the rush*, had appeared to denote the morning and evening congestions created by all these people getting to and from work. One contemporary said, " 'The rush hour' is a slogan peculiar to New York."[11] In Manhattan the factors of population size, density, and movement interacted in a truly spectacular way. Art soon followed to interpret the verbal sign in visual terms. Max Weber's painting, *Rush Hour, New York* (1915), abstracts the human tumult and exposes a new dimension of its meaning. *Rush* and *hurry* were cultural bywords in New York. In 1915 *Variety* wrote that the frenetic vaudeville singer and dancer Eva Tanguay was "the spirit of the Subway Rush" and "admirably personifies the American ideals of hurry."[12]

If the *rush*, a word of the el phase of the rapid transit era, denotes the volume of human traffic, the opening of the subways increased the density and defined the *crush*. "The subway crush, of course, is unmatched anywhere; but the Times Square crush is one of the worst," two travel writers warned in 1929.[13] Grand Central Terminal is properly distinguished from

FIGURE 8. T. de Thulstrup. *A Station Scene in the "Rush" Hours on the Manhattan Elevated Railroad.* The phrase *rush hour* was coined by 1890 to denote the new urban phenomenon of several hundred thousand workers and shoppers crushing onto mass transit to go to and from the center each weekday morning and evening. *Harper's Weekly,* February 8, 1890.
(*Collection of the author*)

its companion Grand Central Station, the busy subway stop that funnels subway riders to and from trains and other destinations. Yet people use "station" for both. The simile *Grand Central Station,* alluding to its rush and crush, early in this century became a slang term for any busy, crowded, hectic place: "It's like Grand Central Station in here!"

The story of rapid transit actually started earlier. The primitive, originally cable-driven, elevated railway began operations in New York in 1868 with a short line up Greenwich Street, from the Battery to Dey Street. Steam locomotives replaced the cable system in 1871 and new lines were started. The name of the new elevated railway was soon shortened to the *elevated* and then to *el,* which was sometimes written even more compactly as *L.* In Brooklyn, however, some people incongruously referred to the *elevator.* The noisy els were an inescapable part of the city's surroundings and became a literary symbol of the aural background of urban living. Edith Wharton in her novel *The House of Mirth,* in a scene set in the 1880s, wrote: "In the street the noise of wheels had ceased, and the rumble of the 'elevated' came only at long intervals through the deep unnatural hush."[14]

The new electric els of the 1890s were not so dirty as the sooty steam engines, but they were still noisy and unsightly and destroyed the open view along major avenues and cross streets. The els ran at the second- or third-story level of buildings, creating noise, flashing light, blocking the sun from flats, and casting the streets below into shadow. Henry James in *The American Scene* spoke of New York's systems of streetcars and els as "the awful hug of the serpent."[15] Yet the el is one of the enduring nostalgic images of New York. The elevated ride did afford an unusual view of the city and, especially at certain corners, gave a little thrill, like a very tame ride at Coney Island; the "S" curve at Coenties Slip was famous. In *A Hazard of New Fortunes,* William Dean Howells's fictional March couple were newly arrived from Boston and liked to ride the elevated for the perspective it gave them on the city and for sheer fun. Mr. March said "those bends in the L that you get in the corner of Washington Square, or just below the Cooper Institute—they're the gayest things in the world."[16] Writers on the New York scene in the 1910s, such as Edna Ferber and Ernest Poole, also reflected on the view from the el.

The urban realist painters and printmakers, such as John Sloan, Edward Hopper, Reginald Marsh, and early modernists like Stuart Davis made many images of the el—from inside and from outside, in day and at night, and in summer and in snow storms, especially as it roared up and down Sixth Avenue and curved into and out of Greenwich Village at Third Street. John Sloan's painting *The Sixth Avenue Elevated at Third Street* (1928), one of his several paintings of the el at night, captures the lighted el roaring above and the urban gaiety in the street below that many older New Yorkers still remember. Edward Hopper, on the other hand, painted the solitary, domestic life of the city that he saw from the windows of the el. *Night Windows* (1928) and *Room in New York* (1932) could easily be scenes inspired by nocturnal glimpses of private lives as he rode past the windows of city flats.

The Sixth Avenue el was torn down in the late 1930s. Ogden Nash's verse "What Street Is This, Driver?" (1942) said "farewell" to the Sixth Avenue El: "No more the El careens." Lawrence Ferlinghetti in *A Coney Island of the Mind* (1958) recalled the El "careening thru its thirdstory world." King Kong, in the movie of 1933, acted out the repressed desire of many New Yorkers, by smashing the Third Avenue el like a great serpent in the urban jungle, but not before he peered into the windows at the terrified passengers—us. The Third Avenue line, the last in Manhattan, was torn down in 1953. But in Brooklyn the elevated tracks are still used by the subway trains, and the ride on the F train gives spectacular views.

In the early buses, trolleys, cable cars, and els, passengers who did not have seats on the crowded vehicles stood and supported themselves by holding—or "hanging"—onto straps of leather or webbing. William Dean Howells in an essay about New York life in the early 1890s described "people standing, swaying miserably to and fro by the leather straps dangling from the roofs."[17] When the New York subways were opened in 1904, the straps for standing passengers were again installed. By 1905 *straphanger* had been recorded to denote that mass of urban humanity that rode rapid transit standing and hanging onto a strap, though it probably originated in pre-subway days. The strap hanger is the symbol of stressed humanity in visual and verbal representations of subway riders. Though subway cars in New York today have either hinged loops of steel or fixed vertical and horizontal metal bars, which standing passengers use to support themselves, subway riders remain "strap hangers."

The subway was also a pejorative symbol and succeeded the el in popular consciousness as a lower form in every respect. While many New Yorkers hated the el, even more seemed to hate the subway, and it did seem a polar comedown from above ground to below, from light to dark. A Lorenz Hart lyric from the musical *Sky City* of 1929 drew the contrast between the El train above and below, "The Hell train!" All New Yorkers today call the subway *the subway,* except of course when they are not calling it "The World's Largest Urinal." Yet the subway system, whose bad reputation began soon after it opened in 1904, got a few ephemeral names. *Sub,* shortened in the predictable way, was in use by 1910 but did not last. The derogatory term *chute* was also used passingly. A travel writer in 1909 caught the sense of *chute* when he described downtown commuters who "keep disappearing down subways steps, like pieces of coal running down a chute."[18] The *tube,* borrowed from the London Underground, was imported and used now and then, but it was just a passing affectation. New York, of course, has its *tubes* (always plural), the PATH trains that run to New Jersey under the Hudson.

Around 1900, the financier Russell Sage remarked on plans for the subway, "New Yorkers will never go into a hole in the ground to ride." But

FIGURE 9.   Isabel Bishop. *Single Straphanger* (1950). The word *straphanger*, first found printed in 1905, came to signify the mass of working people who rode New York's elevateds and subways. The woman in the etching, in addition to hanging onto a strap with one hand, is with the other hand holding a tabloid folded in the customary New York manner for convenient reading on the crowded cars. *Associated American Artists.*
(Collection of the author)

they most certainly did and they tried to name the experience just that. *The hole* for the subway had early use by pickpockets and by subway track workers who spoke of working "in the hole." *The hole* is still used by New York's Transit Authority Police, who also call it *the electric sewer*. *The hole* is a natural, and in the climate of public convictions about subway deterioration, it seems destined for wider popular use. Thanks to Adolph Green and Betty Comden, who wrote the lyrics of "New York, New York!" for Leonard Bernstein's 1945 musical "On the Town," the idea, if not the name, of the New York subways as a "hole" is further imbedded in popular culture each time we sing of straphanging New Yorkers as "the people [who] ride in a hole in the ground."

Hacks, Cabs, Hansoms, and Taxis.   The old two-horse, four-wheeled carriage for hire that served New York through most of the nineteenth century was called a *hack,* from *Hackney,* the name of a town near London where working horses were once bred and trained. A lighter type of vehicle was called a *cab,* short for *cabriolet,* a European one-horse, two-wheeled carriage with a folding hood. Cabriolets were never widely used in New York, though the term *cab* caught on generally. The most familiar type of the New York cab in the late nineteenth century was the one-horse, two-wheeled, two-passenger *hansom cab,* or just *hansom*. Art and photographic images of New York streets in the 1890s and even into this century showed the striking profile of the hansom cabs with its driver perched on top. Though long associated with London streets, the hansom was not introduced to New York until the early 1890s. The name *hansom* is that of the English architect Joseph Aloysius Hansom who patented an early design of the vehicle. Its distinctive feature of the driver's seat high at the rear, however, owes to a design modification by David Chapman in 1836.[19]

The hansom became the preferred cab of the well-to-do and, especially, of lovers who sought its cozy seclusion. The writer Kate Simon characterized their doubtful contribution to the ambience of Fifth Avenue. "The Hansom Cab Company sent out its conveyances to help clot the chaotic traffic, insupportably noisy with the rusty groan of thousands of iron-rimmed wheels and the strike of iron horseshoes."[20] Drivers of hansoms themselves became a street type noted for their presence around stations and terminals, their persistent calls of "Keb, sir, keb, keb," for their aggressiveness, and often for their sharp practices. Nonetheless, the popularity of the hansoms was great enough that the first motorized cabs—the "electric hansoms"— were both modeled and named after them.

The hansoms remained a symbol of shadowy urban romance well into this century. They could be seen waiting across the street from the Plaza Hotel, outside expensive restaurants, and in major squares. Professional countryboy O. O. McIntyre in the 1920s wrote that his "first impression of New York was a single horse, drawing the swank, two-wheeled hansom cab. That impression remains—the two-wheeler is still the swankest thing in

New York to my rustic mind."[21] F. Scott Fitzgerald in *The Beautiful and Damned* (1922), in a passage set in the early 1910s, wrote of "when the lovers sought the romantic privacy of hansom cabs," a "quaint device" even then. Years later in the story, in the early 1920s, Fitzgerald told that the hansoms as well as the romance of his lovers had faded. He wrote of the old worn-out hansoms and their equally aged drivers and horses standing in front of Delmonico's hoping for a drunken fare. "A relic of vanished gaiety!"

Hacks and cabs that traveled city streets at night, taking their fares here and there, were by the 1880s called *nighthawks,* sometimes *night owls,* or just *owls,* and the romantic black hansoms fitted this image perfectly. Each of these names was transferred from the earlier senses of a seemingly nocturnal person who lived in contradiction to diurnal rhythms. Stephen Crane's essay "In the Broadway Cars" mentioned how the "nighthawk cabs whirl by the cars on their mysterious errands."[22] George Luks, to mention just one artist, painted a nighthawk cab. The name *nighthawk* has stuck to night-cruising cabs and their drivers to this day.

Nighthawk cab drivers, true to the habits of the bird, have acquired two related reputations over the years, that of nighttime cruising and of preying on customers. Writers of the period described the nighthawks as "prowling" darkened streets, "lurking" under elevated stations, or "cruising" through the Tenderloin. Nighthawks generally had a bad reputation for cheating naive customers and servicing an evening trade in search of vice. The hansoms were especially popular for making "the rounds" at night. A magazine article on New York cabs in 1906 said that "not even for the sake of acquiring 'local color' will we go down into that nocturnal world where the night-hawk circles for his prey."[23] But all were not bad. O. Henry in "From the Cabby's Seat" (1906) wrote: "Close to the curb stood Jerry O'Donovan's cab. Night-hawk was Jerry called; but no more lustrous or cleaner hansom than his ever closed its doors upon point lace and November violets."

The new horseless carriages or automobiles were soon adapted as vehicles for public hire, so-called electric hansoms in one early version. The gasoline-powered cabs with meters came later. The first taximeter motor cab was introduced to the streets of New York in 1907 by the entrepreneur Harry N. Allen. *Taximeter,* the name of the meter itself, is from French *taximètre* and means a device that measures, a "meter," the rate of travel and its charge or "tax." The short form *taxi,* applied to the whole vehicle, was in use by 1910. A yet slangier one-syllable *tax* was occasionally used in later years. *Hack,* for the large four-wheeler vehicles for hire of an earlier day, was revived and applied to the motorized cabs around 1912. Today New Yorkers from curbside sometimes shout "cab!" but more often "taxi!"

Some of the occupational jargon of *hacking* escaped and became known to riders.[24] Experienced passengers call the drivers *cabbies, hackeys, hackers,* or *hacks*—among other things. A *hack stand* is an assigned place for

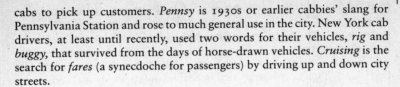
cabs to pick up customers. *Pennsy* is 1930s or earlier cabbies' slang for Pennsylvania Station and rose to much general use in the city. New York cab drivers, at least until recently, used two words for their vehicles, *rig* and *buggy*, that survived from the days of horse-drawn vehicles. *Cruising* is the search for *fares* (a synecdoche for passengers) by driving up and down city streets.

Eating on the Run

Commuting and the accelerated pace of city life brought commercial innovations for dispensing food to hurried urbanites, especially the mid-day meal. *Lunchtime* is a word of the late 1850s and is quite likely of urban origin. New sorts of eating places to service the lunchtime trade multiplied throughout the last half of the century. The Child's Quick Lunch chain flourished in the 1890s. Generic signs that said "Quick Lunch" were a common sight in Manhattan. The quick lunch had begun in railroad-station cafés for the convenience of tightly scheduled travelers. The idea was equally compatible with the time-oriented pace of city life generally. Businessmen's stand-up lunch counters became popular with frenetic Wall Street workers. Everything about the new eating customs connoted motion in contrast to sedentary, more conventional habits of dining. The names of these new restaurants allude to eating, perhaps with one hand, while either standing or sitting on a stool. The stool soon was made to revolve for quicker entry into and exit from the row of eaters. A *one-arm lunchroom,* or *one-arm joint,* was a cheap lunchroom with chairs having wide arm-rests, like students' desk-chairs, for eating quick meals and encouraging an equally quick departure.

Foreign visitors as late as the 1940s were struck by the penchant of New Yorkers for grabbing a bite in cafeterias and automats. The American *drug-store* always amazed Europeans as a place where one could buy nearly anything, including a quick lunch. Soda-water dispensaries had been around since the 1820s and were spurred on by the Temperance Movement of the 1870s. By 1900 New York had about 7,000 soda fountains, or about as many as saloons. The name of their attendant, *soda jerker,* one who "jerked" up soda water, appeared in the 1880s and was shortened to *soda jerk* by 1915. The soda fountain became part of the city's social scene. William Glackens painted *The Soda Fountain* in 1935, with a soda jerk(er) and two Renoir-like young women on stools. Isabel Bishop, one of the urban realists of the Fourteenth-Street School in the 1930s, also made several etchings and drawings of young women sipping sodas while perched on revolving stools.

Early fast-food places, in which one could get a meal for one cent in the 1820s, were called *lunch rooms* and slangily *lunches.* The innovation of counter service by the 1860s led to *lunch counters* and *lunch stands* and by 1895 to *snack bars.* By 1880 the usual sort of hole-in-the-wall for lunch, predictably, was a *lunch joint*. Many small establishments sleeked up and by the early 1930s were called *luncheonettes*, but the register was then lowered to just *lunchettes*. By 1910 some humbler eating places put up a sign, later and unforgettably in neon, that simply said *EATS,* or more commandingly *EAT*. In the opening of John Dos Passos's *Manhattan Transfer* (1925), the first thing Bud Korpenning saw when he hit town was "EAT on a lunchwagon halfway down the block."

Highly oral barkers stood outside downtown eating houses and chanted to whip up the appetites of passersby. Journalist George G. Foster in the *Herald Tribune* recorded in 1850 that they called:

Biledlamancapersors

Rosebeefrosegooserosemuttonantaters—

Biledamancabbage, vegetables—

Walkinsirtakeaseatsir.[25]

In 1868 the journalist Junius Henri Browne wrote of the efforts of waiters to communicate with cooks in the noisy, rushed eating houses of the Wall Street area. "The waiters must be endowed with extraordinary, and the cooks with miraculous, power of hearing. How could any one expect them to comprehend, "Ham-eggs-for-two-oyster-stew-coff-and-ap-pie-for-three-pork-beans-ale-cigars-for-four-beef-steak-onions-porter-cigar-for-five-mut'n-chop-mince-pie-black-tea-for-one," all pronounced in one word, in various keys and tones, with the peculiar recitative of eating-houses?"[26]

Since the 1850s or earlier this slurred abbreviated speech of eating-house employees had been also developing into a special vocabulary that reflected local dialect and culture. *Slaughter in the pan* was beefsteak; *red mike wit a bunch o' violets* was corned beef and cabbage; *drop one on the brown* called for hash with a poached egg (in Bowery joints hash was significantly called *mystery*); *eggs in the dark* meant eggs fried on both sides, or on the Bowery *two shipwrecked*, while *white wings with the sunny side up* was eggs fried on one side only; *two of a kind* was fishballs. Coffee was never ordered by that name, but was just *draw one* and black coffee was *draw one in the dark*. Some of the lingo voiced the common ethnic prejudices of the day: a black coffee was also *one nigger* and a *sheeny funeral with two on horseback* was roast pork and boiled potatoes.[27]

By the 1930s this lingo was called *hash-house Greek*—in the sense of any unintelligible choctaw. These words and phrases were useful and fun for the customers, too, and the most common items leaked into general slang. Countless word lists of lunch-counter lingo were published as light features in newspapers and magazines over the years and undoubtedly helped its spread. Some of the terms today are widely used, such as *BLT* (a *b*acon, *l*ettuce, and *t*omato sandwich), *sunny-side up* (eggs fried on one side with the yolk unbroken), *O.J.* (a glass of orange juice), *a stack* (of pancakes), and *a cuppa* (a cup of coffee).

City life routinely varied the diurnal rhythms established for centuries in agrarian society and this cultural contradiction, as we have already begun to see, is reflected in popular speech. Industry often worked on three shifts. Many other jobs, necessary to keep the business of the city operating on an orderly schedule, required many *night people,* such as deliverers, policemen, cabmen, and newsboys, to be up and out on the streets late at night or well before dawn. And this was to say nothing of all the people, including the streetwalkers, kept up by the electrically lighted entertainment life of the city. The western *chuckwagon* and urban *lunch stands* combined in concept to give us *lunch wagon* in the 1880s. Certain of the new lunch wagons began staying open late at night. By the late 1880s they were called *night owls* or *owl wagons,* after the 1840s slang name, *night owl,* or just *owl,* for a nocturnal person who frequented such modest eating places.[28]

The rollable lunch wagons were positioned at night in Union and Madison squares. In the 1890s writer Brander Matthews had one of his story characters, a park-bench sleeper in Union Square, say to another, "When the owl-wagon is here, you can get a late supper—if you have the price of it. I haven't."[29] Everett Shinn painted an atmospheric night scene, *The Lunch Wagon, Madison Square* (1904), depicting in watercolor a lighted, mobile owl wagon. One of Edward Hopper's most famous paintings, *Nighthawks* (1942), another name for a "night owl," is of lonely figures, seen through plate-glass windows, sitting at a late-night lunch counter. The painting is now a cultural icon of this urban institution.

In the 1890s, New York City and other large eastern cities sold off most of their old horsecars and replaced them with electric trolleys. Restaurant operators bought the old streetcars for a song and converted them into stationary *lunch cars* (apparently from word elements of *lunch wagon* and *streetcar*) and they became popular places to grab a bite. But many women felt that perching on top of stools in their floor-length skirts, as though lining up at the bar with men, was both awkward and unladylike. The row of stools also made it strategically difficult for families to sit together. Soon larger, shiny and always stationary lunch cars were especially manufactured and modeled after the gleaming, fastidious railroad dining cars. They were also equipped with booths to seat ladies and families. Just after 1900 the new lunch cars were called *diners* because of their resemblance to railroad diners, and the term remained popular. Two well-preserved examples still operate in Manhattan: the gleaming black and chrome art-deco Empire Diner on Tenth Avenue at 22nd Street and Munson's Diner at 600 West 49th Street near Eleventh Avenue.

The quick meal, whether lunch or dinner, in rolling (or in formerly rolling, or designed to look like they had once rolled) establishments changed urbanites' way of eating out and set the stage for yet more informal and convenient food services. As early as the 1880s, various kinds of self-service or cafeteria-like arrangements permitted downtown eaters to move even faster. One type of the early establishments was called a *conscience joint* because, wrote Stuart Flexner, "customers themselves added up the items on their trays and paid for what they said they had taken."[30] William Dean Howells in *Letters of an Altrurian Traveller* described these lunch rooms on the honor system as entirely workable in the public moral climate of the early 1890s.[31]

The gleaming, coin-operated, self-service Automats of the Horn and Hardart Baking Company, introduced in Philadelphia in 1902, were soon in New York and there grew to forty by 1933; the chain was never extended to other cities. New Yorkers often as not called the nickle-in-the-slot restaurants *Horn and Hardart's*. Or they called them *the Automat*. The Automat was generally a respected institution and not often slanged. Yet the Automats were sometimes called *slots*. By the 1890s any coin-operated vending machine was called a *slot machine,* not just the one-arm bandits we know today. *Slot,* the vertical opening to insert coins, became figurative for the whole machine. By the 1930s the name *slots* for the Automat was perhaps reinforced by the same name for old-fashioned slot machines, for there was a certain comedic visual and mechanical similarity between the two devices. The Automats began to close in the 1940s and 1950s and soon all were gone.

The Automat once was a cultural symbol of upward mobility, a benchmark of where one had been. James T. Farrell reminisced: "When I first came to New York, before the publication of *Studs Lonigan,* I ate out of those slots. I allowed myself 50 cents a day for food. For breakfast, coffee and muffins for a dime; for lunch, a bowl of pork and beans; for dinner, the same."[32] For many New Yorkers, as well, the Automat was a humbling reminder of a struggling youth when pennies mattered. Others would not let them forget it, either. O. O. McIntyre once quipped, "If he dines at the Ritz there are those who remember—ha, ha—his favorite slot at the Automat."[33] Lorenz Hart's lyric from "The Lady is a Tramp" went: "I wouldn't know what the Ritz is about./I drop a nickel and the coffee comes out."

Several Hollywood movies sought out the novel setting of the Automat for comedy situations, and it was a natural. Many New Yorkers perversely learned to love the Automats, if only because of the weird impersonality of the process. The slots became a tourist attraction and a symbol of modern New York, especially catching the fancy of children. Automats are part of today's urban nostalgia and older people sometimes say they regret their passing. One of the original Automats is installed in the Museum of American History in Washington, D.C.

New York is famous for its *delicatessens,* which often have tables and chairs for eating on the premises, and the institution and its name were firmly in the city by 1900. According to the etymologists at Merriam-Webster, "*delicatessen* is a plural noun, reflecting its origin in German *delikatessen,* the plural of *delikatesse.* The German is a borrowing from French *délicatesse,* meaning 'delicacy.' In English a second sense of *delicatessen* developed when it was understood as a singular noun used to designate a store were delicacies are sold."[34] New York's Ashkenazic Jews, on the other hand, called the same sort of shop an *appetizing store.* The slangy shortening to *deli* apparently did not come along until the early 1960s, and it is now a modifier, as in *deli sandwich* and *to eat deli.*

The *candy store* is another New York institution and it usually included a soda fountain. On the Lower East Side between about 1890 and the First World War the candy stores were also called *cheap charlies* and served as social centers of Jewish life. The candy store in fact sold more newspapers, magazines, tobacco, and egg creams than candy. *Egg cream,* a famous and complete misnomer, is possibly the result of a so-called folk etymology, or a specious word origin suggested by the sound of a word or phrase, in this case perhaps from the name of a French concoction *chocolat et crème.* Or perhaps someone named it *egg cream* to make it sound as "rich" as possible, for both eggs and cream connoted luxurious living in poor neighborhoods. The refreshing drink has neither eggs nor cream but is simply a special syrup and a little milk frothed with lots of seltzer water. Traditionally, people drank egg creams while standing and talking. One of the last archetypes of the candy store in Manhattan is Gem Spa on the southwest corner of St. Marks Place and Second Avenue. Gem Spa still serves a competent egg cream, though in a paper cup.

The City Inverted at Coney Island

One historical and cultural meaning of Coney Island is that of the conventional, everyday, work-a-day city turned upside down and inside out. The organized fun and games at Coney Island parodied the city's public transportation vehicles that carried the masses to and from work and burlesqued many other aspects of city life. Normal rules of behavior in public places were suspended for an interlude at Coney. Even the semiotic of *hot dog,* as we will see, threw humor into New Yorkers' "alienation" from their food. In yet other ways Coney represented a symbolic comment, not usually lexical, on the stresses and repressions of the modern city. Early in this century moral reformers, intellectuals, Progressives, political radicals, and artists mulled on the meaning of the vulgar scene at Coney Island. They generally found what their ideologies directed them to see, whether common sin, cynical commercial manipulation, a clever capitalist "opiate of the masses," a surrender of reason, the excesses of mass society, or Democratic Vistas.

The resort area and its amusement parks grew and declined with the metropolitan center, roughly mid-century to mid-century. Coney started as a middle-class beach and hotel resort and over the years became a playground for the masses of working-class and immigrant New Yorkers. In the 1890s preachers called the beach resort "Sodom by the Sea," alluding to its wild sporting life of gambling, drinking, and prostitution. Weekend crowds, greatly aided by Brooklyn's extended streetcar lines, reached 100,000 by 1900 and a million by 1914. The subway was fully extended to the site in 1920 and the boardwalk was completed in 1923. Even more of the masses came, although the heyday of the resort had passed. On July 3, 1947, the crowds peaked at 2.5 million, but thereafter declined with the growth of suburbs and increased auto travel in the 1950s. Coney Island today is not in the urban experience of most New Yorkers and is remembered mostly by social historians and the nostalgic.

The proper name *Coney Island* was associated in slang with things that were loud, gaudy, insubstantial, and cheap. The modifier *Coney-Island* was widely used to denote any such thing, a little like *Hollywood*—Tinsel Town—is sometimes used today. Competitive Coney Island vendors broke the tradition of the dime beer, along with that of the dime hot dog, and reduced it to a nickel. The public learned once again that "you get what you pay for." This is the pejorative idea behind the name *Coney Island* for a glass of beer with much foam and little beer. The offensively large head itself was called a *Coney-Island head*. In the late nineteenth century *Coney* Island (whose named derives from *coney,* an old name for the rabbits that once inhabited the island) was by many New Yorkers pronounced to rhyme with "money," "honey," or even "looney." Wallace Irwin's *The Love Sonnets of a Car Conductor* (1908) has the line "I went and gave the boss a cooney con." But through the years and for a variety of reasons it came to rhyme, as though fittingly, with "baloney."

By the 1930s the bathing beaches were polluted with sewage and garbage, which gave rise to much bleak humor about what one might find on the beach and how to regard such things. Coney Island also gave its name, probably in the 1930s, to the *Coney-Island whitefish,* a used condom floating in the water at the bathing beach—a common sight then and now.[35] Or it could also refer, I suppose, to a beached whitefish disposed of on the sand under the boardwalk at the *Underwood Hotel,* that gritty al fresco house of assignation, which was much in use long before the slang name for it finally appeared sometime before 1950.

Social commentators and culture critics have long tried to unravel the social symbolism or, as it is fashionable to say today, the semiotics of Coney Island in its heyday. Social historian John F. Kasson believes that the spirit of a secular carnival is the best analogy. Coney was not a date on the calendar but a place on the map—at the south beach of Brooklyn—where urbanites could for a day or two relax certain strictures and suspend certain "categories" of their ordinary lives, usually with impunity. "It attracted people because of the way in which it mocked the established social order. Coney Island in effect declared a moral holiday for all who entered its gates. Against the values of thrift, sobriety, industry, and ambition, it encouraged extravagance, gaiety, abandon, revelry. . . . It served as a Feast of Fools for an urban-industrial society."[36]

Coney Island created a carnival spirit by turning the work-a-day, duty-laden, predictable world of the city upside down. Coney was a fun-house mirror image of the straight city. People found thrills in perversions of recognizable, everyday experiences, or of their anxieties. Twice a day Luna Park staged a spectacle called "Fire and Flames" in which men dressed as firemen battled flames in a stage-set representing a New York tenement house. The rides in the amusement parks were a topsy-turvy, absurdist comment on public transportation in the city. The roller-coasters, switch-backs, scenic railways, toy trains, "Loop the Loop" railways, "Leap-Frog" railways that created the illusion of an impending head-on collision, and other twisting, bone-jarring, stomach-wrenching rides seemed wild parodies on the trolleys, els, and subways back in town. Indeed, the main street in one of the parks was called "The Bowery"—all surrounded with shows, "rides," and hokum.

Darkened tunnels of love, whirling giant tubs in which people were pressed against the bodies of strangers, surprise blowholes that sent skirts over heads (a concerted, sanctioned version of the naughty, windy corner at 23rd Street and Fifth Avenue where updrafts, after the erection of the Flatiron building in 1902, lifted skirts to the titillation of male watchers), disorienting halls of mirrors—all can be seen as sanctioned burlesques of everyday urban situations in which decorum was required. Never-realized romantic encounters in public places with interesting strangers, the inter-mittent darkness of the subway, crowding, pushing, and pressing together in mass transit, fantasies of frottage, the chagrin and delight of windy street corners, fantasies of free-falling elevators, the fun of escalators, the silliness of revolving doors—all seemed recapitulated just for fun at Coney Island.

The vulgar social scene on the beaches and boardwalks and in the fun-houses was grist for the mill for the urban realist artists. Reginald Marsh, in particular, made a major and sustained study of the scene in the 1940s, reveling in the mass and variety of flesh. His men are virile and muscular and his women, sprawled in the sand, nearly nude, and in every position, or in disarray in whirling rides, often as not, have their legs apart, suggesting abandon. His crowd scenes on the beaches also catch the topsy-turviness of Coney Island. All this, of course, was quite in the tradition of Walt Whitman's celebration of the urban crowd. Marsh paid curious homage to Whitman by placing him as a figure in a beach crowd in his painting, *Coney Island Beach* (1951).[37] Old Walt sits in a beach chair, wearing a sun hat, looking at his beloved, anonymous masses, just as his spiritual heir was doing.

Kasson argues that Coney Island was a commercial response to the turn-of-the-century transition from a society that emphasized values of produc-tion to one that celebrated consumption and leisure. Coney was an early, space-bound, manifestation of an urban mass culture that has ceased to exist and cannot be recreated; that kind of city is no more. The radio and movies in the 1920s and 1930s, as well as changing times, eventually sapped the life from the attraction of Coney Island. The automobile physically dispersed its audience and brought other beaches and attractions within reach. Television made surprise, novelty, and the wild juxtaposition of images ubiquitous and so a bore. Disneylands and theme parks, sanitized for the middle classes, later revived certain attractions of Coney Island, but they have had a different meaning for a different society. "A harbinger of the new mass culture," writes Kasson, "Coney Island lost its distinctiveness by the very triumph of its values."[38]

The Story of Hot Dog.   Perhaps part of the early fun of eating the "hot dog" at Coney Island was the idea of an inversion of eating proper, sanctioned meat. The origin of the name *hot dog* until recently has been shrouded in spurious folklore. Etymologist Gerald L. Cohen, continuing his work with the late Peter Tamony, has pieced together a jigsaw puzzle that is beginning to reveal the true story of *hot dog*.[39] The story is rich in middle and late nineteenth-century urban folklore, some about the fate of city dogs.

The earliest found printed instance of *hot dog* is 1896 where it was used as an adjective for good or superior. By 1900 *hot dog* had printed use for the sausage, though it probably had such oral use several years earlier. The invention of the hot dog and, so, the slang term *hot dog* has been traditionally but without proof placed at Coney Island. Hot dogs replaced fried clams at Coney Island as the favorite food of the summer weekend refugees from the steaming city streets. *Coney Island* itself was one of the several names for a hot dog, and this name persists today in some parts of the country for an extra-long hot dog. After 1900 or so the hot dog was also called a *Coney-Island red hot, Coney (Island) chicken,* a *New York tube steak,* and other names.

The hot-dog sandwich, like the American hamburger sandwich, is of German ancestry and of the same period and urban culture. In this country, before the sausage was called a hot dog, at least in respectable print, it was a *frankfurter,* "one from Frankfurt." It was also called a *wienerwurst* (i.e., "Vienna sausage"), which was shortened to *wiener* and more slangily to *wienie.* The slang name *hot dog* either originated in, or was greatly influenced by, mid-nineteenth-century urban humor, and it was often very nervous humor, about sausages being made from dogs, cats, horses, and even rats. Cohen shows how a well-publicized dog-meat scandal in New York in 1843 may have been the beginning of the idea. The muckraking Mike Walsh, reporting the scandal, referred to the "spurious dog sandwich." By the 1850s the odious suggestion was widespread, fact mixing with humor and rumor.

German immigrants in New York in the 1860s humorously called smoked frankfurter sausages *hundewurst*, "dog sausage" or *hündchen*, "little dogs," while larger bologna-type sausages were called *pferdewurst*, "horse baloney." Later, small sausages were humorously called *dogs* and *doggies*. Popular culture, too, supported the notion in the late nineteenth century. Cartoons in humor magazines and low theatrical skits had images of butchers stuffing puppies into sausage grinders and strings of sausage links coming out the other end. The German dachshund, because of its round, elongated, sway-backed shape, was irresistibly made to be *the* dog in the hot dog, and graphic and spoken humor made the sausage-dachshund connection, too. In 1914, Charles McCarron, Thomas J. Gray, and Raymond Walker's song title declared "Fido Is a Hot Dog Now."

The true hot dog is not just a sausage. It is a spiced, heated sausage served on a split roll, classically garnished with *rags and paint* (sauerkraut and mustard), a slang complement from its earliest days. New Yorkers probably began to speak of the edible "hot dog" in the 1890s. "We deal here," says Cohen, "with irreverent American humor in its purest form."[40] The allusion was shocking enough that it probably took several more years before someone dared to set *hot dog* in print for public consumption. *Hot dog* was also 1890s slang meaning good, superior, or the best, but this does not seem to be the primary source of the name. At any rate, *hot dog!* became the uniquely American exclamation of delight, perhaps by way of *hot damn*, a euphemism for *goddamn*, further euphemized to *hot dog*. And *hot dog* is the progenitor of other and recent American slang uses of the term with a surprisingly wide variety of referents.

The name *hot dog* for many years remained in disrepute at the beach resort because of its canine connotations. In 1913 the Coney Island Chamber of Commerce passed a resolution banning the use of the name by their member merchants. But the concern had been completely set aside by 1939 when President Franklin Roosevelt and the visiting King and Queen of England sampled the all-American dish. That put the hot dog into ultimate respectability.[41] On July 23, 1939, Coney Island officially observed "Hot Dog Day" to mark the supposed Golden Anniversary of the hot dog and to claim the invention of the sandwich in 1889; the event was presided over by Milton Berle.

An invention associated directly with Coney Island was the sidewalk stand with the built-in cooker from which the dog on a bun was served. For this reason, small lunch counters and wagons with such cookers all across the country came to be called *Coney Islands, hot dogs,* or just *dogs,* and *dog wagons,* recalling *lunch wagons* from the 1890s. A good many dog wagons remained small, wheeled carts that vendors pushed to set up at a good corner of city streets. Photographer Berenice Abbott saw them as a part of New York street life in the 1930s and captured one on film, *Hot Dog Stand,* on April 8, 1936. Similar pushcarts, but now of stainless steel, with a large umbrella are today a familiar sight in the streets of New York and still serve hurried lunch-hour eaters.

Modern Communications

Popular and lexical culture responded effusively to the innovations in mass communication most closely associated with the classic cycle of the metropolitan center—the modern newspaper, the telephone, and the movies. The formal terminology for the telephone and the moving pictures, themselves recent lexical innovations, were quickly shortened to informal forms for everyday use. In addition, outright slang names were substituted and reflected popular meanings of these new ways of living. The instruments of communication—newsprint, telephone sets, and motion picture theaters—became objects of folklore and humor and stories about their early days set their popular names into the context of their origin.

Newspapers. Alexis de Tocqueville in *Democracy in America,* written about his nine-month visit to America in 1831–32, noted the intrinsic and pervasive role of the press in our politics and community life. Compared to France, he thought that American newspapers were incredible in number; every city and town seemed to have one. Unlike the press in Europe, the American papers were also given to muckraking, which in the big cities after 1850 was to become a national sport. A century later sociologist Robert E. Park emphasized the importance of the newspaper in metropolitan life.[42] Many studies stemming from Park's influence have shown the role of newspapers in urban social, political, and economic integration and how the papers made the workings of the huge, diverse city imaginable to the masses of people. Newspapers were the first true mass medium and their content interacted inextricably with popular speech. At one time in the second half of the nineteenth century, New York had fourteen dailies, more or less, nearly as many semi-weeklies, and several score of weeklies, many serving immigrant communities in their own languages.

The act of newspaper reading in public places, selling papers in the streets, and even the physical presence of newsprint itself have been close to the consciousness of everyday city life and have influenced popular speech. Discarded newspapers, blowing whole in the streets or left behind in subways, are an abiding part of the disordered urban scene. Many modern artists have used newsprint, or pieces of it, in collages to say things about modern life. The papers "are themselves the city's detritus because yesterday's newspaper is a synonym for waste and the city's amnesia," wrote Peter Conrad in his analysis of New York art and literature.[43] The indifferent city custom of commuters leaving their papers behind on seats or on the floor of els and subways was probably formed in the early days of mass transit. In "The Tunnel," wrote Hart Crane, "Newspapers wing, revolve and wing" in a barreling subway car.[44]

Not surprisingly, people gave slangy names to the ubiquitous product of newsprint itself, which was so visible at newsstands, hawked continuously by newsboys, or held in the hands of straphangers, some of it ending in sidewalk refuse bins, or carelessly discarded, when not put to a number of practical uses. Because newspapers were printed on a large sheet, folded in the center, and designed be spread out, they were in street speech by 1850 called a *spread.* Early in this century newspapers were commonly called a *sheet,* as well. A verse of 1908 mentioned the newsboy "Calling the news that will sell the sheet."

The speech of the large German settlements in New York and other cities in the nineteenth century also influenced slang words for newspapers. One of the largest dailies in New York was the *Staats Zeitung.* The German presence probably accounts for the slang *blat* for any newspaper, from German *Blatt,* which means a newspaper as well as a page or "sheet." Writer Damon Runyon used *bladder,* and this form may have had wider currency, too. *Blab sheet* and *daily blab,* silly names for a gossipy newspaper, are from *to blab,* 'to speak,' especially indiscriminately. Such scandal sheets were also called *rags,* or *dirty rags,* if they were bad enough. These names are apparently from the sense of "rag" as something of contemptuously small value and not, as it might seem, from the rag content of the paper, which in the case of newsprint was becoming mostly wood pulp, anyhow.

Tabloid, originally, a trademark of the 1880s for a tablet, or a little pill, was applied, amid law suits, to other concentrated things. *Tabloid* was extended in a slangy way around 1906 to the new newspapers of the half-size format. Pulitzer's New York *World* had introduced the tabloid-size newspaper on January 1, 1901, in response to the fierce circulation battles of the period. A British newspaper, first published in 1902, actually used the word in its title. By the 1920s a tabloid newspaper in New York was called a *tab* for short. Tabloids, true to their name, compressed the news and (with many pictures) made it graphic and easy to swallow.

Because of its small size, the tabloid was popular with straphangers, who managed to read it while holding the folded paper in one hand. Seated passengers could also spread out the little tabloids without intruding on the social space of their fellow riders. Subway readers of the traditional large format of the *New York Times* were self-reliant and learned a folding technique for reducing the paper to smaller than tabloid size and, moreover, allowing them to read continuously by turning and adjusting the fold. The technique, especially when done with one hand while holding onto a strap, rail, or bar, is genuine city culture. The exact technique is illustrated for out-of-towners and learners in a guide to New York.[45]

The kind of sensational, gossipy news favored by some of the tabloids was by 1898 dubbed the *yellow press.* Joseph Pulitzer had bought the New York *World* from Jay Gould in 1883 and set a new course for American journalism with livelier language, political cartoons, and colored comics. The first comic strip to run successfully in an American paper was the *Yellow Kid* introduced by Pulitzer's *World* in 1895. "To attract attention to the feature, yellow ink was used, and the *World,* which was pretty sensational in those years, became known as the "yellow paper"—an epithet later extended in the term *yellow journalism* to any sensation-mongering newspaper," explain the lexicographers William Morris and Mary Morris.[46]

There is a little more to the story. Richard F. Outcault, the originator of the "Yellow Kid" at the *World,* left and took the strip with him to Hearst's New York *Journal.* George Luks, later to become known as one of the Ashcan painters, was hired to continue a nearly identical cartoon series in the *World,* as if Outcault had never left. The two "Yellow Kid" comics flourished side by side, despite law suits. "Other papers referred to the *World* and the *Journal* as 'Yellow Kid journals,' and soon dropped 'kid' from the phrase, so that 'yellow journalism' came into popular parlance, referring to the competitive sensationalism of the press."[47] The expression was probably influenced even earlier by the traditional yellow paper covers on cheaply bound, sensational books and pamphlets that had been published since mid-century.

After being read or "looked at," newspapers were circulated to a variety of other uses, such as food wrappers. Harry Golden in *Only in America* recalled that street vendors in New York once rolled newsprint into a cone, as is done traditionally for British fish and chips, and dispensed hot chickpeas.[48] Children on the Lower East Side called these horn-like cones *toots.* Certain newspapers were disparagingly called *fish wrappers,* suggesting what they were mainly good for, and there has been a worse suggestion of a fitting use for yet other papers. New York housewives of two generations ago, as it is told by their children, spread newspapers on the linoleum of the kitchen floor after mopping to soak up water and prevent tracking.

Bums and other down-and-outs used newspapers to line their clothing against wintry blasts, to line their shoes against holes in the soles, and not infrequently as blankets for sleeping in doorways and on park benches. The practice has been recorded as early as the 1860s when James D. McCabe, Jr. writing of bums sleeping on park benches, noticed that "most had old newspapers under them."[49] O. Henry in "The Cop and the Anthem" (1906) wrote: "On the previous night three Sabbath newspapers, distributed beneath his coat, about his ankles and over his lap, had failed to repulse the cold as he slept on his bench." Theodore Dreiser in *The Color of A Great City* recalled a scene from about 1910 of an old woman preparing to sleep on a park bench. "And now she is stuffing old newspapers between her dress and her breast to keep warm."[50] In the cheapest flop houses, a place on the floor was first covered with newspapers. Reflecting all these images, newspapers were called *bum fodder, bum wad,* and *bum's comforter. Blanket* was a hoboes' term for an overcoat and so newspapers were also known facetiously as *California* or *Tucson blankets.*

The Movies. The motion-picture industry, its technology, and its occupational culture have had an enormous impact on American English, giving us many new expressions and some old expressions with new meanings.[51] The content of the movies, their photographic images and especially their dialogs, particularly in the talking pictures after about 1928, had the greatest impact of all. The movies spread subgroup speech and its writers coined new slang, and to this day the movies interact with popular speech.

The movies gave us, too, several originally slangy words for the new entertainment medium itself, whose presence was so great in the cities in the first half of the twentieth century. The motion pictures, or by 1898 "moving pictures," were called *movies* by 1906 and the theater building itself was, too, by 1913. The Strand Theater on Broadway opened in 1914 as the city's first true motion picture palace and was, we may assume, called "the movies." Tin Pan Alley advised us in 1919 to "Take Your Girl to the Movies If You Can't Make Love At Home." "As late as 1926 the movie industry opposed the word *movie* as slangy and degrading," noted Stuart Flexner.[52] Yet the public's instinct for the new, low-register form *movie* was fitting for the new, highly informal medium. To this day words like *cinema* and *film* sound stilted and stuffy, except for the most ponderous products. Unlettered vernaculars degraded the medium even more by calling it the *mo'on pictures* in the late 1920s and even later had jocular use by those who knew better. Another slang term in use by 1910 was *flickers*. The projected images of the silents were said to "flicker" on the screen; the variant *flicks* was used briefly in the camp speech of the 1950s and 1960s.

The Golden Age of the movie house came in the 1930s with the advent of *talkies,* a term first recorded in 1928. The cinematograph by 1899 was called the "cinema" and by 1908 the "cine," pronounced "sinney," whence the recent stunt word *sin-ema* for X-rated films. About 1930 the talking pictures, in New York at least, got even more slangy abuse with the ephemeral terms *chin-ema* (a pun on *cinema* and the old slang verb *to chin,* to talk) and *yawpie* (probably a pun on *talkie* and the old verb *to yawp,* to talk loudly, to talk foolishly).[53] The eminently American institution of the *drive-in movie,* a nexus of the automobile, the movies, and teenage mating customs, by the late 1930s gave us the slang expression *passion pit* for a drive-in, alluding to the window-steaming activity in the cars.

Artists liked the subject of the old downtown movie houses, especially the rapture of the audiences in the interiors and the colorful, often bizarre exteriors. Artistic treatments of movies in the urban scene started early, especially in the work of John Sloan. His etching *Fun, One Cent* (1905) shows laughing young girls cranking the moving picture machines, one of the earliest forms of the medium, in an establishment on 14th Street near Third Avenue. Reginald Marsh in the 1930s, during the decade when New York was transformed by movies, radio, and advertising, painted the gaudy exteriors of movie houses (some called *grind houses* or *grinders*) plastered with posters; *Twenty Cent Movie* (1936) is the most elaborate.

The early nickel movies or nickelodeons, sometimes called *nickel dumps,* were a favorite of the city's youth. They were disparaged with this lowest of appellations for urban joints, and not without reason. They were crowded, poorly ventilated, and on hot summer days apparently rank places. Harry Golden recalled that "during the movie, and especially in the summer, a fellow would go up and down the aisle with a sprayer like a flit gun and spray some perfumed antiseptic stuff over the heads of the audience."[54] John Sloan's painting *Movie, Five cents* (1907) shows the interior of a crowded, makeshift movie house, with an electric fan turned on the audience. Later he twice painted the gaudy exterior of the little Carmine Theater in Greenwich Village.

The little Variety Photoplay Theater at 110–112 Third Avenue, just below 14th Street, opened as a nickelodeon in 1914. When it finally closed in 1989, it may have been the city's oldest, continually operating movie house. Its name uses an all but forgotten word for the silent movies, *photoplays*. Young people called any such place *The Dump* into the 1930s.[55] The modest nabes did contrast sharply with the new uptown movie palaces. The later neighborhood movie houses all over the city, many of them not dumps at all, were eventually called *nabes*, which persists as slang to this day.

The Telephone. For a final word, the introduction of the telephone in the late 1870s soon caused another flurry of popular word-making.[56] The first private telephone was installed in New York in 1877, the first one-page directory of mostly commercial entries was issued in 1878, and a small city-wide network was in place a few years later. *Telephone* was shortened to *'phone* by 1884, but in print tended to keep the elliptical apostrophe for several decades. But just *phone* eventually got tiresome for slangsters. For several years after 1939, a telephone set was called an *Ameche*, because Don Ameche played the lead role in the movie *The Story of Alexander Graham Bell* about the inventor of the telephone.

Around 1900, a popular song by Charles K. Harris, sung in a mock voice of a child, made capital of the mythical reach of the telephone: "Hello, Central, Give me Heaven, for my mama's there." The novelty of the telephone, as it spread into private use, led to adult behavior wittily termed *phonomania* or *telephonitis*, which today usually affects only adolescents. People by 1910 were speaking of giving their friends *a buzz, a ring, ringing them up*, or *getting them on the line, on the wire*, or *plugging in* to them and other expressions of the little drama of using the new technology. Yet old values endured and every girl knew, as the 1911 song title said, that "A Ring on the Finger is Worth Two on the Phone."

The use of the telephone more generally entered the consciousness of popular speech, as in the expression *hold the phone!*, to ask for a moment of respite after too much information or a surprising turn in a conversation. The expressions *to hang up* the phone and *to hang up on* someone, the latter an aggressive act contrary to the new telephone etiquette, are from the days of the hook-on-the-wall phones when one literally "hung up" the receiver. The new telephone was put to every social use. The telephone even changed the meaning of *call girl* from a woman who was "called upon" to that of one who was just "called up."

The phone booth made its own contribution to the language. The principle of paying for a call dates to 1878 or before, though coin-operated public phone stations or booths did not appear until about 1890. A social type in this century, once called a *fanner,* could not walk by a pay phone without flipping or "fanning" the coin-return lever in hope of a windfall. The name *telephone booth* was in use by the late 1890s, and it was then also called a *telephone box,* as it is today in the U.K. The first phone booths in New York were very large, had conventional hung doors, high latticed windows with curtains, and carpeted floors. The shrinkage of the telephone booth to a tiny cubicle in later years inspired much urban folk humor and countless cinematic images of comic, erotic, and outrageous situations in these small, glassed-in enclosures. Public phone booths were once disparaged as *sweatboxes,* but today many people would like to have them back from (the late) Ma Bell. The era of the nickel phone call, *It's your nickel—so talk* and other phrases, ended in 1951 when the toll was raised to a dime.

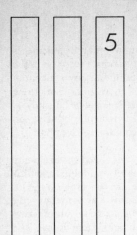

5
Tall Buildings

City people regarded tall buildings for living and working with wonder and pride but had mixed feelings about what the new vertical city meant and how they should relate to it. The tall buildings necessitated a perceptual reorientation and required new words and extended meanings of old words. Word images of tall buildings and of the new ways of living in and around them reveal some of the popular meaning of social change in the private world of domestic life and in the public world of the streets.

New technologies of building and new applications of electricity, especially to elevators, enabled the city to grow vertically at an astounding rate, piling people and economic activities on top of one another to an extent before undreamed of. The visual effect alone required new words, such as *skyscraper*, to make sense of the up-ended cityscape. The imposing presence of skyscrapers, and to a lesser extent large apartment houses, hotels, and department stores, spawned an urban mythology of their relation to Nature and provided a popular iconography of the meaning of modern life. Tall buildings, living and working in them, especially nearer and nearer the top, became a metaphor of social mobility in modern life. In the movie *Baby Face* (1933), Barbara Stanwyck figuratively and literally, floor by floor, sleeps her way to the top of a New York office building. But the story of tall buildings begins at home.

From Tenements to Apartments

For the city's working classes, communal living in a single multi-family building was established by mid-century. One of the first such buildings for working-class people was built in 1833 on Water Street, just east of Jackson Street (today in Corlears Hook Park). Gotham Court, built in 1850 at 36–38 Cherry Street, was intended as model housing for the working classes but soon deteriorated. The 1850s saw a number of other tenements for the working classes of the city. The word *tenement* came into use in the 1850s and was initially a New York legal term specifying any residential rental building with more than three family units. Tenement housing grew rapidly after mid-century. *Frank Leslie's Illustrated Newspaper* on July 1, 1865, reported that New York had over 15,000 tenements, housing on average more than seven families each, and all containing over half the city's population.

Only working-class families, often very poor ones, lived in tenements and the term came to mean any overcrowded, generally inadequate, multi-family building constructed for the usually immigrant working classes; a *tenement district* was understood to be a slum, though it was not yet exactly called a *slum*. Especially airless and dark *rear tenements* were substandard structures built in the back courtyards of tenement blocks. Jacob Riis in *The Battle With the Slum* wrote that over 2,000 rear tenements were still in use as late as 1900; he called them "caves."

Conditions of life in the tenements by the 1860s were perceived as a social problem and a subhuman, even animalistic way of life. Reformers and journalists referred to the worst of the tenements as *kennels, lairs, warrens, rookeries,* and *hives,* to suggest that the poor residents lived like animals. The tenement was the mode of working-class housing for the rest of the century. The old duality of sunshine and shadow, light and dark, alluding to the contrasts of wealth and poverty and, so, of virtue and depravity, took its negative pole here in the crowded, airless, lightless, squalid tenements of the East Side and other parts of the city.

A New York law of 1879 prohibited any further building of the old, prototypical tenements constructed with little thought for public health or safety. The rooms were arranged like cars in a train, one behind the other. Living quarters built on this plan retrospectively became known as *railroad flats,* though the term is not known to have been recorded before the 1920s. Residents, in order to go toward the front or back of the layout, had to pass through all the rooms between. The uniform floor plan was a cheap, efficient way to build but at the cost of privacy, light, and ventilation.

The barely restrictive new plan of 1887 inspired the popular term *dumbbell tenements*. The standard floor plan of family units roughly resembled the shape of a exercise dumbbell with a narrow middle and a bulge at each end. The new plan still required only a minimum of ventilation, chiefly through deep, sunless vertical airshafts in the two concave sections of the floor plan. By 1891 one-third of the city's population lived in dumbbell and older tenements. The dumbbell plan was eventually called the Old Law tenements, for the law was changed again in 1901. The new, third-generation plan, which required yet better ventilation and separate toilets for each flat, became known as New Law tenements and a good many of these stand today.

Around 1850 many middle-class New York families were living in hotels

and genteel boarding houses, seeming trapped halfway between the tenements of the poor and the large single-family houses of the affluent that lined
the city's fashionable avenues and cross streets. The city's less affluent but
nonetheless middle classes ardently aspired to the brownstone style of row
housing because it symbolized respectable family life and class standing.
Such housing was one important way the city's middle class defined itself
and its neighborhoods.[1]

London and later Paris provided New York with its basic models of
middle-class housing in the nineteenth century. Middle-class London was a
city of houses while Paris was a city of apartments, a significant measure of
the two cultures. Bourgeois life in Paris was more oriented to the streets and
more public, partly in response to the spatial constraints of apartment living
and to the social mix within buildings. Middle-class life in London, where
private houses were the mode of living, was more seclusive and neighborhoods more homogeneous. At mid-century well-to-do New York society
generally tried to model its way of life after London, including its housing
and neighborhood styles. When Parisian-style apartment living was introduced in New York, it exposed a certain anxiety in the middle classes.

The Stuyvesant Apartments, built in 1869, was the first building erected
in New York specifically as an apartment house for middle-class familes.
The five-story building, financed by Rutherford Stuyvesant, stood at 142
East 18th Street on the south side, about 100 feet west of Third Avenue, and
was built from the designs of Richard Morris Hunt, the first American
student at the École des Beaux-Arts in Paris. Hunt also designed the centrally
heated Stevens House that was built in the early 1870s on the south side of
27th Street, filling the block between Broadway and Fifth Avenue. Both
buildings were complete successes. But only the two such apartment houses
stood in Manhattan until 1875 when in that year alone an astonishing 112
new apartment buildings were erected.[2] In the next five years, or by 1880,
over 1,200 new apartment houses were built and New York was well on its
way to becoming a city of apartment dwellers.

Cultural adjustments had to be made, including new names for this kind
of living space. The new *flats* (a term commonly used in nineteenth century
New York much as it is still used in Britain today) were in so-called French-
flat buildings. The individual units were called *French flats* in their first
decade of the 1870s because of their association with the Parisian style of
life, and the New York building department had adopted the term in the
early 1870s.[3] "The name [*French flat*] itself," wrote architectural historians
Christopher Tunnard and Henry Hope Reed, "suggested a dangerous and
racy way of life."[4] Prudish New Yorkers were said to be embarrassed at the
very mention of "French flats" and were vastly relieved when *French* in the
phrase was dropped in the 1880s.[5]

New Yorkers who had been to Europe had also encountered the indomi-
table Parisian concierge and, indeed, the new Stuyvesant had provided a
room for one of these meddlesome French social types. But New York

apartment houses never got the dreaded concierge but rather the originally uniformed superintendent, who later became slangily known as the *super*. Like the concierge, the super also became a legendary figure on the fringes of New York domestic life.

Some middle-class New Yorkers in the 1870s and 1880s were concerned about the reputational consequences of, as one said, "living on a shelf under a common roof." After all, only the working classes lived in flats and in tenement-like buildings. Against the backdrop of the nearby tenements, the thought of living in flats symbolized reduced status, even the meanness of poverty.[6] The new French flats, according to historian Elizabeth Collins Cromley, "blurred the line between middle class and working class."[7] Apartment houses were suspected, moreover, of being like hotels, or dubiously transient and sleazy.

American divorce rates had climbed alarmingly in the 1880s and 1890s and as today people were concerned with the perennial breakdown of the family. The aversion to living under a common roof with other families stemmed in some part also from the notion that living cheek-by-jowl with strangers somehow encouraged sexual immorality and threatened the institution of the family. Social respectability was an ideal closely attached to the model of the large, single-family Victorian house and the family life and social control it stood for. The new French flats were spacious by today's standards but they did not afford the same separation of family and household activities as the large brownstones. Some people were concerned, for example, about the proximity of bed chambers to parlors and the idea of living on the same floor with servants.

These exaggerated concerns were expressed chiefly by male writers and critics. Women, on the other hand, generally welcomed apartment living as a modern labor-saving way of life, as it indeed was.[8] Despite the misgiving of some, the new French flats, some of them quite grand, became quickly popular with fashionable young couples. Middle-class New York was soon in the throes of *flat fever* or the *flat craze*, as the new way of living was called by amused observers.

Real estate developers in the 1880s resorted to all sorts of design modifications, architectural symbols, promotional persuasions, and linguistic ruses to create the impression that the new French flats were exclusive, separate, individualized units, offering as much privacy and seclusion as traditional townhouses. Grander flats were soon called *apartments,* which seemed to Americans a more refined term than just *flats. Apartment house* is an Americanism of the early 1870s. The word *apartment* is much older and in New York had meant any suite of rooms in a hotel or floor of rooms in a townhouse but did not yet mean a set of rooms in a building built for this purpose. This new, refined sense of the old word *apartment* was apparently introduced by developers to suggest a larger, more exclusive and private living space, often with maid's quarters, but still usually on one floor.

The social stigma of living in apartments lessened through the 1880s and

1890s, only in some small part because of these semantic blandishments and changing ideas about modern living. The greater reason was accommodation to the changing economic realities of land values and the cost of building and maintaining commodious single-family houses in the city. In 1900 only ten single-family houses were built in Manhattan, and apartment houses, the first wave erected only twenty-five years before, finally dominated the island.[9]

Apartment eventually also became a euphemism for a small flat and, as euphemism is wont to do, patently came to stand for what it was meant to obscure. Nowadays even the smallest flat is called an apartment, unless it is of only one room and euphemistically called a *studio* (apartment) in New York or an *efficiency* (apartment) in other parts of the country. A studio apartment was originally a large, one-room flat with a very high ceiling and especially large windows or skylights, as might suit an artist's studio; such a desirable space today is likely to be called a *loft*. Today a "city apartment," in the minds of most people, is a small, cramped living space in a building with "paper-thin" walls, and it is not far from the truth.

Many architectural critics, Lewis Mumford and Frank Lloyd Wright among them, deplored the characterless high-rise apartments built after the Second World War as *filing cabinets* for human beings; the trope has otherwise caught poetic and political imaginations. Gerald Raftery's verse "Apartment House" (1968) envisions "A filing-cabinet of human lives" and likened apartment houses to bee hives. The notion applied even more to those latter-day tenements—the alienating housing *projects* of the 1950s and 1960s. The Puerto Rican-born poet Pedro Pietri in "3170 Broadway" (1973) wrote of "these human file cabinets." Out-of-towners shudder at the way New Yorkers live in their "little boxes." Yet city people of modest means have always lived in cramped quarters and, in this fact, popular culture has found humor, as well as making a literary situation for writers on the city scene.

Apartment living also occasioned several new words and phrases from the twentieth-century experience of ordinary city people. Around 1920, older tenements and other low-rise apartment houses without elevators, of up to six stories, began to be called *walk-ups* because elevator apartments had become so common. Soon a basement apartment was a *walk-down* and a rear unit, perhaps a better structure than the old rear tenements, was a *walk-back*. By 1945 well over 100,000 walk-up units remained in New York. The refinements of modern plumbing still had not reached the older walk-up buildings and such apartments were called *coldwater walk-ups*. But ordinary New Yorkers saw redemption in the most taxing physical surroundings. After 1920 when women's skirts climbed up to the knees and above, folklore had it that so many of the city's young women had shapely legs because they had to climb the walk-ups.

The novelty of large apartment houses for the middle classes was high in the cultural consciousness of New York life through the 1940s. Popular books, such as Simeon Strunsky's *Belshazzar Court: Or Village Life in New York City* (1914) and Alan Dunn's *East of Fifth* (1948), portrayed life in the great "pre-war" (i.e., those built before the Second World War) apartment houses as walled, citified small towns where diverse lives occasionally touch in highly segmental ways. But the sheer verticality of New York apartments was the dominant image. Apartment dwellers occasionally said to their friends, "If you're passing by, just drop *up*."

Cliff Dwellers. By about 1890 the growing number of residents in apartment houses were sardonically called *cliff dwellers,* after the image of the cliff-dwelling Native Americans in the Southwest. New York's old aristocracy, the Four Hundred, mostly lived on Murray Hill and Fifth Avenue in deep, dark, cool, cave-like mansions of grey stone and white marble. Wags, probably also by about 1890, were calling them *cave dwellers,* a term used for the older nobs down to the 1930s. It was often their children who so notably went to live in the new apartment houses and made cliff dwelling respectable. In the Great West the two ancient housing arrangements were, indeed, built into the sides of cliffs. Popular books about the Great West, such as William M. Thayer's *Marvels of the New West* (1887), fired people's imagination with photographs and descriptions of cave dwellings and cliff dwellings.

In the decades around 1900, the tall buildings of Manhattan were frequently compared to natural cliffs. Literary people loved the trope, especially in its extensions. In 1899 Brander Matthews wrote that "the cliff-dwellers who inhabited the terraces of this man-made gorge, and who spent the best part of their lives a hundred feet above the level of the sidewalk, were no peaceable folk withdrawn from the strife of the plains; they were relentless savages ever on the war-path, and always eager to torture every chance captive. Wars . . . [were] as meanly waged as any Apache raid."[10] Indeed, the whole new cityscape created by the tall buildings, as we will soon see, was elaborately compared, both critically and admiringly, to the jagged landscape of the rock country in the Great West. The architect Herman Lee Meader was perhaps alluding to this popular notion in his embellishment of an apartment building, erected in 1916 at 243 Riverside Drive, on the northwest corner at 96th Street. The building is humorously decorated in a "frieze that depicts motifs from the lives of the early Arizona Cliff Dwellers, with masks, buffalo skulls, mountain lions, and rattlesnakes. . . . designs more than symbolic to our contemporary 'cliff dwellers'."[11]

Cliff dwellers was used mostly in the New York context and this sense might have originated in the city. The journalist Julian Ralph, visiting Chicago in the early 1890s, remarked of the housing styles: "They are not cliff dwellings like our flats and tenements; there are no brownstone cañons like our up-town streets."[12] George W. Bellow's 1913 painting of teeming street life in a New York tenement district is titled *Cliff Dwellers* and reflects the slang of the day.

The term also had early associations with Chicago skyscrapers but in different senses. The title of Henry Blake Fuller's 1893 novel *The Cliff-Dwellers* denoted the businessmen who worked in Chicago's first skyscrapers. The name was popularly extended to the new business society developing around the tall office buildings. In 1909 Chicago's famed social and professional club, the Cliff Dwellers, took their name directly from the cliff-dwelling Native Americans of the Southwest, probably with no thought to the slang term for apartment-house dwellers. Parenthetically, the New York pigeon, whose proper name is the Rock Dove, is the city's original cliff dweller. The rock dove migrated to New York and other cities because the tall buildings simulated its natural environment of high open spaces and many cliff-like ledges to roost and nest on.

The Culture of the Rooftops

City people turned the empty, flat rooftops of tall buildings to a variety of social and mostly pleasurable uses as evening roof gardens, residential penthouses, and playgrounds for children.[13] In the years between the two world wars, the tall city apartment house, especially its penthouse, became an object of glamour and prestige and a symbol of sophisticated living. Song lyricists, such as Irving Berlin and Cole Porter, helped embed in popular culture the idea that the penthouse apartment was the standard for elegant city living and the metropolitan ideal.[14] Movies emphasized their luxury, spaciousness, and the always spectacular views of the cityscape through the floor-to-ceiling windows, by day the skyscrapers, by night their lights. The penthouse became the new, lofty setting for drawing room comedies; everyone seemed to live in one.

A bit ironically, the root sense of *penthouse* is that of a lowly lean-to or attached shed. *Penthouse* was in English by the early 1500s and is an alteration, by the sound confusion of folk etymology, of Middle English *pentis* or *pentice,* a lean-to or shed attached to a larger building. The modern sense of a penthouse as a rooftop apartment seems to have emerged in the late nineteenth century, probably by association with the shed-like utility housing that covered stairwells or elevator machinery on the roofs of tall buildings. Or more directly it may have sprung from the simple living quarters provided for janitors and their families on top of early office buildings. Their children grew up here and had the run of the streets in the deserted business district on weekends. This was the first "penthouse society." Only later did the owner of a new office building in midtown or downtown (stories vary) have the bright and prescient idea of building a luxurious private apartment on the roof.

In the new apartment houses of the 1880s, the lower apartments were considered more desirable because elevators were new, somewhat threatening, and often unreliable. Improved elevator technology inverted this value and made higher floors more desirable. As the symbolism of high living grew more closely associated with actual high living in this century, penthouses were more often built atop tall apartment buildings. They were frequently the most expensive unit in the building and the most prestigious, if only because of their height. In New York today, an apartment on the highest floors of an apartment house, especially the rooftop penthouse, is still associated with status and prestige. All things considered, highly situated apartments progressively cost more, though perhaps only because of the better views, garden patios and set-backs, cooler air, and distance from the noisy streets.

Meanwhile back downtown, tenement dwellers during *hot spells* slept nights on fire escapes and on rooftops to escape the still night heat of the city. Other tenement families slept on stoops or even on the sidewalks at the front of their buildings. Yet others retreated to green parks and wharfs on the water fronts to escape the sweltering heat. On weekends whole families traveled to Coney Island and slept on the beaches. Heat waves, such as the one in the summer of 1896, took their toll in the deaths of infants and the elderly in the tenements. Fire-escape and rooftop sleeping continued well into this century, for air conditioning was not common until after 1950. The Yiddish-speaking poet Moshe Leib Halpern wrote of tenement life on hot summer nights and compared the children sleeping on fire escapes with monkeys hanging in trees. Michael Gold in his novel *Jews Without Money* gives a passionate, personal description of tenement roof-sleepers, a "mélange in the starlight" heaped against the "city of towers" that "reared about us."

A few people had small electric fans in their homes as early as the 1890s, but they were not common and, anyhow, would not have helped much in airless tenements. A journalist in 1904 mentioned the "hundreds" of electric fans in New York City—but these did little to cool the Four Million. It was so hot, O. Henry said tongue-in-cheek in "A Midsummer Knight's Dream" (1907), that "Philanthropists were petitioning the Legislature to pass a bill requiring builders to make tenement fire-escapes more commodious, so that families might die all together instead of one or two at a time."

The well-to-do on hot summer nights often repaired to one of the city's many roof gardens to dine on cold suppers and sip cool drinks. Tenement folk had their own version. Stephen Crane in the 1890s wrote of tenement roofs as the "roof-gardens" of the poor. "Down in the slums necessity forces a solution of problems. It drives the people to the roofs. An evening upon a tenement roof, with the great golden march of the stars across the sky and Johnnie gone for a pail of beer, is not so bad if you have never seen the mountains nor heard, to your heart, the slow, sad song of the pines."[15]

The rooftops more generally and in all seasons served in tenement life as a common area for socializing, night and day, and were used by boys for keeping and flying pigeons, an indigenous city game.[16] Rooftop scenes of whole families sleeping, people talking, lovers at rendezvous, and young women drying their hair—favored images of John Sloan and Edward

Hopper—now seem richly nostalgic of the old East Side. The suntan became fashionable attire in the 1920s, as soon as the new bathing-suit styles allowed the possibility. The fashion spread to working-class men and women in the 1930s and 1940s. Young women, many of them descendents of people who spent nights on roofs to escape the heat, began to spend days on the roofs of their apartment buildings to tan those legs made trim by the walk-ups. John Sloan in 1941 etched his *Sunbathers on the Roof,* a couple reclining beach-style on a blanket. Sun-tanning on the roof was often in preparation for display during visits to Coney Island. By the 1940s city rooftops, those ersatz beaches, were given the fictitious place name *Tar Beach,* alluding to the black tarred and graveled rooftops.

The Hotel Life

The early, great urban hotels were imposing edifices on the cityscape and were a democratic fantasy in the popular imagination. Henry James, as an American expatriate returned home in 1906 for a visit, wrote in *The American Scene* "that one is verily tempted to ask if the hotel-spirit may not just *be* the American spirit most seeking and most finding itself."[17] Hotel lounges, lavish dining rooms, and roof gardens were part of the city's nightlife and were a public arena for conspicious consumption. Historian Bayrd Still wrote that "not only were the first-class hotels among the 'sights' of the city; they also were symbols—with their steam heat, toilet facilities, gas lighting, and elevators—of the comforts and conveniences of city as opposed to rural residence, and of the glamor and conviviality of city life."[18]

The Astor House was New York's first big, modern, luxury hotel and reigned for a generation. Built in 1836, the Astor filled the block on Broadway between Vesey and Barclay streets. In the 1850s a boom in building luxury hotels located a cluster farther up Broadway. Establishments like the St. Nicholas at Spring Street were the wonder of the city. Foreign visitors thought New York hotels rivaled and often exceeded the best hotels of London and Paris. The buzz of activity in and around New York's grand hotels and, especially, their unparalled luxury, total service, and innovative technologies were all taken as evidence of the city's—and the nation's—prosperity. The city reveled in its vigorous commercial enterprise, modern inter-city transportation, and the upward mobility of the expanding middle classes. Popular fiction of mid-century, which bears comparison to the best-selling novels of today, often set scenes in the sumptuous and expensive restaurants in the famous hotels of New York, Boston, New Orleans, and Chicago.[19] Urban color and travel writers always described the grand hotels, some with stories of how many of their guests had risen from rags to riches.[20] The Broadway *hotel swell* was a distinct social type on parade in lobbies and lounges.

These palaces of luxury and splendor held out to ordinary men and women the possibility, at least in their dreams, of living like the swells. Years later O. Henry in "An Unfinished Story" (1906) had a humble shopgirl, Sadie, exclaim the prospect for her friend Dulcie: "Piggy's an awful swell; and he always takes a girl to swell places. He took Blanche up to the Hoffman House [in Madison Square] one evening, where they have swell music, and you see a lot of swells. You'll have a swell time, Dulcie."

Midtown hotel life was continuous with the nightlife of the city. The reputations for elegance and luxury of the Ritz hotels in Paris, London, and later in New York gave American slang in the 1920s a whole array of words and phrases derived from the proper name *Ritz*. The Ritz hotels were named after their founder, the Swiss César Ritz. New York's Ritz-Carlton, built in 1910 at Madison Avenue and 46th Street, reached its height of fashion during the First World War. Bayrd Still observed that "like the phrase 'Park Avenue' the name 'Ritz,' too, came to stand colloquially for the highest fashion of the time."[21]

The rich and elegant of the city were collectively known as *the ritz* and *the ritzies* (collective nouns), who sometimes *ritzed* (transitive verb) their social inferiors. *Ritzy* (adjective), *ritzier* and *ritziest* (comparative adjectives), *ritziness* (abstract noun), and *ritzily* (adverb)—all mean high style and conspicious spending. The style of the Ritz inspired several whole phrases in slang: *in the ritz* (in fat city); the complaint *this ain't the Ritz;* the reproachful observation *acting ritzy;* the gentle warning *don't get ritzy with me;* and, well, getting ritzy in *put(ting) on the ritz* was in the language by 1921. Irving Berlin's song of 1929, "Puttin' On the Ritz," either introduced or more probably echoed the popular phrase. At any rate, Harry Richman's rendition of it in *George White's Scandals* enormously popularized the title phrase. *Ritz* and its variants, as we can see, had both approving and disapproving senses that witnessed the opposing and ambivalent responses to conspicuous consumption and to those who so ostentatiously enjoyed and flaunted it, or who aspired to it.[22]

Meet me at the Waldorf was one of those "meet-me" phrases that New Yorkers used so much to make social contacts in public places in the years around 1900. Others were *Meet me at the Fountain* in the Siegel-Cooper department store's atrium, later *Meet me under the Clock* at the Biltmore Hotel and sometimes under the clock in Penn Station, and still today *Meet me between the Lions* in front of the New York Public Library. The original Waldorf and Astoria hotels, both at Fifth Avenue and 34th Street, merged into a joint company in the 1890s. The resulting Waldorf-Astoria Hotel around 1900 was slangily and popularly named *The Hyphen,* from the new "hyphenated name" that caught the public fancy. A joke of that day went something like this: *Q.* "Where shall I meet you?" *A.* "At the Hyphen." *Q.* "Where?" *A.* "Between the Waldorf and Astoria!" Tin Pan Alley came up with a new song, "The Waldorf-Hyphen-Astoria," which also helped the nickname stick for a while.

The Waldorf-Astoria was renowned for its dining room and its approach through a 300-foot corridor at the 34th Street lobby. This promenade of swells was dubbed *Peacock Row* and also more slangily as *Peacock Alley* by the newspapers. Ordinary people from the streets gathered every night, wrote James Remington McCarthy, to see "the women come in, their long trains draping the floor, the diamonds and pearls and necklaces gleaming, or their generously feathered hats bobbing up and down as they moved with stately tread along the corridor" to the famous Palm Room restaurant.[23] Kate Simon described Peacock Alley as a "theater and nonstop fashion show, which was a high-class meat rack of sleek, eager-eyed ladies and school to the many poorer girls who studied their dress and technique. . . . The Waldorf-Astoria was the court that fed America its fantasies of the good life."[24]

The old Waldorf-Astoria was razed to build the Empire State building on the site in 1931; the new Waldorf-Astoria was soon built on Park Avenue north of Grand Central Terminal. The old Ritz-Carlton was razed in 1951 for an office building; its successor never equaled the reputation of the namesake. The Plaza, built in 1907 and facing the Grand Army Plaza on Fifth Avenue, has survived as a luxury hotel from that period. That era of the grand hotels in New York—the Ritz, the Waldorf-Astoria, and the Plaza—is remembered in the high-sounding phrases, so often mocked by hoi polloi: lunching out at the Waldorf and having tea at the Ritz, or at the Plaza.

The Department Stores

Department stores helped bring women into the everyday life of the city and created a democratic atmosphere where working-class women, the "shawl trade," shopped alongside the "carriage trade."[25] A. T. Stewart opened his famous department store—a drygoods palace—in 1846. Macy's, McCreery's, and Arnold Constable's opened in the 1850s and 1860s. The term *department store* itself is an Americanism and dates to 1887 when a New York store first advertised itself in print as a "department store," though the merchandising principle was decades older. Popular speech soon varied the phrase with *big store,* though the earliest instance I have seen is in 1910. Siegel-Cooper and Company, built in 1896 on the east side of Sixth Avenue between 18th and 19th streets, took the new expression *The Big Store* as their advertising slogan. Years later a Marx Brothers romp was titled *The Big Store* (1941) and exploited every possibility for mischief in the setting of a modern department store.

The city's most famous concentration of elegant department stores from about 1880 to 1900 was on Broadway, from 8th Street up to Madison Square at 23rd Street. *Ladies' Mile,* as the row came to be called, had most of the city's great department stores and was a shopping paradise for middle-class women. Ladies' Mile later spread over to Sixth Avenue where many grand emporia were built. Ladies' Mile was a promenade for fashionably dressed women and became symbolic of New York as a woman's world of consumption. The term *window shopping* may have arisen here. The man's world was Downtown and had to do with making money to support this consumption. A light verse of the day went: "From Eighth Street down, the men are earning it,/From Eighth Street up, the women are spurning it;/ That is the manner of this great town—/From Eighth Street up and Eighth Street down."

The dark side of this world of elegant consumption was—and remains—the infamous *rag trade* (a Britishism of the 1840s) on the East Side of Manhattan, just as it was traditionally in the East End of London. New York recapitulated that industry as well as some of its vocabulary wherein the idea of sweat is key. The city's clothing industry, supported by the needle trades, operated the notorious *sweatshops,* a term of the late 1860s. The system also operated as an urban cottage industry where immigrant labor, women and children alike, were *sweated,* that is, exploited in their squalid tenements. *Sweaters* (a term of about 1850) gave them piece work for appalling low wages. The so-called *Pig Market* on Essex and Hester streets was where sweaters hired Jewish immigrant labor in the 1880s. This nineteenth-century institution of the sweatshop is still alive and well, still on the Lower East Side, mostly in Chinatown.

The Elevator

After 1890 the new electric elevators, successors to the steam-driven and hydraulic ones that had amazed the generation before, allowed buildings to go even higher—beyond five or so stories—to the height of true skyscrapers. The first passenger elevators were steam operated. The first commercial elevator was built in 1850 and was used only for lifting freight between two floors. In 1852 the inventor Elisha G. Otis demonstrated a passenger elevator at New York's Crystal Palace Exhibition on the present site of Bryant Park. This new "vertical screw railway" had a safety device to prevent its falling, which greatly increased public confidence in the contraption. He established the Otis Elevator Company in Yonkers, N.Y., and installed the first real passenger steam-elevator in the five-story Haughwout Building at 488–492 Broadway. But better known in its day was the one installed in 1857 in the six-story Fifth Avenue Hotel on the northwest corner of Fifth Avenue and 23rd Street. It was described as a "perpendicular railway intersecting each story." New York's first office building with an elevator was the six-story (but tall, 130 foot) Equitable Life Assurance Building, completed in 1870 at 120 Broadway.

Quaint old names like *vertical railway* and similar terms for the early steam and hydraulic installations soon gave way to *elevator,* which became standard in American English. Tall buildings continued to be metaphorized by writers as vertical street grids and their elevators were compared to streetcars moving on their tracks up and down the avenues; the tallest buildings even had separate elevators for "express" and "local" stops. The British *lift* was occasionally used, often with quotation marks, but it was soon rejected as an English affectation. Longer names like *aerial elevator* were also dropped in time.

The first hydraulic elevator was installed in 1878 and hydraulic models became common in the 1880s. Some were installed in the new buildings of French flats where they became part of the new culture of apartment living. The elevator was entering urban folklore in all major cities, especially by way of stories of their imperfect operation, the novel and awkward social situation in the cars, fears of falling, and anecdotes about getting stuck between floors. In 1884 William Dean Howells, who personally feared the new elevators, wrote his play "The Elevator," a farce about people stuck between floors in a fashionable Boston apartment house.

The passenger elevator also became part of the glamorous, fantasy world of hotel life. O. Henry in "Transients in Arcadia" (1908) wrote of a hotel on Broadway where guests could "mount its broad staircases or glide dreamily upward in its aërial elevators, attended by guides in brass buttons, with a serene joy that Alpine climbers have never attained." Elevators in the tall office buildings were a different matter, but were an exciting experience, for better or worse. Henry James found upon his return to New York that the "great religion of the Elevator" assaulted his sensibilities. He saw the elevator as a symbol of the city's "herded and driven state" and despaired "to wait, perpetually, in a human bunch, in order to be hustled, under military drill, the imperative order to 'step lively,' into some tight mechanical receptacle, fearfully and wonderfully working."[26] Poet Sara Teasdale in "From the Woolworth Tower" wrote of the thrill of the "flight" to the top and therein found a romantic thought.

The elevator, ascending skyscrapers and tall apartment houses from bottom to top and all stations between, became a metaphor of uneasy and erratic mobility in urban life and appears as an iconograph in modern literature. What goes up can come down; and if it goes up fast, it can come down even faster. (Free-falling elevators are an abiding fear in the back of an older urban mind, like the anxiety that once followed too-quick success.) The ascent by elevator to the lofty top is almost too easy, unlike earning one's way by the steady, labored climb up the staircase. The traditional work ethic said that one should *get in on the ground floor* and work one's way up, presumably by climbing the stairs. At the same time, elevator cars, in giddy ascents, are very sexy places when two or more people share the hermetic ride. Elevator riders developed a little urban culture of etiquette, or "civil inattention," to defuse the eroticism of this daily, even hourly situation. Movies and television still trade on this happy arrangement.

Over the years the elevator, its cars, and its operators collected a few slangy names of limited currency and early demise. The elevator, by the way, was never called an "el," a form whose meaning was utterly preempted by the popular name of elevated trains. Young people today sometimes refer to the *'vator,* but the older names are more fun. The seemingly baby-talk pun *alley-waiter* appeared by 1896. This form is apparently a blend of *alley* and *dumbwaiter,* while phonetically designed to recall *elevator.* Dumbwaiters were also a feature of the new apartment houses and were much noted in descriptions of apartment living in the period, for residents sometimes met their neighbors face-to-face through the two sides of the shaft. A dumb-waiter, like an elevator, traveled up and down a vertical shaft or "alley," as it was sometimes called. By the 1920s, an elevator was sometimes called a *heist,* a slang variant of *hoist,* a name for a freight elevator of primitive technology.

Bird cage for an elevator car is obviously from the image of the grilled, often ornate open cages of early elevators, and the allusion disappeared with the introduction of closed cars. By 1920 elevator operators or "runners" were nicknamed *indoor aviators,* sometimes just *aviators,* expressions that operators and riders probably thought were as funny as their old quip, "This job has (must have) its ups and downs." Irving Berlin wrote the song titled "The Elevator Man: Going Up, Going Up, Going Up, Going Up!"

The escalator and the revolving door are the two other innovations for movement within modern buildings. The Otis Elevator Company bought the patents to the early moving stairways, or escalators, and installed their first model at the Paris Exhibition of 1900 and soon thereafter in the New York subways and in Bloomingdale's department store. The word *Escalator* was also introduced in 1900 and is a trademark of the Otis Elevator Company, but the name became generic as famous brand names are wont to do. Apparently, it is a blend of *escal*(ade) + (elev) *ator.* Other brands were called "an inclined elevator," "a moving stairway," and "a reversed treadmill." No slang name has been recorded, though *escalator* itself found extended meanings. The imagery of the common arrangement of side-by-side, up-and-down escalators, for example, has become a cinematic and video sign of frustration, of people moving at cross purposes on treadmills in opposite directions, passing one another helplessly—conveyed by the "machine" of urban life.

The first revolving door in the city, it is said, was installed in 1899 in Rector's Restaurant, one of the early lobster palaces on the Great White Way in Longacre Square. On opening night, guests played in the revolving door and went around more times than necessary. The revolving door and, to a lesser extent, the escalator have been much used for low comedy and as a symbol of absurdist contradiction in the movies. Yet the revolving door, like the escalator, for all its prominence in the popular imagination, was never named in recorded slang. But *revolving door* itself became a slang metaphor for any Sisyphean situation in urban life—where one tries to enter but is propelled back out, again and again.

Skyscrapers

The technology for erecting the first tall buildings that seemed to scrape the city's sky evolved in New York after the Civil War and in Chicago after the Great Fire of 1871. The two essentials of a true modern skyscraper are the skeletal steel frame that fully supports the curtain walls and floors of the building, first employed in the mid-1880s, and the new generation of electric elevators. Earlier tall buildings sometimes had primitive elevators and reached up to ten or so stories. But the structures were supported by their own masonry, though some with the help of interior ironwork.

There is an old argument about whether Chicago or New York saw the rise of the world's first true skyscraper. Architectural historians now give the distinction to Chicago's Home Insurance Building, which was designed by William LeBaron Jenney and erected in 1884–85. The Home Insurance Building was, writes Paul Goldberger, "the first tall building to be supported on a skeleton frame, in this case a mix of iron and steel."[27] (The Home building was demolished in 1931.) Yet New York in important respects pioneered the modern skyscraper and perhaps contributed significantly to the adoption of its most popular name—*skyscraper*. In 1870, the first of two "Equitable" Buildings in New York, the Equitable Life Assurance Building, was built to 130 feet with six unusually tall stories and, moreover, was the first office building with an elevator. The Equitable made it fashionable to have an office and work on a high floor.

The full steel frame, however, did not come to New York until 1888–89 in the construction of Bradford Gilbert's Tower Building at 50 Broadway, though the principle had been used incompletely in other buildings in the city. Significant for their symbolism of power and prestige, many of the early tallest buildings in New York were built by insurance companies and by competitive newspaper magnates, such as the Tribune Tower in 1875 and Pulitzer's sixteen-story New York *World* building in 1889 on Park Row opposite City Hall.[28] Yet Chicago clearly led New York in building skyscrapers through the 1880s and 1890s. But New York's building after 1900, especially the Flatiron in 1902, its similarly shaped Times Building in 1904, the Metropolitan Life Building in 1909, and the Woolworth Building in 1913, reestablished New York as the city of the world's tallest buildings.

The originally slangy but romantic word *skyscraper,* applied specifically as a noun to a tall building, first appeared in print in 1888.[29] The first dictionary to record it was James Maitland's *The American Slang Dictionary* of 1891: "a very tall building such as are now being built in Chicago." However, the adjectival phrases *sky-scraping* and *sky-scraper* had been used since about 1883. Since the late eighteenth century, the term *skyscraper* had been applied to a variety of unusually tall or high things other than buildings, so naturally the word was in turn applied to unusually tall buildings. The noun was commonly printed with a hyphen, *sky-scraper,* until 1915 or so. *Skyscraper* spread to "colloquial" usage by about 1920; and the dictionaries labeled it "standard" only in the 1930s. But this may not be the full story.

The word *skyscraper* for a tall building may have been most immediately and perhaps decisively influenced, especially in New York, by nautical slang for the main mast on the sailing ships and for the tall stack on steam ships. Lewis Mumford asserted that the city's tall buildings of mid-century were "called the skyscraper after the topmost sail of its [i.e., New York's] old clipper ships."[30] The ships with their "skyscrapers" were plentiful at the South Street seaport and were in sight of the first tall buildings in Manhattan. Ships' masts were indeed among the tallest objects in the city, rivaling even Trinity's spire, and Walt Whitman was struck by the image of "mast-hemmed Manhattan."

Foreign visitors to the city sometimes ridiculed the name *skyscraper* and suggested other names, often derisive ones, upon their first impression of tall buildings. The English writer G. K. Chesterton wrote in 1922 that "the tall building is itself artistically akin to the tall story. The very word skyscraper is an admirable example of an American lie."[31] Another Englishman, Ford Madox Ford, in 1927 liked the skyscrapers but not the word—"its suggestion is one of ugliness that makes the superior European hug himself for his superior virtues." (He thought something like "cloud-houses" better.) Ford allowed however that the sibilant *skyscraper* was suitable for hurried, everyday New York use—"the initial of the word in common use taking the sound along faster."[32]

Proposed *cloud-* words lost out to the more lofty and ambitious *skyscraper*. *Cloud-supporter* briefly competed with *skyscraper* around 1889. A later suggested *cloud-scraper* seemed to recall the standard German *Wolken-kratzer*, literally "cloud-scraper." But the "sky" was higher than the "clouds." *Sky-sweeper* was recorded just after 1900. The French writer Paul Morand in the 1930s said they should be called "sky-batterers." An elliptical *'scraper* was recorded and even a derogatory *rock pile*. Slangsters recently tried out a retrograde *cloud-buster,* apparently modeled on *gang-buster* and *ghostbuster,* but such lame words only set into relief the dignity and romance of the century-old expression—*skyscraper*.

More elaborate metaphors were applied to the skyscrapers to make sense of their novelty and complexity. They were often seen as cities in microcosm, though up-ended. In the late 1890s, a visiting British journalist, William Archer, remarked on the new perpendicular life of the city. "When they find themselves a little crowded, they simply tilt the street on end and call it a skyscraper."[33] A vertical street grid, perhaps with a "vertical railway" or elevator, is a good mechanical definition of a skyscraper. The rival imagery of organicism, which was so influential in social thinking early in this century, also was to have an influence. Journalist, essayist, and novelist Simeon Strunsky made out the skyscraper to be a giant organism. The glorious stone-work lobby and its crowds "would be the heart, the great pumping station for the entire circulatory system. The elevators are the arteries." And the "nerves" are the telephone wires.[34]

In recent decades New York and Chicago, "the second city," renewed their rivalry in the competition for the "World's Tallest Building." The 102-story Empire State Building, completed in 1931, had dominated for nearly four decades. Chicago's John Hancock Building took the title of "The World's Tallest Building" away in 1969; New York took it back briefly with the twin towers of the World Trade Center, but lost it again to Chicago with the completion of the Sears tower in 1974, and there the game mercifully ended. But not to worry. The crestfallen Empire State Building is still a masterpiece of art-deco architecture and, some say, the world's most handsome skyscraper—as well as being the only building in the world equipped with a needle intended (and actually used a few times) for dirigible moorings. On July 28, 1945, at 9:52 on that Saturday morning, the Empire State Building became the first skyscraper actually crashed into by a large airplane, a U.S. Airforce B-25 Mitchell bomber. The Empire State was also the fabulous perch of King Kong. Yet the flamboyant, jazz-modern, 77-story Chrysler Building completed a year earlier in 1930, and for a single year the world's tallest building, is for many New Yorkers the quintessential symbol of the gay spirit of New York between the wars.

Sidewalk superintendent is the humorous name for a pedestrian observer at the edge of a construction site. The social type has been long recognized and was caught in photographs around 1900, though the term was not recorded in print until the late 1940s. (The slang name was soon extended to any kibitzer from the sidelines of any activity.) Excavation and construction sites were usually surrounded by a solid fence that completely closed the site from public view, much to the frustration of sidewalk superintendents. The now customary eyeholes in the fence, arranged for viewers of different heights, were not common until the 1930s. John D. Rockefeller formally accommodated the sidewalk superintendents with a viewing area for pedestrians at the construction site of Rockefeller Center and is said to have established the practice. The semiotician Dean MacCannell found great significance in this little custom. "The becoming public of almost everything—a process that makes all men equal before the attraction—is a necessary part of the integrity of the modern world."[35]

The Flatiron Building and Its Folklore.   The earliest, still-standing, true skyscraper in New York is architect Daniel Hudson Burnham's twenty-story Flatiron Building, which was completed in 1903 at the southern triangular crossing of Broadway and Fifth Avenue at 23rd Street. In its early days the building was officially called The Fuller Building after its builder, the George A. Fuller Company. A popular story holds that *Flatiron Building* was a derisive nickname imposed when the public saw its unconventional, triangular shape and was reminded of the old smoothing irons, or flatirons, used by housewives and tailors. But that name in fact appears on specifications drawn up by Burnham and Fuller in 1902 and, evidently, they were the first reminded of a flatiron and gave its subsequent popular name.

Nautical tropes, perhaps also like *skyscraper* itself, were then popular to describe tall buildings. Some likened the Flatiron to the prow of an ocean liner with Broadway and Fifth Avenue shaping its hull. Photographer Alfred Stieglitz wrote that, viewing the Flatiron from the park of Madison Square, the Flatiron "appeared to be moving toward me like the bow of a monster ocean steamer—a picture of new America still in the making."[36] This image was also celebrated in the impressionist manner by Edward J. Steichen in his famous photo, *The Flatiron Building—Evening* (1905). John Sloan painted the Flatiron in *Dust Storm* (1906) (the area was notorious for the dust blown up from the streets). Other artists in other styles pictured the new building time and again in its first decades. The Flatiron became a symbol of the city in national popular culture and its image was engraved on postcards, stamped on silver spoons, tranferred on china plates, and appeared on other souveniers. Berenice Abbott also notably photographed the Flatiron in 1936, while its fame lingered on.

The street corner at the prow of the Flatiron Building was famous as the City's best spot for girl-watching from 1902 to about 1920 and spawned a spurious lexical tale. The old slang phrase *twenty-three skiddoo,* which was popular from the 1890s to about 1910, is traditionally but falsely associated with an environmental and social phenomenon at Flatiron corner. The construction of the Flatiron in 1902 created down-drafts at the corner of 23rd Street, which New Yorkers have fluttered in for ninety years. The famous "Flatiron breezes" sometimes blew up women's long skirts to the delight of male gawkers. A ditty of the period, no doubt popular with mothers, went: "The Devil sends the wind to blow our skirts knee-high,/But God sends the dust to blow in the bad man's eye." Cartoons, postcards, photographs, and humor about the spectacle of exposed ankles and knees made the corner even more famous, even in Europe. In 1905 Crescent Films produced a risqué little flicker called *The Flatiron Building on a Windy Day*. The Flatiron corner was one of the must-see sights of the city until after the First World War when skirts went up on their own.

The clutches of men standing in the sheltered doorways and on the corner watching the show created a nuisance at times and police had to shoo them away, so the story has it, with the expression *twenty-three skiddoo!* The *twenty-three* supposedly derived from the name of 23rd Street where they stood and were shooed away from. The story, which is still told today, is not true. The phrase was popular before the Flatiron was built in 1902 and the numeral 23 probably was an 1890s catch-phrase of stage or newspaper origin and, in any event, of wholly other associations.

Men did hang out on the corner at the Flatiron and, apparently, specially assigned police did chase them away, quite possibly now and then with the expression *skiddoo*. In a roundabout way, *skiddoo* probably derives from the older *skedaddle,* 'get away,' which was variegated to *skadoodle,* and then shortened to *skiddoo.* The critic Benjamin De Casseres wrote that the Flatiron corner as late as the 1920s was "on a windy day ... the bald-headed row in the vaudeville show of New York life."[37] This ritual aspect of Flatiron corner, I suspect, was continuous with the popularity of the blow-hole theater at Coney Island, which sanctioned the scene of ballooning skirts and feigned surprise for the entertainment of men and women alike.

On April 17, 1907, John Sloan wrote in his diary, "A high wind this morning and the pranks of the gusts about the Flatiron Building at Fifth Avenue and 23rd St. was [sic] interesting to watch. Women's skirts flapped over their heads and ankles were to be seen. And a funny thing, a policeman to keep men from loitering about the corner. His position is much sought, I suppose."[38] The fashion in skirts had just cleared the ground in 1905, but were not above the ankles until about 1913. Sloan was drawn to the spot, and on July 15, 1908, he wrote, "A beautiful day and the breezes about the Flatiron Building show the beautiful forms of the women in their summer gowns. There are so many lovely women in New York and they dress so very charmingly, I'd like to spend hours watching them."[39]

The Social Meaning of Tall Buildings

The skyscraper, more than any other symbol of the metropolitan center, inspired popular ideas, aesthetic criticism, and intellectual interpretation. A variety of popular expressions, including the word *skyscraper* itself, is also part of the mythology—the romantic, prideful, dubious, even frightening idea of reaching for the sky. The skyline and cityscape created by the sky-scrapers, moreover, inspired an elaborate popular, journalistic, and literary metaphor expressed in a vocabulary that compared New York and its tall buildings to the rock country of the American West.

Observers of the city's skyline from the harbor, or of the tall buildings rising from the city streets, tended to be divided in their aesthetic judgment and intellectual interpretation according to how they felt about the very idea of the modern, capitalist city. More matter-of-fact observers either disap-proved of the new heights and feared the building trend would "shut out the sky," or they simply found the tall buildings thrilling symbols of "progress." On the eve of the skyscraper period in 1878, Walt Whitman was already thrilled by the "cloud touching edifices" of "tall topt Manhattan." But most literary observers, like William Dean Howells and Henry James, found the view troublesome. In *The American Scene,* James described the skyline as a "pin cushion in profile," the "huge jagged city," and a "colossal hair-comb turned upward, and so deprived of half its teeth."[40]

The new skyline was also much criticized by literary-left political sensi-bilities, especially by Europeans, and it has never let up. Maxim Gorki, the Russian playwright who visited New York in 1906, decried the ugliness of the "twenty-story houses" and "dark soundless skyscrapers" and generally found in New York the most base expressions of capitalism.[41] Politically minded Americans also saw symbolized in skyscrapers—and the skyline they created—the egotism and greed of capitalist society and the imbalance of corporate power in a democracy; the skyscraper stood for nothing more than the worship of the almighty dollar. Indeed, the management of Cass Gilbert's Gothic-style Woolworth Building, one of the tallest skyscrapers of the time, proudly adopted the nickname "Cathedral of Commerce" in 1917. Popular Freudianism did not fail, either, to see the skyscrapers as giant phallic symbols, making the connection among sex, money, and power, as well as reminding of the rapaciousness of the robber barons and of their corporate successors.

The urban historian Sam Bass Warner has written about the tensions between two cultural readings of the skyscraper and the new urban skyline they made.[42] The oldest meaning conveys the mythology, as Roland Barthes might have called it, that human works and Nature are in harmony. This image of the city is rooted in the civic pride of merchant capitalists and the public who echoed and affirmed the ideology. Several generations of artists in the eighteenth and nineteenth century encoded their portrayals of the urban skyline with various signs that reveal the prevailing ideology of their time. Warner's other major reading of the giant vertical shafts is as a symbol of corporate power that poses a problem of dominance in democratic society.

Twentieth-century skyline artists and photographers, unconsciously responding to the prevailing myth of their time, artistically resolved the conflict between capitalist and democratic elements of contemporary ideology by dissolving a troublesome social fact into a traditional aesthetic object, "cleaning it," and returning it to the older notion of civic pride. The modern skyline and its skyscrapers early in this century were portrayed by painters and photographers in ways that stressed the harmony of economy and civil society. Impressionist renderings of about 1900 dissolved into cubistic images of the cityscape after about 1914. Abstract images, as Peter Conrad has also noted, "clean" the city.[43] I will also add to Warner's thought that later art images in the Machine Age of the 1920s and 1930s also ideologically cleaned the city. The Precisionists Charles Demuth, Stuart Davis, Niles Spencer, Georgia O'Keeffe, Charles Sheeler, and Louis Lozowick suggested that the city was a beautiful, clean, shining machine and so otherwise an object of modernity and civic pride.

Yet the capitalist skyscraper is a prosaic, utilitarian thing. The urban geographer Jean Gottman (who set New York at the center of his concept of "Megalopolis") argues that the modern skyscraper is nothing more than a highly rational structure to facilitate contact and communication—the perfect machine for a "transactional society."[44] Gottman also reminds us that it was no accident that the early ones were built by insurance companies, which are enterprises particularly dependent on generating and exchanging information. An even more basic interpretation has to do with the economics of urban land use. Skyscrapers are economically rational structures, up to certain heights and varying with time and place, which reflect the market for office space. The skyscraper can symbolize many different things to many people, and it has.

The Canyons of the New Metropolis

The word *cityscape,* an Americanism and possibly a New York word from the late 1850s, is modeled on *landscape,* a much older term. The city planner Charles Abrams defined *cityscape* as "the urban equivalent of a landscape—the shape a city (or one of its parts) presents to the eye, particularly from a distance."[45] *Cityscape* appeared in the language at mid-century with the rise of the popular, journalistic, and sometimes literary image of the modern city as a skyline of tall buildings. The word *skyline* means the horizon of earth and sky, a line made jagged by natural objects, such as mountains, hills, trees, rocks, but, in the city, by the jut of buildings. Perhaps the first effort to capture the image of the New York skyline in a photograph was published in *Harper's Weekly* on August 11, 1894. According to historian John Kouwenhoven, "The first use of the word 'skyline' in a picture title seems to have been in Hearst's New York *Journal,* May 3, 1896, which included as a pictorial supplement a panoramic drawing of 'The Skyline of New York' by Charles Graham."[46] The observation in the years around 1900 that the New Metropolis had a skyline, a cityscape, an urban silhouette, prompted the thought that the appearance of the modern city was at one with, or perhaps a parody of, the works of Nature.

An elaborate trope of the cityscape arose in popular speech after about 1890 and accompanied the building of the early skyscrapers. The metaphor was much fueled by, or possibily originated in, journalism, literature, and art. The analogy of cityscape and landscape was extended to compare the new appearance of the artificial city with the popular image of western rock country by means of the vocabulary of natural topography. Even before the building of skyscrapers, the analogy between cityscape and landscape came easily to the reflectful eye. Herman Melville in his poem "The House-Top: A Night Piece" (1863), looking out over the city, wrote: "Beneath the stars the roofy desert spreads/Like Libya . . . ."

City streets, imaged with tall buildings on both sides, were called *canyons* and *concrete canyons,* as well as other names that compared the city with the American Southwest. *Canyon* was especially popular down to about 1930 and was a direct lexical response to the newness and impressiveness of the tall buildings. The slang name *cliff dwellers* for people living in tall apartment houses was part of this elaborate trope. The imagery of canyons was most often used to evoke the feel of the narrow streets of New York's financial district where so many of the early skyscrapers were built.

The figure of speech reflected and influenced popular consciousness of the big city and colored its social meaning. The trope is now rarely heard among urbanites jaded by tall buildings, except now and then in the expression "canyons of Wall Street."

A city street, particularly one with drinking establishments, was less admiringly but more humorously called a *gulch,* as though it were a ravine. The humor might be etymologically deep throat. *Gulch* in roundabout ways is probably related to *gulley, gullet,* and *gulp. Gulch* is also an old slang term for a drunkard, a "throat"; a *gulley,* a small gulch, is apparently a variant of *gullet.* The extended urban meaning of *gulch,* a slangier synonym of *canyon,* can be construed to have the delightful double meanings of a street and of drinking. Though Times Square was famous for its river of wine, theatrical people called it *Orange Juice Gulch* because, writes show biz lexicographer Don B. Wilmeth, "of the large number of fruit-juice stands that were there."[47]

Yet other popular, journalistic, and literary usages elaborated the idea of the New York cityscape as comparable to the Great West. The tall office buildings and apartment houses, after all, were faced with natural stone. Stephen Crane, in his newspaper piece about riding a cable car in Manhattan, wrote of New York streets as "these jungles of men and vehicles, these cañons of streets, these lofty mountains of iron and cut stone—a ride through them affords plenty of excitement. And no lone panther's howl is more serious in intention than the howl of the truck driver when the cable car bumps one of his rear wheels."[48]

The urban canyons were also spoken of as *gorges.* Crane's cable car "enters the gorge made by the towering walls of the great shops." Henry James wrote of "gorges of masonry." Few writers about the New Metropolis seemed able to resist the temptation to call the towering walls *cliffs* ("cyclopean cliffs, crowded canyons," a magazine of the period gushed). Or the silhouette of the skyline reminded writers of a *range* of mountains. William Dean Howells in the early 1890s wrote that "these edifices swaggering upward unnumbered stories, look like detached cliffs in some broken and jagged mountain range."[49] O. Henry in "The Caliph, Cupid and the Clock" (1906) wrote: "The moon was just clearing the roofs of the range of dwellings." Mountain ranges have *passes* through which travelers can pass. Albert Halper in *Union Square* (1933) repeatedly wrote of the "passes" and "steep canyons" where the police gathered like hostile Indians to charge and attack political demonstrators in Union Square.

Tall buildings with flat tops were called *mesas,* though *butte* would have been truer to geographical terminology, and some writers did use *butte.* Early in this century, the poet James Oppenheim in "New York, From A Skyscraper" wrote of a "Plateau of roofs by canyons crossed." But more often the reference was to the *asphalt mesas,* the streets of New York in, as it were, concrete canyons. Here, too, the figure of speech is not true to geography. A mesa is either a plateau or a plain, but never the floor of a canyon.

Truer to the image of a canyon, which might have a river running through it, we all speak of the "streams of traffic" that "flow" through the city streets, as through canyons. The newspapers that "wing" whole through New York streets, we might concede, are urban tumbleweed that is blown, rolling through concrete canyons. The western image can be stretched yet further with the utter coincidence that *potholes* in city streets take their name from the natural phenomenon of rounded depressions in the rock of a stream bed, such as might flow through a canyon. And, as we saw in an earlier chapter, thirsty urbanites in dry times roam these canyons in search of *watering holes,* if only in Orange Juice Gulch.

The popularity of these Western word images of New York in the decades around 1900 also sprang from the public's interest in the vast Western landscape and the development of the National Park System and several National Monuments of great Western imagery. Millions in the east had stereotypical images of the West from photography and travel writers and extended these ideas to their urban surroundings. New Yorkers surely mused on these images and wondered how their own city related to the great scheme of things.

But the metaphor was mostly a bit of urban gaiety in language, a fashionable figure of speech, to express the notion that New York, which is not to be surpassed in anything at all, has its own version of the much-admired Western landscape, and that the big city is every bit as wild and woolly. A related metaphor in New York humor writing of the same period had New York as a "Wild West" where one "roughed it," dodging rampaging bull-vehicles on one hand and bandits on the other. Not much has changed since.

O. Henry in "Thimble, Thimble" (1909) briefly exploited the whole thing: "You follow the Broadway Trail down until you pass the Crosstown Line [14th Street], the Bread Line [11th Street], and the Dead Line [Fulton Street], and you come to the Big Cañons, of the Moneygrubber Tribe. Then you turn to the left, to the right, dodge a push-cart and the tongue of a two-ton four-horse dray, and hop, skip, and jump to a granite ledge on the side of a twenty-one-story synthetic mountain of stone and iron."

PART III

The Shadow Worlds of Social Class in City Life

6

Mean
Streets

*I find letters from God dropt in the street, and
every one is sign'd/ by God's name . . .*
WALT WHITMAN, "Song of Myself"

The old expression *mean streets* signifies the
worlds of urban poverty. It is another term that takes the trope of city streets,
with all its negative connotations, to stand for exposure to the cruelties of
poverty. The meanings of *mean streets* emerged primarily with reference to
the nineteenth-century classic slums of English and American cities and to
an older type of skid row of transient but employable men. In this century its
meaning was transferred to the poverty of utter despair, to the crime, violence, and drugs in black and Latino ghettos, and to the condition of homeless and often mentally ill men and women on American city streets. Mean
streets is the thought behind this chapter mainly in the older sense of Manhattan's classic slums and the intersecting social worlds of transient and often
homeless men and women on the Bowery.

The old skid rows and surrounding poor neighborhoods attracted certain businesses that catered to the special needs and wants of these popula-
tions. In historical New York, these activities were concentrated on the
Bowery, from Chatham Square up to Cooper Square, and in the mix of
surrounding areas, chiefly Chinatown and the variety of East Side ethnic
neighborhoods. Old Hell's Kitchen on the West Side and the Gas House
District on the East Side were similar neighborhoods. The stresses and requirements of hand-to-mouth ways of life prompted a great deal of pejorative naming of the particulars of these social worlds. Middle-class social
worlds sometimes touched the worlds of the down and out, either directly
through intersections of their cultures or vicariously through realistic fiction
and the newspapers. In these ways the lexical culture of the poor diffused
into the city's popular speech of those days.

Slums and ghettos in the several decades around 1900, however impoverished, were communities based on family life and ethnic neighborhood,
more or less permanent residence, and nearby employment, no matter how
marginal or interrupted. Skid rows, inhabited mostly by unattached and
homeless men and a few women, were usually close to the slums. In the late
nineteenth century, every large American city that was a hub of regional
labor migration developed these gathering places for migrant and seasonal

workers who came into town to look for work through the employment agencies or to put up for the winter. These districts were marked by a concentration of low saloons, cheap eating places, cheap lodging houses, and pawn shops. The early skid rows, not unlike the social reality of the nearby slums, were functioning, semi-autonomous communities with a distinctive culture, folklore, and language of the men and women who made up their floating population.

From Skid *Road* to Skid *Row*

The story of *skid row* starts in Seattle, moves to Chicago where it was greatly elaborated, and finally takes on one of its several local versions in New York. *Skid road,* later to be skid *row,* originated, all authorities agree, in the logging towns of the Pacific Northwest. The first urban neighborhood of transient men to be called *Skid Road* was in Seattle along Yesler Way, a street now in that city's preserved historical district. The early form, *skid road,* is still preferred by purists of local usage, not least because it recalls the social and industrial history of the region. In logging jargon of the 1880s, a skid way or skid road was a greased, corduroy track of saplings over which logs were skidded toward water to be floated to sawmills.

Around 1915 *skid road* was extended to mean the area of a town with cheap bars, eating places, and sleeping houses to which loggers drifted for entertainment or when they were out of work. Arrival on skid road implied that these men were on their way down to, or at least flirting with, dissipation and yet further decline—going on the skids. By the 1930s the term had moved eastward and was extended to denote the run-down section of any city where homeless and unemployed men congregated. By 1940 the predominant form had shifted to skid *row,* using the old phrase-forming device -*row* to denote the concentration of special social and business activities along certain city streets.

The subculture of the transient unemployed, including some of its lexical culture, came to public attention in the 1870s with the perception of the "tramp evil" following the economic depression of 1873. Even when prosperity returned in 1878, the upheaval had prompted a new way of life, wandering in search of work and hitching rides on the newly expanded railway system. The big cities spawned large numbers of young tramps and hoboes in the wake of the industrial conflicts and business cycles of the 1880s and 1890s. In 1893, one estimate set the number of tramps in the nation at nearly 46,000, or one percent of the male labor force. Skid rows of large cities, including New York, became communities of tramps and hoboes, some of them settling into permanent residence there. By 1900 the national tramp and hobo culture was full-blown and their argot was leaking into urban popular speech.

The rise and decline of skid rows in American cities occurred through three discernible periods, and these generalizations are no less true of New York's Bowery.[1] The first period, the great hobo era whose heyday was around 1900, was from about 1880 to the First World War. The noun *hobo*, first recorded in 1889, and the verb *to hobo*, recorded in 1906, are of this period. The origin of *hobo* is uncertain, though etymologists have advanced several hypotheses.[2] For example, it might be from the greeting "Ho, boy!," an occupational cry of northwestern railway mail handlers in the 1880s. By 1900 *hobo* was clipped to *'bo* or *bo* and it was so used by Jack London and Josiah Flynt, both chroniclers of hobo life ways. The hoboes in this period were chiefly young men looking for work or putting up between seasonal employment. Hoboes called the thoroughfare of skid road the *main drag* or *main stem*, that is, the main street of their world. Josiah Flynt said of the Bowery in 1900: "This is the most notorious tramp-nest in the United States."[3] The tramps then called the city *York* for short.

The second period was from about 1920 to 1940 when the population of migrant laborers began giving away to aimless, unemployed men noted for their drinking and shiftlessness. The terms *skid road* and, especially, *skid row* diffused into general use in the 1930s. When the form of the expression, probably in Chicago, shifted to the now predominant skid *row,* it also lost its thought of logging and the Pacific Northwest.[4] The prophecy in the metaphor of *skid road* or *skid row* was fulfilled in the complete transformation of these neighborhoods during the Great Depression of the 1930s. E. Y. Harburg and Jay Gorney's 1932 song, "Brother, Can You Spare a Dime?," expressed the shock and pathos of mass unemployment.

The third period was from about 1941 to 1960 when skid rows became smaller, less dense, and the men became older, less mobile, and more indigent. Alcoholics, drug addicts, and the physically and mentally handicapped became more frequent among them. The "community-care" programs that released many custodial patients from mental institutions in the 1960s and 1970s increased the numbers of homeless men and, now, women on city streets. Skid row has become more of a dispersed social condition than a distinctive place and community, and this is no less true of the Bowery.

New York journalists in the nineteenth century, as a stunt to generate quick stories for a public hungry for tales of the underside of the cities, posed for a few hours or a day as a tramp, as a street beggar, standing in breadlines, or sleeping a night in a flop house. Even Walt Whitman, in his early newspaper days, humorously wrote of a night spent in a male lodging house where he was kept awake by five or six snorers. The classic study of the homeless man in social science is Nels Anderson's *The Hobo*, published in 1923, about Chicago's skid row. In the tradition of London's Henry Mayhew and Charles Booth and of New York's Jacob Riis, Anderson's study is a disciplined version of the intellectual slumming in cities made famous by Jack London and Josiah Flynt and later by England's George Orwell.

Anderson, among others, called the hobo community *Hobohemia,* a blend of *hobo* and *bohemia.* Skid rows were usually close to the bohemian quarter in a city's low-rent zone. Chicago's area of homeless men intersected the city's bohemia, or the artists' quarter called Tower Town. New York's Bowery was similarly near the city's traditional bohemia—Greenwich Village. By 1917 *hobohemia* had been used by Sinclair Lewis in his fiction to criticize the pretentious artistic life of Greenwich Village. *Hobohemia* eventually entered popular speech also in the sense of the raffish yet stylish underside of the city. In Lorenz Hart's song "The Lady Is a Tramp" (1937), a line goes: "My Hobohemia is the place to be."

Other than the name *skid row* itself, the name of New York's *Bowery,* not the proper name of either Chicago's Halsted or Madison Street, became the nation's popular generic for a skid row, the social meaning of a real place projected onto other similar places.

Anderson drew a sharp distinction between three types of homeless men—the hobo, the tramp, and the bum—all of whom were in these districts. He liked the definition: "The hobo works and wanders, the tramp dreams and wanders and the bum drinks and wanders."[5] A popular saying put it more cruelly: "A hobo will work, a tramp won't, a bum can't." Hoboes sometimes ceased to work and became tramps and some took to drink and descended to bums. The relative representation of hoboes, tramps, and bums on skid row at different times during its history remarkably corresponds to each of its three successive periods; these three classes of men and women are the human correlates of the decline of the place of skid row.

The word *tramp* has been traced in English back to the 1660s but was not used in the United States until the 1880s. *Bum* is an Americanism of the 1860s and probably came about by shortening its predecessor *bummer*. In 1872 James D. McCabe, Jr. described at length the *bummer* as a New York street type; he also used the new slang names of their middle-class counterparts who renege on cab fares: " 'slouches,' 'bums,' and 'beats.' "[6] The quintessential bum in American popular speech is the alliterative *Bowery bum*. This expression has the popping sounds that often connote pejoration in speech.

Skid rows, as a distinct community and culture, tend to take on certain common institutional characteristics. The Bowery had a classic concatenation of skid-row businesses along its length. These included multiple cheap restaurants, barber colleges, fortune tellers, missions, saloons, cigar stores, cheap clothing stores, drug stores, cheap hotels, gambling houses, and employment agencies.

Skid rows usually had a row of employment agencies called the *slave market* for a bitter comment on the low wages and exploitation offered and hard to refuse there. Nearby green parks were often taken over by hoboes, tramps, and bums, much to the annoyance of local families. Union Square, Madison Square, and until recently Bryant Park still serve as *bum parks;* in the 1930s such a park in Harlem was locally called *Scratch Park*. In 1868 James McCabe, denoting park-bench sleepers as *benchers,* wrote that "the only method our Metropolitans [police] understand of arousing a man is by beating a réveille on his feet with a club."[7] By 1900 *bench warmers* awakened in this crude manner said they had been *fanned*. By the 1920s the sitting offender was also called a *free bencher,* perhaps prompted by *freeloader,* which seemed to express public resentment of their occupancy of taxpayers' benches.

Skid rows traditionally had a speakers' corner, usually in or at the edge of a public park. New York's best known *Bughouse Square* was Union Square. It collected Hobohemia's full array of characters who had something to say, or who wanted to listen. A *soap-box* speaker in Union Square was called a *spouter* by the 1920s; a *soap box,* a meaning transferred from the soap box he stood on to the speech he made, was any such street-corner speech. The Union Square neighborhood and its mix of diverse lives, including political events in the Square itself, was treated atmospherically in Albert Halper's "proletarian" novel *Union Square* (1933).

Open spaces of no formal use became sites of outdoor squatter settlements, camps, and social centers. Yet another sense of the urban *jungle* (see Chapter 2) was employed here to denote the squatter settlements where hoboes slept, ate, and lived. In the 1930s, Camptown was one such in-town jungle that sprang up in Hell's Kitchen on 38th Street, between Tenth and Eleventh avenues. Others were in various vacant lots and open spaces; Reginald Marsh pictorially treated one in his 1934 etching *East Tenth Street Jungle,* a squalid, violent hell of homeless men. Jungles also appeared on the edges of smaller towns and cities and were sardonically called *suburbs*.

Tramps often walked the city streets at night, for the police harassed those who settled in doorways and alleyways. *To carry the banner,* meaning to walk the streets all night and used in accounts of Bowery life, may have been introduced from British tramp's argot. "I with the figurative emblem hoisted went out to see what I could see," wrote Jack London in *The People of the Abyss* (1903), his book about the down and out of London. The expression seems to be an ironic extension of banner-carrying at political-protest meetings and marches for unpopular causes—such as unionization or socialism.

Standing in a breadline, a soup line, or a bed line are other popular images of the poor and unemployed. Affluent New Yorkers first became dimly aware of mass urban poverty about 1830 and began to make charitable gestures. Such lines for charitable dispensation did not become an object of great public awareness until the 1840s. The aftermath of the Civil War and the onset of severe business cycles caused even more highly visible unemployment in the cities. *Soup lines* formed outside charitable *soup kitchens,* the latter term first recorded in 1851. In this century Albert Halper in *Union Square* wrote of one of his characters who "passed a few soup-lines and saw men shoving and arguing to keep their places. The line went raggedly around two corners, like a long, disjointed tapeworm."[8]

Down and out men in the 1890s lined up to get a place to sleep in one of the charitable shelters, especially in winter. One of the best known *bed lines* in New York of that period was a private appeal. The miserable line formed nightly in Madison Square and was described by way of resolving the fate of Drouet in Theodore Dreiser's *Sister Carrie* (1900). O. Henry a few years later in "A Madison Square Arabian Night" also wrote of men standing in "bed lines." A *mission stiff* was a man who regularly frequented the charitable missions of skid row in search of food and shelter, standing in the bed lines, soup lines, and breadlines.

The phrase *breadline,* an Americanism, was popularized and given its modern meaning in New York in the late 1890s. In *The Color of a Great City,* Theodore Dreiser recalled a scene from about 1894 of a breadline of several hundred men that formed every night to collect day-old bread from a bakery on Broadway near Grace Church. "And now it is a sight, an institution, like a cathedral or a monument," wrote Dreiser of the sorry spectacle.[9] He was referring to the famous breadline at Fleischmann's Vienna Model

FIGURE 10. Charles Broughton. *A New York Charity—Distributing Bread at Tenth Street and Broadway after Midnight.* The scene is at the backdoor of Fleischmann's Vienna Bakery whose practice of feeding the unemployed and homeless in the 1890s imparted the modern meaning to the term *breadline. Harper's Weekly,* December 17, 1892. (*Collection of the author*)

Bakery on Broadway at 10th Street; he recounted it by name in the last chapter of *Sister Carrie*. The actual line formed at midnight on 10th Street, starting at the side door of the Bakery, and stretched from just east of Broadway over to Fourth Avenue. Though breadlines had been a common sight in New York for many years, the Fleischmann's breadline in the 1890s established the phrase in American English.

Louis Fleischmann, the bakery's owner, began the private charity in the 1890s and it was continued for several years after his death in 1904. Incidentally, the Fleischmann fortune was used by his heir to establish *The New Yorker* in the 1920s. Fleischmann's breadline was also made famous by pictorial treatments and commentary in magazines and newspapers. Albert Bigelow Paine's novel *The Breadline: A Story of A Paper* (1899) and his short story, "The Bread Line," in McClure's in 1900 are the first known uses of the phrase in print. The novel is a literary "round" that begins and ends in the breadline at Fleischmann's. O. Henry soon spoke of "bread lines" in his New York stories. Years later Reginald Marsh rendered scenes of lines of depressed men in his etchings *Breadline* (1929) and *Breadline—No One Has Starved* (1932).

Low Establishments

The businesses that cater to the creature needs of the poor, the marginal, the homeless, and also of ordinary working men and women are places to eat, to drink, and then to sleep, and sometimes pawnshops to get quick cash. Urban folk speech has elaborated names for these places and their associated activities, not least because they are the establishments that most negatively symbolize the most stressful aspects of the hand-to-mouth existence. Few if any slang names denote schools, churches, hospitals, and other institutions in the same neighborhoods that were seen as supportive rather than exploitative. Slang sometimes serves a pejorative function in social discourse and may be interpreted as a kind of social criticism by the poor and down-and-out.

The generic names for these seemingly exploitative businesses express the bitterness and resignation, sometimes expressed in derision, of the people dependent on them to keep body and soul together. Simple moral oppositions are frequent in the lexicon and articulate the keen awareness of the difference between the haves and the have-nots. Many of the terms originated in the loosely connected subcultures of hoboes, tramps, and generally the poor. Other names were coined by ordinary working people, usually with less resentment, for the places they frequented in their everyday lives. All these social strata and groups borrowed useful terms from one another. These words expressed the commonalities of their urban experience, and some of the terms diffused into general slang. Locutions borrowed from down-and-outs served middle-class people to disparage facilties they considered unworthy of their patronage by means of making an association of a thing with the lower classes. They could irritably or humorously label a restaurant a *greasy spoon,* a hotel a *flea bag,* or a bar a *gin mill*. The more arcane the subcultural borrowings the greater the cachet of the term.

Joints, Dives, Holes, and Dumps

Many of the semi-public places associated with mean streets and, in the next chapter, with the sporting life were named in popular speech according to their social level and type. The names, taken together, make up a word map and social model of low establishments in the nineteenth-century industrial city. Many of the denotations are compound phrases that use the terms *-joint* and *-dive,* and sometimes *-hole, -dump,* and *-trap*. Each of these elements also occurs alone as a noun. A social status hierarchy is implicit in the aggregate of places so named; a vertical, spatial hierarchy also underlies the several terms. Joints and dives, generally, are better (higher) places than holes and dumps; joints are usually better (more elevated) places than dives; and even holes (sometimes to the side as *holes in the wall*) are a step up from dumps, though this tempts the reader to think of many exceptions. *Joint* and *dive* in particular occur so frequently that their word histories warrant a further note.

The Oxford English Dictionary's earliest citation for *joint* for an enclosed urban place is American slang and dated 1883. Earlier and more generally a joint was a coming together, a meeting. Eventually *joint* came to denote the place of such a meeting. *Joint* appeared first in underworld cant where it often denoted a meeting place of criminals for illegal activities, but the expression soon spread into slang where it has persisted in more general senses. Before about 1950, *joint* was most often applied to eating houses, bars, and nightclubs, though today it is applied, with only slight pejoration, to virtually any place. John O'Hara used it repeatedly in *Pal Joey* (1940). Actor George Raft, who was raised in Hell's Kitchen early in this century, always pronounced it "jernt" in the movies. John Ciardi summarized that *"joint* came into slang originally with the sense 'place where things meet': What I didn't learn at my mother's knee, I picked up at other low joints."[10]

Dive, as its meaning evolved, first specified a drinking place in a basement and came to mean any socially low-down place, regardless of its physical level. *Dive* in this sense seems to have originated in American English by the late 1860s, quite possibly in New York, for a drinking place located a flight down from street level. In 1869 the pseudonymous George Ellington in *The Women of New York* wrote of young prostitutes "in such company as grace Chatham Street 'dives.' "[11] The term probably was in use by the mid or even early 1860s. In 1872, George Crapsey in *The Nether Side of New York* also used it in inverted commas, which suggests that it was still considered new: "And here let me explain that in detective parlance every

FIGURE 11. John Sloan. *Bandits Cave* (1920). "Uptown thrill seekers . . . about to venture into a basement 'tea room' in Bohemia," Sloan wrote of this Greenwich Village scene set in the first year of Prohibition. That era revived *speakeasy*, an Americanism of the 1880s, and invigorated the use of *dive*, an Americanism of the 1860's. *Dive* originally denoted a disreputable drinking place, often in a basement, that one figuratively "dived" into, as though to escape public view. (Courtesy of Delaware Art Museum)

foul place is a 'dive,' whether it be a cellar or garret, or neither.[12] Wentworth and Flexner's *Dictionary of American Slang* summarized that a *dive* is "a disreputable, cheap, low-class establishment or public place, esp[ecially] a bar, dance-hall, nightclub or the like; a place of bad repute." The *OED* defines *dive* in the U.S. as "an illegal drinking-den, or other disreputable place of resort, often situated in a cellar, basement, or other half-concealed place, into which frequenters may 'dive' without observation."

Key in the notion of a dive is its physical as well as its social lowness. *Dive* in its subterranean senses is nascent in descriptions in New York in the 1840s and 1850s and reflected the arrangement, uses, and the social meaning of local architecture. Manhattan townhouse architecture, influenced by the Dutch colonists, usually had a ground floor half a flight down from street level and a parlor floor at the top of a high stoop. When commercial activity invaded residential neighborhoods in the rapidly changing city, the ground floor of former private family houses was often given over to a restaurant or drinking place, often a so-called oyster cellar or, more euphemistically, oyster saloon. High elevation in "tall" buildings meant privacy and high status; street-level space was associated with semi-public, usually respectable commercial establishments. Low commercial activities, such as dives, were in basements below the street level into which one "dived," and not usually for oysters. But, as Crapsey wrote, a dive would be any foul place, regardless of its elevation.

After *dive, hole* is fairly obvious. The earliest citation of a related sense in the *OED* is 1483. The term is defined as "a secret place, a hiding-place; a secret room in which an unlawful occupation is pursued." By 1616, a *hole* was "a small dingy lodging or abode; a small or mean habitation; an unpleasant place of abode; a term of contempt or depreciation of any place." Wentworth and Flexner define a *hole* as "any small, dirty, crowded public place." Significantly, the city's subway is called *the hole,* at least by the people who work in it.

Hole in the wall is a singularly urban and very old expression of British origin. It is still widely used for any small, dirty, unpleasant place, especially a residence or place of business. Either one of two hypotheses might best account for the term. One says it derives from the holes in the walls of old English debtors' prisons through which inmates received gifts of food, drink, and money. The other attributes it to the warrens of shops and hovels that were once imbedded in massive medieval city walls. The name long has been popular in American English to disparage small dives and other establishments. In the 1860s 'The Hole in the Wall' was actually the name of a low resort on Water Street at the corner of Dover, one of the most violent and notorious dives in the city. The proprietor was Gallus Mag, a huge Englishwoman who bit the ears off obstreperous customers and kept these bits of flesh preserved in a pickle jar behind the bar.

Dump, the lowest of any sort of place, is even more disparaging by the equation of an establishment with a place for the deposit of refuse. *Dump* for a low lodging or eating house was in use by 1899 and this sense may have originated in U.S. tramp's slang. The term soon came to mean about any sort of low commercial establishment, including low dives. Around 1900 one such joint at No. 9 Bowery was actually called 'The Dump' and was a rotten hangout for panhandlers as well as a flophouse. Wentworth and Flexner write that the "most common use" of *dump* is for "any unattractive, cheap, shabby, or wretched house, apartment, hotel, theatre, or the like; a joint" or, less often, as "any building," irrespective of its quality. By the 1920s or so working-class teenagers in New York were using *dump* for their parents' low-status households, which they so fervently wished to escape.

A dump was more than just a metaphor for low places. Jacob Riis described and photographed people who lived in the refuse dumps at Rivington Street on the East Side and on West 47th Street. Women and children, who picked bones and sorted rags, were found living at some of the dumps, a condition we associate a century later only with the refuse pickers of Manila, Cairo, and Mexico City. Whole rag-picker families worked on the garbage scows and lived under the wooden chutes used to convey refuse from carts down to the scows. Indeed, the word *chute* itself was also a disparaging word for a disliked place that dispensed food and drink, as though garbage, in a rough and indifferent manner. *Trap*, in certain senses not unlike those of *chute*, was similarly used for any place that congregated and intensified the most disliked features of any urban enclosure, such as a *flea-trap hotel*. All these terms were—and still are—applied ironically to better establishments to express disapproval of them.

Bad Eating Places. Eating places of every level called themselves "restaurants" by the 1850s, but city folk never bought this pretense of lesser establishments. The slang names for bad restaurants, as well as names for bad hotels, expressed acute consciousness of the collapse of the social boundary between clean and dirty. The key ideas that reoccur in slang names for low eating places are greasiness and dirtiness, fast and rough service, and the Hobson's choice of fried foods, especially hashes. The contemptuous, negative names drew a dual opposition between slop and appetizing food, greasy and clean food, and such as hash and prime food. These terms, thus, make an implicit comment on life in mean streets.

George W. Matsell recorded the tenor of the rough eating house in the 1850s when he listed *slap-bang*, "an eating-house; a restaurant." The ideas of grease and often dirtiness are also conveyed in *grease joint*, but today most commonly in *greasy spoon*, which has persisted in slang from the early 1920s. Only a *cockroach joint*, an exceedingly filthy eating place, is worse. The cockroach, an eminently urban creature and constant companion that even the poets have addressed, symbolizes both filth and low social status. A *cockroach business* is a small, mean enterprise, but not necessarily a dirty one.

Quite clean and even respectable restaurants were sometimes humorously named "Sloppy Joe's," "Sloppy John's," or "Sloppy" whoever was held to blame. Though in this context *sloppy* is not usually an earnest comment on the quality of the food or service. Yet a dubious place called The Slop Shop was once a restaurant for sailors near the Hudson River docks on West Street. The world's most famous of this naming order is New York's Sloppy Louie's at 92 South Street, the superb seafood restaurant near the corner of Fulton Street and just down the street from the old fish market—all now in the South Street Seaport historical district. Writer Joseph Mitchell told the story of Louis Morino who purchased the restaurant around 1930. The predecessor business had been called "Sloppy John's." When Morino took over, the fishmongers who came in to eat began calling it "Sloppy Louie's." Morino did not like the name, but finally relented and hung out a sign, "Sloppy Louie's," and the landmark restaurant is so called to this day.[13] The men of skid rows had less humor about the idea of slop when they coined similar names for bad restaurants. The graphic term *slop joint* and occasionally *slop chute* became generic of a certain kind of restaurant whose name is its best description.

Early in this century *mulligan stew* symbolized the dish of the poor and humble and was commonly heard in New York speech. A *mulligan joint* was a low eating house. Lorenz Hart in his 1937 song "The Lady Is a Tramp" includes the line, "I've wined and dined on Mulligan stew," as a stylish constrast of plain and fancy. No one knows the origin of *mulligan*, though it is usually said to come from the surname of some long-forgotten Irish cook. *Hash* by the 1860s had become the word for all mean food, not just specifically the fried dish of chopped and sometimes leftover meat and vegetables. *Hash house* and *hashery* also appeared in the 1860s. A waiter in one of these *hash joints* was by 1880 called a *hash slinger*, which again conveys the idea of having a meal all but thrown at you. A character in Dos Passos's *Manhattan Transfer* said, "You put yer clothes on a[n] take a walk round the block to a hash joint an eat up strong."

Closely akin to hash were the new ethnic notes of chop suey, chow mein, chili, and spaghetti that appeared in the years around 1900. Eating places called *chili parlors* or *-joints, spaghetti joints,* and *chop suey joints,* or just *chop sueys,* appeared in poor neighborhoods and on skid rows in the first decade of this century; all were variants on the style and quality of the older hash joints. In the 1920s a *red-ink spot* or *-joint* (referring to cheap red wine) was any of the many small Italian restaurants in Greenwich Village that served a meal for 40 cents.

The name *chop suey* dates in print from 1888. Some stories place the invention of the dish and its name in San Francisco, others in New York, and both cities did in fact have the nation's largest Chinatowns of chiefly Cantonese immigrants. The name is from Cantonese *shap sui,* 'odds and ends,' where *shap* is "miscellaneous" and *sui* is 'bits.' The dish was the result of an effort to concoct an inexpensive commercial dish that would be palatable to non-Chinese Americans of indiscriminate taste; chop suey is Chinese hash. The term *chop suey* though became a synecdoche for the whole menu in these places; some people used to call any Chinese dish *chop suey*. Chop suey joints were also called *chow meineries* and, whatever their names, became popular with ordinary New Yorkers. By the 1930s chop suey joints were thriving even on Broadway at Times Square.

Low Drinking Places. Through the nineteenth century, low saloons were ubiquitous and concentrated near skid rows and tenement districts, as reformers knew well. Jacob A. Riis in *How the Other Half Lives* reported in 1890 that 4,065 of New York's 7,884 drinking places were below "the Line" of 14th Street. In addition, the city accommodated about 1,000 unlicensed saloons.[14] Other studies reported that in the 1890s there was one saloon for every 177 people—man, woman, and child. In one neighborhood on the East Side, within the 42-square-block area bounded by the Bowery and Essex Street and by East Houston and Hester streets, there were almost 300 licensed saloons, as many as fifteen to a square block and seven to a single block face. Small wonder that Stephen Crane could write in *Maggie* that "the open mouth of a saloon called seductively." One gaped from nearly every doorway.

A generic name for a Bowery saloon was *distillery*. Many more names of low dives and joints denote the kind of alcoholic beverage that is dispensed, such as *beer joint*. Early nineteenth-century terms were *rum shop, grog mill,* and *groggery*. Grog was originally a mixture of rum and water, but became a slang generic for any rough alcoholic beverage. *Gin mill* was in American speech by 1865 and is still much used for urban bars that cater to drifters and keep long hours. Gin mills were associated chiefly with the Irish, as beer halls were with the Germans, cafés with the Italians, and so on.

The hoboes spoke of gin mills as *skee joints*, from *-sky* in *whisky*. More generically, they spoke of *alky joints, juice joints,* and *boozeries*. The idea of the low bar room as a place where drink is swilled is heard in *guzzlery* or, slurred, *guzzery,* and in *guzzle shop*. The hoboes also named such places *lush drum* and later *lush dive* and *lush joint*. *Lush* is of unknown, late eighteenth-century origin and means alcoholic drink. *To lush* soon meant to drink heavily and by the 1880s a *lush* was an alcoholic person.

Low drinking places on the Bowery and nearby that dispensed especially poisonous brews and zombifying mixtures were called *morgues* or sometimes *dead houses*. One such saloon on the Bowery was actually named 'The Morgue.' The ominous names came from the popular notion that the drink served in these places worked equally well for drinking oneself into a stupor or for embalming a corpse. This notion may have been helped along by the popular story of how Admiral Nelson's body was shipped back to England from Trafalgar perfectly preserved in a cask of fortified sherry. A dead house on 18th Street in the Gashouse District dispensed their evil brew from a barrel on high shelf down through a rubber hose directly into the mouths of customers. For five cents, a drinker could consume all he could swallow before having to take a breath.

The *stale-beer dive* was a similar type of saloon that was photographed and much scorned by Jacob Riis. The name came about because the proprietors collected exhausted beer kegs from regular saloons, laced the flat dregs with various powerful intoxicants, and sold the admixture at a very low price. Riis's photo of the interior of a stale-beer dive shows customers who look not long for Potter's Field. Riis's words with equal vigor described the squalor of one of these places near the infamous Bend of Mulberry Street.

> Usually, as in this instance, it is in some cellar giving on a back alley. Doctored, unlicensed beer is its chief ware. Sometimes a cup of "coffee" and a stale roll may be had for two cents. The men pay the score. To the women—unutterable horror of the suggestion—the place is free. The beer is collected from the kegs put on the sidewalks by the saloon-keeper to await the brewer's cart, and it is touched up with drugs to put a froth on it. The privilege to sit all night on a chair, or sleep on a table, or in a barrel, goes with each round of drinks.[15]

The stale-beer dives disappeared around 1905 with the introduction of an improved beer pump that drained the keg dry. But low saloons on the Bowery later sold a poisonous distillate called *smoke*. Reginald Marsh's tempera *Smokehounds* (1934) shows a drinker of smoke collapsed on the sidewalk and being helped by his shaky friends under the el near No. 8 Bowery.

Black-and-tan dives was the late nineteenth-century name given to low saloons where black and white people mingled and drank together. An interracial saloon was a noteworthy and scandalous idea in those days and denoted a very low establishment. Black-and-tan dives were noted in New York as early as the 1860s but were not so called; apparently the first use of the term in this sense was in the 1880s. 'The Black-and-Tan' was the usual name of a concert hall at 153 Bleeker Street. The establishment featured, according to contemporary descriptions, scantily clad black dancing girls for the entertainment of its mostly white customers. New York Chief of Police George W. Walling wrote in his memoirs a variant account of the racial mix and their respective gender roles. "It would not be difficut to say where the Black-and-Tan got its name. It is the resort of black men as well as white, but the girls are all white!"[16] Jacob Riis wrote of other such places on nearby Thompson Street, then a black neighborhood: "The moral turpitude of Thompson Street has been notorious for years. . . . The border-land where the white and black races meet in common debauch, the aptly named black-and-tan saloon."[17]

The adjective and noun *black-and-tan* somehow gained two distinct meanings over the years, that of a mix of white and black and, on the other hand, that of a mix of light and dark complexioned African Americans.

Duke Ellington composed the jazz piece "Black & Tan Fantasy" in 1927, as well as "Black, Brown, and Beige" in 1943. Cab Calloway in his *Hepster's Dictionary,* first compiled in 1938, protested that the noun denoted "dark and light colored folks, not colored and white folks as erroneously assumed."[18] Yet from the 1880s the term has more often meant a low drinking place frequented by both blacks and whites and the later Harlem pattern in the 1920s of a place with black entertainers and a white audience. Other Harlem black-and-tans entertained men and women of both races. But the stigma of racial mixing remained and Harlem black-and-tans were known as places where white men "dealt in coal" and "changed their luck."

Low saloons on the Bowery and in tenement districts could be dangerous places for outsiders who might be sized up as profitable to rob. Vicious bartenders or other criminal persons sometimes gave victims a *mickey* or a *mickey finn,* that is, a dose of chloral hydrate in a drink. Rendered unconscious, the victim was then dragged into a back room, robbed and, if not murdered, put out in an alley to sleep off the potion. Many stories purportedly account for the names *mickey* and especially *mickey finn* for knock-out drops. The person of Mickey Finn (actually, an old generic name for any Irishman) is usually an unscrupulous bartender on the Barbary Coast of San Francisco, near the stockyards or on skid row in Chicago, or on the Bowery in New York. But the variant form mickey *flynn* for knock-out drops casts doubt on even his surname. The first recorded uses of *mickey* are around 1915, much later than most of the stories about the late nineteenth-century barkeeps. Alvin F. Harlow, writing in 1931 on the history of the Bowery, said that the practice of doping drinks in low saloons began around 1870 or before and continued for forty years, but was much exaggerated by writers of crime fiction and the newspapers.[19]

Saloons once dispensed beer in two-quart buckets or cans, known as *growlers,* to be consumed off-premises by working men on the job and by men and women in the tenements. Young boys and girls called *rushers* were hired *to rush the growler, to rush the can, to chase the can,* or sometimes in New York *to rush the duck* to their customers. A rusher became known more slangily as a *lush trotter,* someone who goes to bring back the lush, hopefully in a fast trot. This social role, wrote Riis, began many a boy's path "to a bad end in the wake of the growler. . . . Fostered and filled by the saloon, the 'growler' looms up in the New York street boy's life, baffling the most persistent efforts to reclaim him."[20]

The name *growler* in this sense is an Americanism and was first recorded in the 1880s, though its origin is unknown. The word may derive, as Flexner speculates, from the sound of the bucket or can that "made a growling, grating noise when slid across the bar."[21] Or, perhaps more likely, it may derive from the surly dispositions resulting directly and indirectly from the can, but especially from drinking its considerable contents. *Growler,* I note in this connection, is also an old slang term for a mean dog and, later, for a professional wrestler, one who grunts and growls. The old British term *growler* for a four-wheeled cab derives, some say, not from the noisy sound of the vehicle but from the famed surliness of its drivers. New York journalist Julian Ralph in 1897 speculated freely that

> The word 'growler' is accounted for in two ways, both of which credit the term with a humorous derivation. A 'growler,' be it known, is any vessel—pail, pitcher, or can—that is sent to the corner saloon for the family supply of lager beer. It is said that the term grew out of the protests of the girls who did not like to be sent to the saloons, or out of the 'growling' (slang for grumbling) of the children whose play in the streets was interrupted by their having to perform similar errands. On the other hand, the quarrel that followed too frequent emptyings of the can by "gangs," or social coteries of drinking men, is said to have given the beer vessel its nickname.[22]

Jacob A. Riis photographed at least two growler gangs of that period. It is easy enough to imagine a low growl emanating from these toughs when they had emptied a few cans, but this is exactly how specious etymology is made.

A low establishment that sold spirits by the "bucket," which may have been just an extra large glass or mug, was known as a *bucket shop* by the 1860s. James McCabe wrote that "from Franklin to Chatham street there is scarcely a house without a bucket shop or 'distillery,' as the signs over the door read, on the ground floor. Here the vilest and most poisonous compounds are sold as whiskey, gin, rum, and brandy."[23] A. Pember in *Mysteries and Miseries of the Great Metropolis* wrote that "at the bucket-shop a man gets a tumbler or bucket of stuff containing every fiery stimulant but whiskey, though whiskey it is professed to be, for five cents."[24] The slang term *bucket shop* was transferred, along with its low connotations, to small, sometimes shady brokerage houses that operated unregulated curb markets. The slang name drew a parallel between bucket-shop dives in contrast to ornate and affluent saloons, or to the big, respectable brokerage houses.[25]

The word image of *bucket,* again connoting excess, later had yet other uses in naming the low saloon, though this time in order to take account of its reputation for violence. The blood spilt in brawls is the allusion of the informal New York saloon names *bucket of blood* and, more profusely, *tub of blood.* Riis mentioned a dive in the old Fourth Ward actually named 'The Tub of Blood.' Another dive of the same name, reputedly the West Side's toughest saloon, once stood on the present site of Penn Station. Artist George Luks made drawings in 1934 of yet another 'Tub of Blood' on West 36th Street, perhaps the successor of the one destroyed by Progress.

Drugs other than other than alcohol have always been part of the scene in mean streets. *Opium dens* or *drug dens,* phrases akin in thought to *hole,* flourished in the late nineteenth century. Opium dens also served as cheap lodging houses and sometimes brothels. Opium addiction increased after the Civil War, generally by the pressures of the burgeoning, world-wide opium trade. The city's Cantonese tolerated an uneasy tradition of opium use and some of the early opium dens were in Chinatown adjacent to the gin-soaked Bowery. Riis spoke of the "opium joints of Mott and Pell Street" near the Bowery and Chatham Square. But drug dens appeared anywhere in the city where despair and the desire to escape reality were greatest. It is from opium use and addiction that the word *yen,* 'a craving,' came into English about 1908, from Cantonese *in-yăn (in,* opium, + *yăn,* craving).

Hop is older slang for the prepared paste of opium. Drug dens were also called *hop joints* by about 1887. *Pad,* whence *opium pad,* is a very old word from cant for the couch or pallet on which one reclined to smoke in an opium den—*to hit the pad. Pad* in the 1950s was revived and extended in beat and later hippie usage but in the 1960s benignly denoted only one's bed or apartment. A *tea pad* in the 1960s, however, was a place for smoking marijuana, once called tea. The clandestine nature of the traditional opium den is evidenced in the old name *three-tap joint,* referring to the three raps of the knuckles to request admission.

Cheap Lodging Houses. Hoboes sought in cheap hostelries a bed, warmth, safety from the *jack rollers* (by 1915, and probably from *rolling* lumber*jacks* in Seattle), and a place to keep their few belongings. These establishments abounded in areas of homeless men, especially after the Civil War. In the lowest lodging houses scores of men slept in common rooms. The linens, if any at all, were seldom changed and vermin flourished. In the old lodging houses operated by the New York police in order to clear the streets on cold nights, the unfortunates were given simply "the soft side of a plank" to sleep on. But it was at least, as the weary said, a warm place *to kip* or *to doss,* 'to sleep,' two terms taken from old British cant. In this country it was more common in the American manner *to flop,* 'to lie down and sleep,' as though folding from exhaustion.

Riis reported that 234 cheap lodging houses were located below New York's 14th Street. "The caravanseries that lined Chatham Street and the Bowery" harbored a nightly "population as large as that of many a thriving town. . . . The calculation that more than nine thousand homeless young men lodge nightly along Chatham Street and the Bowery, between the City Hall and the Cooper Union, is probably not far out of the way." Riis recognized that most of the lodgers were young men who were migrants to the city, some from abroad, some from the rural hinterlands of New York and from elsewhere in the country who had come to the big city in search of work. "Few of them have much money to waste while looking around, and the cheapness of the lodging offered is an object. Fewer still know anything about the city and its pitfalls. They have come in search of crowds, of 'life,' and they gravitate naturally to the Bowery, the great democratic highway of the city, where the twenty-five-cent lodging-houses take them in."[26]

By the 1890s a cheap lodging house was known among hoboes as a *flop house,* a *flop joint,* or just as a *flop. Doss house* or just *doss* had some New York street use at this time, but was more common in England where it was recently used in fashionable slang. Riis described six grades of flops according to the price of a night, ranging from twenty-five cents, fifteen cents, ten cents, seven cents, down to five and even three cents. The twenty-five-cent lodging kept up "the pretence of a bedroom." But the seven-cent accommodation was "a strip of canvas strung between rough timbers, without covering of any kind." Riis's photo of Happy Jack's Canvas Palace on Pell Street is a stark image of one such seven-cent lodging house. The Bowery also offered even cheaper, though unlicensed accommodations. "One may sleep on the floor for five cents a spot, or squat in a sheltered hallway for three," wrote Riis.[27] Another of his photos recorded the crowding and squalor of a "five-cents-a-spot" place, an unlicensed establishment on Bayard Street.

Our present-day slang vocabulary used to disparage less than satisfactory hotels is mostly derived from the speech of the poor and homeless who had first-hand experience with really bad places. The most pejorative terms for cheap lodgings alluded to the fleas, bedbugs, and lice that abounded in the mattresses and bed linens. Again, the vocabulary draws a moral and practical contrast between clean and dirty. The best-known terms denoting this condition are *fleabag*, as in *fleabag hotel*, which dates in related senses from the late 1820s. Around 1910 'The Fleabag' was the functional name of a low saloon at No. 241 Bowery, a dump with a dirty, smelly flop behind it. Vermin-infested flops were also called *flea houses, flea boxes, flea traps, bug houses, louse traps, louse cages, scratch houses*, and *chinch pads*. A chinch is a bedbug in American regional dialect, from Spanish *chinche*, "bedbug."

Albert Halper in *Union Square* described a fictional flop on the Bowery, and gives a sense of lying down with the vermin. "A few blocks south, broken men were snoring in the 15-20-30¢ flop-houses; each man had a tiny booth, sprawled on a hard iron cot, and if he wasn't drunk spent most of the night scratching himself until he drew blood. All the mattresses were old, discolored, spattered with years of tobacco stain, nasal excretion, and vomit; and bedbugs, like systematic squads of marines, scoured each hairy leg and chest."[28]

A certain type of flop house was known as a *cage hotel*. Its windowless, wire-covered cubicles were known as *cages;* heavy wire mesh served as subceilings to protect the person and possessions of the tenants. On the Bowery around 1900, the cage arrangement was used to evade the City's Sanitary Code and other laws governing hotels. A concerned observer noted in 1909 that "the partitions between the 'rooms' do not extend to the ceiling, as that would legally make them bedrooms, violating the sanitary code. Wire networks extend over the top of the partitions, instead of a ceiling, to prevent guests from making surreptitious visits to their neighbors' rooms when the latter are out."[29] A surreptitious visitor bent on stealing was called a *lush diver*, one who climbs over the top, dives in, and robs the sleeping or absent lushes.

Pawnshops. Poor, marginal, and occasionally embarrassed middle-class people sought the services of one other institution of mean streets—the pawnbroker. Again, it was a tense, negative relationship between the needful customer and the rational business that offered relief for a price. Walt Whitman, when he wrote briefly for the New York *Aurora* in 1842, commented that "the magic 'three balls' hold out hope to those whose ill luck makes them grasp at even the smallest favors."[30] The lexical culture of pawnshops is an eminently urban story, going back to the medieval city and, in its social diversity, to the flowering of modern slang itself.

The business of lending money for interest upon the security of small articles of personal property arose with the commercial city in the middle ages and proliferated in the modern city. Knowledge of the pawnbroker and his establishment was a common urban experience of the poor and nearly poor. In 1889 New York had 110 pawnshops, 59 of them below 14th Street; the total more than doubled to 250 by 1906. The institution sharply declined later in this century with the spread of governmental social services. The number had declined to 150 by 1960 and thereafter even faster. Today only fifteen pawnshops are scattered throughout the city and they bear little resemblance to their nineteenth-century predecessors. Before pawnshops were widely regulated by state laws, many were usurious, hence their notice by the poor, and some were fences for stolen property, hence their notice by the underworld and by the police.

The homeless men and women of skid row seldom used pawnshops, for they usually had little or nothing to pawn. But pawnshops served down-and-outs in other ways. Many on the Bowery could not afford to buy new clothes, even in the *cheap johns,* the local name for inexpensive clothing stores on the street since the 1850s. *Cheap john* was the generic name of a proprietor of such an establishment. Some pawnshops took used clothing in pawn and, moreover, served as a cheap clothing exchange. The poor could pawn any good clothing they had as well as buy unredeemed clothing. The basic services of skid row combined in sometimes fiendish ways and a few low saloons entered the clothing-exchange business. *Reliever shops* on the old Bowery were, said historian Alvin Harlow, "basement doggeries where the outcast sot could exchange his shoes for a pair still more badly worn plus a drink of corrosive whiskey."[31]

Pawnshops tended to locate near skid rows and slums but drew clientele from far and wide. Pawnshop owners liked to emphasize their varied clientele of women as well as men, transients, low speculators and gamblers, vaudevillians and musicians between jobs, and now and then even a society woman short of cash to pay a bridge debt. While in some large part true, this description of clients also served to detract from the embarrassing fact that most borrowers were simply desperate and in need of quick cash. Most of their business came from the poor and marginal, which accounts for the locations of pawnshops near their expected clientele. On skid rows the main source of business was men getting quick cash for liquor, drugs, or food. Decades later pawnshops were still located near slums and skid rows and their customers and services remained about the same.

Pawnbrokers long have had a bad reputation, whether wholly deserved or not. The popular image is of a mean, unfeeling, and rational exploitation of people who must turn to the pawnshop as a last resort. The pawnbroker was a lightning rod for the hostility directed toward all slum businesses that seemed to exploit the poor. A pawnshop scene in Hollywood movies was a symbol of personal desperation, approaching the *last stop* or the *end of the line*, perhaps on *skid road*. The older image is that of a Shylock-like character seeking his pound of flesh and of similar impressions from the nineteenth-century reading of novels. The 1965 movie *The Pawnbroker*, set in New York and starring Rod Steiger in the title role, reactivated part of the old image of the pawnshop in the slum.

Late nineteenth-century newspaper and magazine cartoons, illustrations, and stories were clearly anti-Semitic in portraying pawnbrokers. The popular books warning of the traps of New York often had a description of a pawn shop and a shrewd Jewish pawnbroker, whose ethnicity was identified with a mocking sample of Yiddish-American dialect, cheating people out of their small possessions. Stephen Crane in *Maggie* wrote that Mrs. Johnson, the drunken mother, "carried the lighter articles of household use, one by one, under the shadows of the three gilt balls, where Hebrews chained them with chains of interest."[32] But all pawnbrokers were not Jewish, and most of the early people in the business were not. The first pawnbroker in New York to make it an exclusive business, William Simpson, was English and presumably of Christian background. He established a pawnshop at 25 Chatham Street (now Park Row) in 1822 and his descendants built the business into one of the city's largest and most successful. It was held in the Simpson family until the middle of this century.[33]

Pawnbrokers recently have tried to change their public image in the American manner by changing the name of the business. H. L. Mencken noted how proprietors of pawnshops euphemistically starting calling their establishments "loan offices." New York pawnbrokers, as few as they are now, persuaded the Consumer Affairs department in 1981 to change their name to "collateral loan brokers" and that of their commercial organization to the Collateral Loan Association. Their ancient symbol of the three balls was modified to a sanitized logo of a triple spiral. While the neighborhood pawnshop is dying out, the businesses have consolidated, gone corporate, formed chains, and today sell their stock over the counter on Wall Street—with the symbol PAWN. Pawnshops are setting up in suburban shopping malls and courting people in the middle classes who need quick, small loans.

City folk have always favored colorful terms for pawnshops and pawnbrokers, some of the expressions telling of their stressful relationship to them. Some of the names are rich in yet older folklore.[34] The verb *to hock* is an Americanism dated to 1859 and derives ultimately from the Dutch *hok,* 'hovel' or 'prison.' By a slang association with debtors' prison, *to hok* came to mean 'to put in debt.' Since the 1870s pawnshops have been called *hockshops,* a term of unflattering allusion but nonetheless informally used in the business itself. Pawnbrokers also called their customers *hockers.* In cant, a pawnbroker, who was also often a fence, was called a *hock master,* among other names. The contemporary slang expression *in hock,* meaning in debt or mortgaged, comes more proximately, writes lexicographer Laurence Urdang, from the jargon of the "card game of faro, in which the last card in the box was called the *hockelty card,* the card said to be *in hockelty* or *in hock.* When a player bet on a card that ended up *in hock* he was at a disadvantage, was himself *in hock,* and at risk of losing his bets."[35]

Several old British cant and slang terms pertaining to pawnshops were used in New York in the 1840s and 1850s: A *pop shop* was a pawnshop. The verb *to pop,* 'to pawn,' might be the usage in the old English song "Pop Goes the Weasel." *Weasel* was cockney slang for an overcoat, in this case one taken off to be pawned for quick cash to spend, as the song goes, "In and out of the Eagle," a pub on the City Road. In New York by mid-century and probably earlier, a *lumber* was a pawnbroker or a fence. A *lumber crib* was a broker's or fence's place of business, usually a small room, or crib. The broker's place of business was also called a *shelf,* from the sense of *on the shelf,* 'in a pawnshop.' The shop was also called the *spout,* drawn from the phrase *up the spout,* 'in pawn.' Two of these old expressions, *up the spout* and the verb *to lumber,* related to *lumber,* have considerable stories behind them.

The now obsolete verb *to lumber,* meaning to pawn or to fence at a pawnbroker's (which at one time in British slang also meant to arrest, to imprison), has an unusual urban word history. *To lumber* and *lumber* ultimately derive from the proper name *Lombard,* that is, a resident of Lombardy, the region and former kingdom in northern Italy famous in medieval times for its banking and money-lending activities. A *Lombard* today still informally means a banker or moneylender. A *Lombard room* was a place where medieval bankers and pawnbrokers stored their articles of pledge. In British English this became the *lumber room,* any storage room. Simply the *lumber* was in cant specific for the storage room of a fence. British speakers may have encountered *Lombard* in its French pronunciation with the silent *d,* and there is evidence that London's Lombard Street was occasionally and phonetically spelled "Lumber" Street. Hence, the modern *in lumber,* 'in pawn,' and *to lumber,* 'to pawn.'[36]

In this context, we can also better understand the old sense of *to lay (out) in lavender,* meaning to pawn. The Lombard pawnbrokers used to sprinkle and fold in lavender with fine linens and silk to keep them fresh while in pawn. The practice became traditional among pawnbrokers and eventually was brought to this country. Late nineteenth-century cant in New York kept this allusion in the elliptical phrase *to lay (out),* 'to pawn,' and in the name *lavender cove,* 'pawnbroker,' where *cove* is an old word meaning 'guy' or 'fellow.' Apparently today's slang expression *to lay someone out in lavender,* 'to scold or rebuke them severely,' 'to put them in the dog house,' etc., somehow arose from this old meaning, conceivably from a parallel sense of *to lumber,* 'to arrest,' 'to imprison.'

The slang term *up the spout* today seems to be the synonym of *down the drain,* however paradoxically of direction. *Up the spout* means 'in pawn,' which I suppose is, practically speaking "down the drain," given the low rates of redemption among hockers. The term is a historical "allusion to the 'spout' up which brokers sent the articles ticketed. When redeemed they return down the spout—i.e., from the storeroom to the shop."[37] Funk adds that "the real spout was, in former days, the hoist or elevator within a pawnbroker's shop by which articles pawned were carried to an upper floor for storage. Such articles literally 'went up the spout.' "[38] As late as the 1950s some pawnshops had an electrically operated transit device (like some department stores used earlier to make change) for sending small articles, such as watches and jewelry, straight up through a hole in the ceiling to the storeroom.

The three golden balls have been for centuries the sign of the pawnbroker, traditionally displayed in a triangular arrangement, hanging like a cluster of three gilt cherries on their stems. Early in this century the familiar sign had inspired the slang term *three balls* for a pawnshop, and the expression has been more recently used in New York. The sign of the three balls, it is traditionally said, was taken from the coat of arms of the Medici family and first brought to London by Lombard bankers and money lenders. Stories vary as to exactly why the Medicis had the symbol and why the balls were three in number. One story says that the Florentine Medicis' insignia was six red balls on a field of gold and that, somehow or the other, three balls were lost and the remaining three changed to gold.

By the 1850s a pawnbroker or his shop in New York was slangily called a *two-to-one.* One old story says the term refers to the triangular positioning of the three balls. Another attributes it to the popular saying that the chances were "two to one" that the goods pawned would never be redeemed. Some concerned reports in the 1920s said that two to one was about the actual rate of nonredemption in tenement districts. Yet a prominent New York pawnbroker claimed that the redemption rate was from 50 to 95 percent, depending on the shop.

Since the eighteenth century a pawnbroker and his shop have been fancifully called *uncle's,* often *my uncle's,* as if the pawnbroker were a generous relative one turns to when in need or as if one sent one's belongings to an uncle for safekeeping. In French slang the generous relative is the feminine counterpart, *ma tante,* meaning a pawnbroker, whatever his or her gender. Some have doubted so plain an origin of *uncle* and searched for more "scholarly" Latin sources.[39] But consider that an *aunt,* a brothel madam, presides over another stigmatized institution, much as *ma tante* presides over a French pawnshop. The term *uncle* served an ironic function as well as a euphemistic one for the financially embarrassed. Pawnbrokers have been known humorously to adopt the title in their business dealings and even to name their shops "Uncle" this or that. Comedians and vaudevillians, who of necessity had a lot of dealings with pawnshops, helped popularize the name by using it in their stage routines.

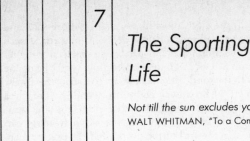

7

The Sporting Life

Not till the sun excludes you do I exclude you.
WALT WHITMAN, "To a Common Prostitute"

Other attractions of the bright lights of city life, these catering chiefly to men, were the companion activities of public drinking, gambling, and prostitution. Around 1850, the expressions *the sporting life, sporting* for short, or just *sport* came to denote, from the male point of view, the comradery of drinking establishments, the action of betting in gambling houses, and the cynical use of prostitutes. These incongruous labels emerged because competitive athletic and other sporting events became an occasion for gambling; drinking in saloons was associated with betting on sporting events and other gambling; and loose women inevitably came into the picture. A *sporting gentleman* had meant a gambler since the 1830s. A *sporting house* by the late 1850s was an establishment catering to gamblers and drinkers and by the 1870s the phrase patently denoted a brothel. A *sporting lady,* of course, was a prostitute, especially one in a brothel. A *sportsman,* or just a *sport,* was an avid gambler, drinker, and brothel patron.

The sporting life had a high and low side, reflecting mostly the social class and spending abilities of sportsmen. Many affluent out-of-town sports came to New York to see the elephant. The better saloons, gambling houses, and brothels were always in easy walking distance of the big hotels on lower Broadway and later on Madison Square. By the late nineteenth century the Tenderloin on the West Side had the most elegant gambling houses and expensive brothels. New York's old sporting life and its scandals, or at least publishable aspects of them, were at once titillatingly "exposed" and glorified by the *National Police Gazette,* which had begun publishing in 1845; Police Chief and slang collector George Washington Matsell was once its owner.

The lowest version of the sporting life, with emphasis on gambling, was the spectacle created by sportsmen in the late 1860s who bet at well-attended dog, rat, and cock fights; dogs fought dogs, dogs fought rats, and cocks fought cocks.[1] Kit Burns's Sportsman's Hall at 273 Water Street was one of the most popular pits, or small arenas, where untold numbers of animals died in combat like miniature gladiators before reformers got this particular sport banned, at least legally, about 1870. The interest of sportsmen then turned to betting on the manly art of boxing, especially in the saloons along the Bowery, such as in Steve Brodie's joint.

As late as 1900 many of the city's most infamous neighborhoods and activities still lay, in the Bowery phrase, "below de line" (of 14th Street). Middle-class men often went slumming *below the line* in search of rougher and cheaper vice. Fourteenth Street, *the Line,* had become symbolic of the divide between the old city to the south and the new city to the north.[2] By the 1840s, the northward growth of Broadway and Fifth Avenue had reached 14th Street and the beginning of the rigid grid. Fourteenth is the southern-most street to go in a straight line completely across the island, from river to river. The modern city, the regular grid to the north, and the pre-modern, irregular city to the south represented the contrasts between the lives of the middle classes and those of the working classes and, so it seemed to some, between virtue and vice. Jacob Riis in *How The Other Half Lives* (1890) wrote: "The city is full of such [vice and slums] above the line of Fourteenth Street, that is erroneously supposed by some to fence off the good from the bad, separate the chaff from the wheat."[3] Both the notorious Tenderloin and large slums, such as Hell's Kitchen, were then north of 14th Street.

From the uptown view, 14th Street was sometimes called *the deadline,* the crossing of which suggested a breach of class lines.[4] In 1927 journalist Will Irwin wrote of Broadway: "Union Square forms at first the southern terminus, the dead-line, of the smart shopping district, and then fades into dingy decadence."[5] Yet fashionable women from above 14th Street regu-larly ventured below the deadline looking for shopping bargains on the Bowery, while in the evening some of their husbands searched below the line for bargain-basement vice.

The Bowery, whose northern terminus is at Cooper Square just a few blocks south of 14th Street, bore the main reputation for working-class vice below the line. As early as the 1830s the street was famous for its beer halls, brothels, and street gangs—especially the Bowery B'hoys. The residential slums in the side streets and back streets of the area, the neighborhood of Crane's Maggie, more generally bore the neighborhood name of The Bow-ery and signified working-class street life and tenement-house poverty. The admonishing expression *Don't act like you were born on the Bowery!* was common by the late 1840s. The Bowery itself with its early bright lights was also the city's first large entertainment district and, in important ways, a precursor of Coney Island's rough bars, dance halls, brothels, variety theaters, and other sensations. The Bowery was fast becoming a skid row by 1890. Yet its fame was now world-wide and the area, including Chinatown at its southern end, was a tourist and slumming attraction, a modern Baby-lon on the cheap.

Charles H. Hoyt and Percy Gaunt's popular song, "The Bowery," from the musical *A Trip to Chinatown* produced in 1891, humorously colored the fame of the street. The Bowery merchants, however, were distressed by the peccable image the song promoted. Harry Conor sang the song, adding "a touch of the coster" that "virtually created a new style."[6] For years after-ward the song was in movies and radio a popular symbol of the city's Lower

East Side. The lyrics satirize the astonishment of a rustic on his first visit to the city, which made it all the more delicious. The chorus and six verses are also a little archive of popular speech associated with the area. The first verse and chorus go:

Oh! the night that I struck New York,
I went out for a quiet walk.
Folks who are "on to" the city say
Better by far that I took Broadway.
But I was out to enjoy the sights,
There was the Bow'ry ablaze with lights—
I had one of the devils's own nights!
I'll never go there any more.

The Bow'ry, the Bow'ry!
They say such things,
And they do strange things
On the Bow'ry, the Bow'ry!
I'll never go there any more.[7]

But they did, and many of the locutions of the sporting life associated with New York south of 14th Street and, farther uptown, with the Tenderloin passed into popular speech.

Saloons

Popular names for urban drinking places alone, without broaching the vast slang vocabulary of drinking itself, encompass a lexical world of their own. In the early tenement districts, ubiquitous corner groceries, some specifically greengroceries, sold liquor and foodstuffs to the neighborhood poor. Most were Irish owned. At night many had little bars at the rear and were hangouts for people on the block.[8] After the city opened the big public markets for meat and vegetables, many corner groceries took further advantage of their corner location and became outright barrooms. By this time many were German owned. Some people continued to call them *groceries,* in part for euphemism. The term may also have been influenced by *liquor grocery,* a common name for a place that dispensed liquor by the bottle and often by the drink. Years later during Prohibition *grocery, greengrocery,* and even *delicatessen* and *confectionary* were recalled from the good old days and used as humorous synonyms for *speakeasy.*

The word *saloon,* from French *salon,* a hall, entered American English around 1840 and was standard for a drinking place until Prohibition in 1920. In 1850 George G. Foster in his book *New York by Gas-Light* complained of the rage in the 1840s to grandiloquently change to *saloon* the name of every honest drinking and sporting establishment in town.[9] By the end of the century, taking the inevitable turn of euphemism, the saloon—and the word itself—had become a sign of working-class ruination in the minds of temperance leaders, and voices for Repeal promised not to revive the old-style saloons. After 1934, the genteel word *lounge,* often as *cocktail lounge,* originally a hotel's public room where light refreshments were served, became one of several euphemisms for both *bar* and *saloon.*

The old saloons, both as a social institution and as a physical presence in the streets, were a pervasive influence on city life. The eye could not escape them, nor the ear. Around 1900 greater New York had 10,000 saloons, and they were on nearly every street in working-class neighborhoods. Remarkable numbers were on street corners, hence the *corner saloon.* Prominent corners were ideal locations to catch traffic in two directions and to accommodate a discreet side door for women patrons or for quick access to back rooms. In the ten block stretch from 43rd to 53rd streets and between Eighth Avenue and the Hudson River, almost half of the 92 street corners were occupied by saloons and many more were between corners.[10] William Dean Howells in his essay "New York Streets" wrote of a walk along Sixth Avenue in the mid-1890s: "There is scarcely a block on any of the poorer avenues which has not its liquor-store, and generally there are two; wherever a street crosses them there is a saloon on at least one of the corners; sometimes on two, sometimes on three, sometimes, even, on all four. . . . In a stretch of some two miles I counted nearly ninety of them."[11]

The Concert Saloon.   After the Civil War, a new type of saloon called a *concert saloon* was a popular place for sporting men to spend an evening of wine, women, and song. The first concert saloon in New York appeared about 1860 and the city soon had 75 such places that employed 747 *waiter girls.*[12] (A German variation was called a *stube,* probably pronounced "stoob" by many non-German New Yorkers, from German *Bierstube,* "tap room.") Yet their primary purpose, exactly as the regular saloons, was to sell liquor. One early proprietor said, "A concert saloon is a gin-mill on an improved plan—that's all, my friend."[13] By 1905 or so the concert saloons had all but disappeared, but they had established a style of working-class nightlife for nearly half a century.

Concert saloons, unlike ordinary neighborhood saloons, offered music or "concerts" for drinking and dancing and they were open only at night. The better concert saloons were on Broadway and its side streets. Lower establishments were on the Bowery, around Chatham Square, and on the waterfront. Some concert saloons hired musicians, if only a piano *professor;* he was an occupational type that was later associated more with the parlor entertainment in brothels. Other places entertained drinkers with the mechanical music of a player piano. The bad music gave a decided aural cast to the Bowery. Stephen Crane wrote in *Maggie:* "A concert-hall gave to the street faint sounds of swift, machine-like music, as if a group of phantom musicians were hastening."[14]

The concert saloons were described by contemporaries as usually in basements and were disparaged, moreover, as "dives." "You descend the steps, and are in a vast hall filled with small tables, at which men and women are seated, chattering like monkeys and drinking like doves," wrote journalist Junius Henri Browne.[15] Sidewalk *barkers* or *pullers-in* called to passersby "Free show inside!" Lighted signs promised all-night music, drink of every sort, and "the prettiest waiter-girls in the City." Contemporaries, however, described the *waiter girls* as often dissolute, fallen women growing hard and old before their time. The waiter girl's job was to sell drinks, and many were casual prostitutes as well. The concert saloons appealed chiefly to the many unattached and lonely men in the burgeoning industrial city.

Throw the Bums Out!. The *bouncer*, a word in American English since 1865, was another type of personnel in concert saloons and like establishments; he was less often called a *chucker-out*. The puller-in stood outside to hook customers in; the bouncer threw them out—"bounced them"—if they got unruly, or did not buy enough drinks. (In later speakeasy days he was called a *gorilla*, which completes his image.) Charles Hoyt's 1891 song "The Bowery," describing what happened to the heckler of a female singer, goes: "I got up mad and spoke out free./ 'Somebody put that man out,' said she./A man called a bouncer attended to me—/I'll never go there any more." The bouncer also was a kind of headwaiter who had other duties. In *Maggie*, Crane described "a 'bouncer,' with an immense load of business upon his hands, [who] plunged about in the crowd, dragging bashful strangers to prominent chairs, ordering waiters here and there, and quarrelling furiously with men who wanted to sing with the orchestra."[16]

The better saloons and hotels put up a splendid *free lunch*, a term of about 1840, to attract liquor patrons. The wisdom of economist Milton Friedman notwithstanding, there once was such a thing as a free lunch, or apparently so. In 1904 Rupert Hughes wrote: "At some of these places a free lunch is served of surprising quality. Judging by the prices for the same things in the restaurant of the same hotel, the profit is hard to understand."[17] The free lunch was a celebrated institution and an urban folkore developed around it.

Even low saloons had a free lunch, though a less appetizing one. Stephen Crane, again in *Maggie*, described a free lunch on the Bowery. "Across from the bar a smaller counter held a collection of plates upon which swarmed frayed fragments of crackers, slices of boiled ham, dishevelled bits of cheese, and pickles swimming in vinegar. An odour of grasping, begrimed hands and munching mouths pervaded all."[18] Even in better places, the "free-lunch fork" served the common use of patrons and stood in "a goblet of greasy water" on the lunch counter, recalled Henry Collins Brown.[19] Free lunches, high and low, went into decline after about 1910, largely because of new licensing and sanitation laws, the changing social uses of saloons, and the high cost of food during the First World War.

The best of the free lunches in the saloons of big hotels were described by contemporaries as enormous and varied boards on which bachelors and well-dressed bummers could live and avoid the restaurants altogether. "Indeed," remarked Henry Collins Brown, "the 'free lunch fiends' were recognized as a big nuisance to the bartenders of that mellow day."[20] The *bum's rush* denoted the business of expelling raiders on free-lunch counters, though that expression was not recorded until the early 1920s and after the demise of the institution of the free lunch. Michael and Ariane Batterberry, chroniclers of New York eating and drinking customs, wrote that "the 'bum's rush' was initiated not as a means of expelling drunks but of repelling daring daylight raids by fleet-footed indigents on the free lunch counters. It was the Golden Age of the bouncer's art."[21] *Freeloaders* and unruly patrons in ordinary saloons were often given a brutal form of the bum's rush, sometimes uttered as the *bum rush,* the *bounce,* or the old *heave-ho.* The technique the bouncer used was to grasp the seat of the pants with one hand and the scruff of the neck with the other and walk the offender to the front entrance and out.

The gait forcibly assumed in the bum's rush was known as the *Spanish walk* and recalls, according to lexicographer Robert L. Chapman, a supposed "custom of pirates, in the *Spanish* Main, of forcing prisoners to *walk* while holding them by the neck so that their toes barely touched the deck."[22] Or the expression may have come about, says lexicographer Laurence Urdang, because the gait "conjures up the image of a (male) Spanish flamenco dancer, who characteristically dances on his toes—the way a person who is being *walked Spanish* might do—before stamping down hard on his heels to the . . . music."[23] The indignant expulsion was also called the *French walk* probably because the offender was sometimes carried out face down, his four limbs splayed outward, like a "frog," alluding to the old epithet for any French person. At any rate, the image of a man flying through the swinging doors of the saloon is one of the enduring visual images of urban popular culture.

One type of free lunch was more apparent than real. In 1896 New York State enacted the "Raines Law" to tax and control the retail liquor trade. One provision prohibited saloons from selling liquor on Sunday, though hotels could sell liquor with meals. Many saloons quickly became bogus hotels and began to serve liquor with equally bogus meals. Hence the birth of the so-called Raines Law sandwich or, in slang, the *brick sandwich*. It was two pieces of bread with, it almost seemed, a brick between, though this concoction should be taken more figuratively than factually. This inedible meal was set out on a table for nominal compliance with the Raines rule. The brick sandwich usually had a real filler, but the customer was not supposed to eat it, and contemporaries described it as so repulsive that no one would want to, though a few dared. Jacob Riis in *The Battle with the Slum* tells a story, reported in the New York *Herald* on April 8, 1902, of the police who broke up a fight between a Brooklyn bartender and a hungry customer who had tried to eat the brick sandwich. The police restored the stage-prop sandwich to the bartender and made no arrests.[24]

Gambling Houses

Gambling houses were a prominent aspect of the sporting life of New York. Reformers and critics called them *gambling dens* and *gambling hells*. Popular books of advice to visitors warned of their wiles and gave details of their crooked roulette, faro, and keno games. Around 1870 some 200 gambling houses, up to 400 lottery offices and policy shops, and two or three thousand gamblers were said to be in business.[25] Policy, a numbers game with small stakes and terrible odds, was the preferred form of gambling among the tenement-house poor, and most policy shops were in the slums.

The few high-class, sedate, and "honest" gambling houses were uptown in elegantly appointed mansions near Madison Square and in the Tenderloin. Smaller, inexpensive houses catering to cautious, small-time players, or *pikers,* were called *piker joints,* and many of these were *skin houses* that specialized in *skin games* to fleece tyros. Many lesser establishments were downtown on or near Broadway and the Bowery; the lowest establishments were yet further downtown near Fulton and Water streets. Many were rough *day houses,* so called because, unlike better establishments which operated only at night, they ran their hustles and invariably crooked games during the day to skin the city's unwary clerks and naive visitors.

Tiger dens were gambling houses that ran faro games called *tiger,* a notorious skin game. *Tiger* apparently comes from the 1840s American sense of 'to fight the tiger,' from the image of a tiger on many faro layouts. "In one house," an observer wrote in 1872, "a magnificent oil painting of a tiger is suspended to the wall immediately over the table, so that none of the players can look up without meeting the glaring eye of the beast which is held to be the presiding deity of the game."[26]

Gambling houses relied on independent middlemen—*ropers-in, ropers, pickers-up, steerers,* or *runners*—to bring them customers from among the new arrivals at the city's hotels. More generally ropers-in were confidence men who "roped in" suckers for any swindle. Once in the gambling establishment, suckers were cheated in card games with the help of *cappers,* who made false bids to encourage incautious playing. High-class houses around Madison Square preferred the term *picker-up* for their ropers. They were smoother, better-dressed men who worked hotel lobbies and kept desk clerks and bellboys in their pay in order to spot rich suckers and entice them into the gambling houses.[27] During the years of great municipal and police corruption under Tammany Hall, even the police worked as ropers and steerers to supply customers to gambling houses. The business of steering persisted, even years later after gambling was sharply regulated and driven into private quarters. In the 1920s the columnist O. O. McIntyre mentioned the *tip-off men* of the gambling houses "who stand in front of certain chop-houses to whisper the hotel room numbers of the nightly dice and poker games."[28]

Dance Halls

Mid-century dance halls linked drinking and consorting with strange women. Most dance halls were operated in connection with saloons, and a staggering consumption of alcohol set the tone of these establishments. Women employees served as *decoy dancers*—early *B(ar) girls*—whose real job was to promote liquor sales. Men were required, upon threat of expulsion by a bouncer, to order drinks for themselves and their dancing partners after each dance. Some of the women were candidly prostitutes and made business arrangements while waltzing. In the British-American cant of New York streets in the 1850s, low dance halls were called *stepping kens,* literally 'dancing houses.' Patrons sometimes called them *sporting houses,* the name that was later affixed strictly to brothels. But reformers called them *dancing hells,* for they saw them as Dantean places with lost souls, or rather bodies, writhing in sin.

In the 1860s Harry Hill's and John Allen's establishments were the best-known dance houses in New York. They were variously described for their raffish local color and denounced for their depravity and wickedness. Harry Hill's, the larger and more respectable of the two, was a two-story building on Houston Street, a few doors west of Mulberry Street, and a block east of Broadway.[29] A huge ornamental lamp hung over the Houston Street entrance and beside the door a signboard had a dozen lines of doggerel, two of which went: "Punches and juleps, cobblers and smashes,/To make the tongue waggle with wit's merry flashes."[30] Admission was 25 cents; women on their own were admitted free and by a private door.

John Allen's dance house was a lower establishment on Water Street and was frequented by waterfront *dollymops,* or sailors' tarts. Allen, who affected fits of religiosity, was called "The Wickedest Man in New York." About twenty women regulars made up the attraction of Allen's establishment. "They wear flashy costumes, scarlet and other gay colors, short dresses, red topped boots, with bells affixed to the ankles," reported Matthew Hale Smith.[31] An engraving of the period shows the wild action in Allen's place, dancers whirling, a man throwing a women overhead in a *spiel*.[32] Dancing events at such rough houses were called *high-flyer stampedes*. Hill's and Allen's places closed in the 1870s, as the action moved uptown and north of the line.

In the 1880s the largest and most famous dance hall in the city was the

Haymarket in the heart of the old Tenderloin on Sixth Avenue just below
30th Street. The Haymarket might have been called a *honky-tonk,* whose
origin just after 1890 is a mystery. It was a garish but lively and gay place
that attracted a social cross section and became a tourist attraction in the
1890s. John Sloan retrospectively painted *The Haymarket* in 1907. He
depicts a night scene of the street in front of the dance hall with three
women, perhaps prostitutes, fashionably dressed in white and arriving to
the invitation of a deliciously lighted interior. New York Chief of Police
George Washington Walling wrote in his memoirs of 1887 that the Haymarket exterior, while appearing "rather repulsive" by daylight, at night
"shines with the brillancy of a Broadway theatre and becomes animate
with the licentious life of the avenue."[33] Walling viewed the Haymarket as
a cradle of crime and debauchery and as a social trap for the city's young
men. He claimed he was shocked by the outrageous language and the
seductive behavior of the women he saw there, but he found no fault with
their men friends.

Low dance halls were magnets for men who used young women in
vicious ways. Certain commercial dance halls in New York, some ostensibly
dancing schools, attracted so-called *cadets,* or pimps. *Cadet,* by the seventeenth century and by a complex route, had come to mean a male street
tough and, more specifically, a pimp.[34] The New York Cadets of the 1890s
were an East Side gang who maintained a political club. Their real business
was the scouting, recruitment, and wholesale of prostitutes. The cadets
hung around *dancing academies* (the pretentious name for a dancing school
but also, perhaps not coincidentally, an old slang name for a brothel). They
were said to drug women and sell them into white slavery, a practice of more
reputation than reality, but real nonetheless. Jacob Riis mentioned the heavy
prison sentences meted out to "The 'Cadets,' who lived by seducing young
girls and selling them to their employer at $25 a head."[35] The cadets were
complete *cads,* a word derived from *cadet* by yet another route. *Dance-hall
pimp* was a later, more direct term for a man who tried in various ways to
take away the earnings of the women who worked in dance halls.

A *trottery,* perhaps from *trotters,* an old term for feet, was 1920s slang
for a dance hall where the shimmy and other popular dances were performed, said Clement Wood and Gloria Goddard, the Greenwich Village
poets who compiled a tiny dictionary of period slang in 1926. During Prohibition New York also had *roadhouses,* a term revived from the 1850s but in
the 1920s so called because they were on a road discreetly outside of town.
The most popular roadhouses, that is, suburban speakeasies, were on Long
Island and several others were on Pelham Parkway, Sheepshead Bay, and
Coney Island.

Ten Cents a Dance. After the First World War,
the *taxi-dance hall,* or *dime-a-dance hall,* a new form of commercialized
dancing, appeared in large cities and gave us new images of the rougher side

of urban nightlife. Paul G. Cressey's book *The Taxi-Dance Hall* (1932) is still the preeminent study of the urban dance hall and, though set in Chicago, its sociology applies equally to New York.[36] These places were also called *closed dance halls,* because they admitted only men as customers. Men bought a string of dance tickets for a dime each, which entitled the patron to one dance with any available *taxi dancer,* a term that dates to the late 1920s. Cressey explained that the taxi dancer is "like the taxi-driver with his cab, she is for public hire and is paid in proportion to the time spent and the services rendered."[37] She took one-half of each ticket, which she later redeemed with the management for a nickel each. She often tucked the ticket stubs into the top of her stocking; the night's accumulation made a bizarre lump on her thigh.

The institution of the taxi-dance hall had migrated eastward from San Francisco and Seattle to Chicago, Kansas City, New Orleans, and New York. Cressey saw the predecessor of the taxi-dance hall in San Francisco's "Barbary Coast" or "forty-nine" dance hall, which was a type of rowdy establishment associated with the hard-drinking and whoring of sailors on shore leave and of miners in the California gold rush of 1849.[38] The Barbary Coast district was "closed" in 1913 and dancing barred, for the same reasons—the brothels and sailors—that New Orlean's Storyville would be closed by the Navy in 1917. The Barbary-Coast style of dancing further evolved in the Seattle dance halls of the original Skid Road, this time with loggers instead of sailors and miners. Seattle's was the prototype of the taxi-dance hall, said Cressey, that was introduced to Chicago in 1921 and about the same time in New York. By 1930, nearly 100 taxi-dance halls were in New York, especially around Broadway and Seventh Avenue.[39] Seventeen of these were on Broadway between 42nd and 57th streets and they flourished throughout the Depression of that decade.[40]

The taxi dancer and taxi-dance halls inevitably were portrayed in the art, literature, and popular song of the period. Edmund Wilson in *Memoirs of Hecate County,* in a passage set around 1930 or just before, describes taxi-dance halls in New York and their "glamorless and garish" atmosphere.[41] Many were near Union Square, and novelist Albert Halper wrote that through the din of 14th Street

> you could hear the taxi-dancing jazzbands in the middle of the block blaring strong, urging the couples on. Ten cents a dance . . . pick your hostesses, boys, here they are, lined up and waiting for your manly arms. The girls, mere kids with painted faces, stood around in long, three-dollar sweat-shop dresses, giving the lads a dreamy, Greta Garbo glance, looking the boys over, trying to find out who had the most tickets (the girls went fifty-fifty with the house). Some of the men gripped the girls too tightly, pawing a bit, but that was to be expected . . . . On the dinky platform the jazzband blared—hot, slow music, the wailing, sobbing blues. The numbers were short, a couple of squeezes, a whirl, and another ticket please.[42]

Reginald Marsh painted and etched two affecting pictures of taxi dancers in the 1930s and 1940s. A tempera, *Ten Cents a Dance* (1933), depicts a group of lurid and eager taxi dancers gesturing to customers from behind a rail in a dance hall. His etching *Diana Dancing Academy* (1939) is a similar scene with a man in glasses responding eagerly to those gestures by reaching across the rail and embracing a dancer. Rodgers and Hart's song, "Ten Cents a Dance," from their musical *Simple Simon* (1930), was most memorably interpreted by Ruth Etting, the co-star of the show, who solicited: "Come on, big boy, ten cents a dance!"[43]

Taxi dancers were more pejoratively called *monkeys,* as were New York chorus girls of that period. A *monkey chaser* was a man sexually interested in taxi dancers. The activity of the dance hall was a *monkey hop.* Since the women often earned only a nickel a dance (not "Ten Cents a Dance")—one

FIGURE 12. Reginald Marsh. *Diana Dancing Academy* (1939). *Taxi dancers were so-named because, like a taxi cab, they are for public hire and charge, so to speak, by the distance covered. Here they stand behind a rail and beckon to prospective dancing partners.*
(*Courtesy of the William Benton Museum of Art*)

half the dime ticket—they were called *nickel hoppers,* and the metered service they performed was called a *nickel hop.* In the depths of the Depression, the price of a dance in some places dropped to one cent.[44] These terms are as obsolete today as the value of nickels and dimes in the Depression economy.

Burleycue

The fringes of the sporting life also offered to working-class and lower middle-class men more passive, spectator forms of contact with women, laughter, music, and dancing. Burlesque in America began as a stageshow of bawdy jokes, slap-stick comedy, and chorus routines by scantily dressed women, the girls eventually becoming the main attraction. The word *burlesque* itself was taken directly from French and originally referred to theatrical parodies, or burlesques of traditional genres.[45] Variety theater that featured the undraped female form and appealed exclusively to men began appearing in New York after the Civil War and, if anything, parodied Victorian sexual attitudes. Naughty American burlesque split from but grew alongside more respectable vaudeville that appealed to the whole family. Some of the early girl shows on the Bowery and 14th Street were simply called *leg shows,* as female legs were an unusual sight in those days. The spelling of *burlesque* was Americanized by theater managers and columnists to *burlesk* and shortened to *burley,* much as *vaudeville* became *vodvil* and *vaud(e).* The humorously said and spelled *burle(y)cue* predates 1931; the variant *burly-Q* appeared in the 1940s.

The words and phrases from burlesque paint a theatrical setting in which daring women titillated passive middle-aged men and inept young men under the disapproving eye of moral society. Reginald Marsh, the American Daumier, was the preemiment artist of the burlesque theater, painting and etching the naked strippers and their leering audiences. *Striptease,* the name of the dance that burlesque featured, is an Americanism of the late 1930s, and *stripteaser* and *stripper* are of the same period. The object of the dance was to strip down to the G-string in as tantalizing a way as possible. New York strippers called the tiny triangles with strings attached *gadgets,* though its initial letter is probably not the source of *G-string.* This Americanism may derive from *gee-string,* found printed in 1877 as a name for the Native American male's loincloth. Yet *G-string* did not appear in the burlesque context until the 1920s. Older businessmen could afford seats on the front row. The strippers referred to *bald-head(ed) row,* alluding to their view of the balding pates below the runway. During intermissions *butchers* hawked candy, sheet music, and risqué books and pictures. During the performance, as bare skin appeared and more was promised, the audience traditionally shouted *Take it off!, Take if off!*

As urban spectacle, burlesque was an offshoot of low variety theater. In the early days, burlesque theaters held amateur nights when the local performers of every kind could try out their acts before an audience. Some of the amateur acts were very bad and inspired calls from the audience—*Get the hook!* The phrase folklorically, perhaps actually, comes from an incident at an amateur night at Miner's Bowery Theater in 1903. An intolerably bad amateur act was being booed and hissed by the audience. The manager, who was standing in the wings, had a long pole with a hook at the end, much like a shepherd's crook, and used it to collar the offending performer and pull him off the stage by the neck. The supposed incident was remembered, and thereafter bad acts prompted audiences to shout *Get the hook!* The strip shows, no matter how badly done, were always more entertaining, and *Take it off!*, referring to the bra and G-string, not the girl, became the enduring cry of the burlesque houses.

The 1920s and 1930s were the Golden Age of burlesque in New York. In 1930, six large houses were near Times Square and another, some say the

FIGURE 13. Reginald Marsh. *New Gotham Burlesk* (1932). The *stripper* is down to her *G-string*. She looks down upon *bald-head row*, the dancers' name for the balding middle-aged men who bought the more expensive seats on the front rows and nearest the runways.
(*Courtesy of the William Benton Museum of Art*)

best, was the Irving Place Theater just north of 14th Street. Most were under the management of Billy Minsky.[46] For years New York was a *strong city,* as people in the business said, where laws governing theatrical nudity were weak or not enforced and *strong* performances were tolerated, such as dropping the G-string and *flashing.* Mayor La Guardia's attacks on burlesque in 1937 closed New York houses and drove the theaters across the Hudson to Union City and Newark, New Jersey; Reginald Marsh followed with his drawing pad. Less "strong" acts reopened in New York, but were shrouded with euphemisms like *veil dancer, exotic dancer,* and *snake dancer.* Even the word *burlesque* was banned on theaters.

H. L. Mencken in 1940 coined *ecdysiast,* from Greek *ekdysis,* the stripping of an outer layer of skin, but it never caught on in slang, only in books. The famous stripper and author Gypsy Rose Lee scorned Mencken's coinage: "We don't wear feathers and molt them off." Maybe she had never seen stripper Sally Rand's famous fan dance with the large, white feathered fans that she used so skillfully to barely cover herself, with an occasional feather flying loose. Around 1950 certain of the nightclubs on 52nd Street were devolving into *strip joints.* In 1952 *Variety* suggested a name change for 52nd Street to *Strip Row* and the columnist Louis Sobol suggested *Stripty-second Street.*

Prostitution

Nineteenth-century urbanization in New York interacted with demographic, economic, and cultural factors to increase and change female prostitution. Social historian Christine Stansell in her book *City of Women* has made a critical analysis of prostitution in New York from 1789 to 1860.[47] Most of the slang vocabulary that denoted the street-side of prostitution emerged from and expressed social situations. Prostitution was engendered by working-class poverty, the lack of legitimate economic opportunities for young women, the anonymity and opportunities afforded by diverse city life, the amorality of the market, and the tacit acceptance of prostitution by all social classes. Prostitution in New York was defined as a social problem in the 1850s, but only after it began to move out of the brothels and into the public life of the main streets. Police Chief George W. Matsell estimated there were 5,000 "women on the town" in 1856, though only a tenth of these were walking the streets. Concerned citizens, such as William Sanger, George Templeton Strong, and Charles Loring Brace, were nonetheless disturbed by the sight of young women and sometimes troops of barely pubescent girls aggressively soliciting in Broadway.

Prostitution was a way working-class women, from a position of traditional social disadvantage, bartered with men to attain a level of living better than the prospect of mere subsistence as wage workers in factories, domestic servants, or working-class wives. Prostitution also was a way to escape the social trap of unilateral relationships with men and convert them into reciprocal exchange. Women in this way gained some of the rewards of city life—not least a private room and a certain independence. Pimps generally did not enter the scene, at least not as protectors, until police and judicial harassment began with reform movements. Prostitution may also be seen as a form of class "discourse" between working-class women and middle-class men. The relationship was a primary exchange, to be sure, but one with a secondary effect to maintain a dominant class relationship, both between the woman and the man and ultimately between the social classes they represented.

Working-class family life was often restrictive and oppressive of young girls, and social control by families was difficult in the city. Working-class families feared the "ruin" of their daughters in their defiance of family authority as much as in their actual sexual behavior. Some girls took to "walking out" at night to the Bowery or Broadway, hanging about on corners, and participating in the youth culture of the city streets. Once in the streets they encountered the social norms to support and justify the exchanges of casual prostitution and even of aggressive streetwalking. Opportunity was plentiful, especially in those many public arenas of main streets, squares, parks, and indoor recreational places where working-class poverty met middle-class affluence. "This class [the prostitutes] throng the watering-places," noted Matthew Hale Smith in 1868.[48]

Red-Light Districts. These watering places, the nearby brothels, and the ever-present streetwalkers followed the logic of the market and the spatial growth in the city. Prostitution generally followed and expanded with the northward growth of the city. Old New York had hundreds of brothels of every class and they clustered with a distinct moral geography in each of various historical periods and were delineated mostly along class and later ethnic lines.[49]

The first principle is that brothels established close to the largest source of their trade, with the nearest slums supplying many of the women for the houses. Early in the nineteenth century, a brothel district stood behind St Paul's Chapel on Church, Vessey, and Barclay streets and near the city's first large hotels on lower Broadway. The better brothels moved uptown with the growth of the city and to be near the newer, fashionable hotels. By the 1850s, 40 percent of the city's brothels and prostitutes clustered in the streets behind the grand hotels on central Broadway, especially on Greene and Mercer streets, or in present-day SoHo. By late in the century, prostitution concentrated within a short walk of major hotels, theaters, and transit stations, especially west of Madison Square and in the old Tenderloin. It became more dispersed in this century and remains so today.

In New York, as in most large cities, the main *red-light district* was usually near or sometimes almost coterminous with the white-light district and its theaters, restaurants, gambling houses, and saloons. Districts that were "wide open" for the sporting life usually had a near proper nickname. The Tenderloin in New York, The Levee in Chicago, the Barbary Coast in San Francisco, and Storyville in the French Quarter of New Orleans were the largest and most famous. The reality of prostitution was always a sordid and often a vicious business. Nonetheless, red-light districts, brothels, and street-walkers were part of the city scene, and the intersection of that world with the public life of the city contributed to popular speech. Those words cast an image of that world, give glimpses of life in it, and in subtle ways shaped perceptions and attitudes toward it.

Red-light district, a phrase first recorded in 1900, is the traditional and still the most general name for an area of brothels. Prostitutes themselves were sometimes called *red lighters* by 1913. Yet the sign of the red light itself is older. The term refers to the red lights that brothels customarily burned in windows as a sign of their business. Manhattan's Greene Street, now in SoHo, had a famous row of brothels by 1850 or thereabouts. Social histo-rian Lloyd Morris wrote that "over the front doors, gas-lamps blazed in bowls of tinted glass, usually red but of other colors also."[50] Reformer I. L. Nascher, who in 1909 wrote of the brothels a few blocks east of the Bowery in his book *The Wretches of Povertyville,* explained his understanding that "the Red Light district was so called because the hall light in disreputable houses had a red globe or shone through red curtains covering the transom of the hall door. A red light before a cigar store, cider room or coffee shop indicated its purpose."[51] The sign of the red light disappeared, at least from the Bowery, in the first decade of this century.

The sign of the red light perhaps either originated or became best known for its use in Paris and was adopted in New York and other American cities. The licensed brothels in France once had a red lantern with the number of the house over the door of each establishment. The red light, however, is not a cultural universal in this meaning. In Cartagena, Colombia, the area is known as the *blue-light district*. Certain variants from white light seem to be the symbol of sexual variance or adventure and the color blue also has erotic connotations in western culture. Red-light districts were also called more slangy names such as *the badlands* or *the jungle,* metaphorically regions where civilization has broken down and licentiousness reigns. *The Jungle,* for example, was an area of saloons and brothels once behind the Brooklyn docks.

The Tenderloin. *The Tenderloin* is preeminent urban slang for the most raffish nightlife district of a city and is an original New York sense of the word. The Tenderloin, as the city's main vice district became popularly known in the 1880s and 1890s, was along Sixth Avenue and its side streets, generally between Fifth and Seventh avenues, and stretched from about 14th up nearly to 42nd Street. The apex of the gradient was Sixth Avenue and 30th Street. Part of the West Side was then a black

neighborhood, especially along Seventh Avenue, and this gave a mixed ethnic cast to the neighborhood and its activities. *The Tenderloin* is one of those
intriguing names, rich with connotation, that gathers various stories of its
supposed origin. The earliest known printed instance is in 1885. The term
apparently first alluded to police graft for protecting illegal vice in the 29th
Police Precinct—"the juicy part of the service," said one police officer.
Tenderloin, an Americanism since the 1820s denoting a luxury cut of beefsteak, was perhaps later unrecorded urban slang for, in the rural expression
of the same idea, living "high on the hog," the anatomical source of luxury
cuts in the Pork Belt.

The slang sense of *The Tenderloin* was soon extended to the activities of
the red-light district as well, in part certainly because of the sexual connotations of *loin*.[52] Sex-as-food metaphors are common in sexual slang and it is
not surprising that such metaphors would be extended to urban areas of
sexual activity.[53] *Tender favor,* I will add, was an early nineteenth-century
term for an act of prostitution; so *tender + loin* apparently completed the
juicy sexual imagery. The first sense of the word as graft, and possibly the
second sexual sense, too, arose in New York in the early 1880s.

Accounts of how New York's Tenderloin got its name almost invariably
tell the story of the corrupt police official, Alexander S. "Clubber" Williams,
who allegedly coined the colorful name of the district. Williams got his own
colorful nickname from his earlier career of prodigious clubbing of bad
elements. In those days, cleaning up an area meant not arrests and convictions, but simply clubbing out the suspected criminals and criminally inclined. Williams on December 28, 1894, in the course of his testimony
before an investigating commission on police corruption, denied that he
directly named the district *The Tenderloin,* as some subsequent accounts
claim. Williams said, rather, that he had eighteen years earlier in 1876, upon
the occasion of his transfer from the poor Fourth Precinct to the prosperous
29th Precinct, used the term in a wider sense in a conversation with an
unnamed newspaper reporter from the *Sun.* Williams said he quipped to the
reporter, "I will have been living on rump steak in the Fourth District, I will
have some tenderloin now." Williams said the reporter "picked it up and it
has been named that ever since."[54] I suspect that the name more spontane-
ously emerged in popular speech, conceivably as early as 1876, but more
likely not until the early 1880s, for it was not found in print until 1885.

The Tenderloin, however, was not the first name for New York's demi-
monde West Thirties. During the corrupt era of the Tweed Ring in the 1850s
and 1860s, reformers sometimes called the area the *Inferno,* drawing a
sharp opposition between the life of the vice district and that of respectable,
middle-class society. The wickedest and gayest area in the city was even
more popularly known as *Satan's Circus,* a name bestowed in the popular
sermons of the Rev. Thomas De Witt Talmage of Brooklyn, who ranted
against sin in the district. That name might have been influenced by the

brothels that warmed up business with broad pornographic performances called "shows" or *circuses*.

The Tenderloin's nightlife was enormously popular with New Yorkers and visitors alike. Most in fact were not pursuing the vice, but the theaters, restaurants, dancing, and gay nightlife with their friends. Stephen Crane in one of his New York City Sketches of about 1900 described the men and women in evening dress riding in cable cars, which resembled "brilliantly-lighted salon[s]," to the restaurants and theaters of the Tenderloin.[55] The notoriety of New York's Tenderloin, however, caused the name to be applied to nightlife districts in other cities, most notably in San Francisco where it is used today.

New York's Tenderloin was already in decline by 1900 or so. The completion of Pennsylvania Station in 1910, but especially the earlier excavation of the open trenches for its tunnels, finished off the old district. The graceful new station building, itself now shamelessly demolished, was bounded by 31st and 33rd streets and by Seventh and Eighth avenues. The construction also destroyed many residential blocks in the area and hastened black migration uptown. Many New Yorkers were pleased to see the old Tenderloin smashed and leveled by the "iron horse" of the Pennsylvania Railroad. A versifier of the period wrote: "Foul Tenderloin! Least wholesome spot in town,/Where vice and greed full many a man brought down,/ . . . The iron horse has sent your dives to join/ The other nightmares of the Tenderloin."[56] The needle trades, too, had taken over the Thirties and the area came to be called the Garment District. By 1915 the Tenderloin as well as its name had passed into history.

Brothels. Outright brothels were called many names in nineteenth-century popular speech. The Anglo-Saxon *whorehouse* sounds too direct and harsh. Victorian prudery and the hypocrisy of middle-class society about prostitution required euphemism. The most euphemistic expression was certainly *ladies' boarding house,* which was used between about 1870 and 1910. *House of ill fame* and *house of ill repute* came into use to avoid mentioning the reason for their ill fame and repute. Exoticism is another way to euphemize eroticism. The French *maison* [de] *joie,* 'joy house,' as well as Italianate *bordello* and *bagnio* were widely borrowed. Whatever their name, warnings of immorality were probably less effective than warnings that some brothels were *creep houses* or *panel houses* wherein visitors were robbed of money and gold watches. While a prostitute preoccupied her customer, an accomplice reached into the room through a secret panel and stole the man's wallet from the pockets of his pants.

Many old slang names for brothels modify *-house* and allude to the class of the establishment. From the late nineteenth and early twentieth centuries we have *sporting house, cathouse,* and *jay house,* the last presumably one that caters to countrymen and other naifs. *Notch house* and *notchery* allude to the singular pursuit of the vulva and, similarly, *can house.* Euphemistically, a brothel is often just a *house*. This unqualified use of *house* is probably one reason American "non-U" speakers avoid the word *house* in favor of *home*. New York madam Polly Adler reminded us with the title of her autobiography in 1954 that, after all, *A House Is Not a Home*.

A *bed house* was an early name used in the city for a cheap "roominghouse," a house of assignation, that rented rooms by the hour to prostitutes, or to trysting lovers. In this century small *free-and-easy* hotels were called *hot-pillow joints* and *no-tell hotels*. In the suburban countryside of the automobile, they were *no-tell motels*. Matsell, as lexicographer, listed a few quaint names for brothels that were used in the streets of New York in the 1850s: *snoozing ken, goosing slum,* and *corinth,* a "bad house," from *corinthians,* "bad women who move in respectable society," presumably an extension of the notion of a "corinthian" as a dissolute man about town. Corinthian Tom was the man about town in Pierce Egan's *Life in London* (1821), a tale of nightly excursions into all the low haunts of the town, and his nickname was generic in New York by 1850.

By the 1860s the higher-class and less common institution of the *parlor house* with its *madam* and *fancy ladies,* or *parlor girls,* was firmly established. A parlor house was so named because its "inmates" gathered in the parlor to receive and sometimes musically entertain their guests. Noted for its clean and attractive women, the parlor house catered exclusively to middle-class men. These brothels were often in a luxuriously appointed townhouse with maids and all the appearances of a fine house of the gentility. The madam was sometimes called an *aunt,* suggesting a bevy of nieces, and somehow inverting the traditional, protectional meaning of kinship. She was sometimes even called *mother*. When the Tenderloin was called Satan's Circus, the Seven Sisters was a huge and famous parlor house—actually a row of seven adjoining townhouses on West 25th Street near Seventh Avenue. The name of *the Seven Sisters,* other than denoting the row of seven houses, was perhaps prompted by the same name of a contemporary play at the Olympic Theater.[57]

Prostitution was interwoven with the social fabric of the city and responded to social change, including new technologies. By the 1890s the telephone was being used by prostitutes to arrange dates; they stayed in their rooms and received men sent to them by bartenders and hotel desk clerks. Arrangements by telephone changed the meaning of *house of call,* or more informally *call house* and later, in the age of apartments, *call flat*. These originally denoted a brothel where men "called upon" prostitutes, usually without prior appointment. By 1910 *call house* denoted a brothel to which women were summoned by telephone when customers arrived and ordered up a particular one, often from a menu of photographs. A woman who worked in such an establishment was a *call girl,* a term that apparently was applied only later and "by confusion and popular misconception," perhaps only since 1935, to a woman who went out to visit her customers in response to telephone calls.[58]

Street Prostitutes. Scores of slang words for prostitutes have appeared in historical popular speech, most of them scurrilous epithets that simply speak contemptuously of the women as low sexual objects. But some of the terms directly reflect the urban context of their origin and reveal a popular image of the lost sisterhood in the public world of city streets. Around 1850 a tenth of New York's prostitutes were streetwalkers; the rest worked in brothels. The streetwalkers, though, were the more visible and considered the greater public nuisance. They cruised in different neighborhoods, streets, parks, but usually near the bright lights, nightlife, and pedestrian traffic. By the 1860s they were also vigorously working the city's vehicles of public transportation. James D. McCabe, Jr. wrote that "at night [the omnibuses] are patronized to such an extent by streetwalkers seeking custom[ers], that the city press has styled them 'perambulating assignation houses.' "[59]

Prostitutes promenaded up and down Broadway, from Canal Street to Madison Square, and in nearby streets and parks. John Sloan's art was the best, most realistic and sympathetic depiction of New York prostitutes in the period of 1907 to 1917, though his portrayals are sometimes coded to avoid objections to the theme. Tenderloin prostitutes around 1910 favored large feathered hats as a sign of their trade and many are so attired in Sloan's painting and graphics.[60] Contemporary writers mentioned the body language, the signal of direct and sustained eye contact, and recorded the very words streetwalkers used to hook their victims. In Broadway around 1850, her familiar greeting was "How do you do, my dear? Come, won't you go home with me?" In later years she seemed to get more informal and brazen: "What's the hurry, sweetheart?," "Warm night, isn't it?," "Busy, honey?," "Lonesome?," or just "Hello, dearie." She seemed to call every man "Johnny," and *John* as her impersonal, anonymous customer survives today. Poet Vance Thompson wrote of the young streetwalkers "In Broadway." "Girls idle for us when the lights/ Are red on the pavement there o'nights./Girls sidle with strenuous eyes for us,/ With gestures urgent and amorous."

Walt Whitman in "Song of Myself" wrote of the streetwalkers in Broadway: "The prostitute draggles her shawl, her bonnet bobs on her tipsy/ and pimpled neck,/The crowd laugh at her blackguard oaths, the men jeer and wink to each other, (Miserable! I do not laugh at your oaths nor jeer you)." In his newspaper article "Street Yarn" of 1856, Whitman wrote with the practiced eye of a street watcher of her image as a sauntering Broadway social type: "Dirty finery, excessively plentiful; paint, both red and white; draggle-tailed dress, ill-fitting; coarse features, unintelligent; bold glance, questioning, shameless, perceptibly anxious; hideous croak or dry, brazen ring in voice; affected, but awkward, mincing, waggling gait. Harlot."[61]

In recent decades, streetwalkers, teenage runaways always among them, have congregated along Eighth Avenue to the west of the theater district, especially between 34th and 55th streets. In the early 1970s the area was passingly called the *Minnesota Strip,* from the local notion that many of the young women were runaways from the Middle West, which was for some reason thought to be epitomized by Minnesota and not, as usual, by Iowa. A related story says the name emerged because many prostitutes, when asked for their hometown, mocked this urban folklore and gave "Minneapolis" as a bitter retort. Local community pride, expressed even in slang, sometimes attributes social deviance to imported, alien influences. In the mid-nineteenth-century, New Yorkers thought that young street prostitutes were mostly runaways from respectable families from farms and small towns upstate and from New England, especially Maine, which is nearly as cold as Minnesota. The "shed" supplying runaway girls and prostitutes, then as now, is mostly the city itself and the surrounding suburbs, cities, and states.

A cultural cluster of nineteenth-century slang terms alludes to the urban prostitute walking the streets or, synecdochically, the pavement. "The pavement is her home," concluded Matthew Hale Smith in 1868.[62] The word *streetwalker* itself appeared in England in 1592 and is still a standard in American speech. In the nineteenth and early twentieth centuries, a *woman on the pave* was also called a *cruiser,* because of her "cruising" up and down city streets in search of men; she was *on the tramp* or *on the pick up.* The whimsical *nymph of the pavement* or *nymph of the pave* was a late nineteenth-century favorite, and it also recalled *nymphomaniac. Nymph of the pavement* is much older in English and is obviously borrowed from the French *nymphe du pavé.*

French borrowings were popular in New York around mid-century; Walt Whitman especially liked *pave, trottoir,* etc. Another French borrowing for a streetwalker, for the French enjoyed a singular reputation for style in such things, is *trottoise,* a phonetic alteration of French *trotteuse,* a street-walker, and from *trottoir,* pavement or sidewalk. *Princess of the pavement* has been in English since the mid-nineteenth century; the variant *pavement princess,* also recent CB radio slang, probably came later. A number of more ephemeral names also placed her in the streets, such as *lady of the pavement, pavement pounder, pavement pretty, sidewalk Susie, curbstone sailor, street sister, (main) stem siren,* and certainly others.

Prostitutes as a social type of the city streets historically have been no-ticed in slang for their nocturnal habits, most directly in such names as *nightwalker.* These names go on to associate the women with darkened public places and nocturnal predation and, so, doubly they stand in opposi-tion to the bright, upright world of middle-class life. The euphemistic, yet sniggering terms *lady of the evening* and *lady of the night,* both popular in the 1870s, are still heard in mock-humorous contexts; *nymph of darkness* was occasionally heard, but was more British.

Several nocturnal animal metaphors make the same point. *Night owl* since the 1840s and later *night bird* denoted a person, usually a man, who stayed up late in contradiction to diurnal rhythms. *Night bird,* usually modified with *little* to make it feminine and thus of clear allusion, was heard around 1900 to suggest that such a woman was a prostitute. Again, feathers. John Reed in a youthful story, "A Taste of Justice" (1913), wrote that the streetwalkers around Union Square were "like dusty little birds wrapped too tightly in their feathers." The notion of a prostitute as a *bird,* in addition to its being reoccurring slang for any young woman, might have been reinforced by the large hats festooned with bird feathers some streetwalkers wore when cruising public places early in this century. Matsell in 1859 listed *owl* and *bat* for prostitutes who walked the streets at night; *bat* in this sense has been in English since the seventeenth century. Matsell also listed *stargazer* for a nocturnal streetwalker, and I like to think the name alludes to her protest, perhaps her posture of innocence when approached by a suspicious police officer.

    Hooker.   *Hooker* is the preeminent word for an urban prostitute, especially a streetwalker. The word as a noun is probably an Americanism; it is certainly American in known word history and, moreover, is perhaps of New York origin, or at least of New York influence. The

FIGURE 14. *Hooking a Victim* (about 1850). These Broadway streetwalkers, called *hookers* by the 1840s, are soliciting clients outside a restaurant, perhaps at the corner of Canal Street. The word *hooker* originated by analogy to one who hooks a fish. Lithograph by Serrell and Perkins. (*Museum of the City of New York*)

earliest written record of *hooker* is in 1845. A college student from Chapel Hill, North Carolina, wrote to a friend, "If he comes by way of Norfolk he will find any number of pretty Hookers in the Brick row not far from French's hotel."[63] The term could have originated in New York and been carried by sailors down the coastal sea lanes to Norfolk, Virginia—from where the first known written record of the word happened to survive and was to surface years later.[64] Other evidence makes a New York matrix a distinct possibility.

The simple idea of "hooking" as coarse sexual persuasion is probably the root sense of the word. A much-reproduced lithograph by Serrell and Perkins, circa 1850, titled *Hooking a Victim,* shows a New York street scene of streetwalkers under gaslight approaching well-dressed men, perhaps at Broadway and Canal Street. In 1850 George G. Foster in *New York by Gaslight* subtitled a chapter on streetwalkers "Hooking a Victim."[65] These titles alone suggest that the word *hooking* for this activity, if not exactly *hooker,* was then on the lips of New Yorkers. A thief was also called a *hooker* in New York by the 1850s, perhaps with little difference seen between them.[66]

Cognates of *hooker,* particularly the verb *to hook* and its gerund *hooking,* may have been imported from British street speech and brought over by immigrants, as were so many other slang terms. *Hook shop,* a brothel, may come from the verb form. Henry Mayhew in his great work *London Labour and the London Poor,* a four-volume oral history and urban sociology, recorded verbatim the speech of street prostitutes. Some of the narratives were collected in the late 1840s, about the time *hooker* seemed to be emerging in the United States. Mayhew's work was first serialized in an English newspaper in 1849–50. One prostitute said, "Some nights we go about and don't hook a soul." And she confessed, "although we musn't mention it, we hooks a white choker [a clergyman, alluding to his clerical collar] now and then, coming from Exeter Hall." Another said, "And I've hooked many a man by showing my ankle on a wet day."[67] The verb remained in cockney until at least 1900.

The adoption and use of *hooker* in New York may have been reinforced by the place name of Corlears Hook, a famous slum and red-light district once on the East Side waterfront. The area was locally known as *The Hook.* John Russell Bartlett in the 1859 edition of his *Dictionary of Americanisms* attributed, without proof, the origin of the word to Corlears Hook: "Hooker. A resident of the Hook, i. e., a strumpet, a sailor's trull. So called from the number of houses of ill-fame frequented by sailors at the Hook (i. e., Corlear's Hook) in the city of New York." The Hook was on the bend or *hook* (from Dutch *hoek,* a corner, a cape) of the East River and at the widest point of the Island. Overcrowded, dirty, and miserable residential hovels were behind the commercial buildings of the wharfs. The brothels, as Bartlett noted, were patronized by sailors; the Brooklyn Navy Yard was just across the East River. Residents of the area, mostly poor Irish, were generally known as the "Hookers," as were the gangs from the neighborhood.

(Note that in the written record of Norfolk *Hooker* is capitalized, suggesting a proper name.) The sailors and others might have applied the name as well to the streetwalkers and to women in the brothels, whence it might have traveled down to Norfolk.

Yet I suspect that *hooker*, with much collateral reinforcement in New York, is ultimately in this sense an agent noun formed from the verb *to hook* and its gerund *hooking*, as one who hooks an eager sexual client as though he were a fish. In 1850 George G. Foster spoke of two New York "sidewalkers" as "fishers of men."[68]

PART IV
The Naming of Social Differences

8
Social Types in City Streets

Come and walk in New York streets, or sit in a restaurant; we will detect some people for you by their uniforms.
WALT WHITMAN, in "Street Yarn," 1856

In 1856 Whitman also wrote his newspaper essay, "Broadway," which opens: "The chief street of a great city is a curious epitome of the life of the city; and when that street, like Broadway, is a thoroughfare, a mart, and a promenade altogether, its representative character is yet more striking."[1] In the 1850s, Broadway proper was the two miles between the Bowling Green and 14th Street and traversed most of the "walking city," as historians now call the old compact cities. Whitman recounted the temporal rhythm of the street around the clock and the synchronized parade of its social types.

After the rumble of delivery trucks down Broadway before dawn, the construction workers appear at about five o'clock on their way to work, followed by shopgirls, then downtown clerks; later in the morning their employers: merchants, money traders, and lawyers. The street is in "high tide" from eleven o'clock to mid-afternoon, full of vehicles and streams of pedestrians on the sidewalks. From two until three or four o'clock appear the fashionable, painted women promenaders, with a few brazen "courtezans" mixing in, and Whitman claimed that, except to the practiced eye, you can't tell them apart. About four or five o'clock the promenaders disappear and "successive waves of the morning tide now begin to roll backward in an inverse order—merchants, brokers, lawyers, first; clerks next; shop-girls and laborers last."[2]

In the early evening the streetwalkers come out under the watchful eye of a few policemen. After supper, the street becomes alive again with sightseers and theater-goers. But after they disperse, the streets are left to streetwalkers, "swearing gangs of rowdies at the corners," and the police—now patroling and watching the scene. After midnight, the streetsweepers appear and do their work, and when they finish, "the circuit of hours is over." Whitman went on to list "various spectacles which diversify this regular routine." These included groups of police marching by, funeral processions and hearses, beggar women, a variety of loafers, walking advertisers, several ethnic types that struck Whitman, ragged shoeshine boys, newsboys shouting "with the voice of steam-whistle," dandies who "spit and swear and giggle," country louts, and a sidewalk medicine showman with a "voluble and senseless harangue of disconnected joke and jargon."[3]

The metropolitan street scene did not essentially change in the century that followed. The curbside array in this chapter is mostly Whitman's cast of characters, their like, and their successors: store clerks going to and from work, corner loafers, dandies, peddlers, hucksters and hawkers of every sort, hustlers and tricksters, walking advertisers, roughs and toughs, a variety of beggars, homeless men and women, ragpickers, street musicians and the neighborhood children who danced around them, ragamuffins, newsboys, the policemen who control the limits of this scene, and finally the municipal workers who clean up after the pageantry of the city. All were precisely and wonderfully named in popular speech.

The Categoric Knowing of Street Types

The bestiary of urban street types has always been a subject of vigorous social classification in language and equally so in art and illustration, fiction, and journalism. Whitman's schema of social types in the streets was continuous with a tradition of urban pictorial caricatures and literary physiognomies that became especially popular in Paris during the 1840s. The culture critic Walter Benjamin has written most famously of categoric knowing of social types by the Parisian *flâneur*, who was yet another street type. The bourgeois *flâneur* saw social variety in public places as a panorama. It was an ideological way to grasp the whole of the modern city.[4] Walt Whitman was certainly not a *flâneur* in the Parisian sense. But his social taxonomies were similar ways to read New York and its emergent complexity. Fifty years later journalist Hutchins Hapgood took the space of a book, *Types from City Streets* (1910), to profile some of these New York social types and their ways of life.[5]

Street types who made their living by catching the attention of passersby were intrusive, often loud sorts and scarcely could be ignored. Artists of the urban picturesque singled out the most colorful among them for humorous, often sympathetic paintings and drawings. Early photographers portrayed galleries of typical street people, often recognizable members of occupational groups, that might be found in London, Paris, Chicago, or New York.[6] The array of street types that Whitman found in the 1850s, had they been photographed, would have been remarkably the same in the 1890s, and it has not changed all that much to the present day.[7] These street types also appeared in fiction, usually as minor stock characters. Writers like O. Henry and Damon Runyon elevated some to noble proportions. Other social stereotypes, especially ethnic types, were butts of vaudeville humor, often abused with the handles of their slang names.

City people assume social knowledge of anonymous others in the public world of strangers by means of many signs of personal appearance and spatial location.[8] Generic names are part of this sign system and are used to identify and 'know' types of strangers in public places. Historically, a shift has occurred from an emphasis on a reliable system of visual signs in the preindustrial city to more emphasis on locational signs in the spatially specialized modern city. Exactly where in the city, at a "good address" or a bad one, one lives, works, or plays is often a more reliable indicator of who a person "is" than how they look or even behave.

Categorizing strangers, however, is still greatly a matter of reading the visual signs of clothing, emblems, stigmata, body markings, physiognomies and other genetic traits, ornamentation, grooming styles, and so on; Walt Whitman considered himself quite expert at this urban skill. Ethnic costumes, occupational dress, certainly police uniforms and the like, the more variable dress displaying social status, and audial speech markers are prominent among such personal appearances. This is what Whitman meant by "uniforms" in the epigraph from "Street Yarn." It "is not only the style and substance of garments, but appearance and carriage."[9]

What people customarily say in the course of going about their business is often among the identifying signs: "Cheese it, duh cops!," "Step lively!," "Watch your step!," "Have a cab?," "What's your hurry, honey?," "Move it along, now," "Brother, can you spare a dime?," "Extra, Extra, read all about it," "Step right this way for the bargain of your life!," and many others. The requisites of modern city life make the human assortment in the streets of any large city a similar cast of occupational and other social types. Most street types had—and still have—popular names in addition to their more formal categoric names.

Shopgirls and Counterjumpers

The expression *working girl* was first used during the Civil War, in part to make a new social category of the increasing numbers of women in the industrial and commercial labor forces. Walt Whitman described the shopgirls passing on the sidewalks at the foot of the Bowery. "Here precipitate themselves, early in the forenoon, hundreds and thousands of delicious New York girls, going to their work, to all kinds of shops downtown; and by this route of course they return, very thick, between six and seven in the evening."[10]

The working girl in New York was often from the countryside of the metropolitan region and she became part of the folklore of the cultural tension between city and country. In the streets she sometimes had to pass through a gauntlet of leering loafers and libertines. Early in this century she was the comic heroine of the popular song, "Heaven Will Protect the Working Girl" (pronounced WOIKing goil), words by Edgar Smith. In the lyric a village mother says to her city-bound daughter, "When you are in the city's giddy whirl,/ From temptations, crimes and follies,/Villains, taxicabs and trolleys, Oh!/Heaven will protect the working girl." Our working girl rejected the villain's offer of a demitasse, which might have led to heaven knows what. In the marketplace of the city, the reputation of even virtuous girls was always being questioned, which our working girl protested in Edgar Smith's song lyric of 1900, "I'm a Respectable Working Girl." *Working girl* did not become a tongue-in-cheek euphemism for a prostitute until the 1960s and is another compliment that vice paid to virtue.

Shopgirls were not always the white-collar clerical and office workers among the working girls. Starting with Whitman's early morning on Broadway, "next come trooping the shop-girls, chatty and laughing, or outworn and weary—some neat, some even sluttish—and hither and thither they disperse to many a bindery and tailor-shop, to attics and back-rooms innumerable."[11] The long working hours in stores and business houses and other rhythms of the city determined the times of their appearances. By the end of the century shopgirls were greatly among commuters who took to the sidewalks at rush hours, swung along with other straphangers on the els and subways, perched on stools at noon at the quick-lunch counters, skillfully managing their long shirt-waist dresses. In the evening certain of them were seen again in the entertainment districts as they stepped out on the town.

Shopgirl, the term itself from the eighteenth century, emerged with extended meanings in the second half of the nineteenth century when expanding commerce and, especially, the growth of retail trade concentrated attention on her presence in the city. Large department stores and other retail businesses employed many young women as retail clerks, not to mention the better-schooled young women working as stenographers and type-writers in offices. The shopgirl was often an object of condescending attention from better-employed, frequently older, middle-class men. A popular song of the day was titled "She Was Only a Shop Girl at Macy's" and speaks to her humble status. Women office and store workers have long been the objects of pejorative social stereotypes. Shopgirls in department stores were frequently characterized as giggling, slangy, clock-watching sorts preoccupied with dating. Some of O. Henry's stories contributed to this image. But in "The Trimmed Lamp" (1907), a bit more sensitively, he criticized the label *shop-girl* in a way that we might even admire in the context of his time: "We often hear 'shop-girls' spoken of. No such persons exist. There are girls who work in shops. They make their living that way. But why turn their occupation into an adjective? Let us be fair. We do not refer to the girls who live on Fifth Avenue as 'marriage-girls.' "

The counterjumper, a derisive name for a male store clerk since the 1820s, became the popular counterpart of the shopgirl in the second half of the century. *Counterjumper* was a word Whitman used, and he viewed the type generally as unmanly. The opinion in Whitman's 1850s bohemian set was that counterjumpers displaced shopgirls in jobs. Young Whitman believed men ought to go into one of the more masculine occupations that he

FIGURE 15. B. West Clinedinst. *The Shop-Girl Released From Toil*. An evening scene at Sixth Avenue and Fourteenth Street. The New York shopgirl, as a regular social type in city streets, was much remarked upon as a sympathetic figure. The visual and word image of the *shopgirl* signified the infusion of women into the public labor force after the Civil War. *Leslie's Weekly*, November 15, 1894. (*Collection of the author*)

admired so much. In "Broadway," he described the "downtown clerks" going to work, just after the lower status shopgirls. He saw them as

> a slender and round-shoulder generation, of minute leg, chalky face, and hollow chest—but trig and prim in great glow of shiny boots, clean shirts—sometimes, just now, of extraordinary patterns, as if overrun with bugs!—tight pantaloons, straps, which seem coming a little into fashion again, startling cravats, and hair all soaked and "slickery" with sickening oils. Creatures of smart appearance, when dressed up; but what wretched, spindling, "forked radishes" would they be, and how ridiculously would their natty demeanor appear if suddenly they could all be stript naked![12]

Counterjumpers, too, were part of the city's folklore of public life, often ridiculed as dupes who got cleaned out in gambling houses and who bought cheap seats in variety houses to gawk at the dancing girls. Whitman, in his early days at the New York *Aurora,* wrote of rube counterjumpers living in boarding houses and getting victimized by skin games in the streets. He faulted "that mischievous idea which makes country people think it is better for their sons to be counter jumpers than American farmers."[13] While certain counterjumpers were seen as naive countrymen in the city, country folk saw them all as city slickers who were apt to prey on country girls in the city. An old comic song, "The Rich Country Girl and the Wicked City Chap," has a line where the girl's father warns her: "Of them counter-jumpers I pray you beware,/You will find them deceitful, I vow and declare."

Well-Dressed Loafers and Libertines

Some men seemed less bound by the strictures of regular working hours and appeared in public places at all hours. Well-dressed loafers, some rumored to be libertines as well, mixed in with women promenaders in Broadway during Whitman's afternoon "high tide" and in the evenings were always to be seen in the streets. Idlers and debauchers abounded in popular fiction as urban folk anti-heroes. "If the libertine defied the Victorian sexual code, the loafer challenged the Protestant work ethic," writes cultural historian Adrienne Siegel."[14] These social types have amazed conventional city people ever since they first appeared in the interstices of the social and economic life of the industrial city.

The *pleasure hound,* where he could afford it, was a regular of the city's nightlife and all its establishments. He was the bon vivant who led women up the great and glittering primrose way of Broadway. He was known chiefly for his fine but gaudy clothes, chasing women, and intemperate drinking. He was known as much by where he was seen as by his appearance. He spent a lot of time in saloons, 'segar' stores, and the theater. His lower-status counterpart, as Matsell recorded in 1859, was called a *hog in togs,* a "well-dressed loafer." He was a *flashman,* "a fellow that has no visible means of living, yet goes dressed in fine clothes, exhibiting a profusion of jewelry about his person." He lived by odd jobs and his wits, by such occupations as roping-in for gambling dens and, it was said, swindling bumpkins. He was to be found around any congregation of women at dance halls or other social events.

His role in the locational order of the city years later got him the name of *Broadway Joe*, a garishly dressed, small-time loafer in Times Square. The general type promenaded up and down Broadway, the Bowery, or any Main Street making gestures and remarks to passing women, hoping to catch their eye and ultimately their attention. Some respectable women found him at once repellent and attractive. Like most complex urban social classifications, the casual male habitué of public places was classified vertically by his social standing and laterally by the particulars of his behavior. Whether they are thought of as loafers or as playboys is largely a matter of their money and social class. And when does the offensive stranger in the inappropriate setting of the street become the intriguing stranger in the more appropriate setting of a hotel lounge?

One such type was named specifically for his behavior toward women. A *masher* was a man who spoke to strange women without an introduction, and his intentions were not honorable. *Masher* was first recorded around 1875 and is related to the noun *mash*, a flirtation, infatuation, or the person of a sweetheart; it is also related to the transitive verb *to mash*, to flirt with. The ultimate etymology of *masher* is uncertain, though it may have been of theatrical or Gypsy origins, possibly from the Romany *masha*, a fascinator. Theodore Dreiser described the drummer or traveling saleman Charles Drouet, Sister Carrie's first suitor, whom she met on the train taking her to Chicago: "He came within the meaning of a still newer term, which had sprung into general use among Americans in 1880, and which concisely expressed the thought of one whose dress or manners are calculated to elicit the admiration of susceptible young women—a 'masher.' "[15] There were worse names for a low street masher. Sylva Clapin's 1902 dictionary of Americanisms defined a *chippy chaser* as "a well-dressed loafer, lying in wait for shop girls or school-children."

Other men "too often" seen in public places, not necessarily masher sorts, were named for their flamboyant dress. A dandy, more slangily a *fancy Dan*, was well dressed and, often, a ladies' man, and generally he had more economic means than other flashy sorts that were to be seen around town; he was a man of leisure. Young Walt Whitman, of course, saw him as a complete wastrel. "The Life of a Dandy: He gets up leisurely, breakfasts comfortably, reads the paper regularly, dresses fashionably, eats a tart gravely, talks superfluously, kills time indifferently, sups elegantly, goes to bed stupidly, and lives uselessly."[16]

The fashionable *dude* (a name of obscure origin) appeared in the early 1880s, a successor to the heavy male figure of the *swell* in the 1860s. In a revolt against Victorian strictures, younger men in the 1880s began to express their personality in clothing and to manipulate the impressions of others with their distinctive dress. The dude took full advantage of the new availability of fitted clothing for men. Some created an extreme, even ludicrous style, which was fashionably extended to his gait and mannerisms as well. Artists of the comic press regarded him with glee. When he was seated in a street car, said one observer, "the head of his cane was usually brought to the mouth and sucked, which completed the effect of inanity."[17] He was a figure of fun on the sidewalks of New York and children followed him down the street, mocking and teasing him. A popular song of the 1880s had him saying, "I'm a dude, a dandy dude." He was such a famous street type that carvers of cigar-store figures put him in their tableaux of American cultural types.

The Street People

The phrase *street people* was first recorded in the 1960s and since has had several turns of meaning. One sense denoted the various sorts who made their living by mixing in the public life of the street or for other reasons were regularly part of the street scene. A second sense denoted people in working-class neighborhoods who, especially in summer, were highly visible sitting on stoops, standing and talking in groups on the sidewalks, or visiting in local shops. By the late 1960s a third meaning denoted young people, some of them hippies and flower children, who survived by cadging food and shelter, some using drugs and begging.

In the early 1970s *street people* came to refer primarily to the many homeless men and women who had recently appeared on city streets, many of them discharged from the custodial care of mental institutions. This fourth sense prevailed into the 1980s. Thoughtful people then suggested that the very name *street people* carried an untoward acceptance that the home of these people is in the streets. The old term *homeless,* commonly used to describe the social problem a century ago, returned to favor and replaced this meaning of *street people.* In the last few years *street people,* at least among urban planners such as William H. Whyte, has come to denote those informal city gatherings and casual passersby that use sidewalks, squares, and plazas. Perhaps the term is finally coming to rest in meaning the diversity of New Yorkers in public places that make up the theater of street life, and this encompasses all the above senses.

Indigents in Public Places. Homeless women began to appear in greater numbers in the 1960s. The shopping-bag ladies, women who raid trash bins, sleep in doorways, wear multiple layers of clothing, and carry their belongings in shopping bags stirred great public interest, not least because of the novelty in recent decades of seeing female indigents in the streets. *Shopping-bag ladies* is now sometimes shortened to *bag ladies,* which in New York causes a confusion with *bag women,* or runners for the numbers racket; both terms are probably of New York origin. Shopping-bag ladies are not new to city streets and were noted in descriptions of New York early in this century. Even then they tended to carry all their possessions in large bags filled to bursting and to wear many layers of clothing. Jacob Riis and other reformers in yet earlier decades regularly found homeless, elderly women on the streets and in the awfullest lodging houses.

The New York police today call the most vagrant of the male homeless *skells.* William Safire informs us that "it is a shortening of *skellum,* meaning a rascal or thief, and akin to *skelder,* 'to beg on the streets,' first used in print by Ben Jonson in 1599, just after the playwright got out of jail for killing a man in a duel; it is possible he picked up the word from a cellmate's argot."[18] The word popped up about 1935 in the short form *skell,* suggesting that *skellum/skell* had underground oral use for centuries. *Skell* is now in popular speech to denote the homeless that are so visible throughout the city.

There are honest beggars and dishonest ones, though it is a tough way to make a living in either case. Beggars' ruses were many and each technique was named in their argot. A few of these subcultural words later passed into slang. Many are old words, often loans from British-Isles underworld cant that were brought to American cities in the early nineteenth century. Matsell in 1859 recorded the now obsolete term *mumper,* a seventeenth-century word for a beggar, which was a century later still used in the streets of New York. He also recorded *palliard,* another old British-Isles word. In New York it had a more specialized denotation of a female beggar who used children, sometimes borrowed ones, tormenting them to make them wince and cry, in order to elicit sympathy for the children and alms for herself.

City people knew at least a few of their tricks, though not usually the names of them. Street-wise pedestrians around 1900 knew, said writer Rupert Hughes, "the famous crumb-thrower who darts into the gutter for a crumb of bread which he has carefully thrown there and now absent-mindedly devours as if unconscious of being observed."[19] Yet the moral dilemma of passersby not knowing which beggars are genuinely destitute (and which are not) long has been a soul-searching topic of discussion, whether to give to all, none, or some—and, if to some, most perplexingly, to whom. As much as anything, the practical motivation for people sorting out and borrowing some of these names was to make sense of the confusing behavior of apparent indigents in city streets.

Some of the old names for beggars are still used today and some were possibily bestowed by pedestrians who were solicited in the streets. *Panhandler,* an Americanism of the 1890s and from *panhandle,* derives most likely from the profile of his extended arm making, so to speak, a panhandle, his torso being the pan. He was also called a *moocher,* from the very old verb *to mooch,* to beg. In the argot, a panhandler might *mooch the stem,* an activity he also called *stemming.* A blind beggar is still called a *cup rattler,* from the practice of rattling coins in a tin cup to get the attention of passersby. The physically handicapped were once in the trade called *gropers, gimps,* and *stumpies,* denoting blindness, lameness, and amputation of legs. *Floppers* positioned themselves in pathetic postures in front of churches and other paths of affluent foot traffic and appeared to be helpless. Most passersby did not care to make the finer distinctions among the apparently maimed they saw sitting on the sidewalks with their hands out and palms up and these words never entered general slang.

Street Vendors and Fakers

A frequent occupation of the poor, then and now, is selling small and cheap goods in city streets. *Street vendors* (an Americanism of the 1890s) usually worked in poor and immigrant neighborhoods. The humblest sidewalk peddlers ran very small, ambulatory operations and gravitated to wherever people thronged. In the 1860s the *patterers* in City Hall Park, Printing House Square, and the Bowery were mostly Irish women and girls who were stand-keepers and petty hawkers of every kind of small merchandise. Their ancient name comes from their stylized patter used to catch the attention of passersby; they did not cry their wares like other street vendors who roamed the city neighborhoods and whose calls were meant to reach people in their houses.

A *pushcart man* was a little more capitalized than the peddlers who carried their wares on their backs, but he was far from being a store owner. Early pushcart men sold about anything but especially foods and dry-goods. They were a familiar sight on city streets, especially before the First World War. Rivington Street on the Lower East Side was called *Pushcart Alley.* Restrictive licensing of all sorts of activities in city streets greatly curtailed their sales, increased police harassment, and drove most into other lines of work. Yet licensed and unlicensed pushcart vendors and increasingly pavement vendors, who simply spread their wares on the sidewalk, still pack certain commercial streets of New York. The new street vendors, while seeming a throwback to an earlier day, have just recreated the street scenes that reflect the origins and customs of the newest immigrants.

In the old days, pushcart vendors of perishable fruit and produce had to be mobile and aggressive sellers to keep their stock fresh, which made them all the more noticeable in the streets. After about 1880 and the New Immigration, their image became prominent in photographs and literary accounts of street life on the old East Side. Today they are a subject of urban nostalgia and many New Yorkers can point to an immigrant grandfather who was a pushcart man on Hester Street or Mulberry Street. Theodore Dreiser recalling the 1890s in *The Color of a Great City* wrote, "I have seen them tramping in long files across Williamsburg Bridge at one, two and three o'clock in the morning to the Wallabout Market in Brooklyn."[20]

Dreiser recalled that the store merchant complained, then as now, that the pushcart men set up in front of his legitimate establishment and took away his business. They were then, as now, of various immigrant nationalities and, then as now, hassled by the police for blocking the flow of pedestrian and vehicular traffic.

Pushcart vendors of ice cream were once called *hokey-pokey men,* from the name of the ice cream sold in this way. They sold penny daubs of ice cream, or hokey-pokey, laid on slips of brown paper. The name was transferred to the little slabs of brick ice cream that were later sold in the streets. The hokey-pokey man was a stock figure on the old East Side and in parks, such as Union Square, and was a favorite subject of street artists and photographers. His popularity with children put him in company with the *candy man* who sold sweets from a pushcart. Stuart Berg Flexner wrote that "children looked for the *hokey-pokey man* or listened for his yell "Hokey-pokey, a penny a lump!" just as today's children watch for the *Good Humor man* and listen for his bells."[21]

One story of the origin of *hokey-pokey,* if true, would be a fetching bit of New York lore. An earlier, 1840s sense of *hokey-pokey* was that of deception and was a playful version of *hocus-pocus. Hokey-pokey* in the sense of ice cream, however, was not recorded until 1884, and thereby hangs a tale. In city lore, with more than a little basis in fact, the hokey-pokey man always seemed to be Italian and to sell his wares in Mulberry Street, the main street of Little Italy. The Italian exclamation *O che poco!,* "Oh, how little!,"— uttered in surprise by Italian children upon getting a dip of disappointing size from the push-cart vendor—might account for the new sense of *hokey-pokey,* the dab or penny portion of ice cream.[22] Otherwise it remains a mystery.

Street selling and peddling was sometimes little different from fraud, truly hocus-pocus. Street *fakers* or *fakirs* were good at spewing *gapeseed,* which Matsell in 1859 defined as "wonderful stories; any thing that will cause people to stop, look, or listen." In those days, New Yorkers went into the streets for excitement and would form a crowd to see a broken window or a dogfight. *Faker,* the word in this sense from the 1840s, is a small-time curbstone swindler or a sidewalk seller of dubious goods. The term, too, seems to reinforce and to be influenced by *fakir,* from Arabic, a poor man or mendicant, which has in English taken on a second, later meaning of an impostor, especially a swindler. The coincidence of sounds and similar spellings of the two names, though they are etymologically unrelated, encouraged their synonymous use. Since about 1965 street peddlers and fakers (fakirs) are once again a familiar sight on the streets of New York.

Nineteenth-century street fakirs ran shell games with the help of a *capper* and a *back capper,* shills whose job was to generate greed in the crowd. They were, of course, the predecessors of today's *three-card monte* players and their confederates. Three-card monte is the same as the old shell game and today is customarily played either with three cards or with three bottle

caps—or with thimbles. Nearly three hundred years ago the English drama-
tist John Gay in his long poem *Trivia* (1716) warned against the "thimble
cheats," the identical skin game in the streets of London. Some things never
change.

Mushroom fakers, Matsell noted, were "umbrella hawkers" and *spunk
fakers* were "match sellers." (*Spunk* was borrowed British dialect for a
match.) *Mushroom* is figuratively an umbrella, and it is also shorted to
mush, hence *mush faker,* an itinerant peddler, tinker, or umbrella mender.
The verb *to mush,* wrote Wentworth and Flexner, is "to earn a living by
grafting or faking under cover of a legitimate occupation, such as umbrella
mending." So, mushroom and spunk faking may or may not be an honest
job. An *arab* or, less often, *street arab* (which usually, rather, denoted a
homeless child) was another name for a wandering vendor. He was sometimes thought to have an exotic countenance, like I suppose that of a fakir.

City streets abounded with every conceivable skin game to fleece
greenhorns, including the ultimate, folkloric one of selling the Brooklyn
Bridge. Some street fakers were smooth, small-time confidence men who
cheated countrymen with the old found-pocketbook game of drops or drop-
pers. More ambitious *con men* in the 1880s made small fortunes selling fake
gold bricks and green goods, or fake securities. Some operated just a step
away inside bogus auction houses, many of which were on Broadway and
Chatham Street. Walt Whitman in his early newspaper days warned visitors
against such *Peter Funk* auction houses. *Peter Funk* was a generic name of
unknown origin for a fake buyer, shill, or puffer, who seemed to buy at low
prices in order to excite the crowd and inflate bidding. Many years later
O. O. McIntyre wrote that "the crudest sort of 'yokel yanking' in New York
is done by the itinerant fur salesmen. They dress as truckmen and stand in
shadowed doorways after nightfall. By whispered implication they give the
idea their furs have been stolen from trucks."[23] Today, they sell fake Rolex
watches.

Peddling slid easily into begging. Some sellers of pencils or shoelaces did
not really expect their wares to be taken when paid for. Their offer of wares
nonetheless helped them keep a certain respectability and not become out-
and-out beggars. Old women, some of them former scrubs now too old and
feeble for stoop labor, nominally sold small items on the streets. Some sold
matches near the theaters to catch gentlemen who stepped out for a smoke at
intermission, and they were invariably called *Matches Mary. Apple Annie*
became a generic for an old woman who sold apples. A similar sort was the
heroine of Damon Runyon's famous story "Madame La Gimp." "Of course
nobody ever takes the newspapers she sells, even after they buy them off of
her, because they are generally yesterday's papers, and sometimes last
week's, and nobody ever wants her flowers."[24] Director Frank Capra made
not one but two movie versions of Runyon's story; she is an indelible part of
New York lore.

Street Advertisers

Established merchants with storefronts added to the disarray of street life. Their displays of goods often went beyond the shop windows and intruded into the public space of sidewalks. It was good merchandising to make an easy continuum from sidewalk to store. Some added to the sidewalk scene a variety of barkers or pitch-men. The *pullers-in* inveigled customers into the store and into the hands of a master salesperson. Clothing stores on Baxter Street, popularly known as *the Bay,* were famous for the skill and aggressiveness of their pullers-in. "Here, in front of every clothing store," wrote Rupert Hughes, "was a rabid puller-in who did not stop at proclaiming his wares or inviting attention, but seized the passer-by and tried to drag him in."[25] Another observer recorded that in nearby Chatham Street pullers-in stood in front of clothing stores and rhythmically shouted "get-your-clothes inside; get'yr'clothes inside." Cheap millinery shops on Division Street had equally aggressive female pullers-in who beckoned from the doorways and sometimes actually pulled at the arms of women shoppers and challenged their male escorts with "Buy the lady a new hat!"

Local advertisers found a new medium in the pedestrian flow of city streets, quite aside from the thousands of signs pasted on every vertical surface and on moving vehicles. A man carrying a sign, it was realized, could expose a much larger street audience to the blandishments of an advertiser. *Banner-man,* a very old word, was applied in a new sense to a walking commercial advertisement in city streets. Bannermen were at times prohibited in New York, but advertisers found devious means of delivering their commercial messages. James D. McCabe, Jr. wrote in 1868 that "since the police have banished the banner-men from the sidewalks, the various trades have taken to representing themselves in odd costumes on the backs of ambitious patterers. Just now walking awnings, barber's poles, whalebones, etc., are the rage."[26] Walt Whitman in "Broadway" mentions "a man with a staring red umbrella containing painted words, dodging the ordinance against walking advertisements, trudges up and down."

The fancifully named *sandwich man,* or more slangily just a *sandwich,* was another sight that struck the walker in the city. The sandwich man was hired by various businesses to be a walking billboard to advertise goods and services of every kind—cheap luncheonettes, manicure parlors, or theatrical productions. The sandwich man wore over his shoulders a hinged pair of sandwich boards, each about two feet wide by three long, with an advertising sign painted front and back; he was, so to speak, sandwiched in between the two boards. Not all were men, however. A close look at Reginald Marsh's tempera *In Fourteenth Street* (1934) (not shown here) reveals a sandwich woman in the crowded sidewalk scene. Early engravings and later photographs of crowded sidewalks in New York frequently show a sandwich man standing about or walking in the sidewalk streams. He was a

FIGURE 16.   W. A. Rogers. *New York Shop-Girls Buying Easter Bonnets on Division Street.* This woodcut illustrates a *puller-in,* a man or woman who stood near the doorways of shops on the Lower East Side and inveigled customers to come in and buy their dry goods. Magazine illustrations of city life in this period sometimes had anti-Semitic overtones, as does this image. *Harper's Weekly,* April 5, 1890.
(Collection of the author)

fixture of street life and, at least once, a simile for wearing one's heart on one's sleeve. Gloria in F. Scott Fitzgerald's *The Beautiful and Damned* (1922), declared "I want to stand on the street corner like a sandwich man, informing all the passersby."

The pay of the sandwich man was low and it was usually down-and-outs who took the job. O. O. McIntyre wrote:

> Each night at six o'clock a tattered group of derelicts gathers in the southeast corner of Bryant Park. They are members perhaps of the poorest club in New York—the Sandwich Men's club. They are the human driftwood of a great city, mostly old men who wander about the streets encased between boards that carry advertisements and picking up at the most seventy-five cents a day. Rain or snow, they meet to talk and puff their ancient pipes, then at eight scatter to their dreary fifteen-cent lodging-houses. Between six and eight is the only time all day that they speak to a living soul.[27]

He became a literary and popular symbol of pathos in public places. In his essay "The Sandwich Man," Dreiser described the misery during a cold Christmas season of the sandwich men he saw in the 1890s walking up and down Ladies' Mile, the fashionable shopping street of Sixth Avenue, between 14th and 23rd streets.[28] A number of poets also addressed his misery. Stephen Vincent Benét in "Notes to Be Left in a Cornerstone" wrote of the sandwich men on a cold winter's day as "overcoatless" and "with the purple hand." Sometimes they moved in groups to advertise theatrical productions. In a verse of seventy-five or more years ago, "Seven Sandwichmen On Broadway," Jefferson Butler Fletcher wrote: "Shuffling and shambling, woebegone, they pass,/Seven in single file, and seven as one." The popular image of the sandwich man also passed into song. Lorenz Hart in his lyric "The Sandwich Men" (1927) spoke for the sorry sight of the human sandwiches in which men were "the piece of cheese."

Street Criers. The cries of street hawkers selling goods and services go back to colonial times in New York. These sounds were among the many aural signs of the city throughout the nineteenth century and well into this century. Street vendors sold about any portable thing—animal, vegetable, or mineral—and each seller had a distinctive traditional cry. Some performed household services with tools they carried about, such as sharpening knives and scissors, repairing pots and pans, or sweeping chimneys. The cries of street hawkers enabled neighborhood residents, even from inside their houses, to know that particular goods and services were at hand. Folklorists have extensively recorded their cries and social historians quote them to recreate the cultural atmosphere of city streets in bygone times. Some of the cries took rhymed-verse form and are now recognized as an urban folk literature in the oral tradition.

Mabel Osgood Wright, in her memoirs of Greenwich Village in the late nineteenth century, recalled the many street vendors, collectors, and other workers and passersby in her middle-class neighborhood on 10th and 11th streets, just off Sixth Avenue and near the Jefferson Market Courthouse. Their cries and distinctive sounds made a vocabulary of the rhythm of street life. The pageantry varied with the season, the day of the week, and with the time of day.

Young girls and women tended to sell prepared foods, such as baked potatoes and fruits, cakes, candies, and boiled corn. *Hot-corn girls* were often mentioned as part of the Bowery street scene, and male city lore had them as pretty and flirtatious sorts. But most were a poor, miserable lot of women and girls, often tiny girls, and were more usually seen as pathetic figures in city streets. A moral tract of 1854 described Katy, a hot-corn girl in the Five Points, crying "Hot corn! here's your nice hot corn—smoking hot, smoking hot, just from the pot!" A more elaborate "song" of the hot-corn girl went

Hot corn! Hot corn!
Here's your lily white corn.
All you that's got money—
Poor me that's got none—
Come buy my lily white corn
And let me go home.

Itinerant chimmeysweeps (often small black boys who were derided in the slang of the 1850s as *lily-whites*) called "Sweepho! Sweepho!" Glaziers, "Glass put'een! Glass put'een." Ragpickers, "Rags-rags-any rags?" Bottle collectors, "Bottles!" Tinkerers, "Pots and pans. Mend your pots and pans." The umbrella fixer, a man of all seasons, "Umbrellas to mend." The knife grinder merely rang a bell. Vendors of fresh fruits and vegetables, which varied by season, seem to have had the most forceful, colorful cries, no doubt with the perishability of their goods in mind. Aside from the ubiquitous "Hot corn: Here's your hot corn," a fruit seller might call "Oranges, sweet oranges," or "Strawberries, any straw be-e-erees!" The fishmonger, "Fresh sha-ad,—fresh sha-aad!"[29]

The Street Children

Newsboys—and newsgirls—added to the raucous atmosphere of city streets. By the 1870s they were called *newsies,* a name that was soon also applied to adult keepers of the newstands that appeared on streetcorners and in lobbies of the new office buildings. The New York *Sun,* first published in 1833, was the first paper in the city to be sold on the streets by newsies. *Newsgirls* (a term of the late 1860s) were also on the scene. Old photographs of New York streets reveal girls of 10 or 11 among the boys selling newspapers. But most were boys, often homeless, many of them younger than 12. They headquartered downtown near Newspaper Row, where they slept, picked up their papers, and fanned out to all parts of the city. Jacob Riis in the 1880s took a special interest in their welfare, photographed them, and described their harsh, animal-like way of life.

Urban color writers, to set the city scene, regularly evoked the vociferous newsboy, often as counterpoint against the rattling streetcars. William Vaughn Moody in his poem "In New York" wrote "Shrill and high, newsboys cry/The worst of the city's infamy." And poet John Hall Wheelock evoked the call of the newsboy as an accent in a romantic memory: "And even the sound of the newsboy's voice in the street/And a rattling car, in that moment of exquisite pain,/Burned themselves like odors into my brain." Stephen Crane in *George's Mother* (1896) wrote that above the din of traffic "could be heard the loud screams of tiny newsboys who scurried in all directions." When they had a special edition, they cried "wuxtree!" (i.e., "extra!") in their variety of English, or so it sounded to one contemporary.

The newsboys, as much as the newspapers they sold, were the heralds of the city and marked its rhythms. In "The Clarion Call" (1908), O. Henry described the sounds of early morning created by the "shrill and yet plaintive" cries of the newsboys. "The comparative stillness of the early morning was punctured by faint, uncertain cries that seemed mere fireflies of sound, some growing louder, some fainter, waxing and waning amid the rumble of milk wagons and infrequent cars. Shrill cries they were when near—well-known cries that conveyed many meanings to the ears of those slumbering millions of the great city who waked to hear them."

The ubiquitousness of newsboys, who incessantly pestered passersby and sitters in public places, surely accounts for the slang phrase *go peddle your papers,* said dismissively and now generally meaning "go away." The anonymous author of the chapter on "The Local Vernacular" in the WPA's (1938) *New York Panorama* added that "*go peddle your papers* is colorful, clear and refers to a precarious, generally humble function of city life; and since its basic sense is universally understood, it lends itself to many nuances of meaning, depending on the individual who uses it, and to whom. It may mean *go away; be a good fellow and leave; go away before you get hurt; mind your own business, you lug* (or *sweetheart*); or *leave us alone, can't you see we're busy.*"[30]

Many of the newsboys and newsgirls came from the ranks of homeless children—gamins, waifs, urchins, or ragamuffins—who roamed the streets in little groups and begged for pennies. Contemporary estimates put the number of street children in New York at 10,000 in 1852, and this already shocking number rose to 30,000 by 1868.[31] These children were also called *street arabs,* sometimes *gypsies,* both an allusion to their nomadic ways of wandering the streets, peddling, and stealing. They made their living other ways, too, by blackening boots, sweeping sidewalks for shopowners, and smashing baggages, as they called it. Some observers distinguished between the older, larger, tougher *street arab* and the younger, smaller, dependent *guttersnipe*. "This little chap," wrote the reformer Helen Campbell in 1891, "generally roams around until he finds some courageous street arab, scarcely bigger than himself, perhaps, to fight his battles and put him in the way of making a living, which is generally done by selling papers. In time the gutter-snipe becomes himself a full-fledged arab with a large *clientèle*, two hard and ready fists, and a horde of dependent and grateful snipes."[32]

The street children were mostly American-born children of mostly Irish immigrants, whom Charles Loring Brace called the "dangerous classes." He thought their presence boded ill for the future stability of society. He called the footloose and sometimes homeless children *street rovers*, at his most generous when using colorful language. "Sometimes they seemed to me, like what the police call them, 'street rats,' who gnawed at the foundations of society, and scampered away when light was brought near them."[33] The police and others did in fact call them *street rats* until politer norms of reform tempered their jargon. Brace was nonetheless deeply concerned with the plight of street children. In 1854 he opened the first lodging house for newsboys and other street boys; in the previous year he had founded the Children's Aid Society.

Homeless girls were probably equal in number, though they were more likely than boys to be gathered into orphanages or put into supervised labor. Even girls with family attachments were in the streets helping in small ways with family incomes. *Crossing sweepers*, for example, were usually young girls who waited at pedestrian crossings and, in the hope of a coin, rushed forward to sweep the path of prosperous-looking adults. The streets of New York after 1850 had become a major employer of child labor. Many young girls were in the streets working as hucksters and peddlers, crossing sweepers, rag pickers, and sometimes petty thieves. The girls quickly gained intimate knowledge of street ways and attitudes. For some, this knowledge prepared the way for a casual transition into prostitution for better and quicker money. Contemporaries reported small gangs of ragged, barely pubescent girls accosting men on Broadway and the Bowery with offers of prostitution, acts of which were usually nothing more than pathetic gropings in alleyways.

Street Musicians

Street musicians were a prominent part of the street scene until they were mostly licensed away. Diarist George Templeton Strong in 1856 complained of the organ grinders, and public criticism of them grew through the rest of the century. The children of the tenements loved street musicians; adults said they found them a nuisance, though contemporaries said a majority occasionally gave them coins. It was the custom to wrap coins in paper before dropping them from tenement-house windows, probably to keep them from rolling away and to make them easy to see. By 1889 city officials had, as one magazine complained, "succeeded in clearing the streets of little German bands, Italian organ grinders, hurdy-gurdy players, and fugitive cornetists." But they soon reappeared, only to be licensed away again early in this century. Street musicians have once again reappeared in streets and subways, some now with licenses and official city blessings. They add a small humanity in harsh public places.

The *hurdy-gurdy man* was once ubiquitous in downtown Manhattan and the strains of "Santa Lucia" and "Funiculì Funiculà" filled the air. He rarely if ever played an actual hurdy-gurdy, which is a medieval, stringed, drone instrument. Rather he played a variety of barrel organs and hand organs, which were also played by turning a crank, hence the popular confusion. The smaller *monkey organ* was mounted on a stick and was transported on the grinder's back; larger organs and street pianos were mounted on wheels. The hurdy-gurdy man's monkey was trained to collect coins in a little cup, was customarily dressed as a Zouave, and invariably was named Jocko. Reformers in the 1890s were concerned that many Italian hurdy-gurdy men were pawns of a vicious padrone system based in Little Italy; they often owned neither their organ nor their monkey; the entire equipment was rented, down to the fez on the monkey.

The hurdy-gurdy man collected around him child *spielers* who danced on the sidewalks and, a little like the story of the Pied Piper, followed his progress down the block and around the corner. The little girl spielers are an enduring folkloric image of New York from the 1880s to around 1910 and are recounted in word and picture. The word *spieler,* either in the sense of an adult dancer given to wild, twirling dances (see Chapter 3), or in the sense here of a child street dancer, appears today in no major dictionary. New York's old unofficial song, "The Sidewalks of New York," published in 1894, words by James W. Blake and music by Charles B. Lawlor, is about the old custom of children and teenagers "waltzing," "twirling," and "tripping the light fantastic," that is, *spieling,* "while the Ginnie played the organ on the sidewalks of New York."

Most accounts of the girl spielers described them as ecstatic dancers. Michael Gold in *Jews Without Money* (1930), a recollection of life on the Lower East Side, described her frenzy. "Her pigtails fly, as she jogs in and out the mazes of a Morris dance. . . . Their little bodies are aflame with rhythm. They have followed the hand-organ from street to street, but after hours of dancing are still unsated." Hutchins Hapgood in *Types From City Streets* (1910) wrote that "she waltzed in the street, to the music of the Italian hand-organ. She avoided by instinct the heavy wagons as they rolled by and the surging mass of men and women."[34] We have at least one personal account of how the dance was actually done just after 1900. Marie Jastrow, a former spieler on East 86th Street, recalled that "foolish, little tripping dances, they were. First on one leg, twirling the other one around and around to the

FIGURE 17. Miss G. A. Davis. *A Harbinger of Spring on the East Side of New York.* This scene is on Hester Street, near Allen. The dancing children, especially the girls, were called *spielers,* a term of the 1880s or earlier. A *hurdy-gurdy man,* Pied Piper like, plays music on his wheeled, hand-cranked organ as the children follow him from block to block. *Leslie's Weekly,* March 28, 1895.
(*Collection of the author*)

rhythm of the music. Then, a change to the other leg, when the whole process was repeated."[35]

Street spielers were naturally a popular subject for realist artists and numerous illustrators. Two tiny girls dancing together are the subject of George Luks's painting "The Spielers" (1905). Jerome Myers, who romanticized tenement life, painted at least three canvasses of speilers. By the First World War, wrote Robert Shackleton, street-organs and street-pianos "to whose music little circles of girls loved prettily to dance on the pavement, have been mostly frowned and licensed away, and no longer do the paper-wrapped nickels and pennies fall like the gentle dew from heaven out of the upper stories of tenements."[36]

Roughs and Toughs

Mean city streets have always been frequented by men prone to crime and violence. The several popular names of such men and their gangs catch the popular meanings of street toughs. A *gang* was many, even hundreds of men and boys who rioted for fun and profit; a *mob* in New York underwold senses was a small group of criminals who set out to commit a specific crime. *Gang* and *mob* (the second shortened from Latin *mobile vulgus,* the moveable, excitable, fickle mass of common people) are old British words. The derivative Americanism *gangster* dates from the 1890s and *mobster* from the 1910s. *Gang* first denoted the famous fighting Irish alliances in the decades around 1850; it later came to mean a smaller neighborhood group of street boys.

Matsell described *roughs,* the most generic term of the 1850s, as "men that are ready to fight in any way or shape." James McCabe in 1872 said that "the New York Rough is simply a ruffian." He was usually of "foreign" [i.e., mostly Irish] parentage "and in personal appearance is as near like a huge English bull-dog [i.e., with a "pug" face, as an accompanying engraving emphasized] as it is possible for a human being to resemble a brute. Of the two, the dog is the nobler animal."[37] He was often illiterate, more or less a pimp, and inclined to violence and robbery, and he was occasionally used by city politicians for dirty work in the wards.

The names for specific gangs refer either to some particular of their appearance—their "uniforms"—or to a locational marker. Gangs were sometimes named for an adopted emblem or for a standard carried into street battles, such as a dead rabbit impaled on a stick, hence the Dead Rabbits. A certain type of street tough afoot in the 1840s was called a *round rimmer,* apparently from a characteristic type of hat. Locational names referred to their home neighborhood or turf. The Bowery B'hoys frequented the Bowery and the Gashousers were from the Gas House District. Other gangs with evocative names such as the Plug Uglies, Shirt Tails, Roach Guards, and Gophers once terrorized the Bowery, Hell's Kitchen, Corlears

Hook, and the Five Points with crime, violence, and day-long brawls in which countless brickbats, or pavings stones and bricks (*Irish confetti* or *alley apples*) were exchanged. The *short hairs* were so called for their practice of keeping their hair clipped short so that it could not be grabbed in street fights; they seem to have anticipated the skinheads of recent years.

Hooligan, first recorded in the 1890s, is perhaps simply after the same Irish surname, one forgotten Hooligan whose behavior somehow gave his name to the category he represented. The word, though, might come from Irish *hooley,* wild drinking party, and came to U.S. cities on the lips of Irish immigrants.[38] So perhaps *hooligans* were originally party-goers noted for their drinking and fighting. The same sorts were also known as *hoodlums,* an Americanism of the early 1870s, and some say it is a San Francisco word. The term is of uncertain origin and has spawned many folkloristic etymologies. But professional etymologists think it from various German dialects. At root it means "ragged" and "disorderly," and only later came to mean a thug.

New York's Bowery was already on the skids by the 1830s, a street of saloons, brothels, and strutting roughs and toughs. A certain type of Bowery rough was the *soap lock,* so named for his greased hair style. The soap locks anticipated the *greasers* of the 1950s and 1960s by more than a century. The greaser was named for his heavily pomaded pompadour and duck's tail hairdo. *Soap lock* was first recorded by John Bartlett in the 1848 edition of his *Dictionary of Americanisms.* A soap lock, he wrote, is "a lock of hair made to lie smooth by soaping it." The name became a synecdoche for "a low set of fellows who lounge about the markets, engine-houses, and wharves of New York, and are always ready to engage in midnight rows or broils. It is, in fact, but another name for a Rowdy or Loafer. Their name comes from their wearing long side locks, which they are said to smear with soap, in order to give them a sleek appearance; whence the name." An eyewitness to 1850s Bowery life recalled the soap lock as wearing "the hair on the back of his head clipped close, while in front the temple locks were curled and greased."[39]

The famous *Bowery Boys,* often called just *the boys,* were a loosely organized gang associated with Bowery life from about 1835 to the 1850s. Many became volunteer firemen and in those days were as famous for fighting other gangs of firemen as for fighting fires. Stuart Berg Flexner explained that "when one referred to such a *Bowery Boy* the fad was then to use a contemptuous or humorous mock Irish pronunciation of 'Bowery B'hoy.' A Bowery Boy's girlfriend or female counterpart was called a *Bowery Girl,* often pronounced 'Bowery Ga'hal.' "[40] The pair were personified and mythologized as *Mose* and *Lize* in Benjamin A. Baker's 1848 play, *A Glance at New York,* staged at the Olympic Theater. This was the first production of an American dramatic work to deal with city street life.

The old Bowery Boys were probably the most romanticized toughs in

urban folklore and popular culture. Yet their public image made them culture heroes in their time. Historian Bayrd Still wrote:

> In temperament, they were the urban counterparts of the rough but self-reliant
> figures who were pushing forward the agricultural frontier. Independent with a
> "pride and a passion," if uncouth in manner, Mose, Jake, and Sykesey were the
> Davy Crocketts of mid-nineteenth-century urban America. At their rowdiest,
> they were problems of public order, apt to organize gangs, such as New York's
> Bowery Boys, Philadelphia's Dead Rabbits, and Baltimore's Plug Uglies, to
> participate in riots, to patronize groggeries and "tiger dens," and to take advan-
> tage of country greenhorns. But in their often helpful services in fighting fires
> and in their distaste for pretense and aristocracy, they exhibited attitudes ad-
> mired by most Americans of their day. By the mid-1860's, the increasing size
> and changing composition of the nation's large cities made the type virtually
> extinct.[41]

The name *plug ugly* emerged in the 1850s and became a slang generic for
a particularly brutal street fighter in any large city. The New York Plug
Uglies may have gotten their name from the gang of the same name in
Baltimore. The etymology is uncertain in the face of several utterly different,
all unproven stories that declare the origin of the term. Most say the name
comes from *plug* in the old slang sense of a face, an "ugly plug," with *plug
ugly* just being a reversal in the occasional fashion of folk speech. A much-
quoted 1876 citation in the *Oxford English Dictionary,* however, says the
name derived "from a short spike fastened in the toe of their [the gang's]
boots, with which they kicked their opponents in a dense crowd, or, as they
elegantly expressed it, 'plugged them ugly'." Another story is that they got
their name "from their enormous plug hats, which they stuffed with wool
and leather and drew down over their ears to serve as helmets when they
went into battle."[42] Jacob Riis did mention a rough saloon named the Plug
Hat in Hell's Kitchen of the 1880s.

At any rate, the New York Plug Uglies gained a well-earned reputation.
According to Herbert Asbury, the chronicler of the city's old street gangs:

> The Plug Uglies were for the most part gigantic Irishmen, and included in their
> membership some of the toughest characters of the Five Points. Even the most
> ferocious of the Paradise Square eye-gougers and mayhem artists cringed when
> a giant Plug Ugly walked abroad looking for trouble, with a huge bludgeon
> in one hand, a brickbat in the other, a pistol peeping from his pocket and
> his tall hat jammed down over his ears and all but obscuring his fierce
> eyes. He was adept at rough and tumble fighting, and wore heavy boots stud-
> ded with giant hobnails with which he stamped his prostrate and helpless
> victim.[43]

Toughs by the mid 1890s were also called *mugs* because of their ugly
faces or "mugs"—or "plugs." The police were making extensive use of

photographic rogues' galleries by the 1880s and this array of mugs may have influenced the use of *mugs* for the toughs who wore them. *Mug* has meant face since the 1840s, wrote Stuart Flexner, "probably because drinking mugs were often made to resemble faces, as were the famous 'Toby mugs.' "[44] In today's older slang a *mug ugly* is still an ugly person.

An early pugilistic sense of the verb *to mug* was "to strike in the face.' *Mug,* in the nounal sense of a person's face but more proximately in the verbal sense of hitting someone in the face, is the source for the 1840s term *mugging*—the act of criminal assault and robbery in city streets. *Mugging* then originally meant the act of striking a victim in the face or mug. Thus, street criminals, sometimes working in small gangs and who robbed people with violence or with the threat of violence, came to be called *muggers,* regardless of exactly how they did it. An alternative technique of mugging, grasping the victim from behind and around the neck in an armlock, or sometimes using a rope or stick, and choking him into submission, was in other cities called *yoking*. By the 1970s the victim of a mugging was called a *muggee* in this all too frequent urban transaction.

Early in this century *apache,* in the sense of an urban gangster, had a passing panache in American English. The curious name is reflected, for example, in the title of Alfred Henry Lewis's *The Apaches of New York* (1912), an anecdotal treatment of some famous gangs of the city. The name was taken directly from the same French slang word for a Parisian gangster. The French had a great interest in the tales of James Fenimore Cooper and liked to find parallels between the so-called Red Indians of the American wilderness and the unruly underground gangs of Paris. *Apache* in this latter-day sense was introduced by the French journalist Émile Darsy. The French word, pronounced roughly a-PASH, was of course borrowed from the name of the ethnic group of Native Americans, whose name in American English is conventionally pronounced a-PATCH-ee. By 1914 or so the term was better known in the expression *apache dance,* a style supposedly originating in low Parisian cafes. In the movies at least, men apache dancers wear berets, T-shirts, and red bandannas, and the women black slit skirts.

Cops

Roughs and toughs and other low street elements were chased about by the police, whose presence in the streets gave policemen a dozen or more disrespectful names. (It is significant that firemen, who were local heros in the fire-endangered city, were virtually never called derisive names until the 1960s.) Names for policemen were mostly invented and used by the people they pursued. This slang was passed around in that intersection of street cultures. The police themselves borrowed a few of the names, most notably *cop*. Some of the names were picked up by the general public from crime fiction and other sources. Most current slang terms for the police and their street-associated activities are of mid- and late nineteenth-century origin.

The first big-city police force was formed in New York in 1845. But they did not wear uniforms until 1853 and not full uniforms until the new Metropolitan Police was created in 1857. Earlier in the century New York's police were little more than nightwatchmen who carried lanterns and wore a leather helmet much like that of firemen. This distinctive headgear got them the early slang name *leatherhead*. The historian Henry Collins Brown wrote that he came out "soon after dark and patrolled the streets till near daylight. Their rounds were so arranged that they made one each hour, and as the clocks struck they pounded with their clubs three times on the curb, calling out, for example, 'Twelve o'clock, and all is well,' in a very peculiar voice."[45] The notion of policemen having a leather head may have served a double meaning to derogate them; by 1839 a stupid person, perhaps coincidentally, was also called a *leatherhead*.

After the Civil War, the fully uniformed policeman on the block became a prominent feature of street and neighborhood life. Their uniforms, their techniques, and even their frequent Irish ethnicity, gave a variety of slang synonyms to popular speech, some of which have endured. Police in large cities since the 1870s have been called *bluecoats,* from the traditional blue uniforms, which also account for other phrases, such as *men in blue* and the recent slang *blue man*. New York police since the 1890s have been, of course, traditionally and respectfully called *New York City's Finest,* though in the 1960s this usage took on ironic overtones. *The Finest* was used slangily and sneeringly in that period of troubled police-community relations and is sometimes still so used.

Pigs, which protestors in the late 1960s may have thought was a new epithet, dates back more than a century to about 1840. The popular synonym *bull,* however, does not really derive from police bullishness, but comes from the Spanish Gypsy *bul,* a policeman, and dates in American English to the early 1890s. Yet the idea of bullish methods and, as a curious coincidence, the nickname of the late Theophilus Eugene "Bull" Connor, the police chief of Montgomery, Alabama, and villain of the black struggles there, probably have influenced the recent vitality of the word. (In French slang, the police are not bulls, but *les vaches,* "the cows.")

Flatfoot and *flatty* come from a whimsical notion of the 1890s that policemen got flat feet from pounding their beats. Old techniques of arrest and shackling gave the police several now obsolete names. By the 1850s, New York police were also sometimes called *frogs,* from their reputation for suddenly leaping on criminals; their brutal techniques of arrest also apparently earned them the occasional name of *crusher. To collar,* to arrest a criminal by seizing him by the collar, gave the police the occasional name *collar.* Their *billy clubs, billies,* or around 1850 *bills* presumably come from clubbing generic Billies, an old name for any unclubbable man.

The verb *to cop*, to arrest, gave the police the Americanism *copper* in the 1840s and its short form *cop* in the late 1850s. The verb *to cop* and its derivatives stem, through the Scots, back to the Latin verb *capere*, "to catch, capture." The expressions *to cop a plea* and *to cop out* also derive from *capere*. *Cop* for a police officer is now merely an informal usage accepted among the police themselves, while the older *copper* remains more slangy and hostile in tone. Over the years spurious etymologies have associated *copper* and *cop* with the copper buttons perhaps once on police uniforms, or more often with copper badges supposedly once worn by policemen, though in New York the old badges were usually brass. Yet their badges did get them another name. Walt Whitman in 1858 wrote of "the 'shields' in the Station Houses," a classic metonym in slang.[46]

The obsolete British verb, *to peel*, to arrest, and the noun *peeler*, a policeman, were both imported from British English and used in New York from the 1860s to about 1890; *peeler* was recorded as slang as late as 1919. Both come from the name of Sir Robert "Bobby" Peel (1788–1850), the British statesman and reformer who instituted the Irish constabulary called *peelers* and reorganized the London police force; his nickname is also the source of British *bobby*, a policeman, which, with the French *gendarme*, is also occasionally used jocularly in this country.

New York's special squad of park policemen in the 1890s were humorously called *sparrow chasers*, or just *sparrows*. Their derisive name is obviously from their constant companions, the lowly grey English or house sparrows in city parks. The fact that these finches were an imported pest did not help either. The park police's grey uniforms surely also reinforced the nickname *sparrows* and, too, distinguished them pejoratively from the blue of regular policemen. Their job was to keep order in the public parks, but they had a status problem in the hierarchy of uniformed city employees and, so, were the butt of jokes. Their popular image was one of flirting with nursemaids in the parks and of rapping their billy clubs on the thin shoe soles of bums sleeping on park benches.

When *the law*, or sometimes *John Law*, as the toughs also called the cops, *nabbed* or *pinched* (all mid-nineteenth-century words) a criminal, they took him to the *booby hatch*, a slang term for a station house. *Booby hatch* of course is now better known as a slang term for an insane asylum and, having nautical allusions, is figuratively a hold, better a hole, into which an inmate is tossed and locked in.

The prisoner was taken there in a horse-drawn police van called a *Black Maria*, another familiar sight in mean city streets. A Black Maria also transported prisoners from jail to the courthouse; and it was once a name for a hearse. The origin of *Black Maria*, however, is uncertain. *Black* apparently refers to the traditional color of the vehicle, but the source of *Maria* seems to be lost. The term is U.S. in origin and has been used since the late 1830s. The earliest found printed use of *Black Maria* is in a story, "The Prison Van; Or, The Black Maria," by Joseph C. Neal, published in *Godey's Lady's Book*,

November 1843. The story was set in Philadelphia and the name may have been coined there in connection with transportation to Moyomensing prison, though *Black Maria* had vigorous use in New York as well. The twentieth-century automotive *paddy wagon* got its name in the 1920s. It either came from the notion that Irish Paddys were greatly among those hauled off to jail or from the popular knowledge that many policemen were Irish, or both. Any Irishman, including Irish policemen, was called *Paddy*, which is a nickname for *Padraic* or *Patrick*, among the Irish a common given name, from that of St. Patrick.

Cleaning the Streets

Now we are at the end of Walt Whitman's Broadway "circuit of hours" and the day's activity has left much refuse in the streets. Only a few major avenues and streets were swept nightly. In most of the city, the inorganic matter was taken away by *rag pickers* who eked out a living by collecting and selling, or "recycling" as we say today, bits of cloth from household and street trash, but also bottles, china, bones, nails, and scraps of wood and metal, sorting them and selling bulk. The men and women in New York today who pick through trash cans on the streets for refundable aluminum cans are classic though more specialized rag pickers.

Until close to mid-century, most New York streets were cleaned, insofar as they were cleaned at all, by peripatetic swine, which were usually called *street hogs*. These animals were usually owned by the poor of the city and, along with their dogs and goats, ate the household wet garbage of discarded fruit, vegetables, and meat that was customarily thrown into the streets. In 1817 there were 20,000 streets hogs at large in New York streets. An argument for tolerance of the hogs reasoned that, since the garbage was thrown out against the unenforced law, the hogs performed a public service. The hogs also provided a certain amusement, at least for children. Youngsters liked to chase after the hogs and lassoed them for fun.[47]

Visitors from Europe in the early nineteenth century recounted their surprise, disgust, but sometimes humor at encountering the New York street hog. One described how the hogs wandered onto the sidewalk and disrupted the fashionable promenade on Broadway by brushing against the finery. In 1842 Charles Dickens in *American Notes* described the New York street hog as "a republican pig, going wherever he pleases, and mingling with the best society, on an equal, if not superior footing, for every one makes way when he appears, and the haughtiest give him the wall, if he prefers it."[48]

Little changed until about 1845 when the city began a somewhat more vigorous campaign of sweeping the streets. Mayor James Harper, elected in 1844, banished the street hogs and hired 350 human street sweepers, as well as forbidding driving cattle below 14th Street during daylight hours. Yet corruption and bureaucratic inefficiency often as not left the streets very dirty, especially in poor neighborhoods. Photographs as late as 1890 show trash and garbage piled waist-high in certain streets, looking much like one of the city's sanitation strikes of recent decades. In 1893 William Dean Howells, as the Altrurian visitor to New York, complained of piles of seething garbage in even uptown streets. Relief was soon to come.

Since the early 1850s, *white wing* has been a slang name for any person who wears a white uniform. The name was most famously applied to New York's street sweepers after Colonel George F. Waring reformed the street cleaning department in 1895. Waring ordered the street cleaning brigades to wear white duck uniforms because, it was said, the white represented cleanliness, and the conspicuousness of the uniform was intended to raise their visibility. Photographs of the period show Waring's White Wings in their equally white pith helmets—always alertly standing up—beside their trashcans on wheels and with pushbrooms in hand, or even on parade in miltary style. The public reaction to the white wings was sometimes amused but always positive. The white wings, indeed, changed the appearance of New York as it entered the twentieth century. Jacob Riis credited Waring and the White Wings with doing as much as the public health doctors in improving sanitary conditions in the slums, not least by reducing the trash piles that bred and harbored the rat population.

9

Us
and Them

Of every hue and cast am I, of every rank and religion.
WALT WHITMAN, "Song of Myself"

The new industrial order after mid-century created and aggregated new economic classes and enlarged and segregated them into adjacent and highly visible neighborhoods. Popular labeling of urban social groups burgeoned after about 1880 in response to the New Immigration from southern and eastern Europe and, in the case of class, to the harsh political ecomony of the Gilded Age.

City people coined a multitude of informal and slang names, often outright slurs, for the diversity of social classes and ethnic groups around them and for the corresponding mosaic of neighborhoods. Social diversity is one of the most abundant themes in urban popular speech and tells its own story of social change, emerging neighborhoods, and the accompanying thoughtways. Popular names for social groups are directed at either poor or rich social classes or, closely related to class, at various ethnic groups. Over a thousand ethnic slur-names for more than 50 different ethnic groups have occurred in historical American English, and that story has been told elsewhere.[1] All popular names for social groups and their neighborhoods signify dual oppositions—Us versus Them—and illustrate that the dualities can be expressed as either vertical or lateral metaphors, though dominance and subordinance are always implied.

Pejoratives directed at social groups have their immediate social uses as well as their delayed and indirect social effects. Name-calling is a social act in speech, a weapon used against outgroups and their individual members. The aggregate and cumulative effect on social relations goes far beyond. All terms of abuse for unlike social groups serve to establish, justify, and maintain the social pecking order, or to protest it. Name-calling marks, articulates, and so reinforces the social boundaries between ingroups and outgroups, or challenges the justice of these boundaries. The exchange of these names shapes the collective social reality of all participating groups and of individual perceptions within them. We make the words and, then, to an extent the words make us and our society.

The thinking that underlies name-calling is that They are not Us, and that We take our identity in part as not-Them. They are the opposite of Us, or at best somewhere between Us and Them. When the informal name of a social outgroup or ingroup is uttered, it is understood in relation to its unspoken opposite. To name Them implicitly names Us, if only as Us. Or to name Us with an ironic epithet given to Us by Them, which people sometimes do, implicitly names Them. Each name makes sense only in relation to other names in this aggregate-level discourse.

Epithets for the Working and Lower Classes

We can be sure that in history the better-offs and the dominant ethnic groups invented and used most of the names to disparage their social inferiors. The underdogs, in turn, coined and used most of the labels that expressed resentment and ridicule of the well-to-do and privileged in the city. But the most prolific abuse was heaped on the supposedly shiftless lower classes. A few facetious terms, like *peons* and *peasants,* are deliberately alien to the modern American context. Older, arch-literary phrases like the Greek *hoi polloi;* a historically anxious *The Mob;* Edmund Burke's *The Great Unwashed;* a scholarly left *Lumpenproletariat;* and the more slangy *plebe* from *plebeian* are occasionally heard, though today mostly in humorous, mock-elitist senses. Other pejoratives were heaped specificially on poor people below and outside the economic community of employed workers, owners, and managers, such as *trash, scum, riff-raff,* all with meanings of human refuse.

The historical slang names for employed wage earners tell a related but different story. A *working stiff* is a depersonalized, replaceable proletarian, simply a body, a machine, a hairy ape that does hard and often dirty work. Early in this century, tramps and underworld sorts, whose language sometimes disparaged the work ethic and those who subscribed to it, used a variety of derisive names for honest working men, such as *chump, dinner pailer,* or *square.* White-collar office workers in their false consciousness sometimes thought they were better than their blue-collar counterparts. But they, too, were nicknamed by those who felt superior to them and their humble clerical tasks. As early as the 1920s they were called *white-collar slaves* and later *brown baggers* (compare working-class *dinner pailers*), and by the 1950s *nine-to-fivers. Wage slaves,* from the late 1880s, probably referred to both white- and blue-collar workers and not always as a criticism of their disempowerment.

A View from Bohemia

New York's *bohemians* often identified, politically at least, with the disparaged working class. *Bohemian* in the sense of a person with an unconventional way of life was introduced into British English in William M. Thackeray's novel *Vanity Fair* (1848). *Bohemian* eventually spread to New York to denote a certain set of artists, writers, and left intellectuals, especially those who inhabited Greenwich Village. Bohemians applied several slang terms to disparage the city's vulgarian middle classes whose values they so strongly denied. One of their favorites was the ideology-inspired term *bourgeoisie* and the attributive *bourgeois*. An outsider from the cultural right, H. L. Mencken, coined *booboisie* to denote that crowd and more.

George F. Babbitt, the hero of Sinclair Lewis's novel *Babbitt* (1922), immediately gave his surname to denote any crass, philistine, conformist, smug, self-satisfied, narrow-minded business man. The name was further elaborated to denote his bourgeois style of life and values, called *Babbittry*, and there were half a dozen more passing derivations. George Babbitt was a member of the Elks club. *Elk* became a near synonym of *Babbitt*, though the reputation of the club and its members may have inspired the name as much as Babbitt's affiliation in Lewis's novel. The Babbitts were early *Yuppies* (a New York term of 1983), though more entrepreneurial than corporate, and sixty years apart the two names were similarly used. In 1923 Lorenz Hart composed "Babbitts in Love," which today could be "Yuppies in Love." The epithet *Babbitt* still lives in slang and in 1990 was heard in the serial television drama "thirtysomething."

Maxwell Bodenheim, a writer and professional bohemian, wrote in his memoir, *My Life and Loves in Greenwich Village*, that "in the hierarchy of the Village an 'Elk' (a member of the bourgeoisie) is put a little below the belly of a cockroach unless he is an Art Patron."[2] Village bohemians despised no one more than a *pseudo*, short for *pseudo-intellectual*, meaning a pretender to the arts and the bohemian style of life. Bodenheim described *Elks* as from uptown or the suburbs and as slummers who come to the Village for vice and the aura of the artistic life, more interested in artists' models than in art.[3]

Epithets for the Truly Rich

The slang imagination, almost by definition a view from the bottom up, was most prolific in naming the rich. Scores of pejoratives denote high-status people as a class, especially the newly arrived in high society. Their connotations tell us that the rich and powerful were resented by the name-callers with egalitarian fervor. Popular ideology holds, as the nation's founding documents seem to promise, that everyone at bottom is of equal social worth, regardless of how much money they have. The rich were at once admired and resented for their ostentatious consumption and luxurious ways of life. The only thing that separates Them from Us is money, which is theoretically possible for anyone to attain.

New York produced more of these terms than other metropolitan centers of the nineteenth century. New York elites, unlike the elites of Boston, Philadelphia, or Charleston, were unique in being of several groups, each with its own sphere, and stratified among themselves.[4] New York society was also more open to new money, more showy, extravagant, and seeking of publicity, of more diverse geographic origins, more disposed to internal rivalry for social supremacy, and more indifferent to civic responsibility. New York society was also distinguished in its domination by women, such as *The* Mrs. Astor. But it was also distinguished by its being marshaled by a succession of male major domos—Isaac Hull Brown before the Civil War, Ward McAllister from the 1860s to perhaps 1890, and thereafter less effectually by Harry Lehr until the social scene changed with the emergence of a faster crowd.

Upper crust, loaned into American English in this sense by 1835, is still one of the most prevalent informal names for high society. Other terms derided the incongruity in America of a European-type elite. The upper classes were called *aristos,* a slighting form of *aristocrats.* The so-called aristocracy of ante-bellum New York fell in the 1870s to the so-called plutocrats, who were then slanged as *plutes.* The richest among them were the *robber barons* and various kinds of industrial and merchandising *kings,* who were much criticized and ridiculed in the papers. This new generation of high society reigned until they in turn fell to *Café Society* after the First World War.

The full array of derisive names for the well-to-do still in popular speech reflects nearly every folk notion and media symbol pertaining to wealth, snobbery, elitism, extravagant and fussy consumption, pridefulness and vanity, social climbing, and the follies of the nouveaux riches. The metaphor of class verticality is abundant throughout the vocabulary, most obviously in compound phrases with *better-, best-, up-, upper-, high-, higher-,* and *top-.* The word collector Sylva Clapin in 1902 recorded the forgotten but nonetheless appealing *tippybobs,* which he glossed as a "term of upmost contempt" for the upper classes.

A few examples of major themes conveys the flavor of this speech. Natural layering: *cream* and *cream of society.* Fine clothes: *silk stockings, fancy pants,* and *high hats* (1920). Too clever by half: *know-it-alls* (early 1930s), *highbrows* (late 1890s), *eggheads* (late 1910s), and *so-smarts.* Clubby and cliquish: *country-club set* and *garden-club crowd.* Pretensions to royalty: *bluebloods* and personal names prefaced by: *colonel-, earl-, king-, queen-,* and *princess-.* Too rich: *Mr. Moneybags, Mr./Mrs./Miss Gotrocks,* and *rich-bitches.* Pride and puffery: *snobs, snoots* (by 1900), *stuck-ups* (1829), *stuffed shirts* (late 1910s), *swellheads* (about 1840). Social climbing: *uppities* (by 1880), *would-be's,* and of course the *Joneses* whom the climbers try to keep up with. The expression *keeping up with the Joneses,* an eminently urban game, originated in 1913 with the title of a new comic strip by Arthur R. "Pop" Momand.

Some of the the best known expressions for elites have specific New York associations and tell their own stories of class relations. By 1798 *silk stocking* was used attributively for wealthy people who dressed expensively, including in silk stockings. Thomas Jefferson commented in 1812: "I trust . . . the Gores and Pickerings will find their levees crowded with silk-stocking gentry, but no yeomanry."[5] Down to 1900 or so *silk-stocking man,* or just the noun *silk stocking,* was used in New York for a man of expensive tastes. Although *silk-stocking* originally referred to the hosiery of men, the term was reinforced early in this century by the affluence of the women who wore fine silk stockings instead of more ordinary cotton ones that did not rustle. The term today is used mostly in informal place names for wealthy neighborhoods, usually to modify *row, avenue,* or *district.* Several old down-town neighborhoods were once called *silk-stocking* areas. Their most famous successor, the *Silk-Stocking District,* is today's affluent upper East Side of Manhattan, which is largely coterminous with the 15th Congressional District.

By the 1840s Fifth Avenue was gaining the reputation as the city's most wealthy and stylish street; the aura lingers to this day. Fifth Avenue, as its wealth moved farther uptown, became the axis of the fashionable district whose boundaries extended to Third Avenue on the east and to Sixth Avenue on the west. "West of Sixth Avenue no true codfish likes to swim," observed the New York *Herald,* apparently indicating as well that Boston's naming of the *Codfish Aristocracy* was being generalized to New York's elite.

Fifth Avenue became equally well known in the city as just *The Avenue,* as though there was only one in the city. Rather, just one mattered to the rich and their admirers. The long-forgotten but fetching slang name for the residents of the street, *Fifth Avenoodles,* or just *Avenoodles,* appeared by the 1850s. Apparently, *Avenoodles* is a burlesque of a certain New York two-syllable pronunciation of *avenue* as "AVE-noo." In 1856 Walt Whitman wrote of downtown neighborhoods "formerly as aristocratic as 'Fifth Avenoodledom.' "[6] As late as 1900 *Avenoodles* was still being applied to residents of the Avenue above 59th Street.

The slang names of the city's most famous rich, all seemingly residents of Fifth Avenue, made sardonic comment when one was called *Mr/Mrs./Miss Astor, Vanderbilt,* or *Rockefeller.* These expressions were used facetiously, in mock admiration, or to scold people rising above their station. By the 1880s a portmanteau *Astorbilt* had appeared to do generic service for the whole crowd on Fifth Avenue, no matter what their names. *Astorbilt* became a slang favorite and evoked a complete social caricature of the rich, haughty, and pretentious social set.

New Yorkers also admired and envied sheer, countable wealth, so it is not surprising that its owners should be named for that quality—and for its multiples of increase. Journalism quickly supplied popular expression with *millionaire,* from French *millionnaire,* which entered English in the 1820s and flourished after mid-century. The Americanism *multimillionaire* appeared in the 1850s and may have been a New York word, for it was most vigorously applied retrospectively to John Jacob Astor (1763–1848). *Billionaire,* a millionaire a thousand times over, first appeared in 1861, but had to wait to be applied to John D. Rockefeller (1839–1937), the world's first billionaire.

By 1844 the upper classes in New York were popularly called the *Upper Ten Thousand,* which by 1848 had been shortened to *Upper Ten.* The term is usually attributed to Nathaniel Parker Willis (1806–1867), an editor, author, and journalist, who in *Necessity for a Promenade Drive* wrote: "At present there is no distinction among the upper ten thousand of the city." By the early 1850s the name was appearing in the press, in book titles, and presumably in popular speech as well. In 1863 Tony Pastor published a song, "The Upper and Lower Ten Thousand," that began:

The Upper Ten Thousand in mansions reside,
With fronts of brown stones, and with stoops high and wide
While the Lower Ten Thousand in poverty deep,
In cellars and garrets, are huddled like sheep.

E. Idell Zeisloft in *The New Metropolis* (1899), an influential book celebrating end-of-the-century New York, detected seven social classes in the city. The top two, "the very rich" and "the rich," which had in common annual incomes of more than $100,000, were together, he said, roughly ten thousand in number. If his estimate was a deliberate allusion to the famous phrase, he was already too late. In 1898, Brander Matthews had a story character say, "I've been mostly in the society absurdly called the Four Hundred; it used to be called the Upper Ten Thousand."[7]

The New York newspapers in the 1890s made much of the implied shrinkage of the city's elite and helped to socially construct the much smaller crème de la crème. The expression *The Four Hundred* soon spread nationwide, and a century later it is still occasionally used for the city's elite. *The Four Hundred* referred to the supposed size of the exclusive circle around Caroline Schermerhorn Astor (1792–1875), the first *The* Mrs. Astor and the daughter-in-law of John Jacob Astor. The ballroom of her mansion on Fifth Avenue at 34th Street held the greatest event of the social season and an invitation meant acceptance into the exclusive Four Hundred.

The Four Hundred itself was coined by Ward McAllister (1827–1895), the snobbish socialite and sycophant. On March 25, 1888, he remarked to a society reporter from the New York *Tribune,* "Why, there are only about 400 people in fashionable New York society. If you go outside that number, you strike people who are either not at ease in a ballroom or else make others not at ease. See the point?" (McAllister's name was sometimes fittingly punned to *Mr. Make-a-lister.*) City lore says that he was alluding to the limiting size of Mrs. Astor's ballroom. But her invitation lists frequently numbered a hundred more or fewer. The number of 400 "was probably the whim of a moment, under the genial intoxication which a press-reporter always evoked in McAllister."[8] Yet the magic number 400 for the city's elite had a certain establishment as early as 1860. McAllister's predecessor, Isaac

Hull Brown, the sexton of Grace Church, arranged a guest list of 400 top citizens to attend the famous ball for the Prince of Wales at the Academy of Music on 14th Street. At any rate, it was the newspapers' first use of the term in 1888 and subsequent magazine satire and cartoons about The Four Hundred and their doings in the 1890s that fixed the term in popular speech.

O. Henry seized on the popularity of *The Four Hundred* to make an ironic title for his first collection of New York stories, *The Four Million,* published in 1906. In the preface, he wrote, "But a wiser man has arisen—the census taker—and his larger estimate of human interest has been preferred in marking out the field of these little stories of the "Four Million." The reference was to the population in 1900 of "Bagdad on the subway," his nickname for New York, and the allusion was to his Whitmanesque concern with the great mass of ordinary people.

Social Climbing

The greatest contempt, then and now, was held for social climbers and parvenus. The metaphor of climbing the social ladder of Manhattan's street grid, preferably straight up Fifth Avenue, was well established in the city's thoughtways and popular culture. Social climbing in nineteenth-century New York was fiercely competitive and offered climbers dilemmas about which faction of Society to throw one's lot in with. Edith Wharton's Undine in *The Custom of the Country* was chagrined when after three years of marriage "she found out that she had given herself to the exclusive and dowdy when the future had belonged to the showy and promiscuous."[9]

The folk vocabulary of class has a dynamic as well as a static dimension; it also expresses social process, a third, mobile position between low and high. The historical lexicon, in the static way, sees the well-to-do and privileged segregated in one part of town and the poor and the marginal equally set apart in another. In the dynamic way, both the have-lesses and the have-mores contemptuously identify a class of the upwardly mobile, who are leaving the have-lesses and joining, or trying to join, or have recently joined, the have-mores. The whole historical vocabulary of class and ethnic conflict pulsates with the energy of frustrated mobility, indignation, and eventually with ambivalence about finally breaking out and making it in the modern city. It is a simple story, an American story, and close to the bone.

Several tell-tale social labels signify the social in-fighting among the city's rich, especially between the old rich, the *nobs,* and the new rich, the *swells. Nobs* is an old British word of uncertain origin for persons of wealth and importance; *swell* is also an old word that in its original cant denoted a gentleman or well-dressed man. Social ringmasters, such as Ward McAllister, knew "that Society was divided into the 'nobs,' old crustacean families who had position without fashion, and the 'swells,' who had to entertain and be smart in order to win their way."[10] McAllister expressed the usefulness of the distinction in his silly book that caused Society finally to drop him. In *Society as I Have Found It* he wrote:

> It is well to be in with the nobs who are born to their position, but the support of the swells is more advantageous, for society is sustained and carried on by the swells, the nobs looking quietly on and accepting the position, feeling they are there by divine right; but they do not make fashionable society, or carry it on. A nob can be a swell if he chooses, i.e., if he will spend the money; but for his social existence this is unnecessary.[11]

The flamboyant life style of some of the big-spending swells, their conspicious consumption, and especially their extravagant behavior, such as dressing up too much and driving too fast in their carriages, earned a set among them the name of the *Howling Swells*.

The more transparent climbers by the 1860s had become known as the *Shoddy Aristocracy,* the *Shoddy Society,* the *Shoddyites, Shoddydom,* or even more slangily just as the *Shoddies.* In 1872 James D. McCabe, Jr. wrote: "They are ridiculed by every satirist, yet they increase." They "flaunt their wealth so coarsely and offensively in the face of their neighbors, that many good people have become to believe that riches and vulgarity are inseparable."[12] The *Oxford English Dictionary*'s earliest citation is 1862 and remarks that "in the U.S. the word seems to have been first used in reference to those who made fortunes by army contracts at the time of the Civil War, it being alleged that the clothing supplied by the contractors consisted largely of shoddy." The *OED* goes on to cite an 1865 source describing "Shoddyism among a large class of people, corruption in official stations, and absorbing passion for making money . . . are the prevailing characteristics of the day."

The Shoddies were tenacious, thick-skinned social climbers, aspirant swells, who seemed to "bounce back" after each failed attempt to win or buy their way into nob circles; the novels of Edith Wharton also had much to say on this subject. Mrs. Astor's crowd named the upcoming swells the *Bouncers,* "a tribute, naturally, to the way they bounced back after repeated rebuffs."[13] The greater wealth of the bouncers finally overwhelmed Nob Society. From the shoddies descended *lobster-palace society* in the 1890's, *Café Society* in the 1920s and 1930s, and the *jet set* in the 1950s. Old wealth, such as the old families who still lived in the deep, dark mansions on Murray Hill, were ridiculed as *cave dwellers*—who had become a most unfashionable crowd of social troglodytes.

Many fine houses in New York were built with brownstone fronts between about 1850 and 1880. Walt Whitman in 1858 mentioned "brownstone fronts" as the type of house in which the rich lived.[14] Families of the new merchant wealth, some of them not all that wealthy, aspired to live in one of the city's status symbols. The expression *brownstone fronts* became a synecdoche for the town houses that once lined Fifth and to a lesser extent Madison avenues. The rows of brownstone fronts in the miles of "brownstone canyons" came to symbolize the appearance, if not always the substance, of upper-middle-class wealth. The brownstone fronts were rumored, perhaps from envy, to have been shoddily built. But it was thought important that the house be at least veneered with brownstone for a suitable front to the social world.

The miles of brownstone rows along New York's avenues and streets, as much as the gridiron, gave a feeling of uniformity and a distinctive, dull appearance to the city. Edith Wharton in *A Backward Glance* describes "this little low-studded rectangular New York, cursed with its universal choco-late-coloured coating of the most hideous stone ever quarried."[15] The brownstone fronts were nearly identical inside and out. The widening of Fifth Avenue destroyed the stoops or "destooped" many of them and ended what little visual interest they had. Most were eventually demolished. Yet the brownstones held the New York imagination.

Brownstoner became an epithet in the 1870s for a well-to-do person, especially a striver of the merchant class. *Brownstone* also modified things, such as *brownstone club* for a private club or *brownstone vote* for the political inclinations of the parvenu class. After 1950 the surviving brown-stones, many having at one time descended to rooming houses and even to slums, once again came into fashion. Today only the rich, usually the newly rich, some of them Yuppies, can afford to buy and restore them and, once again, to enjoy the reputation of being a brownstoner.

The Names of Symbolic Communities

The popular, informal names for rich, poor, and ethnic neighborhoods are, often as not, yet another way to belittle the groups who lived there. Informal place names and their counterpart group names are closely related in spirit and intent, and this may be seen in the similarity of the labels and in the underlying allusions and metaphors. The words and phrases reflect—or better to say they articulate—popular understandings of the class-ified city as a social terrain that often corresponds to the physical terrain.

Formal and informal place names are given and accepted, among other reasons, because they enable people to decode and make sense of the other-wise lexically undifferentiated social city. The act of naming social areas helps to construct "symbolic communities" that give meaning to the cate-gory of people living there.[16] Area names are status symbols that are used by residents to try to raise or maintain their status and by others to assign high or low status to them. Neighborhood names are denied, changed, and varie-gated; boundaries are dissolved, stretched, shrunken, or gerrymandered to establish and keep the class and ethnic integrity of symbolic communities. Area names, like the names of social groups, sometimes result in self-fulfilling prophecies. Residents under the pressure of social expectations begin to fulfill the stereotype of a Greenwich Villager, a Harlemite, an Upper West Sider, or the style of Gramercy Park, SoHo, or Little Italy.

The Wrong—and the Right—Side of the Tracks

The spatial metaphors in many names of symbolic communities, again, are either vertical or horizontal, though they signify invidious stratification in either case. Most explicitly vertical metaphors place the rich on high ground or the poor on low, and this is historical fact in many cities. Horizontal or lateral figures of speech usually place rich and poor neighborhoods either on this or that side of, in front or back of, or near to or far from features of the urban environment that symbolize class divisions. These features are usually a dirty, noisy, or malodorous industrial activity, such as railroad tracks, stockyards, or the gas works.

The idea of a town physically and socially divided by railroad tracks, usually in the expression the *wrong side of the tracks,* dominates the folk image of class division in American towns and cities. Main Street and isolation from it, as we saw in Chapter 2, signifies the moral divisions of the town; the tracks signifies its major class division. The *right side of the tracks* is the explicit other half of the implicitly dual classification. To say that a group or a person lives on the "wrong side of the tracks" makes clear that the point of view, whether taken for granted or ironically assumed, is from the "right side of the tracks." The *wrong side of the tracks* and its variants *across the tracks* and the *other side of the tracks* are used as often in settings where a railroad never actually divided a town.

The railroads built in the nineteenth century transversed many smaller towns and cities and the well-known social divisions often grew up on either side. The railroad's right-of-ways reinforced socially homogeneous areas already marked off by natural barriers. The railroads often, for example, followed the banks of the river, both to pursue the course of least resistance through the flat bottoms and to provide access to water for the steam locomotives. As a town developed and prevailing wind patterns were noticed, smelly industrial activity was sometimes sited on one side of the tracks to make it downwind of better neighborhoods on the other side. Railroad tracks in New York were a more complex case but at various times segmented the social city, and elevated lines determined neighborhood development. Even today the railway lines to and from Grand Central Terminal mark the beginning of Harlem where they go underground at 96th Street beneath a natural rise in the terrain.

Vertical classifications of rich and poor areas reflect the historical tendency for the rich and powerful to build on high ground, leaving, if not forcing, the poor to live on low ground, such as in bottoms, hollows, and flats, often on the other side of the tracks. Informal and slangy place name-phrases for rich areas often use the element *-hill,* or sometimes *-heights, -point,* and the like. This is no less true of historical New York where the wealthy lived in several places named with *-Hill,* such as Murray Hill and Sugar Hill. According to New York records of 1815, a row of fine houses on the south side of Bowling Green was called *Nob's Hill*, a predecessor of San Francisco's Nob Hill where the newly rich Forty-Niners built their mansions after the Gold Rush.

Very informal, sometimes impromptu place name-phrases for the poor sections, like those for the rich areas, also have vertical elements, such as *down by-, the lower side of-, lower-, -bottom, -hollow,* and *-flats*—all taking the perspective, whether in earnest or in irony, from the higher ground and thus from higher social standing. The metaphor, too, is sometimes turned on its head and denotes poor areas as if they were on a hill—and sometimes they actually were. High elevations in certain geographic surroundings can be undesirable places to live for a variety of reasons, such as difficult access, and locally symbolize low status. *Poverty Hill* was an early name for Nassau Heights in Queens; *Vinegar Hill* was an Irish area around 135th Street and Amsterdam Avenue. *Dutch Hill* around 1850 was a German shantytown on the East River at 42nd Street. The hill more usually was a high-status place to live, as on Washington Heights.

The social symbolism of these names is one of class dominance and subordinance. Many historical and material reasons also lie behind this vertical order and its symbols. In ancient days location on high ground had to do with protecting castles and fortresses and with the association of royalty with deity and, thus, with altitude. In later times elevated sites had to do with mundane but still scarce things like drainage, better air, insulation from the plague, and, when that was all taken care of, the privileged amenity of good views from high places. This tendency is not a cultural universal and varies with settings and local histories. Yet in North America and much of Europe the primitive social symbolism of living on the hill—or high in penthouses—as opposed to somewhere down below remains strong in the modern city.

The vertical metaphor is sometimes turned on its side, though no less stratified, with phrasal elements such as *back of-, across-, beyond-, over-, over in-, over on-, other side of-,* and *out in-*. All denote class separateness and social distance. The dividing line is usually some existing feature of the city that separates class areas. Several old informal place names take account of the proximity of poor neighborhoods to, and implicitly the distance of rich areas from, malodorous industrial activities. By the 1850s Manhattan had neighborhoods blighted by the proximity of stockyards, slaughterhouses, and railway yards, mostly located on the banks of the Hudson River to receive livestock and other goods from New Jersey and the West. Images of generic slums in movies of the 1930s and 1940s, often with New York in mind, sometimes had in the background billowing smoke stacks or other symbols of proximity to dirty industrial activity, and it was not far from the truth.

The industrial gas works were a blight in all large cities in the late nineteenth century. New York had one of the earliest, largest, and most infamous *Gashouse Districts*. Starting in the late 1820s the gashouses supplied the city's need for street and household lighting for much of the century. The first big gashouse in Manhattan was constructed in 1842 at 21st Street on the East River. In the next fifty years or so gas companies built works all along the river from 14th Street north to 22nd Street. The so-called Gashouse District was the tenement-house area from 14th to 27th, from the East River over to Third Avenue. The popular name arose in the decades after the Civil War as the slum reputation of the neighborhood grew. The gashouses blighted the area with their foul odor and leaking gas. The cheapest tenements were built in the area and attracted only the poorest, mostly Irish immigrant families. The slum spawned the famous Gashouse gangs or *Gashousers*. "The young men in this slum environment formed gangs that terrorized the Gashouse district for half a century. In their lighter moments they organized courageous volunteer fire companies and dallied with 'the girls with the swinging handbags.' "[17] In 1895 the sashaying antics of these Bowery-like girls inspired Stafford Waters' tremendously popular song *The Bell of Avenoo A*.

Other implicitly lateral yet stratified classifications of rich and poor areas in New York and other American cities are the geographic names that use the cardinal compass points of North, South, East, West. The image of the city of man having four sides, named for the four cardinal directions, is an ancient one and is found in several cultures.[18] Informal but quasi-proper names, such as *West Side, East End, Northside,* and *South End,* have social meaning only within the context of a particular city and change as the class and ethnic mosaic of a city emerges; they occur as randomly as the rich or poor happen to live on this or that side of the city. Yet one such part of the city is implicitly cast in social meaning against another part in the diametrically opposite direction, north to south or east to west.

Downtown, an Americanism from the 1820s, and *uptown* from the 1830s, are of the same order as cardinal directions but add a vertical suggestion. Insofar as the social connotations of these expressions have any generality, they reflect a common pattern of historical development in cities. A few scholars have sought, moreover, to find universal meanings in *uptown* and *downtown,* much as North and South more generally tend to connote, respectively, things better and worse. North American cities tended to grow from the center outwards (at least in one direction) with the better areas leading the expansion and looking back and, so to speak, down toward the historical center. The newer, higher-status areas are "up" in the hierarchial sense, as reflected in the recent advertising terms *upscale* and *upmarket* and their converse expressions.

The nation-wide naming model may have been influenced by the fame of the historical pattern of development in Manhattan, from Downtown to Uptown, whose direction of growth was so constrained by the skinny island. Downtown was where the money was made and where, nearby, the poor lived. By the 1840s the residental Uptown was popularly associated with wealth and style, while the Old City below 14th Street gained in its reputation for poverty. In other cities *uptown* was also a residential area, which was away from, and opposed to, *downtown,* the busy commercial and entertainment district and their nearby poor neighborhoods. This spatial dichotomy also to a degree separates the public from the private and production from consumption. These two terms, moreover, separate the working class, who were left behind in slums adjacent to downtown, and the middle and upper classes who could afford to migrate upward and eventually outward to the suburbs.

The meaning of directional names, whether vertical or horizontal images, also change with class and ethnic succession in neighborhoods. *Uptown* in New York meant wealth and swank, until the uptown movement of wealth slowed and began to leapfrog to the suburbs. *Uptown* early in this century began to connote Harlem and its life, at least viewed from Midtown and from the east and west sides of Central Park. This usage also came from within Harlem. By 1930 *Uptown* was used among jazz musicians as an adjective to denote the earthy Harlem style of music.[19] Today *Uptown* clearly means Harlem, especially to blacks and increasingly to whites. In 1990 a tobacco company tried and failed in the face of protest in Harlem to market a brand of cigarettes named *Uptown,* directed specifically to African Americans.

Today the term *Downtown,* with historical irony, indicates several expensive residential areas below 14th Street, chiefly Greenwich Village, SoHo, NoHo, Tribeca, and even the "East Village." Before the early 1960s the East Village was just the upper part of the Lower East Side and in many ways a classic "slum." The name *East Village* was given in the 1960s apparently to borrow prestige from the name of Greenwich Village or just *The Village,* which then became known to some by the retronym *West Village.* It is often said that *East Village* was bestowed by real estate interests but I think it was equally given by young new residents who found the housing in Greenwich Village too costly. In the 1980s, actually beginning years earlier, the East Village underwent a partial gentrification but was stalled in the subsequent recession and declining real estate market. The recent gentrification of almost all of Manhattan has nearly stripped *East Side* versus *West Side* and *Uptown* versus *Downtown* of clear class meanings, though they still connote different middle-class styles of consumption.

From *Slum* to *Ghetto*

Slum for over a century has been the preeminent word for the poor and physically deteriorating neighborhoods of a city. By the 1950s, however, a certain liberal reaction was setting in against the harshness and connotations of the word *slum.* Urban planners in the 1950s associated slums with intractable poverty, and spoke of *gray areas* or *blighted areas* that should be subjected to the federal bulldozer and the residents dispersed. Jane Jacobs in

The Death and Life of Great American Cities, in defense of the central cities and using the case of Italian sections of Greenwich Village, argued that many of these "slums," though physically old, were in fact healthy ethnic neighborhoods. She showed that the social process of labeling them as slums was used as a justification for tearing them out of downtown and some said out of the body politic. In the 1960s social scientists and journalists introduced the quasi-euphemism *inner city* for slums in general and began to use *ghetto* for black slums in particular.

The urban historian Sam Bass Warner, Jr., found that the story of the social idea of the slums is told in the deep semantic history of the word *slum* and its succession by *ghetto.*[20] *Slum* tells an unusually revealing story of American urban development, social change, and accompanying ideologies. The semantic changes in *slum* and its partial eclipse by the word *ghetto* in public discourse is an illustration, first, of the relation of class to ethnicity and race and, second, of their recent drawing apart in response to the reality of urban poverty.

Warner first calls our attention to the period between 1850 and 1880 when single images of the city, such as the city as "destroyer of virtue," gave way to multiple images, reflecting the growing diversity of classes, ethnicity, and land uses. Abusive names were soon attached to social groups in their diversity, especially to the poor and the ethnically unassimilated, and to the areas of the city in which they lived. The names reflected and accommodated the class and ethnic divisions of the new industrial order. *Slum,* a slang word of mostly journalistic impetus, was another response to changing economic facts and ideological climates.

Slum entered British English about 1825, though not American English until about 1870. The word is of unknown origin and so is the subject of much speculation.[21] Yet we can reasonably posit that *slum* originally meant a small, low, unclean, and possibly wet place of human resort and was later extended to an urban area of such buildings. The derogating sibilant sound of *sl* conceivably directed its early and subsequent meanings. At any rate, the history and connotations of *slum* all indicate a negative idea. In British English, according to the *Oxford English Dictionary, slum* denoted a "street, alley, or court situated in a crowded district of a city inhabited by people of low class or by the very poor." The noun also referred to "a place where a number of these streets or courts formed a thickly populated neighborhood or district where the houses and the condition of life were of a squalid or wretched character." Warner notes that "in England, the term was generally used in the plural and often as 'back slums,' thereby suggesting courts and alleys behind the main streets and squares."[22]

In America, where the term was adopted at a later stage of urban development than in England, *slum* denoted a whole district of a city and reflected, as well, the different historical urban developments of the two nations. The term was thought slangy well into this century and respectable writers enclosed it in inverted commas. Social changes, Warner shows us, also prompted the appearance of the verb *to slum* and *to go slumming* in both the United States and England in the early 1880s. The new verb forms, like the older noun, were middle-class words and signaled a new relationship and attitude toward the slum. To slum or to go slumming was not to live in a slum, but to visit a slum to do charity work or, increasingly, for fashionable entertainment and to satisfy curiosity about how the other half lived.

The new verb *to slum* and its gerund also signaled the growing class segregation in the city. Warner writes that "slums were strange, novel, large places that people visited as a foreign territory" and "no one went slumming when the poor lived on the alley behind her or his house."[23] By the 1880s the middle classes, through their agents of social control, had seen to it that most low forms of prostitution, gambling, and illegal drinking had been driven into the slums. The well-to-do had to go slumming to find low forms of vice and entertainment. In the 1870s and 1880s, some called prowling around slum and vice quarters *hunting the elephant,* a variation of *seeing the elephant,* or seeing "life" and seeking out shocking and thrilling experiences.

The new slums after about 1947 were something else. They soon became largely native-born and black and Latino and were epitomized by Harlem. Its people seemed locked in a cycle of rural-style poverty and debilitated by drugs, street terror, teenage childbirth, growing welfare dependency, and hopelessness. The color, the relentless intergenerational poverty, and the despair of the new slum seemed to call for a new name. The poor black and Latino areas of the cities were—and still are—called slums. But Warner suggests that the term now seemed to miss elements of a newly emergent ideology, particularly the postwar idea of forced segregation as a simple and direct result of prejudice and discrimination. The word as well as the idea behind *ghetto* was well known to educated liberals most concerned with this problem. Thus *ghetto* soon was given a historic new meaning of chiefly a black slum of the new variety.

The American Ghetto. The history of the word *ghetto,* too, tells a related story of ideology, social change, and popular usage. The word *ghetto,* before its most recent turn of meaning, denoted the Jewish neighborhood of any large city. The word derives from the Middle Ages in Europe when Jews, particularly in Italy, were required to live in segregated quarters of cities. In 1516, the Venetian Senate legislated that the city's Jews, previously forbidden to spend the night in the city, could live together on an island called *Ghetto Nuovo* (New Ghetto), which was adjacent, and connected by a bridge, to an island called *Ghetto Vecchio* (Old Ghetto). The word *ghetto* is not of Jewish but of Italian origin and means "foundry," from the Italian verb *getare,* to pour, to cast. In 1555, Pope Paul IV issued a bull requiring Jews to live in a single quarter of all Papal States. In Venice this quarter happened to be on the site called the *Ghetto,* which at an earlier time was the site of a foundry that cast artillery. In 1562, the Jewish quarter in Rome was by semantic extension called the Ghetto for the first time, and the term soom spread to Florence, Siena, Padua, and Mantua.

In later centuries the name was applied to the Jewish areas of any city, whether legally segregated or not, such as to the famous ghettos of Frankfurt and Warsaw. Etymologist Sol Steinmetz writes that "it was to the East End [of London] that the Anglo-Jewish writer Israel Zangwill applied in 1892 the word *ghetto,* thereby adding to the infamous old word the new sense of 'a city quarter inhabited by poor immigrant Jews.' "[24] Zangwill, too, gave us a new meaning of *melting pot,* a place where immigrant groups, such as Jews, assimilate. In America *ghetto* was applied to the urban neighborhoods where Jews settled after the heavy immigrations from the East Europe in 1880s and 1890s. In New York, the name came into prominence perhaps with the publication in 1902 of Hutchins Hapgood's *The Spirit of the Ghetto,* a study of the Jewish quarter of New York.

The term also took on a variety of negative connotations, such as the so-called ghetto mentality, the supposed mind-set of Ashkenazic Jews. After a generation, though, we heard about *gilded ghettos*—the uptown neighborhoods, such as Riverside Drive and Washington Heights, and later the suburbs of successful and affluent Jews. *Ghetto* in later decades was also extended in the American context to denote a neighborhood densely settled by any ethnic group or, for that matter, any social category, such as women or the elderly, that seemed at all insular, especially if its segregation, even if self-imposed, was believed to result from prejudice and discrimination. By the 1960s *ghetto* had come to rest chiefly on black neighborhoods in large cities.

Ghetto in this new sense carries an accusation of the involuntary segregation of blacks (and of other groups) as a result of prejudice and discrimination, drawing a moral parallel with the Jewish historical experience. In the liberal but not yet radicalized ideology of the early 1960s, poor black neighborhoods and the condition of the people in them were seen as the cumulative and collective effect of white bigotry. The problem of the ghetto, it was thought, could be substantially alleviated by public education and Civil Rights legislation, which would change white hearts and release black potential. Subsequent shifts in popular ideologies have weakened these connotations of *ghetto,* and now seem to be casting about for a new vocabulary to register our beliefs about inequality in America.

The Hells of Poverty. Social reformers and the popular press in the nineteeth century made much of the image of the big city as a destroyer of youth and as a place of sin, depravity, and crime. Some of this imagery stemmed from the ancient cultural conflict between town and country, but much was a concern with poverty drawn in moral and religious terms. The language was often of dramatic contrasts of light and dark, of sunshine and shadow, and of heaven and hell. The areas of shadow, darkness, and hell were, of course, the slums, and light and redemption were to be middle-class piety and behavior, though mindlessly expected to emerge in the midst of economic poverty. Slum enclaves and whole slum neighborhoods in New York and in other cities were called infernal names such as *The Devil's Half Acre, Hell's Half Acre,* or most famously *Hell's Kitchen.* All manner of low establishments catering to vice in these neighborhoods were called *hells.* Preachers called New York's old Tenderloin the *Inferno* and *Satan's Circus.* Stephen Crane in *Maggie* gave the name *Devil's Row* to his fictional Irish slum enclave near the old Bowery; he later told an interviewer that his fictional street was not modeled on an actual street but on a condition. Social scientists in the 1920s were also occasionally attracted to the Dantean metaphor to describe urban slums.

Hell's Kitchen, at least as a name pertaining to a neighborhood, is possibly indigenous to New York. Applied to the notorious slum on the West Side, it was probably just a period metaphor, though several dubious etymologies of a different sort have been offered. *Hell's Kitchen* pertinently was used as a metaphor for a brutal prison as a place of embitterment and a school for crime; it was also the name of a low saloon in Corlears Hook. I can only add, taking a lesson from the way similar names have evolved, that the original *Hell's Kitchen* might have been a local name for a single festering tenement house, or perhaps of a particular row of them, and spread to the whole neighborhood. No one knows for sure.

Hell's Kitchen, a mixed black and Irish slum, arose in the late 1850s. The area grew until it was bounded roughly by 39th and 59th streets, from the Hudson River to Eighth Avenue. The decline of the bucolic areas began about 1851 with the building of railway yards, stockyards, and other dirty industries near the river. Then came the tenements for the poor and immigrants who worked in these industries. The name, because of its fame and mythical status, became a slang generic for a slum in any large American city. Hell's Kitchen epitomized the equation of the classic nineteeth-century slum with a social hell. The late John Ciardi, a Dante scholar, called Hell's Kitchen a "hot, steamy, stinking, infernal place. The kitchen would certainly be the hottest part of hell. Hot, by transference, teeming, and in context, evil."[25]

For those who like to stretch a metaphor, Hell's Kitchen had a subdistrict apparently known, according to O. Henry in the short story "Vanity and Some Sables" (1907), as "The Stovepipe," from which a probably fictional Stovepipe Gang took its name. This was "a narrow and natural extension" of the neighborhood that "runs along Eleventh and Twelfth avenues on the river, and bends a hard and sooty elbow around little, lost homeless De Witt Clinton Park. Consider that a stovepipe is an important factor in any kitchen and the situation is analyzed. The chefs in 'Hell's Kitchen' are many, and the 'Stovepipe' gang wears the cordon blue."

Hell's Kitchen served up vicious gangs and became part of the city's folklore and influenced the notions of popular culture. In 1936, Richard Rodgers wrote the music for the gangster ballet "Slaughter on Tenth Avenue" in his show *On Your Toes.* Rodgers' mythical tale took its inspiration from the romanticized apache culture of the slum. After an ethnic succession by Puerto Ricans in the 1950s, the neighborhood was again mythicized in Leonard Bernstein's musical of 1957, *West Side Story*. All this had as little to do with the real neighborhood as its name had to do with the reality. Theodore Dreiser in *The Color of A Great City*, recalling his period of residence in Hell's Kitchen years earlier, wondered "why they saw fit to dub it Hell's Kitchen, however, I could never discover. It seemed to me a very ordinary slum neighborhood, poor and commonplace, and sharply edged by poverty, but just life and very, very human life at that."[26]

Most of that Hell's Kitchen is gone today. The gangs were mostly broken up around 1910, though remnants were active through and encouraged by Prohibition. The neighborhood remained poor until recent years and small parts of it still are. Today, Hell's Kitchen is gentrifying and the tenements are becoming co-ops or being replaced by corporate skyscrapers. The real-estate interests and aspiring residents in the neighborhood, hoping to supplant the old reputation of Hell's Kitchen, have taken the new, more genteel name of *Clinton,* an early name for part of the area when it was farms owned by the distinguished Clinton family of New Yorkers.

Streets and alleys of slum neighborhoods in the nineteenth century were given all manner of colorful names, sometimes by the residents themselves, to denote the vice and squalor of life in tenement districts—their hell-like quality. A number of these names use the phrasal elements *-row* and *-alley,* which have long been common in making informal urban place names.[27] *Poverty Row* was the most popular and genteel generic name for the old slums of New York. Gussie L. Davis and Arthur L. Trevelyan's song of 1895, "Down in Poverty Row," romanticized slum life; note the word *down.*

More realistic reformers used harsher names. Charles Loring Brace mentioned *Misery Row* on Tenth Avenue between 17th and 19th streets. Jacob Riis and other writers of the period used names "of the local street nomenclature, in which the directory has no hand"—*Bone Alley* (once near Houston Street), *Bottle Alley, Bandits' Roost, Thieves' Alley, Battle Row, Murderers' Alley* (once off Baxter Street), *Mixed-Ale Flats, Shinbone Alley, Bummers' Retreat, Mulligan's Alley, Rag Pickers' Row, Cockroach Row,* and *Dead-Cat Alley.* Of *Kerosene Row,* Riis wrote, "Everywhere is the stench of the kerosene stove that is forever burning, serving for cooking, heating, and ironing alike, until the last atom of oxygen is burned out of the close air."[28] The connotation of these names, taken together, is one of poverty, crime, violence, drink, and filth.

The Dead End, nearly forgotten as a once real name of a Manhattan slum, denoted a geographic reference and, like *Hell's Kitchen,* also suggested a social condition. Early in this century The Dead End was an Irish slum in midtown on First Avenue overlooking the East River. The name arose because the neighborhood was as far east as one could go on the crosstown streets short of the river—The Dead End. Social status was also measured by the distance east or west from Fifth Avenue and the river was as far as one could get from Fifth Avenue. The phrase *dead end* also connotes a social condition of thwarted lives and despair and, I think, in this double sense was taken as the title of Sidney Kingsley's play *Dead End* (1935) and its even more successful movie version of the same title in 1937. Thereafter a series of movies, beginning with *Angels with Dirty Faces* (1938), featured the famous Dead End Kids, who became America's sanitized image of slum boys.

Names for Rich Areas. *Millionaires' Row* was most famously applied to rich areas in New York, though the name and close variants occur in several cities. Rich areas in New York and other cities, notably Chicago, after about 1920 were also called *the Gold Coast*. It derives from the name of the Gold Coast of West Africa, a source of wealth for British colonials. One of the earliest so-named Millionaires' Rows in New York was a block on West 23rd Street, a development formally called London Terrace, between Ninth and Tenth Avenues. People started calling it Millionaires' Row shortly after the row-house development for the city's affluent was completed in 1845. But the city's most famous Millionaires' Row was Fifth Avenue. As its reputation grew, The Avenue became the city's social ladder and the site of a succession of Millionaires' Rows. The homes of the wealthy at mid-century had started at No. 1 Fifth Avenue at Washington Square.

In later years, Millionaires' Row stretched from 24th to 59th streets. The center was around 34th Street on Murray Hill, occasionally called *Quality Hill,* where the Astor family and others built mansions. The famous Marble Row on Fifth between 57th and 58th streets later was distinctly a Millionaires' Row. The main Millionaires' Row of the Gilded Age was the mansions north of 59th Street, eventually stretching to 96th Street, overlooking the east side of Central Park. It was from this context of a mile or two—in its heyday more—of granite and even marble mansions, and the style of life in them, that *uptown* and sometimes even the name *Fifth Avenue* were extended to mean well-to-do areas in any city.

The heart of New York's extended Millionaires' Row was at one stage of its development more than a mile in length and, so, was also called *Millionaires' Mile.* By the late 1890s popular expression in New York referred to "a mile and a half of millionaires" on Fifth Avenue, or even "two miles of millionaires." The old nobs, of course, looked askance at the row of millionaires that could be measured by the mile and especially at their vulgar mansions copied, often with embellishments, after every imaginable French or Italian grand style, and some designs were freely invented. Ralph Marvell in Edith Wharton's *The Custom of the Country,* on the steps of his genteel, old red-brick row house in Washington Square, mused on the "social disintegration expressed by widely-different architectural physiognomies at the other end of Fifth Avenue."[29] The disparate and eclectic palaces on Fifth Avenue were often the subject of low doggerel and much folk humor during the Gilded Age.

Names for Minority Ethnic Neighborhoods

Konrad Bercovici in *Around the World in New York* fancifully suggested that ethnic settlement in Manhattan, as it appeared to him in the 1910s, had recapitulated the ethnic geography of Europe.

> A map of Europe superposed upon the map of New York would prove that the different foreign sections of the city live in the same proximity to one another as in Europe: the Spanish near the French, the French near the Germans, the Germans near the Austrians, the Russians and the Rumanians near the Hungarians, and the Greeks behind the Italians. People of western Europe live in the western side of the city. People of eastern Europe live in the eastern side of the city. Northerners live in the northern part of the city and southerners in the southern part. Those who have lived on the other side near the sea or a river have the tendency here to live as near the sea or the river as possible. The English, islanders, living on the other side of the Hudson as if the river were the channel that separates them from the rest of Europe.[30]

More realistically, two large trends, both more economic than ethnic, determined the social mosaic of Manhattan and later of the New York metropolitan area. First, by 1850 the compact, socially mixed Old City below 14th Street was beginning to break up toward larger and more homogeneous social areas. Throughout the rest of the century, there was a transition from a diversified to a segregated pattern of occupation and residence and the ethnic mosaic variegated with it. The close association of ethnicity and immigration with the class hierarchy of the city made the burgeoning new neighborhoods more homogeneous in language, culture, religion, and national origin. Second, by 1900 the trend of decentralization was already well underway. For Manhattan, this was mostly a movement uptown and then northward and outward to the suburban boroughs and beyond.

The inhabitants of early neighborhoods of great wealth and fame, it went without saying, were all white, Protestant, and of old immigrant stock, though they were nonetheless "ethnic" in their way. White Protestants in New York used to be known simply as *Americans* and, in the nativist atmosphere of nineteeth-century immigration, this is also what they called themselves. From the 1860s to the 1890s, Greenwich Village was known as the *American Ward,* then the city's prestigious Ninth Ward. Greenwich Village had a distinctive Anglo-American ethnic character and way of life that was disrupted after about 1890 by the New Immigration from especially Italy.

When the ethnicity of a neighborhood was otherwise made explicit in

popular names, the neighborhood was usually poor, often immigrant, and
the name often as not was derisive. These popular locutions, it bears repeat-
ing, are the urban place-name counterparts of ethnic slurs and behave similarly. Most form with a popular name for the group to modify -*town* or
sometimes -*ville*. Low register nicknames for ethnic neighborhoods thus
contain the most offensive names for the resident groups themselves, such as
Nigger Town, Kike Town, or *Wop Town. Chinatown* might be thought
derogatory and at one time was, for the same reason that *Chinaman* is
pejorative, but it is now generally accepted. New York's Chinatown also
was occasionally called *Pigtail Town,* sometimes *Pigtail Alley,* which is a
reference to the old-fashioned pigtail hairstyle that was worn by some Chinese men on the streets of Chinatown down to the early 1890s. *Chow-Mein
Stem* and *Poppy Alley* (from opium *poppy* and an allusion to opium dens)
were also ephemeral names for Chinatown and its main stem of Mott Street.
They probably were of newspaper origin around 1900 when slumming and
a peek at a mock opium den were popular.

Some of these historical names were never particulaly offensive and
served merely as informal place names. In the 1880s, the area of 3rd, 4th,
Wooster, and Greene streets just southeast of Washington Square was called
French Town, because of the French settlement there. The café life and style
of French Town was an early source of nearby Greenwich Village's reputation for Parisian Frenchiness. *Germantown* was the neighborhood mainly to
the east of Second Avenue and centered on Tompkins Square that was settled
after the failed European revolutions of 1848. By the 1860s Avenue A south
of 14th Street was called *Dutch* (i.e., *Deutsch*) *Boulevard*. The Slocum river
boat disaster in 1904, in which over a thousand mainly women and children
from the neighborhood were drowned, hastened the breakup of Germantown in favor of the new German settlement of Yorkville uptown around
east 86th Street.

Other informal neighborhood names were made with *Little-* to modify
the proper name of the group's country of origin. Sizeable sections of Manhattan's Old City below 14th Street were once called *Klein Deutschland,*
"Little Germany." *Little Russia* was the name of the Russian Jewish settlement in south Harlem, which was dissolved by 1930; most of its residents
were migrants from the immigrant Lower East Side. These and other names
have been taken up by the residents themselves and symbolize ethnic pride
and identity with place. Some of the *Little-* names have found so solid a place
in the language that they have become virtually formal place names, such as
Little Italy on and around Mulberry Street.

Some popular place names are, on the other hand, implicitly ethnic, as
are some formal names, such as *Harlem. Shantytown,* a term of the early
1880s, on the face of it refers to any poor section of shacks or shanties. Yet
historically urban shanties and shantytowns are associated chiefly with
poor Irish immigrants, whence the phrase *Shanty Irish*. Until the late 1860s,
a mainly Irish shantytown shambled over much of the East Side, including

Fifth Avenue along Central Park, and harbored some 5,000 squatters. (In the Depression of the 1930s, a new generation of shantytowns of the unemployed appeared in Central Park and were called *Hoovervilles*.) Shantytowns declined quickly after 1870 when gaslight was carried north on Fifth Avenue to 59th Street, then the edge of civilization. Remnants of Shantytown occupied part of the Park itself until almost 1880. The East and Hudson rivers were lined with other so-named Shantytowns.

The Jews of New York were popularly noted for their success and upward mobility. In the Yiddish-American vernacular, an upwardly mobile person, especially one who seemed to have doffed Jewish ways and values in order to assimilate, was rather contemptuously called an *allrightnik,* one who had got himself set up "all right." Etymologist Sol Steinmetz writes that "from *olrayt* 'all right' American Yiddish derived *olraytnik* 'upstart, parvenu' and the feminine *olraytnitse;*" and this was taken into English as *allrightnik.*[31] The slangy street name *Allrightniks Row* was given to Riverside Drive where certain affluent Jews came to live. In the 1920s and 1930s *Wisenheimers* called nearby Washington Heights the *Jewish Alps.* *W(e)isenheimer,* incidentally, was by the 1910s a punning new name for *smart alecks,* itself a New York coinage of the mid-nineteenth century.

The name *Allrightniks Row* is best known from Samuel Ornitz's novel *Hauch Paunch and Jowl,* whose narrator finally mused: "So here we live in *Allrightniks* Row, Riverside Drive. The newly rich Russian, Galician, Polish, and Roumanian Jews have squeezed out the German Jews and their Gentile neighbors. Great elevator apartment structures are being put up to house the clamoring *Allrightniks.* The Ghetto called anyone who was well off—one who is *all right in this world,* that is well fixed, an *Allrightnik.* We moved in the world of the *Allrightniks.*"[32]

Up to Harlem.   Black New Yorkers moved uptown with the rest of Manhattan. In the Federal period several small, free-black settlements were on the southern tip of the island. Soon other black communities, called *Stagg Town* and *Negro Plantations,* were settled near the Five Points and occupied Mulberry Street long before the Italians came. By the 1830s some African Americans were moving farther uptown and by 1865 a quarter of the city's black population had settled in the area around Bleecker, Sullivan, and Thompson streets, just south of Washington Square. The neighborhood was then politely known as *Little Africa,* an early nineteenth-century name for a black district in any city. More slangily, it was called *Coontown.* Another small settlement was also nearby in the two streets together known as The Minettas. By the 1910s tiny, angled Gay Street was the only black block remaining in the Washington Square area.

After the Civil War, many African Americans moved farther uptown to several locations on the West Side between the 20s and the low 60s, including in and around the Tenderloin vice district. It became a mixed area where blacks were segregated from whites block by block, sometimes tenement by tenement. This neighborhood reached its peak about 1890. A settlement of African Americans had also formed west of Columbus Circle in the west 50s and 60s, just north of Hell's Kitchen. The section above West 59th Street, between Tenth and Eleventh avenues sharply bounded an Irish district in the low 60s. This hilly area, sloping toward the river, around 1900 became known facetiously and generally among New Yorkers as *San Juan Hill*. It is traditionally said today that the area was named in honor of the black soldiers who distinguished themselves in the famous Battle of San Juan Hill that was fought in Cuba in the Spanish-American War of 1898. Or sometimes it is said that its was so named because so many black veterans of the War lived in the neighborhood.

The name more probably alludes to the riots between the blacks and the neighboring Irish that were fought up and down the hilly streets of the district. Perhaps the name was initially given by an onlooker or participant who saw a sardonic parallel between the two battles. During the hot spell of August 1900, about the time San Juan Hill was named, one of the city's worst race riots since the Draft Riots of 1863 occurred in the Tenderloin and several incidents also broke out in the West 60s; racial violence was much on the mind of the city in 1900. After the First World War, when the black migration to Harlem was well underway, San Juan Hill became known as Columbus Hill, denying its past.

The suburb of Harlem, named by the early Dutch settlers for their home city or Haarlem in the Netherlands, was annexed to New York in 1873 and developed as a middle and upper class area. Most of the fine old houses standing today were built between 1870 and 1910. By 1900 or so developers had overbuilt Harlem in expectation of an endless demand for luxurious housing by affluent white New Yorkers. Whites began to flee when the blacks came after 1910. The collapse of speculative building and white flight opened to blacks the fine housing intended for whites. But the chief impetus to the new settlement of Harlem was the fact that by 1910 the city's black population had increased to 92,000, mostly by migration from the South. By 1920 black Harlem was bounded by Fifth and Eighth avenues and by 130th and 145th streets and had 73,000 residents, or two thirds of the city's black population. Thereafter Harlem spread mostly southward along the avenues. The onset of the Depression hastened its decline into a slum.

A few blacks had begun to migrate to Harlem as early as 1890, and by 1909 a black settlement had appeared in Harlem around West 133rd Street. West 130th, a tenement street, was called *Darktown* in the 1890s. Similarly, a poor settlement on West 146th Street was called *Nigger Row*. In the 1920s and 1930s whites called all Harlem the *Black Belt* and *Darktown*. Cab Calloway more poetically referred to his Harlem as the *Land O' Darkness*. Yet most often New Yorkers used the old Dutch name *Harlem*, which now had a new ethnic meaning. Other ethnic groups settled on the east side of

Harlem into areas called *Italian Harlem* and *Spanish Harlem. The Barrio,* from Spanish *el barrio,* a neighborhood or quarter, was borrowed into English and applied to New York's Spanish Harlem by the 1930s.

Harlem's *Strivers' Row* is the two block-faces on West 138th and 139th streets between Seventh and Eighth avenues. It was a unified development of 130 tan brick row houses designed by Stanford White and completed in 1891. The row was originally named the King's Model Houses and was built for and restricted to white owners until 1919. The Equitable Life Assurance Society then put them up for sale to anyone with the money; they were all sold to affluent blacks. *Strivers' Row* was applied about 1919 as a black term of derision for the well-to-do who sought yet higher status in the elegant townhouses, often with heavy mortgages. In other American cities heavily mortgaged neighborhoods have been called *Debtors' Row* or *Mortgage Row,* as well as *Strivers' Row.* Countee Cullen in 1931 depicted Strivers' Row and Sugar Hill in his novel *One Way to Heaven.* Popular recognition of the name greatly increased in the 1930s with the production of Abram Hill's play *On Strivers' Row,* which satirized the social set and made the name a trope for Harlem social climbers. Strivers' Row keeps that symbolism today.

Sugar Hill was the name given in the late 1920s to the Harlem neighborhood of grand apartment houses on Coogan's Bluff, the rise along the heights roughly between Amsterdam and Edgecombe avenues, between about 138th and 155th streets. After the whites fled, Harlem's Café Society, among them many black intellectuals, writers, artists, musicians, and politicans, came to live on Sugar Hill and were called *Sugar Hillies.* In "Harlem Sweeties," poet Langston Hughes wrote: "Have you dug the spill/ Of Sugar Hill?/ Cast your gims on this sepia thrill:/ . . . Stroll down luscious,/ Delicious, *fine* Sugar Hill." The *sugar* in the name, of course, is slang for 'money,' and Sugar Hill is figuratively up where the money is. It also connoted the sweet and expensive life that money afforded. "If you want to go to Harlem, 'way up to Sugar Hill,'" composer and lyricist Billy Strayhorn penned in 1941, "you must take the 'A' train."

Historian David Levering Lewis wrote that Sugar Hill was "a citadel of stately apartment buildings and liveried doormen on a rock, [and] soared above the Polo Grounds and the rest of Harlem like a city of Incas."[33] From this vantage point, central Harlem was called *The Valley,* as it lay below them both socially and physically. Down around West 133rd Street was once *Oatmeal Flats,* an area were rents were so high that renters had "to live on oatmeal" and occasionally hold rent parties to pay the landlords.

10

The Contempt
for Provincial Life

Country louts, with heads craned forward and
tow-colored hair, stare and stumble
WALT WHITMAN, ,"Broadway"

The disdain of city people for their country cous-
ins is an ancient story that reoccurs in every urbanizing society. The perennial drama was played out in the century and a half from the emergence of
the early industrial city in the United States, through its evolution into a
metropolis in the decades around 1900, its maturing after 1920, and its
decentralization after the late 1940s down to the present time. The cultural
and political conflict between the City of New York and upstate is a classic
case in point. The cultural conflict between the center and the periphery
arising from these changes was widely reflected in literature and folklore,
including the slang of the day. City people expressed their contempt for rural
and small-town people and places with more than a hundred pejorative
names. Some of the oldest terms are borrowed from British English and were
given new turns of meaning in the American urban setting.

These words and phrases are yet another major case of popular naming
of social variety, this time over the whole metropolitan region. The contrast
of city and country in popular speech, once again, serves to maintain group
identities and boundaries. Urbanites differentiate the space of the metropolitan community ethnocentrically, distinguishing between the center (Us) and
the periphery (Them). The urban name-callers expressed their disaffiliation
from, and superiority to, their provincial opposites. The performance of the
act of name-calling had the effect of shoring up the boundaries of the
group—in this case the moral union of the city itself. Name-calling becomes
particularly vigorous when identities seem threatened and when members
feel marginal to the group. Urbanites, some of them just a step away from
rural backgrounds, thus expressed their identities as city people, not *hicks*,
as people who lived at the center of things, not in *the sticks*.

Yet the big city has been described as a collection of small towns, even
"urban villages," where people in their way are no less provincial than their
country cousins. Popular epithets for country and small-town people are
sometimes turned around and thrown back at equally provincial people in
the big cities, as in *city hick, city jake, city cousin*, or "dumb" this and that.
Gotham, Washington Irving's nickname for New York City, was introduced
with the ironic sense of a city of provincial fools, and more about that

follows. O. Henry in "Innocents of Broadway" (1907) had his narrator comment on a city provincial who "hadn't been above Fourteenth Street in ten years" and as "a typical city Reub—I'd bet the man hadn't been out of sight of a skyscraper in twenty-five years." Broadway columnist O. O. McIntyre, who called New York "Jaytown on the Hudson," quipped, "In New York, Reuben does not come to town. He lives there. Remove the spats and monocle and behold the apple-knocker."[1]

City people may be dimly aware of their own kind of provinciality but nonetheless feel superior to their rural and small-town counterparts. Sociologist Barry Schwartz, writing of the disdain of urbanites for suburbs in the 1950s, observes that "the masses of the city may find in their lives nothing but routine and monotony; but as members of the center, they are part of a collective dynamism which colors and becomes part of their existence. They become the 'city people,' of whom rural and small-town lore has so much to tell."[2]

After about 1830, the urban population, especially in the big cities of the Northeast, grew much more rapidly than the farm population, chiefly from farm-to-city migration. For fully a century or more, migrants were culturally visible and part of the city's social scene. Young Walt Whitman, writing for the New York *Aurora* in 1842, wrote that "you can always tell a rustic in Broadway, from his ill-at-easeness."[3] More experienced New Yorkers berated farm-to-city migrants and immigrants from abroad as newcomers—*greenhorns*. The term had connotations of the country hick, whether from upstate or from eastern or southern Europe. *Greenhorn* is an extension of the same word for a young, inexperienced animal with young or "green" horns before they are hardened and darkened with age and experience. *Greenhorn*, as well as the slangier nounal forms *green*, *greener*, and *greeny*, were much used on the Lower East Side in the decades around 1900. And some of the newcomers, probably with mixed emotions, surely used their new urban vocabulary of disdain to belittle people still in the country or in the old country.

Pejoratives for American Provincials

By 1900 there was an ideological split between city and country that occurred when urban industry finally overtook agriculture and the rural way of life. The cities, New York included, invented and used a torrent of derisive names and pejorative sterotypes of farmers, their families, and their communities. Quite aside from the names like *hick, yokel,* or *hayseed,* popular culture portrayed farmers as stupid but wily, uncouth, coarse, and living in remote communities destitute of civilization. Vaudeville made popular the so-called Rube songs, such as "Wal, I Swan" (1907). The Rube songs were about the idiocy of life down on the farm and were traditionally sung by the comic figure of a toothless farmer in a high-pitched, nasal voice. The farmer, as well as his horse Dobbin, became a stock figure of fun alongside the harsh vaudeville image of the city's ethnic minorities.

The year 1920 was a watershed for American society and culture. When the country settled down after the First World War, it was soon clear that the nation had finally tilted from a predominantly rural-agrarian society to an urban-industrial order. The U.S. Census of 1920 showed for the first time in American history that the majority of the population was no longer rural; by 1930 nearly half of the population would be living in metropolitan areas. The agrarian way of life, which had culturally dominated American society since the colonial period, had lost public esteem in favor of the urban way of life, at least in the cities. And this shift of national values was directly reflected in the growing popularity of ridiculing rural areas and small towns with an imagery of the city turned wrong side out.

The farm and the small town also became objects of scorn among intellectuals and communities of disassociation for many upwardly mobile young people who flocked to the great cities. These attitudes were reflected in and supported by literature, social thought, and popular culture. Main Street was entrenched but by 1920 was actually declining as a social institution. Main Street nonetheless became a negative symbol for disaffected young intellectuals and writers who resented and chafed against small-town dullness, smugness, provincialism, conventionality, and philistinism. A remarkable number of these people gravitated to New York. Or they went first to Chicago and, finding it also too provincial, went on to New York.

Sinclair Lewis's novel *Main Street,* published in 1920, satirized the supposed values of small-town people in the Middle West and made the author famous. The setting was drawn from Lewis's hometown of Sauk Centre, Minnesota. Out of a related critical atmosphere in social science, Robert Lynd and Helen Lynd in 1929 published *Middletown: A Study of Contemporary American Culture,* their famous community study of Muncie, Indiana. The two books were inevitably compared; H. L. Mencken's review, "A City in Moronia" in the *American Mercury* of March 1929, found them to be complementary fictional and sociological portraits of the "booboisie." The titles of the books themselves, *Main Street* and *Middletown,* entered popular language in the 1920s and 1930s as uncomplimentary generics, as did briefly *Gopher Prairie,* Lewis's fictional name of his hometown. *Gopher-prairie dog,* "a countryman," was recorded in a 1926 dictionary of slang.[4] H. L. Mencken about this time coined *Bible Belt* to air his invective against rural and small-town provincials.

Names for Rustics and Farmers. Most of the oppositional terms for country people are male stereotypes. Abusive slang naming social diversity, at least historically, was chiefly a male indulgence used in a competitive social world of men. The urban stereotype of rural women came more often in the form of salacious jokes about country girls or "farmer's daughters." In this folklore young farm women were portrayed as figures of utter, though naive sexual promiscuity, serving at the pleasure of "traveling salesmen" from the city and behind the backs of dumb farmers. Yet taken together the names for rustics and farmers give us a word picture of the provincial as both he and she were imagined, not always actually seen, by city people in the nineteenth and early twentieth centuries.

Explicit in the origins and root meanings of many of these terms is the image of a naive, foolish, unsophisticated, unwary countryman who is an easy prey for city sharpers and swindlers. He was easy to spot in the sidewalk streams of New York and was regularly duped, even if not "sold the Brooklyn Bridge." Yet, like any member of a group held in prejudice, people were sometimes surprised to see him succeed or do well at anything. The counterbalancing image, more often seen in narrative forms of the folklore, is that the seeming dupe is not so dumb as he seems and, indeed, he may be so clever as to outsmart the city dudes and slickers. This is the meaning of his mockmodest exclamation about himself, *not bad for a country boy!*

Derogatory and ridiculing names, when they were used by city people, were reflexive to the collective image of the users. By pejoratively naming provincials, city people said who they were not. City people, the reflexive message said, were at a dignified distance from the earthiness of farms, livestock, and the farm life. Farm people even took on some of the character and behavior of the wild and domesticated animals of their surroundings. City people's dress signified their often white-collar occupations; their physiques, complexion, and graceful body movements also signified a life of shelter; they were worldly, intelligent, educated, and spoke correctly; they knew proper sidewalk manners and did not bump into people. City people, even if they were factory workers, were experienced and thus wary; their behavior was purposeful and predictable, not random and mysterious like certain farm activities. City people did not bear given names, such as *Clem* and *Reuben,* stigmatized with rurality, and if they did, they were embarrassed. City women were sexually modest or at least knew enough to be coy, unlike the barely suppressed barnyard promiscuity of "farmers' daughters" and other country girls. Listen for these reflexive images in the words and phrases of popular speech.

The most genuinely popular American epithets for rural people today, and in just about this order, are *hick, hillbilly, hayseed, rube, clodhopper, farmer, yokel,* and *bumpkin.* Several names of this class were borrowed from the British English where they had been long used for exactly the same purpose to express the tensions between town and country. Some of the most general of the American epithets are modified with *country-,* as though to emphasize their counter location on the periphery, as in *country hick* and many others. More than a hundred other names for rustics and farmers have occurred in regional American English, but were mostly restricted to small town and rural use.[5] Just as many similar names were of journalistic whimsy and never popular, though their use in print shows the proclivity of some writers and what they thought their readers liked.[6]

Certain personal given names that were common in rural America of the nineteenth century probably struck early namecallers as special to the collective object of their contempt. *Hick* is from the old English dialectal nickname for *Richard.* In seventeenth-century British speech, *hick* had come to mean a simple countryman and one who was an easy prey for the city sharpers. *Hick* came into American English in both senses in the 1840s. George W. Matsell reported an apparent variant, *hicksam,* "a countryman, a fool," on the mean streets of New York in the 1850s. The more slangy *wood hick* and the adjective *hicky* eventually appeared. By 1900 *hicktown* for his place of residence was probably in oral use.

Reuben, the Hebrew given name once popular in Protestant America, had become generic for a countryman by about 1850, and its short form *Rube* was in print use by the late 1890s. *Rube* in this sense either originated in or was taken up by carnival, circus, and show biz argot. The cry of alarm "Hey, Rube!" was put up by circus and carnival people when a *local yokel* for some reason complained loudly, threatened, or actually picked a fight. In 1891 Tin Pan Alley published "Hey, Rube," a song by J. Sherrie Mathews and Harry Bulger. One of the best known occurrences of *Reuben* in popular culture is in the lyrics of George M. Cohan's song "Only 45 Minutes from Broadway." New Rochelle, New York, just north of the city, was supposed to be the setting of the musical show of 1906. "Oh! what a fine bunch of Reubens, Oh! what a jay atmosphere/ They have whiskers like hay, and imagine Broadway only 45 minutes from here."

A few other given names for men gathered the same meanings. *Jake,* the old nickname for *Jacob,* was another Old Testament name popular in nineteenth-century America. It came to mean a country sort, often specified in *country Jake,* and dates in this sense to around 1850. Carnies also liked to call the gullible local men *Clem,* a nickname for *Clarence,* another name once common in rural areas; carnies shouted "Clem!" too. The generic *Elmer* was also heard.

The slang name *jerk,* most likely from a dialectal pronunciation of the nickname *Jack,* was occasionally used for a naive countryman, especially one who appeared foolish. Folklorically, a jerk has sustained self-induced feeble-mindedness from "jacking-off" or "jerking off," and that graphic expression has been been in the language for hundreds of years. The urban slang sense of *jerk* as an offensive person became popular only around 1940. None of these *jerks* have anything to do with the origin of *jerkwater town,* as we shall see in a later section. Its short form *jerktown* was in tramps' argot by 1900. *Jerktown* is nonetheless now taken to mean where the jerks, or rustic fools, live. *Herkimer Jerkimer,* a fool, a rustic, is a "jerk from Herkimer," an impossibly remote place. This jerk was, presumably, from his upstate hometown of Herkimer, New York, ZIP code 13350.

Jay and *yokel* may derive from images of rural birds. *Yokel* dates from around 1810 and is of uncertain origin in British English. Webster's Third says it is perhaps imitative of the call of the English green woodpecker. John

Ciardi speculated that it is a "person from out where the green woodpeckers call."[7] Etymologist Gerald Cohen, however, asks if the green woodpecker "really calls out 'Yokel'?" If not, he advances an "alternative, very tentative suggestion" that it may have come from Polish Yiddish *Jukl*, a fool, a country bumpkin, dupe, and was perhaps early "imported by Jewish criminals into English cant," as so many other slang words have come into Anglo-American usage.[8]

Jay, another old name for a rustic or even a city boor, is also of uncertain origin. *Jay* was extremely common in older New York speech. It may be remotely from a man's name or, as others speculate, it may be from the echoic name of the European jay, who supposedly calls *gai! gai!*. It alludes, according to Ciardi, to "one who lives back there among the jays."[9] The jay bird also has a reputation of being loud, squawky, boorish toward other birds, rambunctious, and an impertinent chatterer, and this is perhaps the original allusion of the name. Cohen however reasons that more likely the original allusion was to the bright, striking plumage of the jay bird.[10] By transference, *jay* came to mean, in the words of Webster's Third, (a) a gaudily or flashily dressed person and (b) an unsophisticated, countrified, gullible person. Cohen posits that the first became a popular image of the second, thus *jay* for a naive countryman, but also for the pugnaciousness of the loudly dressed jay bird.

When a country jay comes to town, he wanders without urban purpose, gawking at the sights, walking heedlessly through the city traffic as through his rural fields. For that ignorance of the rules (which was probably misunderstood as deliberate lawlessness) he was by the 1910s called a *jaywalker*. Lexicographer Laurence Urdang agrees with the origin of *jay* from the "noisy, defiant" jaybird and adds that "this is likely to have been reinforced by (or may be a play on) *jayhawker*, an Americanism of unknown origin referring to a member of a guerilla band in eastern Kansas in the 1850s and early 1860s. . . . These notions of lawlessness and the sound of *jayhawker* seem likely to have produced *jaywalker*. The verb *jaywalk* is a backformation—that is, it was formed by the dropping of the *-er*."[11] By way of animal sounds, *yap*, is another name for a country boor and could be at root imitative of the impertinent bark of a dog that does not seem too bright. In the years around 1900 *yap* was a New York favorite, especially in the comic press.

Several names for rustics seem to derive from the notion of their lumpishness and clumsiness. *Hoosier*, an Americanism of uncertain origin, since the 1820s has meant a rustic and was also taken as a proud monicker by residents of Indiana. The word is "perhaps" from English dialect, *hoozer*, denoting anything large of its kind, allows *Webster's Third*. If so, it conceivably alluded to the supposedly larger size of American farm boys who were said to be "corn fed." *Country bumpkin* or just *bumpkin*, which was borrowed from British English around 1782, seems to be from Flemish *bummekjin*, a small cask, perhaps suggesting a stoutish, person who rolls and bumps about, both offending and amusing city people. *Joskin,* a bump-kin, and a loanword from early nineteenth-century British slang, says Random House's Second, is perhaps a blend of English dialectal *joss,* to jostle, to bump, and bump*kin.*

Another class of names for rustics declares that they jump, kick, and hop in frenetic activity that bewilders and amuses more reposed city folk. In the image of these terms, farmers have peculiar forms of locomotion over, around, and through objects of the open fields of upstate. They do this footwork wearing clodhoppers or hobnail boots, whence the old name *hobnail* for a countryman. He was also called *Hob,* but this time from the old nickname for *Robert;* both *hobnail* and *hobb* with two b's, according to Matsell, were on the streets of New York by the 1850s. *Clodhopper* is a British term that goes back to about 1690 and was in the United States by the mid-nineteenth century. Clodhoppers hop like grasshoppers (whence the word seems to be modeled) over clods of earth turned up by plows; the word now refers both to the man and the boots he wears. He is sometimes called just a *clod,* directly from the lumpish clods he hops over so cloddishly.

Stumpjumpers arcanely jump over stumps of trees that were cut to clear new fields for plowing; or perhaps they jump from one stump to another. Equally athletic *gulley jumpers* jump over gullies and *brierhoppers* hop over briers. *Cloverkickers* skip through fields of clover, or perhaps just kick at the feed for the milk cows. A farmer is also known as a *shitkicker,* which has a curious but ultimately understandable double meaning, on the one hand, of a naive country lad, and on the other, of a double-dealer who affects modesty by kicking at imaginary things on the ground and saying "Aw, shucks," using a well-known euphemism for *shit.*

The association of the farm crops of corn and hay with the essence of country people was the source of several other names. The Americanism *corn cracker* dates from the early 1830s and derives from the frontier food staple of cracked corn. This diet also probably accounts for the eighteenth-century name *cracker* for the Scotch-Irish, whip-cracking, hell-raising, boasting, backwoods Georgian. Among the lower orders of New York in the 1850s, according to Matsell, rustics were called *cornthrashers.* In corn grow-ing regions, rustics were called *corn huskers* and *corn tassels,* the second perhaps from the farm job of detasseling corn to keep it from pollinating. All these sorts were said to be *corn-fed,* which supposedly made them as coarse as their food. They were also called *cobs,* from *corncobs,* and the sense of "rough as a cob," was perhaps reinforced by the folkloric use of corncobs in the outhouse. The image of pitching hay led to *haypitcher, hayshaker, hayfoot,* and *haymaker.* The seed that ended up in their hair and on their clothing about 1888 produced the still-popular *hayseed.*

Appleknocker is a chiefly northern slang term for a farmer and specifi-cally for one who picks fruit in an orchard. The term was in use by 1915 and reflects the ignorant city notion that apples are harvested by knocking them down with long sticks. The term was much used in New York and is possibly of city origin. It would appropriately echo the long political and cultural conflict between the City and upstate, symbolized by its famous apple orchards. Dobie's Appleknockers was once the name of a New York vaudeville act. Rustics have also been called *squirrel shooters,* once a common foraging activity in rural areas. The name also suggests an attack on an animal that city people see only as furry friends in city parks.

Yet the term that irked hardworking farmers more than any other was the self-respected name of the occupation itself—*farmer.* By the 1890s *farmer* had become a derisive epithet for a countryman in the city. "In the tenement districts of this city [New York] every countryman is called a 'farmer,'" wrote the journalist Julian Ralph in 1897.[12] Edward W. Townsend's character Chimmie Fadden, the scrappy newsboy from Park Row, always used *farmer* to mean a yokel and in the sense of a fool. Even today *farmer* remains popular in New York street talk to denote a hick or out-of-towner. The image of his riding a plow was expressed in *plow jockey,* which sounds more of this century.

Modern literature and its intersection with popular culture also made contributions to passing as well as to more lasting slang terms. Just one source was the influence of Erskine Caldwell's novel *Tobacco Road,* published in 1932. *Jeeter* for any crude countryman came from the character of Jeeter Lester, the quintessential rural primitive in the novel. The long-running Broadway stage play based on the novel popularized *Jeeter* even more and introduced the name directly into New York speech. The name *Tobacco Road* itself became a name for any backward rural area, but especially one in the South.

Several old regional names for rural Southerners have been recently extended with new meanings in northern urban slang usages, including in New York. The late nineteenth-century terms *ridgerunner* (one who "runs" along the mountain ridges) and *hillbilly* (a Billy from the hills) until the 1950s usually referred to rural people of the highland South. Today *hillbilly,* following in part from the media-promoted image of Appalachia in the 1960s, is one of the most popular terms for a crude country person from anywhere. *Redneck* originally was a rural social type in the Deep South and referred to his sun-burned neck sustained from working in the sun, especially in contrast to the whiteness of his shirted torso. With the migration of Southerners to cities in other regions after about 1950 and the subsequent Dixification of American popular culture, *redneck* has become generic of rough people, rural or urban, anywhere in the nation.

Names for Small-Town People.   Big-city people, most completely New Yorkers, lived at the center of a metropolitan world, not at its periphery or beyond, and altogether had higher values than the boors of Main Street. Residents of small towns also came in for verbal abuse by city slangsters. The name *town hick* is only a slight elevation from *wood hick.* When superior-feeling city people had occasion to visit small towns they sometimes snidely referred to the residents as *natives* and *locals* to make it clear that they regarded them as a breed apart. City namecallers from their distance, moreover, often did not distinguish between small town and medium-size cities, seeing everything and everyone outside the metropolitan center as uniformly and hopelessly provincial. A few words such as *two-stemmer,* a town with *two* busy streets, was about the only concession in slang (and this was perhaps of hobo and tramp origin) to variations in size among towns short of the big city itself.

                             Country Names for City People.   The reflexivity of name-calling works in both directions. When rural people used epithets for city people, they were saying that they, the country people, were plain, simple, unpretentious but proud, hard-working, God-fearing people, whose family farms were the city's breadbasket and an essential part of the national economy. Yet rural and small-town people used few derogatory names for city people as a class of humanity; just calling them *city people* with all its connotations pretty much summed it up. The movies used *city feller* a lot, though I suspect it is synthetic rural dialect. The abundance of epithets for rural and small-town people in contrast to the relatively few rural epithets for city people also seems to reflect the urban enthusiasm for slang-making and the more stable, traditional rural vocabularies.

    In the eyes of rural and small-town residents, city people were noted for their fancy clothes and fine ways, and they were distrusted for both. Country people are popularly thought to have used *city slicker* and *dude* a lot, though the extent of this is not clear. *City slicker* is an Americanism of the early 1920s and also appears as *slicker, city slick,* or *slick.* These expressions sum up rural suspicions of the city type, alluding to his smooth, oily ways and to his slick appearance and dress.

    Dude, as we saw in Chapter 8 on street types, is an Americanism of the early 1880s and of unknown origin. Some etymologists, though, speculate that it is cognate with *duds,* a suit of clothes, and thus might allude to his slick appearance. *Dude* was sometimes specified as *city dude* by country people. *Dude* has had both city and rural uses, and in recent years has had new turns of meaning in urban street venaculars. The word appeared in the 1880s when men's clothing styles were undergoing a change from the dark, baggy, often badly fitting, coarse-woolen suits of the Victorian Age to improvements in style and fit. Younger, more daring city men took up the new styles, but older, more conservative men, especially in small towns and certainly in rural areas, spurned them. Wearers of the new styles became known as *dudes,* a successor of earlier swells and dandies. On the metropolitan periphery, dudes were associated with the fads and artificialities of cities.

    Most labels for city people recorded in dictionaries of slang were probably self-appellations of urban invention and never or rarely used by rural people. They nonetheless convey the tenor of this thinking. *Cit* and *cityite,* the latter modeled on the standard *urbanite,* were recorded but rarely used.

Several uncommon names based on *town*, in the sense of a city, were also recorded: *towner, townie, big towner,* and *townite.* Rural people nonetheless had a rich folkloric image of the city and of city people, a mixture of attraction and repulsion, which was expressed more in stories and metaphors of parasitism and wickedness than in derisive epithets.

Names for Rural Areas and Small Towns

Pejorative placenames for the metropolitan periphery are the counterparts of the epithets for the people who live in these settlements. Popular names for small towns and rural areas are similarly used reflexively, or intending reverse imageries, with respect to the collective self-image of the big-city users. The names say that we city people are at the center of things and live in a big, important place. Our city is a destination of travel, not a place passed through or by on the way to somewhere else. Roads lead to our city, not just through it. The trains not only stop here but this is their terminal. Our world is one of pavement and tall buildings of stone and steel, not a wilderness of woods and brush. People, not farm animals, are central in our everyday life. Our streets are many and wide and our facilities are abundant. Hear all these proud assertions in the following words and phrases.

Names for the Agricultural Hinterlands. Some of the recorded generic names for rural areas in general were flip journalistic coinages with little currency, often just extensions of derisive names for farmers and rustics. A representative several are: *The clods, hayseed country, hickdom, hoosierdom, jakedom, jay country, rubedom, yokelania,* and *youbetcherland.* The image of corn farming reappears in *corn country* and in its feeble variant *maize country.* The long phrase-name *out where they knock the big apple* (alluding to the epithet *appleknocker*) appeared briefly at some time long before the name *Big Apple* for New York city became nationally popular. The phrase seems almost prophetic in view of the way congressional representatives of rural and small-town America talked in the heat of the City's financial crisis in the mid-1970s.

But many terms had—and nearly as many still have—genuine use in popular speech. Certain names for settled rural areas perversely use images of wilderness and wild vegetation. *The sticks* (always with the definite article) is still among the most widely used terms for rural areas. *The sticks* alludes, of course, to the trees or "sticks" of yet uncleared rural areas in contrast to city pavement. *The sticks* may have escaped from lumbermen's jargon for the timberlands around 1900. *Backwoods* and other words with similar references, when used for settled rural areas, are slangy. Other such informal words suggesting uncleared land are *the timbers, the woods, the bush,* or *the bushes,* or *the brush.* (A *brush ape,* of course, is a rural primitive from such a place.) *Bush* is also widely used as an adjective to qualify, usually contemptuously, the provincial character of such places and things, as in baseball's *bush leagues.*

Boondocks is still one of the most popular of these references to supposed wilderness. It has a less than obvious origin from Filipino Tagalog *bundok,* "mountain." *Boondocks* was used by U.S. Marines for rough mountain country in the Philippines during the conflict of 1899–1903 and was later taken into general American slang. During the Vietnam War or before, *boondocks* was shortened to *booneys* or *boonies,* also whence *boonie,* a country person. All these words were probably used with a nod toward the wild regions west of the Hudson.

A rural landscape of grass and unmown fields and meadows is sometimes the theme in these names. *Grassroots* is an informal term of about 1880 and of no particular derogation for the rural areas of a country in contrast to its urban industrial regions and in this sense has come to mean the foundation or source of political society. According to William Safire's *Political Dictionary,* "the phrase began with a rural flavor, implying simple virtues of the land as against city-slicker qualities. Recently the anti-big-city connotation has been disappearing, leaving only an anti-boss, up-from-the-people meaning. Accordingly, politicians seek support 'from the grassroots and the sidewalks of the nation' to cover everybody." Above ground, *high grass,* circus slang for the sticks, stood in contrast to *low grass,* a civilized place where the grass is mowed.

The rhubarbs (always plural) is a still-heard slang term for the sticks that came into oral use just after 1900. It is of uncertain origin and mysterious allusion. *The rhubarbs* is perhaps just a nonsense phrase and of no real kinship, except in spelling, to the vegetable rhubarb. Yet certain rural areas, including some in New York State, specialize to a degree in growing rhubarb; a sense of 'out in the rhubarbs' is easy to imagine. Or the expression might be of baseball origin, where for some reason it was used for the bush leagues.[13] Or it might derive in some way from slang *rhubarb,* a squabble or quarrel, a common event in baseball, perhaps especially out in the bush leagues. It might be a word play on *suburbs,* a place not at the center of things. Or perhaps it anticipated one of the later inventions like *rurban* (1918) for the metropolitan fringe. Or perhaps (I fancy) it formed from something like a "ruburb," which would lie outside the "urb" and somewhere between a "burb" and a *rus,* the Latin word for "countryside" that was smartly used early in this century.

On the streets of New York in the 1850s *daisyville* and *grassville* were slang names for "the country," according to Matsell. Both are early examples of the perennially popular *-ville* suffix used to dub unpopular places and situations. *Hicksville* adjectively means corny, dull, and boring. This word-forming device in slang is revived from time to time, most recently in the 1950s.[14] The *-ville* suffix in generic place names took on the suggestion of a very remote, boring place, like in *dullsville,* or ultimately so in *noplaceville.*

Names for Small Towns. More abundant, varied, and story-laden are the contemptuous names that slangsters gave to small towns. These are to be distinguished from a related class, though the categories overlap, of scores of humorous names for imaginary hick towns, such as *Toonerville*.[15] Most of the names that found a genuine place in popular speech reflect the image of small towns as places on the road to somewhere else or as places of physical isolation and cultural desolation.

Podunk is the quintessential derisive name for a small town and it is wholly American in origin. The distinguished scholar Allen Walker Read in a series of articles traced the word history of *Podunk* in American English to 1841.[16] It was originally an Algonquian word meaning 'marshy meadow' and was applied by Native Americans to several locations in Massachusetts, Connecticut, and New York. The name survived in a few places, even to the present day. Its curious sound to European ears in the early nineteenth century caused it to be used humorously and eventually the name became a derisive term for any small backward settlement. Read also documents its spin-off *Squedunk* (pronounced squee-dunk) around 1907. John Ciardi, for an alternative but not necessarily contradictory view, believed that *Podunk* is at least reinforced by the sound of the bullfrog, dialectally called a *podunker,* who says *po-DUNK, po-DUNK,* and so *Podunk* is "out where the bullfrogs go *po-dunk.*"[17]

Several names for small towns just extend epithets for provincial people, usually forming them with the suffixes *-ville, -town,* and *-burg.* Of this order, only *hicktown, hicksville, rubeville* and the less popular *jaytown, jayburg,* and *rubetown* had much use in speech. "Rubeville" was the name of a popular New York vaudeville act that ran for six years. The use of *hicksville* in New York City was surely reinforced by the fact that the real city of Hicksville (an utterly coincident name) was nearby on Long Island. Around 1920, a judge in the Bronx was said to have ruled favorably for a woman's right to smoke on the street with the comment "What do you think this [New York City] is, Hicksville?"[18]

The form *jaybirdtown* has occurred and the *bird* in the middle may lend a little more support to the credibility of the hypothesis that *jay,* a rustic, is from *jay,* the bird, or at least was understood that way. Most of these slang terms passed through speech early in this century, but *hicktown* and *hicksville* are used to this day. This class of names, too, has its journalistic coinages with little or no real currency. Several of these are: *appleknocker town, chinwhisker town, clodville, clucktown* (from *dumb cluck*), *hayseed town, hoosiertown, jaketown* and *jakeville, yahootown,* and *yokeltown* and *yokelville.*

A View from the Road. Some of the best known generic names for small towns characterize them as anonymous places on the way to somewhere else. The densely concentrated industrial cities were linked to their rural hinterlands by horse-drawn wagons and carriages and later by railroads. The cities saw themselves as "hubs," "crossroads," "hearts," and "centers," and these terms frequently appeared in the booster-ish nicknames that cities all across the country gave to themselves.[19] The new transportation systems radiating out from the cities shaped settlement patterns in the hinterlands. Rural towns tended to cluster along transporta-tion arteries to facilitate exchanges with the city, first along major roadways and later along railway lines.

By 1900 the integrated metropolitan region was clearly emergent and the nation had been declared one of cities. The large central cities, the early suburbs, and the small towns and rural areas in the agricultural hinterland were linked by networks of roadways and railways and, closely associated, by channels of communication, first newspapers and later the telephone. This spatial organization and the dominance of big cities over their regions is clearly reflected in slang names for small towns. A few of the terms date from horse-and-buggy days, several of the best known are from railroad-ing, and later ones reflect the attitudes of early automobilers. In the 1920s, motor cars put Americans on the road in a big way and the popular culture and slang of automobiling coincided with the heady roll of city life in that decade.

A significant group of informal words and phrases characterize small towns merely as places to pause on a journey to somewhere else: *stop, stop off, stopping-off place,* and *stop on the road. Falling-off place* more slangily suggests just rolling off at some likely settlement at the side of the road; conceivably it is from hobo jargon and comes from falling off the so-called sidedoor Pullmans to the side of the tracks. Larger cities actually traded on being a place on the way to somewhere else and boosterishly nicknamed themselves as "Gateways" to here and there. But *jumping-off place* and the slangier thought in *last chance* suggest the last miserable settlements on the road into utter wilderness; indeed, they say that such a town is on the verge of wilderness. *Jumping-off place,* as a last outpost of civilization, has been used at least since the 1820s, and probably was applied to a succession of such places on the frontier during the great migration westward; yesterday's reality is today's humor. If a place is extremely remote, it might be denoted as *the middle of nowhere.* Or worse, if it is so remote that it is seemingly inaccessible, it might be said that "you can't get there from here."

The idea that small towns are apt to have only one of an essential facility inspired *one-horse town* and the less frequently heard *one-lung town.* (*One-lung* is an item of slang from about 1910 and is descriptive of an engine, such as a primitive automobile, with only one cylinder.) *One-horse town* is be-lieved to have been first used in print and possibly coined by Mark Twain in his phrase: "This poor little one-horse town," which appears in his story "The Undertaker's Chat." A popular song of 1920 (words by Alex Gerber) was titled "My Hometown Is a One-Horse Town—But It's Big Enough for Me." The idea of the town with only one street is a secondary allusion in the still popular phrase *wide place in the road*. If the road or street was not surfaced, it encouraged the town to be called a *mudhole* or *mudhole town*. A *crossroads* or *four corners*, two still-used informal names for a hamlet, would have at least two streets, but not the essential of an urban grid, which requires at least two parallel streets and two cross streets.

The transportation era of the railroads contributed several still-popular terms. *Jerkwater town* is from railroading jargon of the 1890s and is one of the best known terms for a small town. *Jerktown* (by 1900) and *Jerkwater* are variants; *jerktown*, as mentioned above, now has the double meaning of a town inhabited by jerks, but that was not the original sense. *Jerkwater town* recalls the railroaders' terms for a town too small for a station, but having a water tower or tank for the thirsty old steam locomotives. It was a town so small and insignificant that trains stopped only for water. A job of the train's fireman was to swing out the watertower's large spigot-like pipe, position and lower it over the train's water tank on the tender, and "jerk" the chain to start the flow of water, hence, "jerkwater." A *tanktown*, often shortened to *tank*, is also from railroader's talk and also refers to the water stops in jerkwater towns out in the middle of nowhere.

A slightly larger town up the line was a *whistle stop*. It had a station but one so small that the trains did not stop to pick up passengers, unless the station master signaled with a flag. The "whistle" in *whistle stop*, though, referred to an action of the train crew. If passengers wanted to get off at an unscheduled stop, they notified the conductor, who pulled the signal cord, and the engineer acknowledged that he was preparing to stop with two toots of the train's whistle. The designation of such whistle-stop towns was *whistle stop* even before the term entered the mainstream of popular speech with its now pejorative meaning. Train crews later referred to "flag stops" or "flag stations," possibly to avoid the acquired pejoration of *whistle stop*.

Urbanites saw small towns as places of physical isolation at great distances from the center of things. *Timbuctoo*, from the name of an actual city of ancient importance in present-day Mali, came to mean the remotest imaginable town, much as *Afghanistan* once meant the remotest country. *East Jesus*, whose allusion eludes me, is a name for such a *god-forsaken place* that is so small that "if you blink your eyes you miss it." Eastern slangsters borrowed from Old Western usage, probably from the movies, the terms *cowtown, ghost town,* and *prairie-dog town* to refer to similarly desolate towns anywhere.

Clearly of the automobile age is *filling station* used in reference to a small town. It derives, according to Wentworth and Flexner, "from the concept that, to one passing through, the filling station is the most important place" and it voices a notion similar to that behind *jerkwater town*, which started in railroaders' jargon. The old automobile expression *greasy spot on the road* seems to deepen the derogation of the thought of a wide place or wide spot in the road. Country hamlets collected greasy spots where the road, actually the shoulder, widened as it passed old-fashioned gas stations and country stores close by roadside and where the stopping, turning, parking, and starting of cars and other human activity left their visible traces on the roadway and its shoulder. The pejoration may have been helped along because the expression also had usage to mean the "greasy spot" left by small animals crushed on highways. The trope of a small settlement as merely a greasy spot on the road, the lowest evidence of human habitation, is concisely offensive.

The popular culture of funny papers and of novels, too, left its imprint. *Dogpatch* was taken directly from the name of the imaginary hillbilly settlement of Al Capp's "Li'l Abner" and was 1940s slang when the comic strip was especially popular. *Dogpatch* was preceded a century earlier by *dogtown,* which is still occasionally heard. *Cabbage patch* since the middle of the nineteenth century has meant a small, unimportant thing or domain and was sometimes extended to such a small town—and is still occasionally heard. A wider familiarity with the term early in this century came with Alice Hegan Rice's enormously popular book *Mrs. Wiggs of the Cabbage Patch* (1901). She described the setting as "not a real cabbage patch, but a queer neighborhood, where ramshackle cottages played hop-scotch over the railroad tracks."

More than a few names for small towns were probably coined or given new turns of meaning by touring theatrical people out of New York. They were condescending, at best, toward the rural and small-town people they entertained. A few of these names became known outside of theatrical circles, though usually in allusion to that life. Vaudeville troupes saw small towns as undifferentiated stops on a circuit, hence the names *kerosene circuit* (alluding to kerosene powered footlights in unelectrified districts) and *straw-hat circuit. Citronella circuit,* I like to believe, alluded to the smell of the crowd, not to the protection used by actors against the roar of mosquitoes. *Dogtown,* according to *Webster's Third,* is also theatrical jargon for "a city commonly used for theatrical tryouts before a play receives metropolitan presentation." Turkeys flop in dogtowns. Domesticated turkeys have a reputation as exceedingly stupid birds and have given their name to many losing enterprises. *Turkey town,* a derisive label for a small town, was in American speech by 1868.

A *stick* (used in the singular and not to be confused with *shtik* of Yiddish origin for a stage act) is theatrical jargon, though undoubtedly borrowed from general slang, for a town outside a large theatrical center; *the sticks* (always plural) is "the road" and also refers to time spent traveling outside the New York metropolitan area.[20] *Sticktown* and *stickville* are variants of *stick* in the talk of show biz. The most famous use of *the sticks* in this context was the headline in *Variety,* the principal newspaper of American show business, that once proclaimed "STIX NIX HIX PIX." The movie *Yankee Doodle Dandy* (1942) has a scene in which Jimmy Cagney holds the issue and translates the mysterious jargon for some kids—who had thought it was "new jive talk"—as meaning, says Cagney, "small towns refuse Rube pictures." More accurately, the famous declaration, attributed to Sime Silverman, founder and editor of *Variety* and himself a slang-maker, conveyed the industry news that box-office receipts in small towns were unexpectedly low for motion pictures about rustic characters and rural themes.

A Few Generic Names for Cities. Just as country people coined and used only a few derogatory names for city people, they must have coined even fewer—none known to me—generic names for cities. The several slang names for cities seem coined and used chiefly by city people. Some seem to reflect the outlook of traveling people who saw most towns and cities as an undistinguished succession of places on the landscape. *Burg* is the only generic name with much currency today. It has been applied pejoratively to towns and cities at least since the early 1840s and, as noted above, is conversely also a popular name for an unimportant or out-of-the-way place. A burg is a place one does not like, big or small. Tough, cynical newspaper reporters in 1930s movies and stories called New York the *Big Burg*. Slangsters took the common ending *-burg* or *-burgh* of the names of many American cities, often unimpressive places; *burg* and *burgh* are German and Scots for "town." Thus, New York as the *Big Burg* is a variant of *Big Town*, another local nickname for the city and of much radio and other media use.

Inevitably, some city slangsters like to play with Latinate coinages and these have had usage chiefly among others of like mind. *Urb*, a shortening of *urban* (and coincidental with the Latin *urbs*, "city"), had some hip use in the 1950s and 1960s for an exciting, diverse, sophisticated city like New York or San Francisco. In the 1970s *urb* gained scattered use in social science jargon as a synonym for *city*, usually as a foil to *suburb*. We will meet this cluster of Latinate coinages again in the suburbs.

The nickname *Gotham* for New York City came into popular use after 1807 when Washington Irving used it as a satirical name for the city in several essays published in his magazine *Salmagundi*. Irving borrowed the name from the real town of Gotham near Nottingham, England, which today has about a thousand residents. *Gotham* is Anglo-Saxon for "goat town." In the Middle Ages, according to folklore, the town's people got the reputation of being "wise fools" by acting crazy and avoiding King John's plan to tax them. By the seventeenth century the village and its people were the butts of many jokes about a village of idiots. Eventually the "fools of Gotham" were ironically referred to as the "wise men of Gotham." Irving seems to have taken the name in the sardonic sense of New York as a city of self-important but foolish people. These pejorative connotations were gradually lost and today *Gotham* is a neutral nickname and sometimes a pseudonym for New York in popular culture. Batman protects Gotham City.

And, Then, the Suburbs

By the end of the Second World War the old industrial cities, particularly in the Northeast, had matured and their decline was already evident. The most recent and massive out-migration to the suburbs, beginning about 1947, has continued to the present day. New York sustained a net loss to the suburbs of a million people, disproportionately middle-class families, between the 1950 and the 1990 Censuses.

In the mid-1950s, when the migration trend was well under way, the suburbs were criticized by urban pundits and derogated and satirized in popular culture. This last wave of name-calling paralleled the assault on rural and small town people and places in the 1920s and recapitulated the old tension between the center and the periphery. "In a dominantly urban society", writes sociologist Barry Schwartz, "the previous condemnation of the 'idiocy of rural life' is reserved for the suburban provinces."[21] Best sellers in social science such as William H. Whyte's *The Organization Man* (1956) and any number of satirical novels, movies, and critical essays, both good and bad ones, in those years portrayed the suburbs as places of middle-class blandness, boredom, teenage misbehavior, and compulsive adult conformity.

The words, *suburb, suburban, suburbanite,* and *suburbia* became pejorative epithets. *Suburbia* is a late nineteenth-century word that took on new, somewhat pejorative uses in the 1950s and 1960s. An echo of this pejoration was heard in the mid-1980s when *'burbs,* shortened from *suburbs,* began to be used in negative contexts from the in-city perspective. The word is already losing its elliptical apostrophe, the turn of meaning hardening up. A sociologist, Mark Baldassare, recently coined *disurbia,* which is essentially what the burbs are thought to be.

The word *suburb* earlier in its long history had derogatory connotations. The root meaning of *suburb,* literally "beneath or near the city," is that of a settlement spatially below a city on a hill, and suburbs were usually regarded as socially below the city as well. Access to the ancient city on the hill often had powerful religious and symbolic significance and was denied to residents of the suburbs below. The *Oxford English Dictionary* gives an old meaning of *suburban* as "having the inferior manners, the narrowness of view, etc., attributed to residents in suburbs." In late sixteenth and seventeenth century England, *suburb* referred to sexual licentiousness, taking this meaning from the vice areas in the suburbs of the City of London; a *suburb sinner* or a *suburban* was a prostitute and the *suburban trade* was prostitution.

In the 1950s, social science and popular culture, as well as a good deal of literary culture, found a consensual negative image of the suburbs, which revisionist critics in the 1960s called the "myth of suburbia." Sociologist Sylvia F. Fava writes that "suburbia [as a pop sociology] has a legitimate claim as the first of the major social changes that attracted broad public attention and was widely disseminated through the mass media."[22] The myth of suburbia fostered a largely incorrect image of the suburbs as homogeneously middle-class communities with an ethos of conformity and a norm of competitive consumption, inhabited by families on the verge of collapse, spoiled children, compulsive adulterers, martini-swilling commuters, and participants in the socially enforced conviviality of block parties and backyard barbecues.

When urban critics spoke of suburbia, most added that it was not only a place but also a state of mind. The presumption was that moving to the suburbs somehow pulled people into the mythical suburban way of life and changed their personalities, I suppose, from alert individualists to dull conformists. Urban folklore, or perhaps mass culture about the suburbs, expressed in novels, stage plays, and Hollywood movies in the 1950s and 1960s, was full of this imagery. The myth of suburbia was no more or less true than the earlier stereotypes of the idiocy of rural life or of the singular backwardness of small towns. But believing in the myth and using the pejoratives associated with it served to express a collective identity with a challenged urban way of life. The critics of suburbia in the 1950s regarded the new suburbanites as having broken a moral bond with the city.[23]

In the 1920s some of the critics of small towns and their way of life as well as, we may assume, some of the pejorative slang-makers, were also ambivalent in their opposition. They were not nostalgically drawn back to the provinces. They were ambivalent, rather, because they were of rural and small town background and were forging a new city identity, in part through symbolic opposition to the hated provinces. A generation later in the 1950s some of the urban critics of suburbia were themselves—or many of their kind—eventually drawn to the ersatz small towns and gentlemen's farms of the suburbs.

In the early 1950s a number of affluent New Yorkers also began to settle in the new commuter suburbs uptrack from the older suburbs surrounding the city. The writer A. C. Spectorsky in his book *The Exurbanites* (1955) dubbed these long-distance commuters as *exurbanites,* their harried way of life as *exurbia,* the places as the *exurbs,* and added the adjective for all, *exurban. Exurbia* popped up in a few dictionaries of slang in the 1960s, though today the word and its cognates are considered standard. Spectorsky described the exurbs of New York in the 1950s as lying in a fan-shaped area generally to the north of the city in northern New Jersey, southern New York and southern Connecticut, and on Long Island; the "suburbs" are the first 25 miles out, the "exurbs" are the next 25 miles out. The first exurbanites, according to Spectorsky, were mostly high-salaried people in the communications industries, such as advertising, publishing, and broadcasting.[24] Life in such high-pressure businesses, the supposedly harried suburban life, hard drinking, and the burden of commuting each day on the freeways, certainly influenced the 1960s expression *life in the fast lane.*

Urban planners and other critics admired the orderly growth of European cities and lamented the missed planning opportunities in the rapid decentralization of the North American city after the Second World War. They were deeply shocked and disappointed by the low-grade, low-density urban sprawl that was surrounding New York and other cities and that appeared to consume open space at an alarming rate. The spectacle of urban sprawl along the coast of California had by the early 1960s inspired *slurb,* a blend of *slum* and sub*urb,* to name a certain type of unsightly new suburb, one stretching after the other, that was the standard product of many real estate developers. The adjective, of course, is *slurban.* The general result of the low-density sprawl was also dubbed *spread city.* Slurbs tended to grow up behind *franchise strips* along major roadways leading out of cities and these elongated settlements were occasionally called *strip city* and *string city.*

Slangy Latinate coinages got at the same idea. The blend *rururban,* "partly urban, partly rural," was recorded as slang in 1934.[25] A social scientist in the 1950s concocted a similar *rurban,* another blend of *rural* and *urban,* for the emerging areas around metropolitan centers that were neither rural nor urban but not yet really suburban. Recently a few journalists have been using *rurb* (compare *urb* and *burb*) for the new high-density suburbs near large metropolitan areas.

In the 1960s and 1970s suburbs came in for a much feebler and last round of moral criticism as safe havens for middle-class white people who, through *white flight,* try to escape the problems and social diversity of the city and insulate themselves with *snob zoning.* But criticism of the suburbs, either by intellectual disdain, popular ridicule, or making pejorative slang, has all but disappeared. The suburbs and beyond are today where most people live and build their community identities, including the slang-makers. Half of the U.S. population now lives in suburbs, more than in either cities or in nonmetropolitan areas. Once a rural nation, an urban nation has become, so to speak, a suburban nation. Moreover, the urban society is now continuous with the whole society and the older distinctions among urban, rural, and suburban are diminishing.

A whole new generation, suburban born and suburban bred, knows little or nothing of classic city life. The popular image of the big cities among many young suburbanites, much of it received through television, is one of congestion, dirt, violence in the streets, and impoverished minorities. The word *urban* has emerged as an euphemism and codeword in public discourse to connote all these things. "The time-honored meanings of 'core' and 'periphery,' 'center' and 'margin,' are reversed,' notes the geographer Yi-Fu Tuan.[26] A few ridiculing place names of probable suburban origin have appeared, such as *New Yecch* and *New York Shitty,* but there is *Filthydelphia,* too. Americans used to say that New York was a nice place to visit but that they would not want to live there. They are now more likely to say that they want neither to visit nor to live in the big city. Yet the attitudes of many others toward the big cities is as likely to be one of indifference as one of hostility. City life is a taste of the few, not the many.

Suburbs in Town. The flurry of "back to the city" in the mid-1970s proved to be an illusion, having been initially confused with a middle-class stay-in the-city resettlement of a few old neighborhoods in New York and in a few other metropolitan cores of great architectural, historical, and social interest. *Gentrification* was an originally pejorative, even slang-like word favored by both urban and suburban critics of the trend, though people who like the trend use it without pejoration. The term is of British origin in the 1960s and was coined to denote the process and result of middle-class Londoners moving into conveniently central working-class neighborhoods, such as Islington, buying and renovating the sturdy old houses, driving up the taxes, and eventually supplanting the population and changing the character—gentrifying—the neighborhood. The newcomers were seen as invaders and snidely referred to as "the gentry," though virtually all were middle class and many were of modest incomes.

Critics of the American version of the trend like the term *gentrification,* for it enhances the observation that big-city neighborhood change of this sort often displaces poor residents and brings an inauthentic and expensive quality to the neighborhood. Echoing a theme of decades earlier, other critics have alleged that the trend represents the "suburbanization" of the city, bringing an exclusive, soulless way of life to "real" working-class neighborhoods. In the 1980s, the adjective *pink* was briefly used to describe such gentrified neighborhoods, shops, or restaurants catering to yuppies flush with new prosperity. The allusion of *pink* is not clear, though it seems fitting for an expensive but pale style of life.

Notes

CHAPTER 1
New York City Life and Popular Speech

1. Bender 1987, 429, 433.

2. See Lofland (1973) on the relative shift from appearances to locational signs of status in the modern city.

3. Allen 1993.

4. Flexner 1960.

5. Flexner 1973, 624–26.

6. Labov (1966) is now the classic study of New York speech and shows its class, ethnic, age, gender, and situational variations of pronunciation.

7. Burke 1967, 4, 27.

8. Strauss 1961, 17.

9. James 1931, 306–09. A New Yorkism of the 1920s is *Bronx cheer,* the withering sound of disapproval issued at baseball games and other occasions where exasperation runs high. The Bronx cheer is classically made by expulsing air through flaccid lips to produce a very vulgar fluttering sound. A synonym is *raspberry,* a crimson word picture that some people associate with the Bronx cheer.

10. McCabe 1868, 18.

11. Brooks 1977.

12. Benjamin 1973, 35–66; Wechsler 1982. Edgar Allan Poe in his short story "A Man of Crowd" (1840) wrote of the ultimate indeterminacy of reading appearances. Also see Whitman's (1936) essays "Broadway" and "Street Yarn."

13. Lakoff and Johnson 1980.

14. Schwartz 1981.

15. Mickelson 1978.

16. Whitman 1885.

17. Gelfant 1954; Zlotnick 1982.

18. Berger 1977.

19. Perlman 1979.

20. Barth 1980, 67.

21. Mencken 1963, 209–10. See Taylor (1992, 163–82) on Runyon's "invention" of Broadway.

22. McIntyre 1929, 89.

23. Tysell 1935.

24. Bogart 1955.

25. Toll 1974, 160–94.

26. McIntyre 1935, 143.

27. Snyder 1989, 12.

28. Mish 1989, 490–92. The form *vaudeville* emerged because a sixteenth-century genre of courtly love songs called *voix de ville* was confused with a genre of folk songs called *vau/x de vire,* "Valley/ies of Vire."

29. Barth 1980, 194.

30. Henderson 1974.

31. Snyder 1989, 124–25.

32. The old but still famous exclamation *cheese it!* variously meaning stop it!, be quiet!, look out!, don't do it!, or run away! dates to around 1810 in British cant, was soon in New York, and is of uncertain etymology. In the 1840s, *gallery gods* shouted it as a disapproving catcall from the uppermost reaches, or *paradise,* of Bowery theaters. The etymologist Peter Tamony speculated that *Cheese it!* derives from the old custom of eating a bit of cheese to conclude a meal, thus, figuratively to stop, to cease, whatever one is doing—*to cheese it.* Tamony's essay is reprinted in Cohen (1989, 109–11). Yet major dictionaries say it is perhaps just a dialectal alteration of *cease it!*

33. Allen Walker Read's article (1963) is the first in his series of six papers on the etymology of *O.K.* that were published in *American Speech* in 1963 and 1964. *O.K.* was attested first in Boston in 1838 as an initialism for the expression *oll korrect,* a facetious phonetic spelling of *all correct.* In 1839 the partisans of presidential candidate Martin Van Buren were said to have named their organization the O.K. Club, but now in allusion to the initials of *Old Kinderhook,* Van Buren's nickname that recalled his birthplace in Kinderhook, New York.

34. Cohen 1985, 85–105.

35. Cohen 1982a; 1984; 1989, 91–96.

36. Mencken 1963, 148.

37. Burke 1967, 301.

38. Thernstrom 1964.

39. Bremmer 1956, 4.

40. Dickens 1842, 89.

41. Partridge 1963, 3, 322.

42. Melville 1852, 276. The word *flash,* usually attributive, is old British cant meaning "of the underworld." Etymologically, it alludes to the loud clothing and jewelry worn by successful criminals who "flashed" their style, especially their jewelry, for the admiration and envy of their fellows.

43. Richardson 1970, 56, 216–17.

44. *Leaves,* a similar resource of mid-nineteenth century street speech, is a long series of underground stories told in cant and was originally published anonymously in the *National Police Gazette* in the 1860s. *Leaves* was reprinted with annotations in *Comments on Etymology* between 1979 and 1989.

45. Gans 1962.

CHAPTER 2
The Social Meaning of City Streets

1. See Sennett (1977) for the historical roots of this bifurcation.
2. Tuan 1974, 27–28.
3. Strauss 1968, 17.
4. Lockwood 1972, 10–11.
5. Gillette 1987.
6. Riis 1890, 119.
7. Crane 1893, 73–74.
8. A contemporary illustration is in McCabe (1872, 684).
9. Howells 1896, 186.
10. The expression was in British English by the 1860s and may have been an inside-out form of the old French proverb *Il faut laver son linge sale en famille.*
11. Wharton 1931, 200.
12. Howells 1890, 61.
13. Wharton 1925, 35.
14. Jacobs 1961, 29–41.
15. Tuan 1974, 248.
16. Ware 1935, 148, 151.
17. Conrad 1984, 213–14.
18. *The jungles,* always in the plural and with the definite article, has been used to refer slightingly to rural districts, *the sticks,* but suggesting only pre-industrial wilderness and dull ecological order.
19. E.g., Lingeman (1969).
20. Suttles 1968, 73–83.
21. The mid-nineteenth-century expression *on* (or *through*) *the grapevine* (i.e., on or through a social network of rumor) is a self-evident metaphor probably taken from the image of a winding, spreading vine. But its popularity in New York may have been influenced by the name of The Old Grape Vine tavern that once stood on Sixth Avenue and 11th Street from 1838 to 1915. It was a hangout and gossip center for local artists, who naturally would have said they heard something "at the Grape Vine" and, thus, make a clever pun. Cf. Miller (1990, 135).
22. Safire 1984b.
23. Odean 1988, 144–45.
24. Wentworth and Flexner 1960.
25. Major 1970.
26. The expression was conceivably applied earlier to the state prison erected in 1797 at Christopher Street and the North River, which was "up the river" from the perspective of the main, downtown settlement of the city around 1800. See Miller (1990, 15).
27. Whitman 1932, 104.
28. Irwin 1931, 66.
29. Harlow 1931.
30. Spaeth 1927, 212–14.
31. Rifkind 1977, 17–23.
32. Lingeman 1980, 293–98.
33. Gold 1985.

34. Tuan 1974, 27.

35. In 1990 the City of New York announced plans to reinstall the original Belgian brick surfaces in part of the Cast Iron Historical District, in Greene and Mercer streets between Canal and West Houston streets.

36. Romains 1942, 54–55. Sartre quoted by Still (1956, 311).

37. Barth 1980, 150–51.

38. Conrad 1984, 25–27, 195–96.

39. Conrad 1984, 42.

40. Dos Passos 1925, 202.

41. Fitzgerald 1922, 10.

42. Morand 1930, 311–12.

43. de Casseres 1925, 70–71.

44. de Casseres 1925, 69.

45. Tuan 1974, 75–77.

46. Gutman 1978, 250.

47. Rifkind 1977, 74.

48. McCabe 1872, 275.

49. Flexner 1982, 540–41.

50. A similar 1905 photograph of curb brokers may be seen in Kouwenhoven (1972, 399).

51. Campbell 1891, 237.

52. Gold 1975, 116–17.

53. Grub Street was an actual street in London where many such writers lived; it was renamed Milton Street in 1830.

CHAPTER 3
The Bright Lights

1. Melbin 1987.

2. Jenkins 1911, 37–38.

3. Bouman 1987.

4. Shulman 1990.

5. Mencken 1936, 546.

6. Howells 1961, 107.

7. Still 1956, 210.

8. Crane 1966, 188.

9. Brown 1919, 281.

10. de Casseres 1925, 211–12.

11. Walter Winchell, who made the area his beat for years, dreamed up many of the names, including *The (Big) Gulch, The Hardened Artery, Grandest Canyon, Bulb Belt, Baloney Boulevard,* and perhaps even the elliptical spelling *B'way* (Beath 1931, 45; Mencken 1963, 209). Winchell also coined the coarse puns *Two-Time Square, Hard-Times Square,* and *Times Queer.* The columnist Louis Sobol seems to have coined *Illuminated Thoroughfare, The Modern Appian Way, The Rue of Roués, The Flamboyant Floodway, The Gay Lit-Up Canyon, Golden Gulch,* and *Mazda Lane (Mazdas* was slang for light bulbs, especially ones on a theater marquee, after the Zoroastrian deity who gave his name to a brand of light bulb) (Conrad 1984, 284). O. O. McIntyre, who wrote for the *New York American,* interpreted Broadway for America in 500 newspapers in his syndicated column, "New York Day

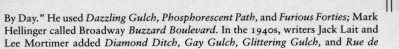
By Day." He used *Dazzling Gulch, Phosphorescent Path,* and *Furious Forties;* Mark Hellinger called Broadway *Buzzard Boulevard.* In the 1940s, writers Jack Lait and Lee Mortimer added *Diamond Ditch, Gay Gulch, Glittering Gulch,* and *Rue de Revelry.*

Many other stunt names by these and other writers had accumulated in print by the early 1940s (Berry and Van Den Bark 1942, 54): *the Alley, the Artery, Artful Alley, Aspirin Alley* (apparently from the treatment for hangovers), *Beer Gulch, the Big Alley, the Big Artery, the Big Drag, the Big Street, Broad, the Broadest Way, Coffee Pot Canyon, Dazzling Gulch, Dirty White Way, the Drag, the Fascinating Forties, Fraudway* (a song in a musical of 1929 goes "Broadway they say its a fraudway./ They play until broad day."), *the Galaxy, Gin Gulch, Glitter Boulevard, the Glittering Stem, Grand Canyon, Hooch Highway, the Incandescent District, the Lane, Levity Lane, the Lighted Lane, Little Old Broadway, Lobster Alley* and *Via Lobsteria Dolorosa* (alluding to the early "lobster palaces" on Times Square), *the Main Alley, the Main Artery, the Main Drag, the Main Stem, Maraudway, the Milky Way, Neon Boulevard, the Noisy Lane, Orange Juice Gulch* (from the many orange juice stands), *the Stem, Street of the Midnight Sun,* and *Tungsten Territory.*

12. Shakespeare, *The Merchant of Venice,* Act I, Scene iii, line 34.

13. Cohen 1991b. Also, Gerald Cohen, *Names,* 41 (March 1993):23–28.

14. Martin 1909, xv.

15. McIntyre 1935, 42.

16. Broadway Association 1926, 35.

17. Broadway Association 1926, 107.

18. Shapiro 1991.

19. McIntyre 1929, 143.

20. Ciardi 1980, 387.

21. Kanter 1982, 24.

22. Erenberg 1981, xii.

23. See Funk (1948, 73–74) for several hypotheses.

24. Hapgood 1910, 131, 134–35.

25. Peiss 1986, 114.

26. Peiss 1986, 101–02.

27. Flexner 1976, 309.

28. Fitzgerald 1945, 29.

29. Armitage 1987.

30. Erenberg 1981, 40.

31. Schuller 1968, 250.

32. Gold 1975, 133–34.

33. Vandersee 1984.

34. Mencken 1963, 195; also see Chapman (1986, 407).

35. See Funk (1948, 82) for possible etymologies.

36. Morand 1930, 175–76.

37. Churchill 1970, 254.

38. Botkin 1954, 428–30.

39. Morris 1951, 327–28.

40. Still 1956, 275.

41. Osofsky 1966, 184.

42. Calloway 1976, 251–61.

43. Hapgood 1910, 74–90.

44. E.g., Smith (1868, 385).

45. Winchell 1927.
46. Erenberg 1981, 218.
47. Irwin 1927, 176.
48. Erenberg 1981, 222.
49. Sobel 1931, 223, 229.
50. McIntyre 1922, 184.
51. Walker 1933, 216.
52. McIntyre 1922, 218–19.
53. McIntyre 1922, 123.
54. McIntyre 1922, 182.
55. McIntyre 1929, 116–17.
56. Erenberg 1981, 83–85.
57. Crockett 1931, 308.
58. de Casseres 1925, 123.
59. See MacCannell (1976) for a supporting view.
60. Mencken 1963, 99.
61. Mencken 1948, 647.
62. Van Dyke 1909, 179.
63. McIntyre 1922, 232–33.

CHAPTER 4
New Ways of Urban Living

1. Dreiser 1923, 82.
2. Whitman 1950, 26.
3. Whitman 1936, 138.
4. Matthews 1912, 177–187.
5. Schlesinger 1933, 92, note 2.
6. Flexner 1976, 186.
7. Berman 1982, 160.
8. Crane 1966, 185–89.
9. Gelfant 1954, 25–27.
10. Tichi 1987, 245–57.
11. Towne 1931, 9.
12. Quoted in Snyder (1989, 150–51). Cf. today's expression *New York minute*.
13. Brock and Golinkin 1929, 76.
14. Wharton 1905, 308.
15. James 1907, 86.
16. Howells 1890, 49.
17. Howells 1896, 193.
18. Van Dyke 1909, 152.
19. Mish 1989, 78–79.
20. Simon 1978, 9.
21. McIntyre 1922, 154.
22. Crane 1966, 189.
23. Thompson 1906, 12.
24. WPA 1938, 158, 358–59; Vidich 1976, 180–83.
25. Foster 1850, 217.
26. Browne 1868, 262.

27. Nascher 1909, 93; Brown 1926, 92–94; Weitenkampf 1947, 93.
28. Flexner 1982, 470.
29. Matthews 1894, 254.
30. Flexner 1982, 470.
31. Howells 1961, 108.
32. Farrell 1979, 46.
33. McIntyre 1929, 80.
34. Mish 1989, 135.
35. Hendrickson 1986, 67.
36. Kasson 1978, 50.
37. Goodrich 1972, 272.
38. Kasson 1978, 112.
39. Tamony and Cohen 1978, 1980; Cohen 1991a.
40. Tamony and Cohen 1978, 36.
41. Pilat and Ranson 1941, 244–46.
42. Park and Burgess 1925, 80–98.
43. Conrad 1984, 302.
44. Crane 1933, 57.
45. Miller 1983, 94.
46. Morris and Morris 1977, 616.
47. Cuba, Kasanof, and O'Toole 1987, 95.
48. Golden 1958, 60.
49. McCabe 1868, 279.
50. Dreiser 1923, 220.
51. Flexner 1982, 372–434.
52. Flexner 1982, 386.
53. James 1931, 307.
54. Golden 1958, 74.
55. Ware 1935, 367.
56. Flexner 1982, 497–505.

CHAPTER 5
Tall Buildings

1. Cromley 1990, 1–10.
2. Boyer 1985, 36.
3. Cromley 1990, 69.
4. Tunnard and Reed 1953, 123.
5. Brown 1936, 45–46.
6. Birmingham 1979, 8, 11–20.
7. Cromley 1990, 2.
8. Cromley 1990, 3.
9. Barth 1980, 52.
10. Matthews 1912, 133.
11. Wolfe 1988, 347.
12. Ralph 1893, 19.
13. Dargan and Zeitlin (1990, 43–85) discuss children's uses of tall buildings for playgrounds, especially their rooftops, walls, and stoops.
14. Stern, Gilmartin, and Mellins 1987, 88–89.

15. Crane 1966, 156.

16. Dargan and Zeitlin (1990, 63–67) discuss the rules of the pigeon-flying game and its jargon.

17. James 1907, 99.

18. Still 1974, 152.

19. Siegel 1981, 139.

20. McCabe 1872, 304–15.

21. Still 1956, 261.

22. Mish 1989, 398–99.

23. McCarthy 1931, 61.

24. Simon 1978, 95.

25. Barth 1980, 110–47.

26. James 1907, 180–81.

27. Goldberger 1981, 22.

28. Domosh 1988.

29. Webster 1960.

30. Mumford 1934.

31. Chesterton 1922, 26.

32. Ford 1927, 61.

33. Quoted in Still (1956, 206).

34. Strunsky 1914, 227.

35. MacCannell 1976, 50.

36. Quoted in Taylor 1988, 241.

37. De Casseres 1925, 75.

38. Sloan 1965, 122–23.

39. Sloan 1965, 231.

40. James 1907, 74, 135, 136.

41. Gorky 1972, 7–41.

42. Warner 1984, 191–95. Also see Taylor (1992, 23–33) for an analysis of skyline views of Manhattan to reveal how they symbolized a succession of different cultural meanings of New York; Domosh (1988) has otherwise analyzed the symbolism of the skyscraper.

43. Conrad 1984, 111. Also see Taylor (1992, 1–21).

44. Gottman 1967.

45. Abrams 1971, 49.

46. Kouwenhoven 1972, 394.

47. Wilmeth 1981, 189.

48. Crane 1966, 186–87.

49. Howells 1961, 38.

CHAPTER 6
Mean Streets

1. Schneider 1984.

2. Funk 1950, 146–47; Mish 1989.

3. Flynt 1899, 97.

4. Tamony 1976, 143.

5. Anderson 1923, 87.

6. McCabe 1872, 680–82, 218.

7. McCabe 1868, 279.

8. Halper 1933, 230.

9. Dreiser 1923, 129.

10. Ciardi 1987, 32.

11. Ellington 1869, 193.

12. Crapsey 1872, 159.

13. Mitchell 1959, 9–10.

14. Riis 1890, 160–61.

15. Riis 1890, 55.

16. Walling 1887, 486–87.

17. Riis 1890, 117.

18. Calloway 1976, 253.

19. Harlow 1931, 409–10.

20. Riis 1890, 163.

21. Flexner 1976, 27.

22. Ralph 1897.

23. McCabe 1872, 401.

24. Pember 1874, 13.

25. Ciardi 1983, 34.

26. Riis 1890, 59, 60, 65.

27. Riis 1890, 63–64.

28. Halper 1933, 189.

29. Nascher 1909, 72.

30. Whitman 1950, 18.

31. Harlow 1931, 525.

32. Crane 1890, 42.

33. Simpson and Simpson 1954.

34. In several Romance languages a pungent thought of pity for the poor is in the traditional popular name for pawnshops: French *mont-de-piété*, mountain of pity, and the same in Italian *monte di pietà* and Spanish *monte de piedad* or *montepío*.

35. Urdang 1988, 79.

36. Cohen 1981a. Cf. *Lombard rate* in banking terminology.

37. Evans 1970, 1029.

38. Funk 1948, 90.

39. John Ciardi (1987, 340) and others, perhaps smelling of the lamp, say that this *uncle* derives from Latin *uncus*, hook, *unculus*, little hook, "because many small pawned items were hung on rows of hooks in the pawnshop." Ciardi notes that Italian *onchia*, claw, fingernail, is reminiscent of the three prongs in the Medici's sign. "A literate British hack pawning some small body ornament would have no difficulty in punning from *unculus*, little hook, to L. *avunculus* or even perhaps to It. *onchia*; whence Uncle Hook or Uncle Claw." An earlier account says that "pawnbrokers employed a hook to lift articles pawned before spouts were adopted" (Redall 1889, 368). Of course, both sources, first, *uncle* as claw and, later, *uncle* as relative in time of one's need, could have influenced the expression.

CHAPTER 7
The Sporting Life

1. Kaufman 1972.

2. Fifth Avenue between Madison Square and 42nd Street was also called *the*

Line early in this century, but in reference to the afternoon fashion parade of rich and beautiful women. One of John Sloan's etchings retrospectively set about 1907, *Up the Line, Miss?* (1930), shows a finely dressed young woman mounting an open carriage for a ride up Fifth Avenue and being addressed so by the driver (Morse 1969, plate 243). The phrase was reportedly borrowed from elegant, fashion-conscious San Francisco (Irwin 1927, 172).

3. Riis 1890, 120.

4. A more official "deadline" was designated at Fulton Street in 1880 by Police Inspector Thomas Byrnes, who decreed that any professional swindler known to the police would be arrested, if he was seen south of the deadline.

5. Irwin 1927, 162.

6. Botkin 1954, 233.

7. Spaeth 1926, 186–88.

8. Batterberry 1973, 101.

9. Foster 1850, 84–85.

10. Peiss 1986, 17.

11. Howells 1896, 201.

12. McCabe 1868, 308.

13. McCabe 1872, 594.

14. Crane 1893, 80.

15. Browne 1868, 329.

16. Crane 1893, 66.

17. Hughes 1904, 71.

18. Crane 1893, 54.

19. Brown 1926, 76–77.

20. Brown 1926, 76.

21. Batterberry 1973, 147.

22. Chapman 1986, 148.

23. Urdang 1988, 144.

24. Riis 1902, 224.

25. McCabe 1872, 715.

26. Crapsey 1872, 94.

27. Fox 1880, 26.

28. McIntyre 1932, 68.

29. An engraving of the busy interior of Hill's place is in Smith (1868, facing page 435).

30. Crapsey 1872, 161.

31. Smith 1868, 632.

32. McCabe 1882, 491. The outrage of moralistic observers with regard to stigmatized lower-class dialect is glimpsed in Crapsey's comment that many of the men "have and expect no better recompense than talking with these painted women in the slang language in which they are alone versed" (1872, 161).

33. Walling 1887, 480.

34. See Mish (1989) for the etymology of *cadet*.

35. Riis 1902, 74.

36. Also see Nye (1973).

37. Cressey 1932, 3.

38. Cressey 1932, 179.

39. Cressey 1932, 222.

40. Walker 1933, 201.
41. Wilson 1946, 126–29.
42. Halper 1933, 78.
43. Etting n.d.
44. Walker 1933, 208.
45. Mish 1989, 75–76.
46. Barber 1960.
47. Stansell 1986.
48. Smith 1868, 429.
49. Gilfoyle 1987.
50. Morris 1951, 46.
51. Nascher 1909, 89.
52. Flexner 1982, 452.
53. A never common twentieth-century term for a brothel, *rib joint,* is a compli-cated pun, say Wentworth and Flexner (1960), deriving "from 'tenderloin,' re-inforced by 'crib joint.' " Yet, I will add, *rib* (from "Adam's rib") is also an old slang term for a woman. A *rib joint* was also a type of eating place, usually in Harlem, that specialized in barbecued spareribs, and *sparerib* is another slang version of *Adam's rib,* a woman.
54. H.M.L. 1945, 73.
55. Crane 1966, 188.
56. Quoted in Mayer (1958, 285).
57. Ellington 1869, 208.
58. Wentworth and Flexner 1960.
59. McCabe 1868, 121.
60. Kinser 1984.
61. Whitman 1936, 129.
62. Smith 1868, 378.
63. Eliason 1956, 124.
64. Smith 1983.
65. Foster 1850, 69.
66. Matsell 1859; Fox 1880.
67. These utterances appear on pages 248 and 256 of the 1861–1862 edition published by Griffin, Bohn, and Company, reprinted by Dover Publications in 1968. Ciardi (1987, 148–49) alerted me to these cognate uses, he by his correspondent Walter Newman, and says it probably comes by analogy to hooking a fish.
68. Foster 1850, 71.

CHAPTER 8
Social Types in City Streets

1. Whitman 1936, 119.
2. Whitman 1936, 121.
3. Whitman 1936, 122–23.
4. Benjamin 1973, 35–66; also see Bergman (1985).
5. Klapp (1962, 1–24) indicates the social utility of such social stereotypes.
6. Hales 1984, 224–76.
7. E.g., Krausz (1891).

8. Lofland 1973, 29–91.
9. Whitman 1936, 128.
10. Whitman 1933, 48.
11. Whitman 1936, 120.
12. Whitman 1936, 120.
13. Whitman 1950, 29.
14. Siegel 1981, 113.
15. Dreiser 1900, 3.
16. Whitman 1921, Vol. I, 163.
17. Weitenkampf 1947, 88.
18. Safire 1983.
19. Hughes 1904, 317.
20. Dreiser 1923, 112.
21. Flexner 1976, 191.
22. Cohen 1988.
23. McIntyre 1929, 121.
24. Runyon 1929, 89.
25. Hughes 1904, 333.
26. McCabe 1868, 511.
27. McIntyre 1922, 135.
28. Dreiser 1923, 260–66.
29. Wright 1926, 93–97.
30. WPA 1938, 156.
31. Still 1974, 164.
32. Campbell 1891, 116.
33. Brace 1872, 95, 318.
34. Hapgood 1910, 21.
35. Jastrow 1979, 166.
36. Shackleton 1917, 247.
37. McCabe 1872, 542–44.
38. Safire 1984a, 213–14.
39. Haswell 1896, 271.
40. Flexner 1982, 226.
41. Still 1974, 140–41.
42. Asbury 1927, 22.
43. Asbury 1927, 22.
44. Flexner 1982, 485.
45. Brown 1935, 101.
46. Whitman 1932, 152.
47. See Schermerhorn (1982, 17) for a contemporary drawing of this hog-lassoing street game; this drawing is also reproduced in Dargan and Zeitlin (1990, 20).
48. Dickens 1842, 85–86.

CHAPTER 9
Us and Them

1. Allen 1983; 1990.
2. Bodenheim 1954, 104–05.

3. Bodenheim 1954, 121ff.

4. Jaher 1973.

5. Mathews 1951.

6. Whitman 1936, 96.

7. Matthews 1912, 78. *Uppertendom* was also recorded.

8. Wecter 1937, 216.

9. Wharton 1913, 170.

10. Wecter 1937, 212.

11. McAllister 1890, 246.

12. McCabe 1872, 139.

13. Churchill 1970, 114.

14. Whitman 1932, 104.

15. Wharton 1934, 55.

16. Hunter 1974.

17. WPA 1939, 187.

18. Tuan 1974, 32–36, 161.

19. Gold 1975, 292–93.

20. Warner 1984, 181–91. The second part of Warner's essay concerns the images of the skyscraper and the skyline in urban culture and it is discussed similarly in Chapter 5.

21. E.g., Abrams (1971, 286); Flexner (1982, 303); Cohen (1982a).

22. Warner 1984, 185.

23. Warner 1984, 187.

24. Steinmetz 1986, 44.

25. Ciardi 1983, 130.

26. Dreiser 1923, 199.

27. Gold 1984.

28. Riis 1902, 92–93.

29. Wharton 1913, 64.

30. Bercovici 1924, 20–21.

31. Steinmetz 1986, 35.

32. Ornitz 1923, 295.

33. Lewis 1981, 217.

CHAPTER 10
The Contempt for Provincial Life

An early version of this chapter appears in J. Levitt, L. R. N. Ashley, and K. H. Rogers, eds. *Geolinguistic Perspectives*. Lanham, MD: University Press of America, 1987.

1. McIntyre 1929, 115.

2. Schwartz 1976, 337.

3. Whitman 1950, 49.

4. Wood and Goddard 1926, 25.

5. E.g., Cassidy (1985).

6. See, e.g., Berrey and Van den Bark (1953, 352–53).

7. Ciardi 1983, 311.

8. Cohen 1981b.

9. Ciardi 1980, 207.
10. Cohen 1987.
11. Urdang 1988, 81.
12. Ralph 1897, 90.
13. See, e.g., Shulman (1951).
14. Wentworth and Flexner 1960, 625.
15. Berrey and Van Den Bark 1953, 41.
16. Read 1939; 1963–64.
17. Ciardi 1983, 222.
18. Walker 1933, 24.
19. Kane and Alexander 1970.
20. Wilmeth 1981, 257.
21. Schwartz 1976, 336.
22. Fava 1973, 124.
23. Schwartz 1976, 338. Today, some Manhattanites call suburbanites *bridge-and-tunnels,* alluding to their routes of entry.
24. Spectorsky 1955, 16–19.
25. Weseen 1934.
26. Tuan 1974, 248.

References and
Bibliography

Alland, Alexander, Sr. 1974. *Jacob A. Riis: Photographer and Citizen*. Millerton, NY: Aperture.

Allen, Irving Lewis. 1983. *The Language of Ethnic Conflict: Social Organization and Lexical Culture*. New York: Columbia University Press.

――. 1990. *Unkind Words*. Westport, CT: Bergin & Garvey.

――. 1992. "*Spieler,* the Neglected Historical Sense of 'Dancer.' " *Comments on Etymology,* XXI (April), 2–6.

――. 1993. "The Sociology of Slang." *Encyclopedia of Language and Linguistics.* Oxford and Aberdeen: Pergamon Press and Aberdeen University Press.

Abrams, Charles. 1971. *The Language of Cities: A Glossary of Terms.* New York: Equinox-Avon, 1972.

Anderson, Jervis. 1982. *This Was Harlem: A Cultural Portrait, 1900–1950.* New York: Farrar Straus & Giroux.

Anderson, Nels. 1923. *The Hobo: The Sociology of the Homeless Man.* Chicago: University of Chicago Press, 1961.

Armitage, Shelley. 1987. *John Held, Jr.: Illustrator of the Jazz Age.* Syracuse, NY: Syracuse University Press.

Armstrong, Hamilton Fish, ed. 1917. *The Book of New York Verse.* New York: G.P. Putnam's Sons.

Asbury, Herbert. 1927. *The Gangs of New York: An Informal History of the Underworld.* New York: Capricorn Books, 1970.

Barber, Rowland. 1960. *The Night They Raided Minsky's.* New York: Simon and Schuster.

Barth, Gunther. 1980. *City People: The Rise of Modern City Culture in Nineteenth-Century America.* New York: Oxford University Press.

Barthes, Roland. 1979. *The Eiffel Tower and Other Mythologies.* New York: Hill and Wang.

Bartlett, John Russell. 1848. *Dictionary of Americanisms: A Glossary of Words and Phrases Usually Regarded as Peculiar to the United States* [4th ed., 1877]. Boston: Little, Brown.

Batterberry, Michael and Ariane. 1973. *On the Town in New York, From 1776 to the Present.* New York: Scribner's.

Beath, Paul Robert. 1931. "Winchellese." *American Speech* 7 (October): 44–46.

Bender, Thomas. 1987. "New York As a Center of 'Difference.' " *Dissent* 34 (Fall): 429–35.

Benjamin, Walter. 1973. *Charles Baudelaire: A Lyric Poet in the Era of High Capitalism*. London: NLB.

Bercovici, Konrad. 1924. *Around the World in New York*. New York: The Century Co.

Berger, Peter. 1977. "In Praise of New York: A Semi-Secular Homily." *Commentary* 63 (February): 59–62.

Bergman, Hans. 1985. "Panoramas of New York, 1845–1860." *Prospects: An Annual of American Cultural Studies* Vol. 10. Jack Salzman, ed. New York: Cambridge University Press. 119–37.

Berman, Marshall. 1982. *All That Is Solid Melts into Air*. New York: Penquin Books, 1988.

Berrey, Lester V., and Melvin Van Den Bark, eds. and comps. 1953. *The American Thesaurus of Slang: A Complete Reference Book of Colloquial Speech*. 2nd ed.; 1st ed., 1942; with supp., 1947. New York: Crowell.

Birmingham, Stephen. 1979. *Life at the Dakota*. New York: Random House.

Bluestone, Daniel M. 1991. "The Pushcart Evil: Peddlers, Merchants, and New York City's Streets, 1890–1940." *Journal of Urban History* 18 (November): 68–92.

Blumin, Stuart M. 1984. "Explaining the New Metropolis: Perception, Depiction, and Analysis in Mid-Nineteenth Century New York." *Journal of Urban History* 11 (November): 9–38.

Bodenheim, Maxwell. 1954. *My Life and Loves in Greenwich Village*. New York: Belmont, 1961.

Bogart, Leo. 1955. "Adult Talk About Newspaper Comics." *American Journal of Sociology* 61 (July): 26–30.

Botkin, B. A., ed. 1954. *Sidewalks of America*. Indianapolis: Bobbs-Merrill.

———, ed. 1956. *New York City Folklore*. New York: Random House.

Bouman, Mark J. 1987. "Luxury and Control: The Urbanity of Street Lighting in Nineteenth-Century Cities." *Journal of Urban History* 14 (November): 7–37.

Boyer, M. Christine. 1985. *Manhattan Manners: Architecture and Style*. New York: Rizzoli.

Brace, Charles Loring. 1872. *The Dangerous Classes of New York, and Twenty Years of Work Among Them*. 3rd ed., 1880. New York: Wynkoop & Hallenbeck.

Bremmer, Robert H. 1956. *From the Depths: The Discovery of Poverty in the United States*. New York: New York University Press.

Broadway Association. 1926. *Broadway: The Grand Canyon of American Business*. New York: Broadway Association..

Brock, H. I. and J. W. Golinkin. 1929. *New York Is Like This*. New York: Dodd, Mead.

Brooks, Peter. 1977. "The Text of the City." *Oppositions* 8 (Spring): 7–11.

Brown, Henry Collins, ed. 1919. *Valentine's Manual of Old New-York*. Vol. 3, New Series. New York: Valentine's Manual.

———, ed. 1926. *Valentine's Manual of Old New-York*. Vol. 10, New Series. New York: Valentine's Manual.

――――. 1935. *Brownstone Fronts and Saratoga Trunks*. New York: E. P. Dutton & Co.

――――. 1936. *From Alley Pond to Rockefeller Center*. New York: E.P. Dutton.

Browne, Junius Henri. 1868. *The Great Metropolis; A Mirror of New York*. Hartford: American Publishing Co.

Burke, Kenneth. 1967. *The Philosophy of Literary Form*. 2nd ed. Baton Rouge: Lousiana State University Press.

Calloway, Cab [and Bryand Rollins]. 1976. *Of Minnie the Moocher & Me*. New York: Crowell.

Campbell, Helen. 1891. *Darkness and Daylight; Or, Light and Shadows of New York Life*. Hartford, CT: A.D. Worthington.

Cassidy, Frederic G. 1980. "Unofficial Sectional City Names." *Verbatim* 7 (Autumn): 1–3. And rejoinder: 1981. "Unofficial Sectional City Names: Postscript." *Verbatim* 8 (Summer): 3.

――――, ed. 1985–91. *Dictionary of American Regional English*. Volumes 1 and 2 [Vols. 3+ forthcoming]. Cambridge, MA: Belknap-Harvard University Press.

Chapman, Robert L. 1986. *New Dictionary of American Slang*. New York: Harper & Row.

Chesterton, G. K. 1922. *What I Saw in America*. New York: Dodd, Mead and Company.

Churchill, Allen. 1970. *The Upper Crust: An Informal History of New York's Highest Society*. Englewood Cliffs, NJ: Prentice-Hall.

Ciardi, John. 1980. *A Browser's Dictionary and Native's Guide to the Unknown American Language*. New York: Harper & Row.

――――. 1983. *A Second Brower's Dictionary and Native's Guide to the Unknown American Language*. New York: Harper & Row.

――――. 1987. *Good Words to You; An All-New Dictionary and Native's Guide to the Unknown American Language*. New York: Harper & Row.

Clapin, Sylva. n.d. [ca. 1902]. *A New Dictionary of Americanisms*. Detroit: Gale Research, 1968.

Clark, Thomas L. 1987. *The Dictionary of Gambling and Gaming*. Cold Spring, NY: Lexix House.

Cohen, Gerald L. 1981a. "(To) Lumber." *Comments on Etymology*. XI (Nos. 1–2): 31; also 1986. "(to)lumber." *Comments on Etymology*. XVI (Nos. 1–2): 20–21.

――――.1981b. "Yokel." *Comments on Etymology*. XI (Nos. 1–2): 76.

――――. 1982a. *Origin of the Term 'Shyster.'* Frankfurt am Main: Verlag Peter Lang.

――――. 1982b. "slum" [note in Glossary for *Leaves*]. *Comments on Etymology*. XI (Nos. 13–14): 30.

――――. 1984. *Origin of the Term 'Shyster': Supplementary Information*. Frankfurt am Main: Verlag Peter Lang.

――――. 1985. *Studies in Slang, Part I*. Frankfurt am Main: Verlag Peter Lang.

――――. 1987. "*Jay* 'Amateur (Derogatory), Greenhorn.' " *Comments on Etymology*. XVI (Nos. 9–10): 20–21.

――――. 1988. "*Hokey-Pokey* Ice Cream: An Example of Multiple Causation." *Comments on Etymology*. XVII (Nos. 11–12): 5–9.

――――. 1989. *Studies in Slang, Part II*. Frankfurt am Main: Verlag Peter Lang.

――――. 1991a. "*Hot Dog* Revisited." *Comments on Etymology*. XX (Nos. 5–6).

──────. 1991b. *Origin of New York City's Nickname "The Big Apple."* Forum *Anglicum,* Band 19. Frankfurt am Main: Verlag Peter Lang.

Cohen, Marilyn. 1983. *Reginald Marsh's New York: Paintings, Drawings, Prints and Photographs.* New York: Whitney Museum/Dover.

Conrad, Peter. 1984. *The Art of the City: Views and Versions of New York.* New York: Oxford University Press.

Cook, Ann, Marilyn Gittle, and Herb Mack, eds. 1973. *City Life, 1865–1900: Views of Urban America.* New York: Praeger.

Crane, Hart. 1933. *The Complete Poems of Hart Crane.* Waldo Frank, ed. Garden City, NY: Anchor/Doubleday, 1958.

Crane, Stephen. 1893. *Maggie; A Girl of the Streets* and *George's Mother* (1896). New York: Fawcett, 1960.

──────. 1966. *The New York City Sketches of Stephen Crane and Related Pieces.* R. W. Stallman and E. R. Hagemann, eds. New York: New York University Press.

Crapsey, Edward. 1872. *The Nether Side of New York; Or, the Vice, Crime and Poverty of the Great Metropolis.* Montclair, NJ: Patterson Smith, 1969.

Cressey, Paul G. 1932. *The Taxi-Dance Hall: A Sociological Study in Commercialized Recreation and City Life.* Chicago: University of Chicago Press.

Crockett, Albert Stevens. 1931. *Peacocks On Parade.* New York: Sears.

Cromley, Elizabeth Collins. 1990. *Alone Together: A History of New York's Early Apartments.* Ithaca, NY: Cornell University Press.

Cuba, Stanley L., Nina Kasanof, and Judith O'Toole. 1987. *George Luks: An American Artist.* Wilkes-Barre, PA: Sordoni Art Gallery, Wilkes College.

Dargan, Amanda, and Steven Zeitlin. 1990. *City Play.* New Brunswick, NJ: Rutgers University Press.

De Casseres, Benjamin. 1925. *Mirrors of New York.* New York: Joseph Lawren.

Dickens, Charles. 1842. *American Notes: A Journey.* New York: Fromm International, 1985.

Domosh, Mona. 1988. "The Symbolism of the Skyscraper: Case Studies of New York's First Tall Buildings." *Journal of Urban History* 14 (May): 321–45.

Dos Passos, John. 1925. *Manhattan Transfer.* New York: Harper & Bros.

Dreiser, Theodore. 1900. *Sister Carrie.* New York: Bantam, 1982.

──────. 1923. *The Color of a Great City.* New York: Boni and Liveright.

Dumas, Bethany K., and Jonathan Lighter. 1978. "Is *Slang* a Word for Linguists?" *American Speech* 53 (Spring): 5–17.

Dunn, Alan. 1948. *East of Fifth: The Story of an Apartment House.* New York: Simon and Schuster.

E.A.A. [initials only]. 1945. "A Neighborhood, an Era, a State of Mind: Informal Notes on the Gas House District." *American Notes & Queries* 5 (October): 99–103.

Eliason, Norman E. 1956. *Tarheel Talk: An Historical Study of the English Language in North Carolina to 1860.* Chapel Hill: University of North Carolina Press.

Ellington, George [pseudonym]. 1869. *The Women of New York; Or, the Under-World of the Great City.* New York: Arno Press, 1972.

Erenberg, Lewis A. 1981. *Steppin' Out: New York Nightlife and the Transformation of American Culture, 1890–1930.* Chicago: University of Chicago Press.

Etting, Ruth. n.d. [ca. 1960]. *The Original Recordings of Ruth Etting*. Columbia LP #ML5050.

Evans, Ivor H. 1970. *Brewer's Dictionary of Phrase and Fable*. New York: Harper & Row.

Farrell, James T. 1979. "The Last Automat." *New York* 14 (May): 44–46.

Fava, Sylvia F. 1973. "The Pop Sociology of Suburbs and New Towns." *American Studies* 14 (Spring): 121–33.

Fitzgerald, F. Scott. 1922. *The Beautiful and Damned*. New York: Collier/Macmillan, 1986.

———. 1945. *The Crack Up*. New York: New Directions, 1956.

Flexner, Stuart Berg. 1960. "Preface." *Dictionary of American Slang*. Harold Wentworth and S. B. Flexner, eds. 2nd supplemented ed. New York: Crowell, 1975, vi–xv.

———. 1973. "Slang." *Encyclopaedia Britannica*.

———. 1976. *I Hear America Talking*. New York: Van Nostrand-Reinhold.

———. 1982. *Listening to America*. New York: Simon and Schuster.

Flynt, Josiah [Josiah Flynt Willard]. 1899. *Tramping With Tramps*. New York: The Century Co.

———. 1901. *The World of Graft*. New York: McClure Phillips.

Footner, Hulbert. 1937. *New York: City of Cities*. Philadelphia: J.P. Lippencott.

Ford, Madox Ford. 1927. *New York Is Not America*. London: Duckworth.

Foster, George G. 1850. *New York by Gas-Light: And Other Sketches*. Stuart M. Blumin, ed. Berkeley: University of California Press, 1990.

Fox, Richard K. 1880. *Slang Dictionary of New York, London and Paris*. New York: National Police Gazette.

Funk, Charles Earle. 1948. *A Hog on Ice and Other Curious Expressions*. New York: Harper & Row, 1985.

———. 1950. *Thereby Hangs a Tale: Stories of Curious Word Origins*. New York: Harper & Row, 1985.

———. 1955. *Heavens to Betsy! And Other Curious Sayings*. New York: Harper & Row.

Gans, Herbert J. 1962. "Urbanism and Suburbanism as Ways of Life: A Reevaluation of Definitions." *Human Behavior and Social Process*. Arnold M. Rose, ed. Boston: Houghton Mifflin. 625–48.

Gelfant, Blanche Housman. 1954. *The American City Novel*. Norman: University of Oklahoma Press.

Gilfoyle, Timothy J. 1987. "The Urban Geography of Commercial Sex: Prostitution in New York City, 1790–1860." *Journal of Urban History* 13 (August): 371–93.

Gillette, Howard, Jr. 1987. "The City in American Culture." *American Urbanism: A Historiographic Review*. H. Gillette, Jr. and Z. L. Miller, eds. New York: Greenwood Press. 27–47.

Gold, David L. 1984. "*Row* in Some English Placenames." *Names* 32 (September): 347–49; and addendum, "More on *Row* in English Placenames." *Names* 34 (March): 101–02.

———. 1985. "Figurative Uses of *alley* in English-Language Placenames." *Names* 33 (September): 209–210.

Gold, Michael. 1930. *Jews Without Money*. New York: Avon, 1965.

Gold, Robert S. 1975. *Jazz Talk*. Indianapolis: Bobbs-Merrill.

Goldberger, Paul. 1981. *The Skyscraper*. New York: Knopf.

Golden, Harry. 1958. *Only in America*. New York: World.

Goodrich, Lloyd. n.d. [ca. 1972]. *Reginald Marsh*. New York: Harry N. Abrams.

Gorky, Maxim. 1972. *The City of the Yellow Devil: Pamphlets, Articles and Letters About America*. Moscow: Progress Publishers.

Gottmann, Jean. 1967. "The Skyscraper Amid the Sprawl." *Metropolis on the Move*. J. Gottmann and R. A. Harper, eds. New York: John Wiley, 125–50.

Gutman, Robert. 1978. "The Street Generation." *On Streets*. Stanford Anderson, ed. Cambridge, MA: MIT Press.

Hales, Peter Bacon. 1984. *Silver Cities: The Photography of American Urbanization, 1839–1915*. Philadelphia: Temple University Press.

Halper, Albert. 1933. *Union Square*. New York: Viking.

Hapgood, Hutchins. 1902. *The Spirit of the Ghetto: Studies of the Jewish Quarter of New York*. New York: Schocken Books, 1966.

———. 1910. *Types From City Streets*. New York: Garrett Press, 1970.

Harlow, Alvin F. 1931. *Old Bowery Days*. New York: D. Appleton.

Hart, Lorenz. 1986. *The Complete Lyrics of Lorenz Hart*. Dorothy Hart and Robert Kimball, eds. New York: Knopf.

Haswell, Charles H. 1896. *Reminiscenses of An Octogenarian of the City of New York (1816–1860)*. New York: Harper & Bros.

Henderson, Floyd. 1974. "The Image of New York City in American Popular Music." *New York Folklore Quarterly* 30 (December): 267–78.

Hendrickson, Robert. 1986. *American Talk: The Words and Ways of American Dialects*. New York: Penguin, 1987.

H.M.L. [initials only]. 1945. "Answers" [to "Red Light Districts" in May 1944 issue]. *American Notes and Queries* 5 (August): 72–74.

Howells, William Dean. 1890. *A Hazard of New Fortunes*. New York: Bantam, 1960.

———. 1896. *Impressions and Experiences*. New York: Harper & Bros., 1909.

———. 1960. *The Complete Plays of W. D. Howells*. Walter J. Meserve, ed. New York: New York University Press.

———. 1961. *Letters of An Altrurian Traveller (1893–94)*. Clara M. Kirk and Rudolf Kirk, eds. Gainseville, FL: Scholars' Facsimiles & Reprints.

Hughes, Rupert. 1904. *The Real New York*. New York: The Smart Set.

Hunter, Albert. 1974. *Symbolic Communities*. Chicago: University of Chicago Press.

Irwin, Godfrey. 1931. *American Tramp and Underworld Slang*. New York: Sears.

Irwin, Will. 1927. *Highlights of Manhattan*. New York: The Century Co.

Jacobs, Jane. 1961. *The Death and Life of Great American Cities*. New York: Vintage.

Jaher, Frederic Cople. 1973. "Style and Status: High Society in Late Nineteenth-Century New York." *The Rich, the Well-Born, and the Powerful*. F. C. Jaher, ed. Urbana: University of Illinois Press, 258–84.

James, Henry. 1907. *The American Scene*. New York: Harper & Bros.

James, Rian. 1931. *All About New York: An Intimate Guide*. New York: John Day.

Jastrow, Marie. 1979. *A Time to Remember: Growing Up in New York Before the Great War*. New York: W. W. Norton.

Jenkins, Stephen. 1911. *The Greatest Street in the World*. New York: G. P. Putnam's Sons.

Kane, Joseph Nathan, and Gerard L. Alexander. 1970. *Nicknames and Sobriquets of U.S. Cities and States*. 2nd ed. Metuchen, NJ: Scarecrow Press.

Kanter, Kenneth Aaron. 1982. *The Jews of Tin Pan Alley*. New York: Ktav Publishing Co.

Kasson, John F. 1978. *Amusing the Millions: Coney Island at the Turn of the Century*. New York: Hill & Wang.

Kaufman, Martin and Herbert J. 1972. "Henry Bergh, Kit Burns, and the Sportsmen of New York." *New York Folklore Quarterly* 28 (March): 15–29.

Kinser, Suzanne L. 1984. "Prostitutes in the Art of John Sloan." *Prospects: The Annual of American Cultural Studies* Vol. 9. Jack Salzman, ed. New York: Cambridge University Press, 231–54.

Klapp, Orrin E. 1962. *Heroes, Villains, and Fools*. Englewood Cliffs, NJ: Prentice-Hall.

Kneeland, George J. 1913. *Commercialized Prostitution in New York City*. New York: The Century Co.

Kouwenhoven, John A. 1972. *The Columbia Historical Portrait of New York*. New York: Harper & Row.

Krausz, Sigmund. 1891. *Social Types of Great American Cities*. Chicago: The Werner Co., 1896.

Labov, William. 1966. *The Social Stratification of English in New York City*. Washington, DC: Center for Applied Linguistics.

Lakoff, George, and Mark Johnson. 1980. *Metaphors We Live By*. Chicago: University of Chicago Press.

Lewis, Alfred Henry. 1912. *The Apaches of New York*. New York: M. A. Donohue.

Lewis, David Levering. 1981. *When Harlem Was In Vogue*. New York: Knopf, Vintage.

Lingeman, Richard R. 1969. *Drugs from A to Z: A Dictionary*. New York: McGraw-Hill.

———. 1980. *Small Town America: A Narrative History, 1620–The Present*. New York: G. P. Putnam's Sons.

Lippard, George. 1853. *New York: Its Upper Ten and Lower Million*. Cincinnati, OH: H. M. Rulison.

Lockwood, Charles. 1972. *Bricks and Brownstones: The New York Row House, 1783–1929*. New York: Abbeville Press.

Lofland, Lyn H. 1973. *A World of Strangers: Order and Action in Urban Public Space*. New York: Basic Books.

McAllister, Ward. 1890. *Society As I Have Found It*. New York: Cassel Pub. Co.

McCabe, James D., Jr. [under pseudonym: "Edward Winslow Martin"]. 1868. *The Secrets of the Great City*. Philadelphia: Jones, Brothers.

———. 1872. *Lights and Shadows of New York Life; Or, the Sights and Sensations of the Great City*. New York: Farrar, Straus and Giroux, 1970.

———. 1882. *New York by Sunlight and Gaslight*. New York: Edgewood Pub. Co.

McConnell, Dean. 1976. *The Tourist: A New Theory of the Leisure Class*. New York: Schocken Books.

McCarthy, James Remington. 1931. *Peacock Alley: The Romance of the Waldorf-Astoria*. New York: Harper Bros.

McIntyre, O. O. 1922. *White Light Nights*. New York: Cosmopolitan Magazine.

———. 1929. *Twenty-Five Selected Stories of O. O. McIntyre*. New York: Cosmopolitan Magazine.

————. 1932. *Another "Odd" Book: Twenty-Five Selected Stories*. (Second Series). New York: Cosmopolitan Magazine.

————. 1935. *The Big Town: New York Day By Day*. New York: Dodd, Mead.

Maitland, James. 1891. *The American Slang Dictionary*. Chicago: R.J. Kittredge.

Major, Clarence. 1970. *Dictionary of Afro-American Slang*. New York: International Publishers.

Martin, Edward S., ed. 1909. *The Wayfarer in New York*. New York: Macmillan.

Matthews, Brander. 1894, 1897. *Vignettes of Manhattan: Outlines in Local Color*. New York: Charles Scribner's Sons, 1921.

————. 1912. *Vistas of New York*. New York: Harper & Bros.

Matsell, George W., ed. 1859. *Vocabulum; Or, the Rogue's Lexicon*. New York: George W. Matsell Co.

————, ed. 1865. "Leaves." Serial in *National Police Gazette*. Republished in *Comments on Etymology*, 1979–89, with notes by Gerald L. Cohen.

Mayer, Grace M. 1958. *Once Upon a City: New York from 1890 to 1910*. New York: Macmillan.

Melbin, Murray. 1987. *Night as Frontier: Colonizing the World After Dark*. New York: The Free Press.

Melville, Herman. 1852. *Pierre, Or the Ambiguities*. New York: Signet/New American Library, 1964.

Mencken, H.L. 1936. *The American Language: An Inquiry Into the Development of English in the United States*. 4th ed. New York: Knopf.

————. 1945. *The American Language; Supplement I*. New York: Knopf.

————. 1948. *The American Language; Supplement II*. New York: Knopf.

————. 1963. *The American Language*. The Fourth Edition and the Two Supplements, abridged, with annotations and new material by Raven I. McDavid, Jr., with the assistance of David W. Maurer. New York: Knopf.

Mickelson, Joel C. 1978. "Correlations Between Art and Literature in Interpreting the American City." *Images of the American City in the Arts*. J. C. Mickelson, ed. Dubuque, IA: Kendall/Hunt. 2–25.

Miller, Saul. 1983. *New York City Street Smarts*. New York: Holt, Rinehart and Winston.

Miller, Terry. 1990. *Greenwich Village and How It Got That Way*. New York: Crown.

Mish, Frederick C., ed. 1989. *Webster's Word Histories*. Springfield, MA: Merriam-Webster.

Mitchell, Joseph. 1959. *The Bottom of the Harbor*. Boston: Little, Brown.

Morand, Paul. 1930. *New York*. New York: The Book League/Henry Holt.

Morris, Lloyd. 1951. *Incredible New York: High Life and Low Life of the Last Hundred Years*. New York: Random House.

Morris, William, and Mary Morris. 1977. *Morris Dictionary of Word and Phrase Origins*. New York: Harper & Row.

Morse, Peter. 1969. *John Sloan's Prints*. New Haven: Yale University Press.

Mumford, Lewis. 1934. "The Metropolitan Milieu." *America and Alfred Stieglitz*. Waldo Frank et al., eds. New York: Doubleday, 33–58.

Nascher, I. L. 1909. *The Wretches of Povertyville: A Sociological Study of the Bowery*. Chicago: Jos. J. Lanzit.

Nye, Russel B. 1973. "Saturday Night at the Paradise Ballroom; Or, Dance Halls in the Twenties." *Journal of Popular Culture* 7 (Summer, No. 1): 14–22.

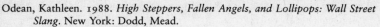
Odean, Kathleen. 1988. *High Steppers, Fallen Angels, and Lollipops: Wall Street Slang*. New York: Dodd, Mead.

O. Henry [William Sydney Porter]. 1953. *The Complete Works of O. Henry*. Garden City, NY: Doubleday.

Ornitz, Samuel. 1923. *Haunch Paunch and Jowl*. Reprinted as *Allrightniks Row*. New York: Marcus-Weiner Publishing, 1985.

Osofsky, Gilbert. 1966. *Harlem: The Making of a Ghetto: Negro New York, 1890–1930*. New York: Harper Torchbooks, 1968.

Paine, Alfred Bigelow. 1899. *The Breadline: The Story of a Paper*. New York: Century.

Park, Robert E., Ernest W. Burgess, and Roderick D. McKenzie. 1925. *The City*. Chicago: University of Chicago Press.

Partridge, Eric. 1963. *Slang, To-Day and Yesterday*. 3rd ed. New York: Bonanza Books.

———, ed. 1984. *A Dictionary of Slang and Unconventional English*. 8th ed. Paul Beale, ed. New York: Macmillan.

Peiss, Kathy. 1986. *Cheap Amusements: Working Women and Leisure in Turn-of-the-Century New York*. Philadelphia: Temple University Press.

Pember, A. 1874. *The Mysteries and Miseries of the Great Metroplis*. New York: D. Appleton.

Perlman, Bennard B. 1979. *The Immortal Eight: American Painting from Eakins to the Armory Show, 1870–1913*. Cincinnati, OH: North Light.

Pilat, Oliver, and Jo Ranson. 1941. *Sodom By the Sea: An Affectionate History of Coney Island*. Garden City, NY: Garden City Publishing Co.

Ralph, Julian. 1893. *Our Great West*. New York: Harper & Bros.

———. 1897. "The Language of the Tenement-Folk." *Harper's Weekly* 41 (January 23): 90.

Read, Allen Walker. 1939. "The Rationale of 'Podunk'." *American Speech* 14 (April): 99–108.

———. 1963. "The First Stage in the History of O.K." *American Speech* 38 (February): 5–27 [Five subsequent articles in *American Speech* in 1963–64 complete the report of this project].

Redall, Henry Frederic. 1889. *Fact, Fancy, and Fable: A New Handbook*. Chicago: A. C. McClurg.

Richardson, James. F. 1970. *The New York Police: Colonial Times to 1901*. New York: Oxford University Press.

Rifkind, Carole. 1977. *Main Street: The Face of Urban America*. New York: Harper & Row.

Riis, Jacob A. 1890. *How the Other Half Lives: Studies among the Tenements of New York*. New York: Hill and Wang, 1957.

———. 1902. *The Battle With the Slum*. Montclair, NJ: Patterson Smith, 1969.

Romains, Jules. 1942. *Salsette Discovers America*. New York: Alfred A. Knopf.

Runyon, Damon. 1929+. *Guys and Dolls: Three Volumes in One*. Philadelphia: J. P. Lippencott, n.d.

Safire, William. 1978. *Safire's Political Dictionary*. 3rd ed. New York: Ballantine.

———. 1983. On Language. "Bag Lady." *New York Times Magazine* (January 2): 6–8.

———. 1984a. *I Stand Corrected: More on Language*. New York: Avon.

————. 1984b. On Language. "Forgive Me, But . . . ." *New York Times Magazine* (October 21): 14–15.

Sante, Luc. 1991. *Low Life: The Lures and Snares of Old New York*. New York: Farrar Straus & Giroux.

Sasowsky, Norman. 1976. *The Prints of Reginald Marsh*. New York: Clarkson N. Potter.

Schermerhorn, Gene. 1982. *Letters to Phil: Memories of a New York Boyhood, 1848–1856*. New York: New York Bound.

Schlesinger, Arthur Meier. 1933. *The Rise of the City, 1878–1898*. New York: Macmillan.

Schneider, John C. 1984. "Skid Row as an Urban Neighborhood, 1880–1960." *Urbanism: Past and Present* 9 (Winter-Spring): 10–20.

Schuller, Gunther. 1968. *Early Jazz: Its Roots and Musical Development*. New York: Oxford University Press.

Schwartz, Barry. 1976. "Images of Suburbia." *The Changing Face of the Suburbs*. B. Schwartz, ed. Chicago: University of Chicago Press, 325–40.

————. 1981. *Vertical Classification: A Study in Structuralism and the Sociology of Knowledge*. Chicago: University of Chicago Press.

Sennett, Richard. 1977. *The Fall of Public Man*. New York: Knopf.

Shackleton, Robert. 1917. *The Book of New York*. Philadelphia: The Penn Publishing Co.

Shapiro, Fred R. 1991. "*Big Apple* 'New York City.' " *American Speech* 66 (Summer): 223.

Shulman, David. 1951. "Baseball's Bright Lexicon." *American Speech* 26 (February): 33.

————. 1990. "*The Great White Way* 'Broadway' " *Comments on Etymology* XIX (No. 7): 33.

Siegel, Adrienne. 1981. *The Image of the American City in Popular Literature, 1820–1870*. Port Washington, NY: Kennikat.

Simon, Kate. 1978. *Fifth Avenue: A Very Social History*. New York: Harcourt Brace Jovanovich.

Simpson, William R., and Florence K. Simpson. 1954. *Hockshop*. New York: Random House.

Sloan, John. 1965. *John Sloan's New York Scene, from the diaries, notes, and correspondence 1906–1913*. Bruce St. John, ed. New York: Harper & Row.

Smith, Matthew Hale. 1868. *Sunshine and Shadow in New York*. Hartford, CT: J. B. Burr.

Smith, W. N. 1983. "Epistolae" [on *hooker*]. *Verbatim* 10 (Autumn): 19.

Snyder, Robert W. 1989. *The Voice of the City*. New York: Oxford University Press.

Sobel, Bernard. 1931. *Burleycue: An Underground History of Burlesque Days*. New York: Farrar & Rinehart.

Spaeth, Sigmund. 1926. *Read 'Em and Weep: The Songs You Forgot to Remember*. Garden City, NY: Doubleday, Page.

————. 1927. *Weep Some More, My Lady*. Garden City, NY: Doubleday, Page.

Spectorsky, A. C. 1955. *The Exurbanites*. New York: Berkley.

Stansell, Christine. 1986. *City of Women: Sex and Class in New York, 1789–1860*. New York: Knopf.

Steinmetz, Sol. 1986. *Yiddish and English: A Century of Yiddish in America*. University: University of Alabama Press.

Stern, Robert A. M., Gregory Gilmartin, and Thomas Mellins. 1987. *New York 1930*. New York: Rizzoli.

Still, Bayrd. 1956. *Mirror for Gotham: New York as Seen by Contemporaries from Dutch Days to the Present*. New York: New York University Press.

———. 1974. *Urban America: A History with Documents*. Boston: Little, Brown.

Strauss, Anselm L. 1961. *Images of the American City*. New York: Free Press.

———, ed. 1968. *The American City: A Sourcebook of Urban Imagery*. Chicago: Aldine.

Strunsky, Simeon. 1914. *Belshazzar Court, Or Village Life in New York City*. New York: Henry Holt.

Suttles, Gerald D. 1968. *The Social Order of the Slum: Ethnicity and Territory in the Inner City*. Chicago: University of Chicago Press.

Tamony, Peter. 1976. "Skidroad's Skidway to Inner City." *Western Folklore* 35 (April): 141–48.

———, and Gerald L. Cohen. 1978. "Contributions to the Etymology of *Hot Dog*." *Comments on Etymology* VII (No. 15): 1–38.

———, and Gerald L. Cohen. 1980. "*Hot Dog* Revisited." *Comments on Etymology* IX (No. 7): 1–15, 22–24.

Taylor, William R., ed. 1991. *Inventing Times Square: Commerce and Culture at the Crossroads of the World*. New York: Russell Sage Foundation.

———. 1992. *In Pursuit of Gotham: Culture and Commerce in New York*. New York: Oxford University Press.

Thernstrom, Stephan. 1964. *Poverty and Progress: Social Mobility in a Nineteenth Century City*. Cambridge: Harvard University Press.

Thompson, Vance. 1906. "The New York Cab Driver and His Cab." *Tales of Gaslight New York*. Frank Oppel, ed. Secaucus, NJ: Castle, 1985, 3–12.

Tichi, Cecilia. 1987. *Shifting Gears: Technology, Literature, Culture in Modernist America*. Chapel Hill: University of North Carolina Press.

Toll, Robert C. 1974. *Blacking Up: The Minstrel Show in Nineteenth-Century America*. New York: Oxford University Press.

Towne, Charles Hanson. 1931. *This New York of Mine*. New York: Cosmopolitan Book Corp.

Tuan, Yi-Fu. 1974. *Topophilia: A Study of Environmental Perception, Attitudes, and Values*. Englewood Cliffs, NJ: Prentice-Hall.

Tunnard, Christopher, and Henry Hope Reed. 1953. *American Skyline*. New York: New American Library, Mentor, 1956.

Tysell, Helen Trace. 1935. "The English of the Comic Cartoons." *American Speech* 10 (February): 45–55.

Urdang, Laurence. 1988. *The Whole Ball of Wax and Other Colloquial Phrases*. New York: Perigree/Putnam.

Vandersee, Charles. 1984. "Speakeasy." *American Speech* 59 (Fall): 268–69.

Van Dyke, John C. 1909. *The New New York: A Commentary on the Place and the People*. New York: Macmillan.

Vidich, Charles. 1976. *The New York Cab Driver and His Fare*. Cambridge, MA: Schenkman.

Walker, Stanley. 1933. *The Night Club Era*. New York: Frederick A. Stokes.

Walling, George W. 1887. *Recollections of a New York Chief of Police*. New York: Caxton Book Concern.

Ware, Caroline F. 1935. *Greenwich Village, 1920–1930*. New York: Octagon Books, 1977.

Warner, Sam Bass. 1984. "Slums and Skyscrapers: Urban Images, Symbols, and Ideology." *Cities of the Mind: Images and Themes of the City in the Social Sciences*. Lloyd Rodwin and Robert M. Hollister, eds. New York: Plenum Press, 181–95.

Webster, J. Carson. 1960. " 'Skyscraper,' etc." *American Speech* 35 (December): 307–08.

Wechsler, Judith. 1982. *A Human Comedy: Physiognomy and Caricature in 19th Century Paris*. Chicago: University of Chicago Press.

Wecter, Dixon. 1937. *The Sage of American Society: A Record of Social Aspiration, 1607–1937*. New York: Scribner's, 1970.

Weitenkampf, Frank. 1947. *Manhattan Kaleidoscope: A Genial, Rambling Account of the New York Scene, 1870–1945*. New York: Scribner's.

Wentworth, Harold, and Stuart Berg Flexner, eds. 1960. *Dictionary of American Slang*. 2nd. supp. ed., 1975. New York: Crowell.

Weseen, Maurice Harvey, ed. 1934. *A Dictionary of American Slang*. New York: Crowell.

Wharton, Edith. 1905. *The House of Mirth*. New York: Bantam, 1984.

———. 1913. *The Custom of the Country*. New York: Collier, Macmillan, 1987.

———. 1925. *The Mother's Recompense*. New York: Scribner's, 1986.

———. 1931. "The Pomegranate Seed." *The Ghost Stories of Edith Wharton*. New York: Scribner's, 1973.

———. 1934. *A Backward Glance*. New York: D. Appleton-Century.

Whitman, Walt. 1855+. *Leaves of Grass and Selected Prose*. John Kouwenhoven, ed. New York: Modern Library, 1950.

———. 1885. "Slang in America." *The North American Review* 141 (November): 431–35.

———. 1921. *The Uncollected Poetry and Prose of Walt Whitman*. 2 vols. Emory Holloway, ed. Garden City, NY: Doubleday, Page.

———. 1932. *I Sit and Look Out: Editorials from the Brooklyn Daily Times*. Emory Holloway and Vernolian Schwartz, eds. New York: Columbia University Press.

———. 1933. *Walt Whitman and the Civil War: A Collection of Original Articles and Manuscripts*. Charles I. Glicksberg, ed. New York: A.S. Barnes, 1963.

———. 1936. *New York Dissected: A Sheaf of Recently Discovered Newspaper Articles by the Author of LEAVES OF GRASS*. Emory Holloway and Ralph Adimari, eds. New York: Rufus Rockwell Wilson.

———. 1950. *Walt Whitman of the New York AURORA: Editor at Twenty-two*. Joseph Jay Rubin and Charles H. Brown, eds. State College, PA: Bald Eagle Press.

Wilmeth, Don. B., ed. 1981. *The Language of American Popular Entertainment: A Glossary of Argot, Slang, and Terminology*. Westport, CT: Greenwood.

Wilson, Edmund. 1946. *Memoirs of Hecate County*. New York: Bantam, 1976.

Winchell, Walter. 1927. "A Primer of Broadway Slang." *Vanity Fair* (November): 67ff.

Wolfe, Gerard R. 1988. *New York: A Guide to the Metropolis*. Rev. ed. New York: McGraw-Hill.

Wood, Clement, and Gloria Goddard, eds. n.d. [ca. 1926]. *A Dictionary of American Slang*. Little Blue Book No. 56. Girard, KS: Haldeman-Julius.

Works Progress Administration. 1938. *New York Panorama: A Companion to the WPA Guide to New York City*. New York: Pantheon, 1984.

———. 1939. *The WPA Guide to New York City: The Federal Writers' Project Guide to 1930s New York*. New York: Pantheon, 1982.

Wright, Mabel Osgood. 1926. *My New York*. New York: Macmillan.

Zeisloft, E. Idell. 1899. *The New Metropolis*. New York: Appleton.

Zlotnick, Joan. 1982. *Portrait of an American City: The Novelists' New York*. Port Washington, NY: Kennikat Press.

Index of Words and Phrases

across the tracks, 226
acting ritzy, 122. *See also* ritz
African Broadway, 42
after-hours club, 73
airing (washing) dirty linen in public, 34
alley, 45, 46, 234; Allee (*German*), allée (*French*), 46
Alley, The (*London*), 39; the (Big) Alley (*Times Square*), 265 n. 11
alley apples, 46, 210
alley bat, alley cat, alley rat, 46
alley-waiter, 126
allrightnik, Allrightniks Row, 238
ameche, 110
American Ward, Americans, 236
Annie Oakley, 10
apache, apache dance, 212
apartment, 116, 117; apartment house, 116
appetizing store, 101
Apple Annie, 200
appleknocker, 3, 247, 250; appleknocker town, 252
arab, 200
aristo, aristocrat, 220
Artery, the (Big), 265 n. 11
Artful Alley, 265 n. 11
asphalt jungle, 38; asphalt mesa, 134
Aspirin Alley, 265 n. 11
Astorbilt, 221
aunt (*brothel madam*), 160, 181
auto(*mobile*), 86
Avenoodles, Fifth Avenoodles, 22, 221
Avenue, The (*Madison Avenue*), 39; avenue, AVE-noo, The Avenue (*Fifth Avenue*), 221. *See also* Fifth Avenue
aviator (*slang sense*), 126

Babbitt, 43, 219; babbittry, 219
back alley, back-alley abortion, 46

back capper, 199
back street, back-street wife, 45
backdoor, backroom, backroom boys, backstairs, 45
backwoods, 250
badlands, 178
bag lady, bag woman, 197
bagnio, 180
bald-head(ed) row, 174, 175 (*caption*)
Baloney Boulevard, 264 n. 11
Bandits' Roost, 234
Banner man, 201
bar, 166; B(ar) girl, 170
barker, 167
Barrio, the; el barrio (*Spanish*), 240
bat (*prostitute*), 46, 184
Battle Row, 234
Bay, the, 201
beat (noun), 40
bed house, 181; bed line, 143, 144
Beer Gulch, 265 n. 11
beer joint, 151
below the line, 164
bench warmer, 143; bencher, 142
Bible Belt, 243
big alley, 41
Big Apple, The, 3, 62, 63, 74, 250
Big Burg, 256
Big Red Apple, Big Red with the Long Green Stem, 74
big spender, 77
big store, 123
Big Street, the, 265 n. 11
Big Town, 256; big towner, 250
bill(*y club*), billy, billy club, 213
bird (*notion of prostitute as*), 184
bird cage, 126
blab (*v.t.*), blab sheet, 107
Black Belt, 239

black joints, 74
Black Maria, 214
black-and-tan (*adj. & noun*), 74, 152
bladder, 107
blat, Blatt (*German*), 107
blighted area, 229
blind pig, blind pigger, blind tiger, 72
blow out, 67
bluebloods, 220
bluecoat, blue man, 213. *See also* men in blue
bo, 'bo, 141. *See also* hobo
bobby, 214
bob-tail car, 87
bohemia, 141, 142; bohemian, 218
boîte, boîte de nuit (*French*), 71. *See also* box; shine box
Bone Alley, 234
booby hatch, 214
boondocks, booneys(ies), boonie (*person*), 251
bordello, 180
Bottle Alley, 234
bottle club, 73
bounce (*noun*), 168; bouncer, 167. *See also* gorilla
Bouncers, the, 224
bourgeois, bourgeoisie, 219
Bowery, the, 41
Bowery Boy (B'hoy), Bowery Girl (G'hal), 210
Bowery bum, 142
box, 71. *See also* boîte; shine box
boys, the (*Bowery*), 210
breadline, 3, 143, 144 (*and caption*)
brick sandwich, 168
bridge-and-tunnels, 274 n. 23
brierhopper, 247
bright lights, 12, 24, 58
Broad, the Broadest Way, 265 n. 11
Broadway Babies, 78
Broadway battleship, 88
Broadway Joe, 195
Brodie, do a Brodie, 20
Bronx cheer, 261 n. 9. *See also* raspberry
brown baggers, 218
brownstone (*adj.*), brownstone club, 225; brownstone front, 224; brownstone vote, brownstoner, 225
brush, the, brush ape, 250
bucket (tub) of blood, 154
bucket shop, 154
bug house, 156
Bughouse Square, 143
buggy (*taxi*), 97
bul (*Spanish Gypsy*), 213; bulls, 9, 213
Bulb Belt, 264 n. 11
bum, bum park, bummer, 142
bum fodder, bum wad, bum's comforter, 108

bum rush, bum's rush, 168
Bummers' Retreat, 234
bumpkin, 244, 246, 247
bundok (*Filipino Tagalog*), 251. *See also* boondocks
burb(s), 'burb(s), 257, 259
-burg, -burgh (*suffixes*), 252, 256; burg, burgh (*German & Scots*), 256
burlesque, 174, 176; burlesk, burley, burle(y)cue, burly-Q, 174
bus, 86, 87; omnibus, 87
bush (*adj.*), the bush(es), 250; bush leagues, 251
butcher, 174
butte, 134
butter-and-egg man, (big), 3, 19, 77
Buttinsky, 20, 21
buzz (*v.t.*), 110
Buzzard Boulevard, 265 n. 11
B'way, 264 n. 11

cab, 86, 95; cab joint, 73; cabby, 73, 96; cabriolet, 95
cabbage patch, 255
cad, 171; cadet, 171, 270 n. 34
Café Society, 73, 74, 220, 224
cage, cage hotel, 156
California (Tucson) blanket, 108
call girl, 111, 181; call house (flat), 181
can house, 180
candy man, 199
candy store, 101
canyons, 11, 133, 134
capere (*Latin*), 214. *See also* cop, copper
capper, 73, 169, 199
carry the banner, 143
cat house, 180
cave dweller, 11, 118, 224
Champagne Charlie, 19, 76
charity girl, 80
chase the can, 153
cheap charlie (*candy store*), 101
cheap john (*clothing store*), 157
Cheese it!, 262 n. 32
chili parlor (joint), 150
chin (*v.i.*), chin-ema, 109
Chinaman, Chinatown, 237
chinch pad, chinche (*Spanish*), 156
chinwhisker town, 252
chippy-chaser, 195
chop suey (*restaurant or dish*), 150, 151; chop suey joint, 150; chop-suey dance joint, 68 (*caption*), 69
chorine, 78
chorus girl, 19, 78, 79; chorus Judy, 78
chow meinery, 151; Chow-Mein Stem, 237
chucker-out, 167. *See also* bounce
chuckwagon, 99
chute (*subway*), 93; chute (*eatery*), 149

cigarette girl, 19, 79
circus (*slang sense*), 180
citronella circuit, 255
city cousin, city hick, city jake, 241
city dude, cit(yite), city feller, city people, city slick, city slicker, 249
cityscape, 133
Clem (Clarence), 244, 245
cliff dweller, 3, 11, 118, 133
cliffs, 11, 134
clip (*v.t.*), 73; clip joint, 10, 73
clodhopper, 244, 247; the clods, 250; clodville, 252
clothesline, 33 (*caption*), 34
cloud-buster, cloud-scraper, cloud-supporter, 128
cloverkicker, 247
clucktown, 252. *See also* dumb cluck
cob, 247
cockroach, 46; cockroach business, cockroach joint, 149; Cockroach Row, 234
Codfish Aristocracy, 221
Coffee Pot Canyon, 265 n. 11
coldwater walk-up, 117
collar, collar (*v.t.*), 213
con(*ductor*), conney, 88
con man, 200
concrete canyon, 133
Coney (*Island*) chicken, Coney Island (*hot dog*), 104; Coney Island (*hot dog stand*), 105; Coney-Island red hot, 104
Coney Island (*glass of beer*), Coney-Island head, 102
Coney Island (*placename*), Coney-Island (*adj.*), Coney-Island whitefish, 102
confectionary (*slang sense*), 165
conscience joint, 100
Coontown, 238
cop, 212; cop (*v.t.*), copper, 214
cop a plea, cop out, 214
corinth (*brothel*), corinthian (*prostitute*), 181
corn (cracker), corn-fed (*adj.*), corn husker, corncob, corn tassel, cornthrasher, 247; corn country, 250
corner boy, corner cowboy, corner wolf, 44
counterjumper, 192
country (*adj.*), 244; country bumpkin, 246; country hick, 244; country Jake, 245
country-club set, 220
cove, 160; coves, let us frog and toe, 23
cowtown, 254
crawl, 41, 42
cream, cream of society, 220
creep house, 180
crib joint, 271 n. 53
cross street, 45; crossroads, 254
crossing sweeper, 206

cruiser (*streetwalker*), 9, 183; cruising (*for cab passengers*), 97
crush (*noun*), 90
crusher, 213
cup rattler, 197
cuppa, 99
curb, 50; curb (*adj.*), 29; curb brokers, 51, 264 n. 50; curb (*market*), curb market, 51. *See also* curbstone
curbstone (*adj.*), 29, 51, 52; curbstone (*cigarette*), 52; curbstone broker, 29, 51; curbstone justice, curbstone meeting, curbstone philosopher, curbstone singers, curbstoner, 51; curbstone sailor, 183. *See also* curb
cut corners, 53

daddy, 80
daily blab, 107
daiseyville, 251
dance-hall pimp, 171
dance in the streets, 65
dancing academy (*brothel*), 171; dancing hell, 170
Darktown, 239
day house, 169
Dazzling Gulch, 265 n. 11
Dead-Cat Alley, 234
Dead End, the, 234; dead end, 235; dead-end street, 53
dead house, 151
Dead Man's Curve, 89
deadline, the (*14th Street*), 164; (*Fulton Street*), 270 n. 4
Debtors' Row, 240
decoy dancer, 170
deli sandwich, 101; delicatessen, 100, 101; delicatessen (*saloon*), 165. *See also* eat deli
department store, 123. *See also* big store
Deuce, The, 63
Devil's Half Acre, Devil's Row, 233
Diamond Ditch, 265 n. 11
dime-a-dance hall, 171
diner, 99
dinner pailer, 218
dirty rag, 107
dirty wash, 34
Dirty White Way, 265 n. 11
distillery, 151
disurbia, 257
dive (*noun*), 146, 147 (*caption*), 148
dog, dog (*stand*), dog wagon, doggies, 105
Dogpatch, dogtown, 255
dolled-up, (all), 65
dollymop, 170
Don't act like you were born on the Bowery!, 164

don't get ritzy with me, 122. *See also* ritz
doss, doss (*v.i.*), doss house, 155
down (up) one's street (alley), 53
down the drain, 160
Downtown, downtown, 228, 229
Do you want to come up and see my
    etchings?, 79
drag, 41; the (Big) Drag, 265 n. 11
draw one, draw one in the dark, 98
Dream Street, 61
drive-in movie, 109
driven to the wall, 53
drop one on the brown, 98
drug den, 154
drugstore, 97; drugstore cowboy, 44
dude, 195, 249; duded-up, 65; duds, 249
dullsville, 251
dumb cluck, 252
Dumb Dora, 79
dumbbell tenement, 114
dumbwaiter, 126
dump, 146, 148, 149; The Dump, 110
Dutch (*i.e., Deutsch*) Boulevard, 237;
    Dutch Hill, 227

East Jesus, 254
East Village, 229
Easy Street, 53
EAT(S), 98
eat deli, 101
ecdysiast, ekdysis (*Greek*), 176
egg cream, 101
eggs in the dark, 98
el, 86, 92; L, 92
electric sewer, 95
electrics, 87
elevated, 92
elevator (*elevated train*), 92; elevator, 124,
    126
Elk, 219
Elmer, 245
end of the line, 53, 89, 158
escalator, 126
exotic dancer, 176
explore every avenue, 53
exurban, exurbanites, exurbia, exurbs, 258

faker, fakir, 199
falling-off place, 253
fan (*v.t.*), 143; fanner, 111
Fancy, the, 42; fancy Dan, 195; fancy
    ladies, 181; fancy pants, 220
fare, 97
farmer, 244, 248
Fascinating Forties, the, 265 n. 11
Fat City, 53
Fifth Avenue, 235. *See also* The Avenue
filing cabinets, 117
filling station, 254

Finest, The, New York City's Finest, 213
first (kid) on one's block, 53
fish wrappers, 108
Flamboyant Floodway, the, 264 n. 11
flapper, 68, 69
flash, 262 n. 42; flashman, 194
flashing, 176
flat, 115; flat craze (fever), 116
flatfoot, 9, 213; flatty, 213
Flatiron Building, 129
flea bag, 146, 156; fleabag hotel, 156; flea
    house (box, trap), 156; flea-trap hotel,
    149
flickers, flicks, 109
flop (*v.i.*), flop house (joint), 155
Forties, The, 60
four corners, 254
Four Hundred, The, 3, 221, 222
franchise strip, 259
frankfurter, 104
Fraudway, 265 n. 11
free-and-easy (*hotel*), 181
free bencher, 143; freeloader, 143, 168
free lunch, 167
French flat, 115
French Town, 237
French walk, 168
frogs (*police*), 213
Fun City, 62
Furious Forties, 265 n. 11

G-string, gee-string, 174, 175 (*caption*)
gadget (*G-string*), 174
Galaxy, the, 265 n. 11
gallery gods, 262 n. 32
gambling den (hell), 169
gang, gangster, 209; gangbuster, 128
gape wagon, 84; gapeseed, 199
garden-club crowd, 220
Gashouse District, 227; Gashousers, 209,
    228
Gay Gulch, 265 n. 11; Gay Lit-Up
    Canyon, 264 n. 11
Gay White Way, The, 59
gendarme, 214
gentrification, 260
Germantown, 237
get in on the ground floor, 125
get off the beaten track, 53
get streets ahead, 53
Get the hook!, 175
get them on the line (wire), 110
ghetto, 8, 230, 231, 232; Ghetto Nuovo,
    Ghetto Vecchio (*Italian*), 231
ghost town, 254
ghostbuster, 128
gigolette (*French*), gigolo, 81
gilded ghetto, 232
gimp, 198

Gin Gulch, 265 n. 11
gin mill, 146, 151
Glitter Boulevard, Glittering Gulch (Stem), 265 n. 11
go in (a) circle(s), 49
go on a spree, go on a tear, 65
go on the street, 28. See also street etc.
go peddle your papers, 205
go slumming, 74, 81, 231
go to town, goin' to town, 65
god-forsaken place, 254
Gold Coast, 235
gold digger, 3, 19, 80
Golden Gulch, 264 n. 11
good address, 42
good-time Charlie, 77
goosing slum, 181
Gopher Prairie, Gopher-prairie dog, 243
gorge, 134
gorilla, 167. See also bounce, bouncer
Gotham, 241, 256
Grand Canyon, 265 n. 11; Grandest Canyon, 264 n. 11
Grand Central Station (slang sense), 92
grassroots, grassville, 251
gray area, 229. See also slum
grease joint, 149
greasers, 210
greasy spoon, 146, 149
greasy spot on the road, 254
Great Tight Way, 60
Great Unwashed, The, 218
Great White Way, The, 3, 58, 59, 61
green (money), 74
green, greener, greenhorn, greeny, 242
green light, 53
gridlock, 86
grinder, grind house, 109
grocery, greengrocery, liquor grocery, 165
grog mill, groggery, 151
gropers, 198
growler, 153, 154
Grub Street, 53, 264 n. 53
gulch, 134; the (Big) Gulch, 264 n. 11
gullet, gulley, gulp, 134
gulley jumper, 247
gussied-up, 65
gutter, 50, 52; gutter language, gutter rat, guttermarket, gutter music, gutterpup, 52; guttersnipe (various senses), 52, 206
guzzery, guzzle shop, guzzlery, 151
gypsies (street children), 205

hack, 86, 95, 96; hack (v.i.), 95; hack stand, hacker, hackey, 96; hackney, 95
hang up (the phone), hang up on (someone), 110
hansom, hansom cab, 95
Hardened Artery, the, 264 n. 11

Hard-Times Square, 264 n. 11
Harlem, 237, 239; Haarlem (Dutch), 239
hash, hash house, hash joint, hash slinger, hashery, 150
hash-house Greek, 98
have one on the city, 72
have one's back against the wall, 53
have their minds in the gutter, 52. See also gutter etc.
hayfoot, haymaker, haypitcher, 247; hayseed, 242, 247, 255; hayseed country, 250; hayseed town, 252; hayshaker, 247
hear it on the street, 39. See also street etc.
heave-ho, 168
Hell's Half Acre, 233
Hell's Kitchen, 8, 233, 234
herkimer jerkimer, 3, 245
hick (Richard), 13, 241, 242, 244, 245; hickdom, 250; hicksam, hicky, 245; hicksville, 251, 252; hicktown, 245, 252
highbrow, high hat, 220
high grass, 251
high-flyer stampede, 170
hillbilly, 244, 248
hit (beat, pad, pound) the bricks (pavement, road, rocks, macadam, sidewalks, turf), 39, 40
hives, 114
Hob (Robert), hobb, hobnail, 247
hobo, hobo (v.i.), 141. See also bo
Hobohemia, 141, 142
hock (v.t.), hock master, hockelty card, hocker, hockshop, in hock, in hockelty, hok (Dutch), 159
hocus-pocus, 199
hog in togs, 194
hoi polloi, 218
hokey-pokey, 199; hokey-pokey man, 3, 199
hold the phone!, 110
hole, 146, 148, 154; the hole (subway), 95, 148
hole in the wall, 146, 148
hollow, 227
Hollywood (adj.), 102; Hollywood Jungle, 37
home, 181. See also house
homeless, 196
honky-tonk, 171
Hooch Highway, 265 n. 11
hoodlum, 210
hook (v.t.) 185, 186; hook shop, 185; hooker, 3, 9, 184 (and caption), 185, 186
hook (topographical noun), hoek (Dutch), 185
hooligan, 210
hoosier, hoozer (British dialect), 246

hoosierdom, 250; hoosiertown, 252
Hoovervilles, 238
hop, 67; hop joint, 155
hot-corn girl, 204
hot damn, 105
hot dog, 3, 101, 104, 105; hot dog (*stand*),
    hot dog! (*exclam.*), 105
hot jazz, hot spot, 71; hot mama, 69
hot-pillow joint, 181
hot spell, 120
hotel swell, 121
hotsy-totsy, 10
house (*brothel*), 180, 181; house of call,
    181; house of ill fame (repute), 180
house hop (*noun*), house really hopped, 75
house-rent party, 75
Howling Swells, 224
hündchen, hundewurst (*Amer. German*),
    105
hurdy-gurdy man, 207, 208 (*caption*)
hurry, 90
hush house, 72
Hyphen, The, 122

Illuminated Thoroughfare, 264 n. 11
in the ritz, 122. *See also* ritz
in the same street, 53
Incandescent District, the, 265 n. 11
indoor aviator, 126
Inferno, the, 179, 233
inner city, 230; inner-city jungle, 37
Irish confetti, 46, 210
Irishman's sidewalk, 46
It's a jungle out there!, 37
It's your nickel—so talk, 111

Jack (Jacob), 245
jack roller, 155
Jake, 245; jakedom, 250; jaketown,
    jakeville, 252
jam (*traffic*), 86
jay, 245, 246, 252; jay country, 250; jay
    house, 180; jaybirdtown, jayburg,
    jaytown, 252
jaywalk, jaywalker, 246. *See also* jay *etc.*
jazz (jass), 71; jazz baby, jazz bo, 69; jazz
    joint, 71
Jeeter, 248
jelly bean, 69
jerk, 245; jerktown, 245, 254; jerkwater,
    jerkwater town, 245, 254
jet set, 224
Jewish Alps, 238
john (*prostitute's client*), 182
John Law, 214
joint, 146
joint really jumped, 75
joskin, joss (*v.t., British dialect*), 247
judas-hole (*adj.*), 72

juice joints, 151
Jukl (*Polish Yiddish*), 245. *See also* yokel
jump, jump joint, 75
Jump Street, 53
jumping-off place, 253
jungle (*tramp or hobo*), 37 (*caption*), 38;
    the (urban) jungle, 3, 11, 36, 37, 143;
    The Jungle (*electronics*), 37; the jungle,
    The Jungle (*brothel district*), 178; Jungle
    Alley, jungle music, 75; the jungles (*rural
    district*), 263 n. 18. *See also* asphalt
    jungle
just around the corner, 53

keeping up with the Jones's, 220
kennels, 114
keptie, 80
kerosene circuit, 255; Kerosene Row, 234
Kike Town, 237
kip (*v.i.*), 155. *See also* doss, flop
Klein Deutschland (*Amer. German*), 237
know-it-alls, 220

ladies' boarding house, 180
Ladies' Mile, 123
lady of the evening (night), 9, 183; lady of
    the pavement, 183; lady of the town, 77
lairs, 114
Land O' Darkness, 239
Lane, de (*the Bowery*), 41; the Lane
    (*Broadway*), 265 n. 11
last chance, 253
last stop, 50, 158
lavender cove, 160
law (*police*), the, 214
law of the jungle, 37
lay (out) in lavender, 159, 160; lay
    someone out in lavender, 160
leatherhead, 213
leg show, 174
Levity Lane, 265 n. 11
life in the fast lane, 258
lift (noun), 125
Lighted Lane, the, 265 n. 11
lilly whites, 204
line, the (*14th Street*), 164; Line, the (*Fifth
    Avenue*), 269 n. 2
line girl, (*chorus*), 78
Little Africa, 238; Little Italy, Little Russia,
    237
little night bird, 9, 183
Little Old Broadway, 265 n. 11
live one, 77
Lobster Alley, 265 n. 11
lobster palace, 70, 265 n. 11; lobster-
    palace society, 224
local yokel, 245; locals, 249
loft, 117

Lombard, lombard room, 159; Lombard rate, 269 n. 36
long green, 74
lounge, 166; lounge lizard, 80, 81
louse trap (cage), 156
love nest, 80
low grass, 251
lower-, lower side of, 227
lower than the belly of a cockroach, 46
lumber, lumber (v.t.), in lumber, lumber crib (room), 159
Lumpenproletariat, 218
lunch (room), 97; lunch car, 99; lunch counter, 97; lunch joint, 98; lunch room, lunch stand, 97, 99; lunch wagon, 99, 105
luncheonette, lunchettes, 98
lunchtime, 97
lush (alcoholic person and drink), lush (v.i.), lush dive (drum, joint), 151; lush diver, 156

ma tante (French), 160, 161. See also uncle
madam (brothel), 181
main alley, 41; the Main Alley, 265 n. 11
Main Artery, the, 265 n. 11
main drag, 41, 141; the Main Drag (Broadway), 265 n. 11
main stem, 141; the Main Stem (Broadway), 41, 265 n. 11; main stem siren, 183
main street, Main Street, 42, 43, 44, 243
maison joie, 180
make the rounds, 66
make whoopee, 65. See also whoopee
mallies, malling, mall rats, 26
man about town, 76, 77
man in the street, 28, 85; man in the cars, 85
Maraudway, 265 n. 11
mash, mash (v.t.), masha (Romany), 195; masher, 9, 195
Matches Mary, 200
matinée girl, 78
mazda, Mazda Lane, 264 n. 11
mean streets, 38, 139
Meet me at the Fountain, Meet me at the Waldorf, Meet me between the Lions, Meet me under the Clock, 122
melting pot, 232
men (women) are like buses (streetcars); there's one by every few minutes, 89
men in blue, 213. See also bluecoat
mesas, 11, 134
mickey, mickey finn, mickey flynn, 153
middle of nowhere, 253
middle of the road, 53
Middletown, 243
midway, 41

Milky Way, the, 265 n. 11
millionaire, millionnaire (French), 221
Millionaires' Mile (Row), 235
Minnesota Strip, 183
Misery Row, 234
miss the bus, 89
mission stiff, 144
Mixed-Ale Flats, 234
mob, mobile vulgus (Latin), mobster, 209; The Mob, 218
Modern Appian Way, the, 264 n. 11
monkey (taxi dancer), monkey chaser, 173; monkey hop, 173, 174
monkey organ, 207
mont-de-piété (French), monte di pietà (Italian), monte de piedad, montepío (Spanish), 269 n. 34
mooch (v.t.), moocher, mooch the stem, 41, 197
mo'on pictures, 109. See also movies
morgue (barroom), 151
Mortgage Row, 240
mother (brothel madam), 181
movies, 109
Mr. (Mrs., Miss) Astor (Vanderbilt, Rockefeller), 221. See also Astorbilt
Mr. (Mrs., Miss) Gotrocks, Mr. Moneybags, 220
mudhole, mudhole town, 254
mug, 211, 212; mug (v.t.), mugee, 212; mugger, 9, 212; mugging, mug ugly, 212
mulligan, mulligan joint, mulligan stew, 150; Mulligan's Alley, 234
mumper, 197
Murderers' Alley, 234
mush, mush (v.t.), mushroom, 200; mush(room) faker, 9, 200
mystery (hash), 98

nab (v.t.), 214
nabes, 110
naked in the streets, 27
natives, 249. Also see local yokel, locals
neon (adj.), 60; Neon Boulevard, 265 n. 11
New York minute, 266 n. 12
New York tube steak, 104
newsboy, newsgirl, newsies, 204
nickel dump, 109. See also dump
nickel hopper, 173
Nigger Row, 239; Nigger Town, 237
night bird (nocturnal person), 183
night club, 72; night spot, 71
night owl (cab or driver), 96; night owl (lunch wagon), 99; night owl (nocturnal person), 99, 183. See also nighthawk; owl
night people, 99
nighthawk (cab or driver), 96. Also see night owl, owl

296

nightlife, 9, 58
nightwalker, 183
nine-to-fiver, 218
no-tell hotel (motel), 181
nobs, 223; Nob's Hill, 227
Noisy Lane, 265 n. 11
noplaceville, 251
not bad for a country boy!, 244
notchery, notch house, 180
nymph of darkness, 183; nymph of the
    pave(ment), 9, 40, 183; nymphe du pavé
    (*French*), 183

O che poco! (*Italian*), 199. *See also* hokey-
    pokey
O. K., 20, 262 n. 33; Old Kinderhook; oll
    korrect (all correct), 262 n. 33
Oatmeal Flats, 240
off one's trolly, 88
olraytnik, olraytnitse (*Amer. Yiddish*), 238
on (through) the grapevine, 39, 163 n. 21
on the pavement (sidewalks), 38, 40; on
    the stem, 41
on the pick up, on the tramp, 183
on the street(s), 28, 38, 40; on The Street
    (*Wall Street*), 39
on the town, 65, 66; out on the town (*of a
    woman*), 77
one nigger (*black coffee*), 98
one-arm joint, one-arm lunchroom, 97
one-horse town, 253
one-lung (*adj.*), one-lung town, 253
one-way street, 53
opium den, 154; opium pad, 155
Orange Juice Gulch, 134, 265 n. 11
other side of, 227; other side of the tracks,
    226
out of town (*to be sent*), 40
out on (in) the streets, 27. *See also* street(s)
    etc.
out where they knock the big apple, 250
owl (*cab or driver*), 96; owl (*nocturnal
    person*), 99; owl (*prostitute*), 184; owl
    wagon, 99. *Also see* night owl;
    nighthawk
oyster cellar (saloon), 148; oyster house,
    70

pad (*noun*), 155
Paddy (Padraic, Patrick), paddy wagon,
    215
paint the town red, 65
panel house, 180
panhandle, 197; panhandler, 9, 197
Panic Beach, 62
paradise, 262 n. 32
parlor girls, parlor house, 181
parlor lizard, parlor snake, 81
party (*v.i.*), party girl, 79

passion pit, 109
patterer, 198
pave (*noun*), 183
pave their own way to success, 53
pavement pounder, pavement pretty, 183;
    pavement princess, 9, 40, 183
Peacock Row (Alley), 123
peasants, 218
peel (*v.t.*), peeler, 214
Pennsy, 97
penthouse, 119
peons, 218
Peter Funk, 200
pferdewurst (*Amer. German*), 105
phone, phonomania, (tele)phonitis, 110;
    (tele)phone booth (box), 111
Phosphorescent Path, 265 n. 11
picker-up, 169
Pig Market, 124
pigs (*police*), 9, 213
Pigtail Town, Pig Tail Alley, 237
piker, piker joint, 169
pinch (*v.t.*), 214
pink (*adj.*), 260
piping the stem, 41
piss on ice, 70
playboy, 19, 77
pleasure hound, 194
plebe, plebian, 218
plow jockey, 248
plug, 211; Plug Uglies, 209, 211. *Also see*
    mug
plug in (*to someone*), 110
plutes, plutocrats, 220
Podunk, 252
political jungle, 37
pop (*v.t.*), pop shop, 159
poppy, Poppy Alley, 237
pothole, 135
pounding the pavement, 38
Poverty Hill, 227; Poverty Row, 53, 234
prairie-dog town, 254
press the bricks, 40
princess of the pavement, 183
professor (*piano*), 166
projects (*housing*), 117
pseudo, pseudo-intellectual, 219
public woman, 77
puller-in, 9, 167, 201, 202 (*caption*)
Pushcart Alley, pushcart man, 198
put it on the street, 39. *See also* street(s)
    etc.
put(ting) on the ritz, 122. *See also* ritz

Quality Hill, 235
Queer Street, 53

racket, 67
rag (*newspaper*), 107

rag picker, 215; Rag Pickers' Row, 234
rag trade, 124
rags and paint, 105
railroad flat, 114
range (noun), 134
raspberry, 261 n. 9. See also Bronx cheer
rat (slang sense), 46
rattle, rattler, 89
red mike wit a bunch o' violets, 98
red-ink spot (joint), 150
red-light district, 177, 178; red lighters, 178
redneck, 248
reliever shop, 157
rent party, 3, 10, 75. See also house-rent party
revolving door (slang sense), 126
rhubarb (argument), the rhubarbs (place), 251
Rialto, The, 61
rib, Adam's rib, rib joint, 271 n. 53
ridgerunner, 248
riff-raff, 218
rig (noun), 97
right side of the tracks, 226. See also wrong side of the tracks
ring (noun), ring them up, 110
ritz, the, ritzily, ritzed, ritzier, the ritzies, ritziest, ritziness, ritzy, 122. See also acting ritzy; don't get ritzy with me; in the ritz; put(ting) on the ritz; this ain't the Ritz
roadhouse, 171
Roaring Forties, 60
robber barons, 220
rock pile, 128. Also see skyscraper
roll up the sidewalks, 57
roof garden, 70
rookeries, 114
roper, roper-in, 169
roughs, 209
round rimmer, 209
rounder, 76, 77
row (phrasal suffix), 140, 221, 234
rub, rub joint, 67
rubberneck, rubberneck wagons (autos, buses), 83
rubbernecker, 3, 10, 82 (caption), 83, 84
Rube (Reuben), 244, 245; rubedom, 250; rubetown, rubeville, 252
Rue de Revelry, 265 n. 11; Rue of Roués, 264 n. 11
rug joint, 70. Cf. sawdust joint
rum shop, 151
runner, 169
rurb, 259; rurban, 251, 259; rururban, 259
rush (noun), rush (hour), 90, 91 (caption)
rush the growler (can, duck), rusher, 153

saloon, salon (French), 165, 166; concert saloon, corner saloon, 166
sandwich man, 201
San Juan Hill, 239
Satan's Circus, 179, 233
sawdust joint, sawdust parlor, 70. Cf. rug joint
schmuck, 10
'scraper (sky-), 128
scratch house, 156; Scratch Park, 142
scum, 218
seeing (hunting) the elephant, 231
sent up (the river), 40. See also up the river
sepia sin spot, 74
Seven Sisters, the, 181
sewer, 50; sewer mouth, sewer rat, 52
Shanty Irish, shantytown, 237
shap sui (Cantonese), 150. See also chop suey
sheeny funeral with two on horseback, 98
sheet, 10, 107
sheik, 69
shelf, on the shelf, 159
shield (noun), 214
Shinbone Alley, 234
shine box, 71. See also boîte; box
shit, shitkicker, 247
Shit Street, 53
Shoddies, Shoddy Aristocracy, Shoddy Society, Shoddydom, Shoddyites, 224
shopgirl, 192, 193 (caption)
shopping-bag lady, 196. See also bag lady
short hairs, 210
shout it from the rooftops (housetops), 34
shouts, 75
show girl, 78. Also see chorus girl; line girl
shyster, Scheisser (Amer. German), 20
side street, 45
sidewalk, 50; sidewalk (adj.), 29; sidewalk superintendent, 29, 129; sidewalk Susie, 183
silk stockings, 220; Silk-Stocking District, silk-stocking man, 221
skedaddle, skiddoo, skidoodle, 130
skee joint, (whi)sky, 151
skell, 10, 197; skellum, skelder, 197
skid road, 140, 141, 158. Cf. skid row
skid row, 4, 9, 140, 141, 142
skin game, skin house, 169
skyscraper, 13, 113, 127, 128, 130, 131; skyscraping, 127. See also 'scraper
sky-sweeper, 128
slang, 22
slap-bang, 149
slaughter in the pan, 98
slave market, 61, 142
slick, slicker, 249
slip (off) one's trolley, 88
slop chute, slop joint, sloppy, 150

slot machine, slots, 100
slum, 4, 8, 229, 230, 259; slum (v.i.), 231;
    slummer, 81; go slumming, 74, 81, 231
slurb, slurban, 259
smart aleck, 20, 238
smoke (alcoholic drink), 152
snack bar, 97
snake dancer, 176
snob zoning, 259
snobs, snoots, 220
snoozing ken, 181
so-smarts, 220
soap box (noun, adj.), 143
soap lock, 210
social gangster, 81
soda jerk(er), 97
soiled linen, 34
soup kitchen, soup line, 143
spaghetti joint, 150
spaldeen (Spalding), 32
Spanish walk, 168
sparerib, 271 n. 53
sparrow, sparrow chaser, 214
speak, speako, 72; speakeasy, 72, 147
    (caption)
spiel, 67, 170; spieler, 3, 66, 67, 207, 208
    (caption); spieling, 67, 207
spitting on the sidewalk, 51
sport, sporting (life), sporting gentleman,
    163; sporting house, 163, 170, 180;
    sporting lady, sportsman, 163
spot, 71
spout, up the spout, 159, 160
spouter, 143. See also soap box
spread (noun), 107
spunk, spunk faker, 200
square (a person), 218
Squedunk, 252
squirrel shooter, 248
stack (of pancakes), 99
stage (vehicle), 87
stage-door Jenny, 78; stage-door Johnny,
    19, 78
stale-beer dive, 152
star gazer, 9, 184
steer joint, 73; steerer, 73, 169
stem, 41, 74; the Stem (Broadway), 265 n.
    11
stemming, 197
step off the curb, 53
step out on the town, 66; steppin' out, 65
stepping ken, 170
stick (place), sticktown, stickville, 255
sticks, the, 12, 241, 250, 255, 263 n. 18
Stix Nix Hix Pix, 255
stoop, stoep (Dutch), stoopers, 29;
    stoopball, 32
stop (place), stop off, stop on the road,
    stopping-off place, 253

straphanger, 3, 9, 93, 94 (caption)
straw-hat circuit, 255
street(s), the, 11, 28, 34, 38
Street, The (Broadway, 52nd Street,
    Madison Avenue, Wall Street), 39, 61
street (adj.), 28, 29
street arab (homeless child), 29, 52, 200,
    205, 206
street blockade, 86
street broker, 51; street Christian, street
    fighter, street ministry, 29; street money,
    29, 38; street name, street theater, 29;
    street vendor, 198
street hog, 215
Street of the Midnight Sun, 265 n. 11
street people, 29, 196
street rats, street rovers, 206
street smarts, street-smart (adj.), street-wise
    (adj.), 39
street talk, 39
street walking, 38
streetcar, 87, 88, 99
streetwalker, 9, 40, 183; street sister, 183
string city, 259
strip, the Strip, 41
strip city, 259
strip joint, 176
Strip Row, Stripty-second Street, 176
stripper, 175 (caption), striptease, 174
Strivers' Row, 240
stroll, the, 42, The Stroll, 74
strong (adj.), strong city, 176
struts, 75
stube, Bierstube (German), 166
stuck-ups, 220
studio (apartment), 117
stuffed shirts, 220
stumpies, 198
stumpjumper, 247
sub(way), subway, 93
suburb, 251, 256, 257, 259; suburban,
    suburbanite, suburbia, 257
suburb(s) (tramp or hobo), 38, 143
suburban (prostitute), suburban sinner,
    suburban trade, 257
sugar, 240; sugar daddy, 79, 80; Sugar
    Hill, 3, 240; Sugar Hillies, 240
sunny side of the street, 53
sunny-side up, 98
super(intendent), 116
sweat (v.t.), sweater (sweatshop owner),
    sweatshop, 124
sweatbox, 117
swell (noun), 195, 223
swellheads, 220
Swing Alley, Swing Street, 39

tab, 10, 107; tabloid, 107
take a flyer, 65

Take it off!, Take it off!, 174, 175
take it to the streets, take to the streets, 28
talk of the town, 39
talkies, 109
tally-ho, 87
tango pirate, 81
tank, tanktown, 254
tar beach, 3, 121
tax, 96; taxi, 86, 95, 96; taximeter, 96
taxi dancer, 172, 173 (*caption*); taxi-dance hall, 171
tea pad, 155
tell someone where to get off, 89
tender favor, 179
Tenderloin, The, 3, 4, 9, 178, 179; tenderloin, 271 n. 53
tenement, tenement district, 114
terpsichorine, terpsichorean, 78
Thieves' Alley, 234
this ain't the Ritz, 122. *See also* ritz
three balls, 160
three-card monte, 199
three-tap joint, 155
thrown out on (in) the streets, 27
tiger (*faro game*), tiger den, 169
timbers, the, 250
Times Queer, 264 n. 11
Tin Pan Alley, 63, 64; tin-pan (*adj.*), 64
tip-off man, 170
tippybobs, 220
Tobacco Road, 248
togged-up, 65
Toonerville, 252
town, towner, townie, townite, 250
town (*phrasal suffix*), 237, 252
town hick, 248
tramp, 142
trap, 146, 149
trash, 218
trolley, 87, 88; trolley dodgers, 88
trotters, trottery, 171
trotteuse (*French*), trottoir, trottoise, 183
tube, the tubes, 93
Tungsten Territory, 265 n. 11
turkey town, 255
twenty-three skiddoo, 130. *See also* skedaddle, skiddoo
two of a kind, 98
two shipwrecked, 98
two-stemmer, 249
Two-Time Square, 264 n. 11
two-to-one, 160
two-way street, 53

uncle, my uncle, 160, 161, 269 n. 39
unculus, (av)unculus, uncus (*Latin*), 269 n. 39
Underwood Hotel, 102
up, upper, upper crust, uppities, 220

up a blind alley, up against the wall, 53
up on the town, 66. *Also see* on the town
up the river, 10, 40, 263 n. 26
upmarket, upscale, 228
Upper Ten, the, 3, 222; Upper Ten Thousand, 222; Uppertendom, 273 n. 7
Uptown, uptown, 228, 229, 235
urb, 259; urban, 256, 259; urbanite, 249; urbs (*Latin*), 256

vaches, les (*French*), 213. *Cf.* bul, bulls
Valley, The, 240
'vator, 126. *See also* elevator
vau/x de vire (*French*), 262 n. 28
vaud(e), vodvil, 174; vaudeville, 18, 174, 262 n. 28
veil dancer, 176
vertical railway, 124
Via Lobsteria Dolorosa, 265 n. 11
Village, the, West Village, 229
-ville (*suffix*), 237, 251, 252
Vinegar Hill, 227
voix de ville (*French*), 18, 262 n. 28. *See also* vaud etc.

waiter girl, 166
walk Spanish, 168
walk-back, walk-down, walk-up, 117
Wall Street jungle, 37
Wall Streeters, 39
warrens, 114
watering hole, 70, 135; watering place, 69; watering spot, 70
weasel, 159
wiener, wienerwurst (*Amer. German*), wienie, 104
w(e)isenheimer, 238
whisper low, 72
whistle stop, 254
white flight, 259
white way, 58, 59. *Also see* Great White Way, The
white wings, 215; white wings with the sunny side up, 98
white-collar slaves, 218
white-light district, 58
whoopee, 10, 65, 66; whoopee mama, 69
whorehouse, 180
wide place in the road, 254
window shopping, 124
Wolkenkratzer (*German*), 128. *See also* cloud-buster, cloud-scraper
woman about town, woman of the town, woman on the town, 77; woman on the pave, 183
wood hick, 245, 248
woods, the, 250
Wop Town, 237
work both sides of the street, 53

working girl, 191, 192
working stiff, 218
would-be's, 220
wrong side of the tracks, 226. *See also* right side of the tracks

yahootown, 252
yap, 246; yap wagon, 84
yawp (*v.i.*), yawpie, 109

yellow journalism, 3, 108; yellow press, 107
yen, in-yăn (*Cantonese*), 155
yokel, 242, 244, 245; yokelania, 250; yokeltown, yokelville, 252
yoking, 212. *Cf.* mugging
York, 141
youbetcherland, 250
yuppie, 219

Author and
Subject Index

Abbott, Berenice, 17, 33, 105, 130
Abrams, Charles, 133
Adler, Polly, 181
African-American neighborhoods, popular
names for, 238–40
Algren, Nelson, 60
Allen, Harry N., 96
Allen, John 170
Alleys, symbolism of, 45–47
American Stock Exchange, 51
Anderson, Jervis, 74
Anderson, Nels, 141–42
Apartments and apartment houses, 114–
19
Armstrong, Louis, 77
Art, and its interplay with slang, 13–17
Asbury, Herbert, 211
Ashcan School of art, 16. *See also* Art
Astor, Caroline Schermerhorn, 220, 222
Astor House Hotel, 121
Astor, John Jacob, 221, 222
Automats, popular culture of, 100

Back streets, symbolism of, 45–46
Baer, Arthur ("Bugs"), 18
Baker, Benjamin A., 210
Baldassare, Mark, 257
Balzac, Honoré de, 11
Barth, Gunther, 18
Barthes, Roland, 48, 132
Bartlett, John Russell, 185, 210
Batman, 256
Batterberry, Michael and Ariane, 168
Beebe, Lucius, 73
Bellows, George W., 16, 118
Bender, Thomas, 4
Benét, Stephen Vincent, 203
Benjamin, Walter, 87, 190
Bercovici, Konrad, 236

Berger, Peter, 15
Berkeley, Busby, 80
Berlin, Irving, 19, 119, 122, 126
Berman, Marshall, 88
Bernstein, Leonard, 66, 95, 234
Big Apple, source idea of the, 62–63
Biltmore Hotel, 122
Bishop, Isabel, 16, 94, 97
Black-and-Tan saloon, 152
Blake, James W., 207
Blizzard of 1888, 88
Bloomingdale's department store, 126
Blue-light district, 178
Bodenheim, Maxwell, 219
Bogart, Leo, 18
Booth, Charles, 141
Bouncers and their art, 167–68
Bowery (Bouwerie) Lane, 41
Bowery, the, 5–6, 40–42; bad reputation
of, 164–65
Bowery Boys and Girls, 210–11
Brace, Charles Loring, 176, 206, 234
Brady, Diamond Jim, 58
Breadlines, 144–45
Brill Building, 64
Broadway, 61–63, 189–90; ephemeral
slang names for, 264–65 n. 11; social
types associated with, 76–81
Brodie, Steve, 20, 163
Brooklyn (Trolley) Dodgers, 88
Brothels, euphemisms and popular names
for, 180–81
Brown, Henry Collins, 60, 167, 168, 213
Brown, Isaac Hull, 220, 222–23
Browne, Henri Junius, 98, 167
Buffet, Bernard, 48
Burke, Edmund, 218
Burke, Kenneth, 8, 21
Burlesque, history and culture of, 174–76

Burnett, W. R., 38
Burnham, Daniel Hudson, 129
Bustanoby, Jacques, 70
Byrnes, Thomas, 270 n. 4

Cab Calloway, 153
Cadets, New York, 171
Café Royal, 61
Café Society, emergence of, 73–74
Cagney, James, 255–56
Caldwell, Erskine, 248
Calloway, Cab, 76, 239
Campbell, Helen, 206
Cantor, Eddie, 66
Canyons, popular notion of urban, 133–35
Capp, Al, 255
Capra, Frank, 200
Carleton, Will, 46
Carmine Theater, 110
Castle, Irene and Vernon, 68
Chapman, Robert L., 168
Chesterton, G. K., 128
Chorus girls, erotic idea of, 78–80
Ciardi, John, 64, 146, 233, 246, 252, 269 n. 39, 271 n. 67
Cigarette girls, image of, 79–80
Circuit of hours or temporal rhythms in city life, 189–90
Cities, generic names for, 256
City people, as provincials, 241–42; rural names for, 249–50
City novel, idea of, 14–15
Clapin, Sylva, 195, 220
Cliff dwellers, popular notion of, 118–19
Cohan, George M., 19, 245
Cohen, Gerald L., 62, 104, 105, 246, 262 n. 32
Coleman, Glenn O., 16
Comments on Etymology, 262 n. 44
Concert saloons, 166–67
Conden, Betty, 95
Coney Island, symbolism of, 101–5
Conner, Theophilus Eugene ("Bull"), 213
Connie's Inn, 75
Conrad, Peter, 48, 106, 132
Corner saloons, 166
Corners, symbolism of street, 44, 49
Cotton Club, 75
Counterjumpers as social type, 192–94
Country people, generic names for, 242–49
Crane, Hart, 106
Crane, Stephen, 14, 28–29, 32–34, 49, 60, 89, 96, 120, 134, 151, 158, 164, 166–67, 180, 205, 233
Crapsey, George, 146, 148, 270 n. 32
Cressey, Paul G., 172
Crockett, Albert, 81

Cromley, Elizabeth Collins, 116
Crysler Building, 71, 129
Crystal Palace Exhibition, 21, 124
Cullen, Countee, 240
Curbs and curbstones, symbolism of, 50–52

Dance craze, 66–68
Dance halls, 170–74
Darsy, Émile, 212
Davis, Gussie L., 234
Davis, Stuart, 16, 49, 92, 132
de Casseres, Benjamin, 49, 60, 81, 131
Dead End, slum neighborhoods as the, 234–35
Delicatessens, origin and culture of, 100–101
Demuth, Charles, 132
Department stores in urban life, 123–24
Dickens, Charles, 22, 215
Dictionary of American Slang, 148, 149, 200, 254, 271 n. 53
Domosh, Mona, 268 n. 42
Donaldson, Walter, 65
Dorgan, Thomas A. ("TAD"), 18
Dos Passos, John, 14, 48, 90, 98, 150
Downtown, idea of, 228–29
Dreiser, Theodore, 14, 85, 108, 144, 195, 198, 203, 234
Drinking places, generic names for low, 151–55
Dumb Doras, pejorative notion of, 79
Dunn, Alan, 118
Dunn, Peter Finley (Mr. Dooley), 19

Eating places, generic names for low, 149–51
Egan, Pierce, 181
Elevated trains, popular images of, 92–93
Elevators, culture and symbolism of, 124–26
Ellington, Duke, 75, 153
Ellington, George (pseudonym), 146
Empire Diner, 99
Empire State Building, 129
Equitable Life Assurance Building, 124, 125
Erenberg, Lewis A., 64–65, 70, 78, 79
Escalators, symbolism of, 126
Ethnic neighborhoods, popular names for, 236–40
Etting, Ruth, 173
Evans, Florence Wilkinson, 52

Farrel, James T., 100
Fast-food services, popular names for, 97–101
Fava, Sylvia, 257–58
Feeney, J. L., 67
Ferber, Edna, 92

Ferlinghetti, Lawrence, 93
Fifth Avenue Hotel, 124
Fitzgerald, F. Scott, 48, 69, 96, 203
Flâneur, social role of the, 11, 190
Flappers, 68–69
Flatiron Building, 103, 127; folklore of,
    129–31
Fleischmann, Louis, 145
Fleischmann's Vienna Model Bakery, 144–
    45
Fletcher, Jefferson Butler, 203
Flexner, Stuart Berg, 88, 100, 109, 153,
    199, 210, 212. *See also Dictionary of
    American Slang*
Flynt, Josiah, 141
Ford, Ford Madox, 128
Foster, George G., 98, 165–66, 185, 186
Fourteenth School of art, 16. *See also* Art
Freddie Keppard's Creole Band, 71
Fuller, Henry Blake, 119
Funk, Charles Earle, 160

Gambling houses, 169–70
Gans, Herbert, 25
Gaunt, Percy, 164
Gay, John, 200
Gem Spa, 101
Gentrification, 260
Ghetto, history of the, 231–32
Gillett, Charles, 62
Glackens, William, 16, 52, 97
Goffman, Erving, 87
Gold diggers, notion of, 80
Gold, Michael, 120, 207
Goldberger, Paul, 127
Golden, Harry, 108, 110
Goodman, Benny, 75
Gorki, Maxim, 131–32
Gorney, Jay, 141
Gotham Court, 113
Gotham, legend of, 256
Gottman, Jean, 132–33
Grand Central Station (Terminal), 90–92
Grand Palace ballroom, 67
Great White Way, history and development
    of, 58–61
Green, Adolph, 95
Gude, Oscar J., 58
Guinan, Texas, 77–78
Gutters, symbolism of, 52

Halper, Albert, 14, 134, 143, 156, 172
Halpern, Moshe Lieb, 120
Hammett, Dashiell, 73
Hanley, James F., 80
Hanson, Joseph Aloysius, 95
Hapgood, Hutchins, 66, 77, 190, 207, 232
Harburg, E. Y., 141
Harlem, 239–40; nightlife in, 74–76

Harlow, Alvin F., 153, 157
Harper, James Mayor, 215
Harris, Charles K., 59, 110
Harry, Hill, 170
Hart, Lorenz, 19, 76, 77, 78, 93, 100, 142,
    150, 173, 203, 219
Haughwout Building, 124
Haymarket dance hall, 170–71
Held, John, Jr., 69
Hellinger, Mark, 265 n. 11
Hell's Kitchen, 233–34
Hells, metaphor of slum neighborhoods as,
    232–35
Henri, Robert, 16
Herkimer, N.Y., 245
Hicksville, N.Y., 252
Hill, Abram, 240
Hirschfeld, Al, 69
Hoag, Aleck, 20
Home Insurance Building, 127
Hooker, notion of prostitute as, 184–86
Hoovervilles, 238
Hopper, Edward, 16, 35, 90, 92–93, 99,
    120–21
Horn and Hardart Baking Company, 100
Hot dogs, folklore of, 104
Hotels in urban life and speech, 121–23
Howells, William Dean, 14, 35, 48, 59, 92,
    93, 100, 125, 131, 134, 166, 216
Hoyt, Charles H., 81, 164, 167
Hudson, Samuel, 72
Hughes, Langston, 240
Hughes, Rupert, 167, 197, 201
Hunt, Richard Morris, 115
Hunter, Albert, 225
Hurst, Fanny, 45

Irving, Washington, 241, 256
Irwin, Godfrey, 41
Irwin, Wallace, 102
Irwin, Will, 78, 164

Jacobs, Jane, 36, 229–30
James, Henry, 32, 35, 48, 92, 121, 125,
    131, 134
Jastrow, Marie, 207
Jazz, 71
Jefferson, Thomas, 221
Jenney, William LeBaron, 127
Jungle, metaphor of urban, 36–38
Jungles, hobo and tramp encampments as,
    143

Kanter, Kenneth Aaron, 64
Käsebier, Gertrude, 78
Kasson, John F., 102–4
Kaufman, George S., 77
Kinderhook, N.Y., 262 n. 33
King Kong, 36, 93, 129

King, Mavis, 79
Kingsley, Sidney, 235
Kit Burn's Sportsmans' Hall, 163
Kouwenhoven, John, 133

Labov, William, 261 n. 6
Lait, Jack, 265 n. 11
Lardner, Ring, 14
Lateral metaphors in names of
    neighborhoods, 227–28
Lawlor, Charles B., 207
Lee, Alfred, 76
Lee, Gypsy Rose, 176
Lehr, Harry, 220
Lewis, Alfred Henry, 212
Lewis, David Levering, 240
Lewis, Sinclair, 43, 142, 219, 243
Lindsay, Vachel, 60
Line, 14th Street as the, 164
Linguistic construction of social reality, 8–
    13
Literature and its interplay with slang, 13–
    17
Lodging houses, generic names for low,
    155–56
Lofland, Lyn, 261 n. 2
London, Jack, 141, 143
Loos, Anita, 80
Lounge lizards, notion of, 80–81
Lozowick, Louis, 132
Luks, George, 16, 89, 96, 108, 154, 209
Lynd, Helen, 243
Lynd, Robert, 243

McAllister, Ward, 220, 222–24
McCabe, James D., Jr., 108, 142–43, 154,
    182, 201, 209, 224
MacCannell, Dean, 129
McCarthy, James Remington, 123
McCrea, Junie, 72
McDonald, John D., 60
McIntyre, O. O., 18, 62, 63, 79, 80, 95–
    96, 100, 170, 190, 200, 203, 242, 264–
    65 n. 11
Main drag and main stem, ideas of, 40–42
Main street, history and symbolism of, 42–
    44, 243
Maitland, James, 127
Marsh, Reginald, 16, 37, 38, 68, 69, 75,
    79, 89, 90, 92, 103, 109, 143, 145, 152,
    173, 174, 175, 176, 201,
Marx Brothers, 123
Mashers and related social types, 194–96
Mass media and slang, 17
Matsell, George Washington, 23–24, 149,
    163, 176, 181, 184, 194–95, 197, 199,
    200, 209, 245, 247, 251
Matthews, Brander, 87, 99, 118, 222
Mayhew, Henry, 141, 185

Meader, Herman Lee, 118
Mean streets, historical idea of, 38–39,
    139–40
Medici family, 160
Melville, Herman, 23, 133
Mencken, H. L., 21, 59, 72, 78, 82, 83,
    158, 176, 243
Metropolian Life Building, 127
Meyers, Jerome, 209
Miller, Kenneth Hayes, 16
Miller, Terry, 263 nn. 21, 26
Minsky, Billy, 176
Mitchell, Joseph, 150
Momand, Arthur R. ("Pop"), 220
Mondrian, Piet, 49
Moody, William Vaughn, 205
Morand, Paul, 48–49, 73, 128
Morino, Louis, 150
Morris, Lloyd, 74, 178
Morris, William and Mary, 108
Mortimer, Lee, 265 n. 11
Movies in urban life and speech, 19–20,
    108–10
Mugging, act of, 212
Mumford, Lewis, 117, 128
Munson's Diner, 99

Nascher, I. L., 178
Nash, Ogden, 93
Neal, Joseph C., 214–15
Neighborhoods, naming of symbolic, 225–
    40
Nesbit, Evelyn, 78–79
New Rochelle, N.Y., 245
New York Stock Exchange, 51, 52
Newspapers and slang, 17–18
Newsprint in urban life and speech, 106–8
Niblo's Garden, 59
Nightlife, 64–80

Odlum, Robert E., 21
O'Hara, John, 146
O. Henry (William Sydney Porter), 15, 29,
    35, 49–50, 67, 76, 84, 89, 96, 108, 120,
    122, 125, 134, 135, 144, 145, 192, 205,
    223, 233, 242
O'Keeffe, Georgia, 132
Oppenheim, James, 134
Original Dixieland Jazz Band, 71
Ornitz, Samuel, 238
Orwell, George, 141
Osofsky, Gilbert, 75
Ossining, N.Y., 40
Otis, Elisha G., 124
Otis Elevator Company, 126
Outcault, Richard F., 108
Outgroups, duality in naming of social,
    217–18

Paine, Albert Bigelow, 59, 145
Palace Theater, 61–62
Park, Robert E., 106
Partridge, Eric, v
Pastor, Tony, 19, 222
Paul, Maury, 73–74
Pavement, symbolism of, 39–40
Pawnshops, history and culture of, 157–61
Peel, Sir Robert ("Bobby"), 214
Peiss, Kathy, 67
Pember, A., 154
Pietri, Pedro, 117
Pines, Anita, 79
Playboys, 76–78
Plaza Hotel, 123
Poe, Edgar Allan, 261 n. 12
Police, popular names for, 212–15
Poole, Ernest, 92
Porter, Cole, 19, 119
Private houses in opposition to streets, 35–36
Prostitution, 176–86, 182–84
Public and private realms of city life, 32–36
Public transportation, popular images of, 86–97

Raft, George, 146
Raines Law, 168–69
Ralph, Julian, 118, 154, 248
Rand, Sally, 176
Rapid transit, cultural influence of, 90–95
Read, Allen Walker, 20, 252, 262 n. 33
Rector's restaurant, 70, 126
Red-light districts, 177–80. See also Blue-light district
Reed, Henry Hope, 115
Reed, John, 184
Reisenweber's Restaurant, 71
Revolving doors, symbolism of, 126
Rialto, social institution of the, 61–62
Rice, Alice Hegan, 255
Rich neighborhoods, popular names for, 235–36
Rich people, generic names for, 219–23
Richman, Harry, 77, 122
Rifkind, Carole, 43, 51
Riis, Jacob A., 16, 22, 24, 32, 114, 141, 149, 151, 152, 153, 154–56, 164, 169, 171, 197, 205, 211, 216, 234
Ritz, César, 122
Ritz-Carlton Hotel, 122, 123
Rockefeller, John D., 129, 221–22
Rodgers, Richard, 173, 233–34
Rogers, W. A., 202
Romains, Jules, 48
Rooftops, social uses of, 119–21
Roseland Ballroom, 68
Rosenfeld, Monroe, 64

Rubbernecker bus tours, 81–84
Runyon, Damon, 14, 18, 61, 72, 76, 78, 190, 200
Rural areas, generic names for, 250–51

Safire, William, 39, 197, 251
Sage, Russell, 93
St. Nicholas Hotel, 121
Saloons, history and culture of, 165–69
Sandwich men and other street advertisers, 201–3
Sartre, Jean-Paul, 48
Schlesinger, Arthur M., 87–88
Schwartz, Barry, 242, 257
Seven Sisters brothel, 181
Shackleton, Robert, 209
Sheeler, Charles, 132
Shinn, Everett, 16, 99
Shopgirls as social type, 191–94
Sidewalks, symbolism of, 39–40
Siegel, Adrienne, 194
Siegel-Cooper department store, 122, 123
Silverman, Sime, 256
Simon, Kate, 95, 123
Simpson, William, 158
Sinclair, Upton, 36
Sing Sing prison, 40
Sissman, L. E., 71
Skid row, history and institution of, 140–45; social types on, 141–42
Skid-row establishments, pejorative names for, 145–49
Skyscrapers, development and culture of, 127–35
Slang, definition of, 6; diffusion of, 4, 8; dual oppositions in, 11–13; social theory of, 6–10; urban matrix of, 4–6
Sloan, John, 7, 16, 36, 83, 84, 90, 92, 109, 110, 120–21, 130, 131, 147, 171, 182, 270 n. 2
Slocum river boat disaster, 237
Sloppy Louie's Restaurant, 150
Slumming, touristic activity of 81–84
Slums, history of idea of, 229–31
Small's Paradise, 75
Small-town people, generic names for, 248–49
Small towns, pejorative names for, 252–56; influences on pejorative names for: automobiling, 252–55; railroading, 254; show business, 255–56
Smith, Edgar, 191, 192
Smith, Matthew Hale, 177, 183
Snyder, Robert W., 18
Sobel, Bernard, 79
Sobol, Louis, 176
Social classes, pejorative naming of, 218–23
Social climbers, generic names for, 223–25

Speakeasies, 72–73
Spectorsky, A. C., 258
Sporting life, notion of, 163
Standard speech versus slang, 22–23
Stansell, Christine, 176–77
Stanwyck, Barbara, 14–15, 113
Steichen, Edward J., 17, 130
Steinmetz, Sol, 232, 238
Stella, Joseph, 16
Stevens House, 115
Stieglitz, Alfred, 87, 130
Still, Bayrd, 59–60, 121, 122, 211
Stoops, in New York life, 29–32
Strand Theater, 109
Strauss, Anselm, 28
Strayhorn, Billy, 240
Street children, 204–6
Street cleaners, 215–16
Street criers, 203–4
Street gangs, 209–12
Street grid, metaphor of, 44–50; as
   gameboard of urban life, 52–53
Street hogs, 215
Street lighting, history of, 57–58
Street musicians, 206–9
Street people, evolution of concept of,
   196–98
Street types, categoric knowing of, 190–91
Street vendors, popular names for, 198–
   200
Streets, symbolism of, 27–32
Strong, George Templeton, 176, 206
Strunksy, Simeon, 118, 128–29
Stuyvesant Apartments, 115
Suburban novel, idea of, 15–16
Suburbia and slang, 25–26
Suburbs, pejorative naming of, 257–60;
   urban disdain for, 257–60
Subways, popular images of, 93–95

Tall buildings, social meaning of, 131–35.
   See also Skyscrapers
Talmage, Thomas De Witt, 179
Tamony, Peter, 104, 262 n. 32
Tanguay, Eva, 90
Taxicabs, popular names for, 95–97
Taxi-dance halls, 171–74
Taylor, William R., 261 n. 21, 268 nn. 42,
   43
Teasdale, Sara, 125
Technological innovation and changing city
   life, 85–86
Telephones in urban life and speech, 110–
   11
Tenderloin, as vice district, 178–80
Tenements, 113–14; lack of privacy in,
   32–34
Thackeray, William M., 218
Thaw, Harry K., 78

Thompson, Vance, 182
Tichi, Cecilia, 90
Times Square, ephemeral slang names for,
   264–65 n. 11
Tin Pan Alley, 17, 61; history of, 63–64;
   and slang, 19
Tocqueville, Alexis de, 106
Tower Building, 127
Townsend, Edward W., 14, 248
Tracks, wrong and right sides of, 226–29
Tramp evil, the, 140
Trevelyan, Arthur L., 234
Tribune Tower, 127
Tuan, Yi-Fu, 27, 36, 259
Tunnard, Christopher, 115
Twain, Mark (Samuel L. Clemens), 253
21 Club, 73

Uncle, notion of pawnbroker as, 269 n. 39
Underworld speech and slang, 23–24
Uptown, idea of, 228–29
Urban novel, idea of, 15
Urbanism, New York's century-long cycle
   of, 20–26
Urdang, Laurence, 159, 168, 246

Van Alen, William, 71
Van Vechten, Carl, 42
Variety Photoplay Theater, 110
Vaudeville and slang, 18–19
Vertical metaphors in names of
   neighborhoods, 226–27
Von Tilzer, Albert, 72
Von Tilzer, Harry, 64

Waldorf-Astoria Hotel, 122–23
Walker, Stanley, 79
Wall Street, 39
Waller, Fats, 75
Walling, George Washington, 152, 171
Walsh, Mike, 104
Ware, Caroline, 36
Waring, George F., 216
Warner, Sam Bass, Jr., 132, 230–31, 273
   n. 20
Waters, Stafford, 228
Weber, Max, 16, 90
Wentworth, Harold. See Dictionary of
   American Slang
Wharton, Edith, 14, 32, 35–36, 48, 92,
   223, 224, 225, 235–36
Wheelock, John Hall, 205
White, Stanford, 78–79, 240
Whitman, Walt, 3, 14, 16, 17, 27, 40, 49,
   57, 69–70, 85, 87, 103, 113, 128, 131,
   139, 141, 157, 163, 182, 189–95, 200,
   201, 214, 215, 217, 221, 224, 241, 242,
   261 n. 12
Whymark, H. J., 76

Whyte, William Foote, 44
Whyte, William H., 196, 257
Wilkins' Exclusive Club, 75
Williams, Alexander ("Clubber"), 179
Williams, William Carlos, 90
Willis, Nathaniel Parker, 222
Wilmeth, Don B., 134
Wilson, Edmund, 172
Winchell, Walter, 18, 62, 66, 74, 77, 264
   n. 11
Wolfe, Thomas, 14

Woolworth Building, 127, 132
World Building, 127
World Trade Center, 129
Wright, Frank Lloyd, 117
Wright, Mabel Osgood, 203–4

Yiddish Broadway (Rialto), 61

Zangwill, Israel, 232
Zeisloft, Idell E., 222
Ziegfield, Florenz, 78

simple story - sadness very found